Betty Siegel

Julie
Vollentine

6/68

A text and guide on child development

These Are Your Children

third edition

GLADYS GARDNER JENKINS
Lecturer in Education and Home Economics, University of Iowa

HELEN S. SHACTER, PH.D.
Consulting Clinical Psychologist

WILLIAM W. BAUER, M.D.
Director Emeritus, Department of Health Education, American Medical Association

SCOTT, FORESMAN AND COMPANY

Foreword

Within little more than a decade, we have been precipitated into a new kind of world, a world of space capsules and astronauts, of independent nations that only yesterday were colonies, of minorities in determined quest of their constitutional rights, of increasingly mobile populations, of heroic projects aimed at providing adequate food, housing, and health for all. How brief a time since such a world was either wholly unknown or considered purely visionary.

Of vital significance are the children of this new kind of world. They must learn more at school. They must adapt to more outside of school. They will face pressures and tensions that demand better training and greater adaptability than were required only a few years ago. To guide these children's development wisely and provide for their individual education adequately, we must seek new areas of understanding, rethink outmoded attitudes, and reach toward concepts and values appropriate to today's world. This is the task that faces us. And this is a task for which *These Are Your Children* offers help.

Puzzling problems face the school and the home daily. Adults are anxious about the neighborhood gang, the school dropout, and the defiant teen-ager. They are troubled by the early dating of boys and girls who are not yet ready emotionally or socially for this experience. They are appalled at the increasing incidence of pregnancies among high-school girls and of teen-age marriages ending in divorce. What can teachers and parents do to prevent such unhappy experiences?

If parents are to accept the responsibility of sending to school children who are physically and morally sound and if teachers are to meet the obligation of furthering the wholesome development of the children in their classrooms, both must recognize the need to truly understand the children in their charge. To understand an individual child and how he has been influenced by the circumstances of his life, parents and teachers must first understand how children develop. The purpose of this book is to help provide that understanding.

These Are Your Children describes and illustrates all four basic aspects of children's growth and development—physical, emotional, social, and mental. There are countless concerns and questions in each of these areas. For example:

How do children grow and develop physically? What knowledge of the biological organism is essential for the wise supervision of physical growth?

How do they grow and develop emotionally? What can be done to encourage controlled direction of emotions so that anger, fear, jealousy, and other expressions of anxiety and insecurity do not win ascendance in the episodes of ordinary daily living?

How do children grow and develop socially? What will further their learning to get along with other people, to recognize other people's rights, and to help other people when they need help?

How do they grow and develop mentally? What steps can be taken to assure each child tasks that are appropriate to his individual abilities and interests?

These are not simple matters, permitting pat explanations. They are of concern throughout all the years of childhood, but they are manifested differently and require different handling at different ages.

In this third edition of *These Are Your Children* the text has been expanded to nineteen chapters organized into six main parts. Part One, "Guiding All Our Children," sets the stage by examining some of the special problems and challenges children face in today's changing world and outlining the basic principles of sequential growth. These introductory chapters stress the importance of keeping the focus on the individual child and helping him to achieve his individual potential.

Parts Two through Five trace the various stages in the process of growth. Introducing this material is a new chapter, "The Very Beginning," which deals with development in the important period between conception and birth. The following ten chapters—each covering a particular age group—describe children's physical, mental, social, and emotional characteristics at successive periods of development from infancy through adolescence. Illustrating and complementing the text in these central chapters are a series of studies of real children. These studies show how problem situations can stem from personal or family factors and lead to undesirable or unacceptable behavior patterns. Some of the stories involve typical situations. Others describe unusual conditions. But each of them illustrates a way to meet certain important needs of children, and each includes practical suggestions for the wise management of children.

Part Six, "Home, School, and Community Work Together," discusses and illustrates the principles of good guidance at home and school. Included in this section is an important new chapter, "When Things Go Wrong," which discusses ways of helping children who have serious emotional problems or physical or mental handicaps.

An entirely new feature of this revision of *These Are Your Children* is the inclusions of questions and projects for thought and discussion at the end of each group of chapters. These should guide the reader toward a fuller understanding of the text and also open up to him new areas for independent investigation. The authors are grateful to Mrs. Susan MacMillan, a teacher of emotionally disturbed children at the Medical Center of the University of Iowa, for her help in developing these questions.

Another new feature at the end of each part is an annotated bibliography which documents the text and suggests avenues for further study. The bibliographies include not only recently published books, pamphlets, and scholarly articles but also classic resources and other resources, whether old or new, that have been found practical in working with children both at home and at school.

Following the main text of *These Are Your Children* is a thoroughly revised Reference Manual which provides some special aids for studying and understanding children:

The "Individual Study Guide" is a tool for investigating the total circumstances of a child's life in order to amass the facts essential to an understanding of his difficulties. Teachers and parents are not qualified to conduct a psychological investigation, of course, but they should be able to distinguish the elements of a situation that have combined to create difficulties for a child. They are then in a position to know when professional help should be sought.

The "Guide for Parent-Teacher Conferences" outlines a method for conducting a parent-teacher conference that will enable parent and teacher to better understand both the child and each other and will help them in planning for the child's future.

"Charting Development" is a pertinent selection of tables, graphs, charts, and even X rays and cartoons depicting children's physical, mental, emotional, and social patterns and reactions. This section was developed with the assistance of Dr. Dorothea Ewers, psychologist in the Flossmoor, Ill., public schools.

The "Summary of Normal Development" provides a succinct overview of children's growth, outlining general patterns of development from infancy through adolescence and noting the special needs of each developmental period. In referring to this summary the reader should remember that it does not indicate the normal expectancy for any particular child, but merely shows what experimental evidence has found to be true of children in general.

Three fundamental points of view underlie the theory and practice exemplified throughout *These Are Your Children:*

First, starting with the story of life even before birth, it shows *the infinite variations on the basic similarity between all children.* The sequences of growth and basic needs are alike for all children, but each child's pattern and rate of growth is individual.

Second, it emphasizes *the continuity of the growth process.* Growth may proceed unevenly—now rapidly, now slowly, often with plateaus. And often stage follows stage so gradually that a succeeding one has almost imperceptibly appeared before parents realize that the passing one has gone.

Third, it stresses *the significant influence of the first years of life.* To understand a school-age child, we must know about him long before he enters school. Nor is it enough to consider the child alone. His experiences at home with his parents and his brothers and sisters, as well as his interpersonal relationships outside the home, have been potent influences. His reactions to those experiences determine in part how he uses his innate capacities and what personality characteristics he acquires. For personality is not static. It develops as the product of myriad experiences, within the controls of the inherited biological structure.

Here, then, is a fresh look at child development. *These Are Your Children* was written for students, teachers, and parents. Readable and readily understandable, it reports the findings of both current and classic research in child development and translates these findings into a practical, usable body of information. It is systematic in approach, warmly human in tone, thoroughly scientific in content, modern in concept. *These Are Your Children* is a new kind of book about children in a new kind of world.

Contents

Acknowledgments

Sources of illustrations are listed below except for the charts and diagrams used in the Reference Manual. These are credited in footnotes on the pages where they appear.

Bob Amft: 148, 263
Eve Arnold, MAGNUM: frontispiece, 19 (left), 29, 34 (both), 35, 291
Charles Biasiny: 7, 17 (right), 18 (left), 19 (right), 174, 175, 203, 318
Rene Burri, MAGNUM: 285 (both)
Cornell Capa, MAGNUM: 286, 289
Carnegie Institution of Washington: 32 (right), 33 (center)
Henri Cartier-Bresson, MAGNUM: 243
Herb Comess: 310
Jerry Cooke: 258
Elliott Erwitt, MAGNUM: 199, 201, 204, 206
Flint, Michigan, Community Schools: 303, 304
Peter Gold: 146, 284
Burt Glinn, MAGNUM: 242
Charles Harbutt, MAGNUM: 17 (left), 18 (right), 37, 49 (both), 61 (both), 67
Erich Hartmann, MAGNUM: 16 (left), 144, 149, 172
Eugen Ludwig of the Anatomisches Institut der Universität, Basel, Switzerland: 33 (left)
Jay Maisel: 278
Grete Mannheim: 265, 311 (both)
Constantine Manos, MAGNUM: 189
Wayne Miller, MAGNUM: 2, 41, 42, 45, 55, 58 (both), 59, 80, 87, 88, 91, 96 (both), 109, 110, 116, 126, 131, 134 (both), 135 (both), 137, 155, 156, 157, 161, 162 (both), 169, 170, 200 (right), 205, 220, 224, 226, 227, 229, 230, 237, 240, 242 (right), 261, 262, 281, 297, 298
National Congress of Parents and Teachers, Chicago, Illinois: 309
E. L. Potter, *Fundamentals of Human Reproduction:* 33 (right)
George Rodger, MAGNUM: 267 (right)
Carroll Seghers, II, ALPHA: 293
Serge Seymour: 84, 92
Morton Shapiro: 5
Landrum B. Shettles: 32 (left, center)
Don Stebbing, 112 (both), 113
Joseph Sterling: 239
Suzanne Szasz: 6, 7 (left), 10, 16 (right), 26, 43, 62, 132, 171, 176, 186, 188, 190, 200 (left), 238, 244, 266, 275, 277, 294, 295 (both), 313
Max Tharpe: 267 (left), 269
Cora Ward: 300

Softbound cover photograph by Wayne Miller

These Are Your Children

Guiding All Our Children

These are your children. These are the boys and girls who are growing up and learning at home, in the classroom, and in the neighborhood. These are the youngsters who we hope—through the guidance of all of us working together—will become healthy, useful, and adequately happy adults, for their own sakes and for the sake of the world of tomorrow.

As teachers and parents, we are coming more and more to realize, as our knowledge of children increases, how great must be our individual concern with the development and guidance of all our children. We have a responsibility to help all children develop to their fullest—those who are slow learners as well as those who are capable students, the disadvantaged as well as the privileged. They cannot do this without the help of adults who will work together to provide an environment which is suitable for the continuing development of each child.

This is particularly true today when guiding a child is complicated by the overwhelming rapidity of social and scientific change in the world. It is probably no longer possible for parents to bring up their children alone, as may have been possible in the past. The impact and pressures of contemporary society have become so strong that it is increasingly necessary for parents, teachers, and the other adults in the community to carry a joint responsibility for the welfare of all the children. The first and major responsibility for child care remains with the parents, but they must have the continuing support of the school, the church, and the community.

While the children who are described in this book may not be in all respects typical of the children in all the communities in our country, the principles of understanding and the processes of growth that are presented apply to all boys and girls, whatever kind of community they may live in and whatever type of racial or cultural background they may have.

3

chapter I

Children in a Changing World

Citizens of tomorrow's world

The heritage of today's children is that of the whole world, for there are few parts of the world left unrepresented in a particular neighborhood or school of our country. Some of our children, and the relatives or ancestors of others, have come from the countries of the north such as Finland, Sweden, Norway, or Canada; others have come from east, west, and south, from such faraway places as Africa, India, Turkey, South America, or the Philippines. We often think of these boys and girls, and even speak of them, as members of their particular racial or cultural group—referring to them as Irish, Chinese, Negro, Indian, German, or Puerto Rican and mentally setting them apart as somehow different from ourselves and from one another.

Yet in spite of such obvious physical differences as color of skin, texture of hair, shape of eye, or size of body, the similarities among children are more basic than the differences. All have the same fundamental needs, motivations, and drives, although no two children have them in the same proportion or express them in exactly the same way. All children need an environment that helps them grow physically and mentally to their fullest potential; the security of being loved, cared for, and accepted by parents and friends; and opportunities to learn and to be rewarded by a sense of accomplishment. All children need these things and many more, but each child needs them in different and constantly changing degrees.

Economic and cultural differences

Of far more significance than the differences of racial background are those differences of community, culture, opportunity, and experience which color a child's reactions, determine in large part his patterns of behavior, and foster the development of his unique traits and characteristics. Many children of all racial backgrounds still grow up in deprived communities in which few of the essen-

tials for healthy development exist. The child in the city slums or in the poverty-stricken areas of a community where there is no work has a very different environment from the child in the suburbs.

A child in a slum area may, of necessity, have developed different values than a child in whose home the necessities of life and protection have been taken for granted. The child who must fight for his place on the street, who has little certainty of shelter or food and little or no privacy, may want to live in the immediate present, with his needs gratified now. He has little incentive to look ahead and plan for satisfactions in the future. He may spend the little he has now—while he has it. He seeks his pleasure *now*—he cannot wait for what may never be.

There are still communities where boys and girls grow up in which, although material needs are satisfied, new ideas are met with suspicion. In some communities parents cling to the past and try to ignore the changes of the present. Some parents prefer to keep their children away from books and too much "learning." Others simply have no interest in education for themselves or for their children. The child who grows up in a home where there are books, where education is valued and learning is encouraged, where new ideas are met with eagerness and

explored, has a start on the road to learning which has been denied to far too many of our children.

If we would understand the children we teach or the needs of the children in the larger community of our country, we must be aware of the influences of the culture in which a child grows up. We can never ignore the background of a child. If we would help a child to grow and develop as fully as possible, we must begin where he is.

Preparing for the space age

The children of today are the same as the children of yesterday in the stages of development through which they will pass as they grow up, but their environment is becoming increasingly complex. The patterns of the past are being disturbed and new directions are not entirely clear. We cannot guide a child today toward a stable, comfortably predictable future for which we can help him to prepare step by step. In the glimpses we have of what the future of the space age may be like, we do know that the children who are growing up today must be prepared to think clearly for themselves, evaluating new knowledge not only in science and technology but also in human relations. For one of the major changes, which is already in progress, is *the shrinking in size of the world* through the expansion of the media of communication and transportation. The people

6

of the world are being brought closer together with an ever-increasing need for understanding one another and for learning how to think together and work together for our common welfare. What affects children across the world affects our children and hampers or encourages their own best development. The boy or girl who grows up unable to appreciate and work with people whose appearance, language, or customs are different from his own will be severely handicapped in the world of tomorrow.

Children everywhere are living in a *nuclear age* under the threat of the mushroom cloud of a hydrogen bomb. They cannot help but be affected in some degree by the constant threat that a disturbance, either in their own country or in some far-off corner of the earth, may trigger bombs far worse than the one which so tragically maimed and destroyed the children of Hiroshima. There are indications that this is the first, though often unmentioned, worry of many youngsters. Asked what he wanted to be ten years from now, one high-school boy perhaps spoke for all our children when he replied "Alive."

Our children must be helped to learn how to meet new problems and as-yet-unknown situations. They will need adaptability, stability within themselves, skills with which to open up and use new knowledge, ethical values to guide them, and the courage of the pioneer. If we as teachers and parents are to be able to guide children in this direction, it is important for us to remain close to the activity of this changing world and to be aware of the new developments, the

7

opportunities, and the possible strains and pressures which may affect the lives of the children in our care.

Health and education

There has never been a time in which more attention has been paid to the welfare of children. We are aware of their *health needs* and are attempting to meet them through many services in school and clinic and through public health nursing. Physically our children are taller and heavier on the average than they were in the past. As a group they mature physically at a slightly earlier age. There is a lower infant mortality rate than at the turn of the century. There is rapidly increasing knowledge of ways to prevent many of the potentially damaging childhood diseases. Physical handicaps are more widely recognized and more care is given to them. Mental handicaps have been taken out of the realm of superstition and disgrace and are receiving scientific study. More attention is being given to the emotionally disturbed child and to the mentally ill child. An increasing number of physical and mental health services are available to help children and to help parents in the better understanding of their children's needs and problems. There has been real progress. Nevertheless, much has still to be done if these services are to reach all the children and parents who need them.

Although thousands of our children are not yet receiving an adequate or appropriate education, there is an awareness of the *educational needs* of many different kinds of youngsters and a movement in the direction of finding better ways to meet these needs. Much thought and experimentation are going into the effort to find more effective ways of teaching, new ways of grouping and of school organization, new curriculum goals, so that the individual differences among children can be taken more fully into account during their school years.

Problems, pressures, and anxiety

There are, however, still too many boys and girls who are defeated and discouraged by their school experiences. The problem of *dropouts* is one of increasing concern. The problems of *vandalism and delinquency* among restless, school-age youngsters cannot be ignored. There is also mounting concern over the *pressures* caused by adult awareness of the vast increase of knowledge, which has resulted in heavy demands for a speed-up of learning during the school years. There are evidences of *increasing anxiety* on the part of some of even the brightest of our children as they face the competitive pressures upon them to succeed academically, so that they may be considered adequate candidates for a college education. Other boys and girls are becoming increasingly anxious because they are not, or fear they will not be, of college caliber. They are told constantly that without a college education the road to success is closed to them.

There are indications, also, of a *vanishing childhood,* at a time when our boys and girls need the opportunity to assimilate the vastly increasing experiences with which they are being bombarded. At the same time that our society is emphasizing the need for education as preparation for life in the space age, we are permitting boys and girls to be pushed into growing up prematurely, with experiences which they are not yet ready to understand or use wisely. They are

8

caught in the midst of the social stimulation and the ever-evident excitements of a materialistic age. Succeeding socially, having money to spend, and owning a car and the other material possessions that spell success in the adult world today are coming to assume more importance in the thoughts of many children than the studies that are vital to their best growth and development.

Toward the end of a youngster's school years we often find a reverse situation. Our older high-school boys and girls are far too often pushed backwards toward childhood, as it becomes increasingly difficult for them to enter fully into an adult world which is not prepared to receive them with adequate jobs and opportunities for full participation as working citizens.

Industrialization, followed by the moving of families and young people to the cities, is spreading throughout the world and changing the patterns of family life. Large family groups are breaking apart and scattering in search of work. It is becoming difficult for family businesses, such as the small shop or plant, to hold out in competition with the increasing number of large corporations. The number of workers needed on farms is constantly diminishing. Rural families are facing a steady loss of their youth.

The family unit is shrinking in size to what has been called the "nuclear" family—father, mother, and children. Many boys and girls do not know their relatives. They rarely feel the support that comes from close relationships with grandparents, aunts, uncles, and cousins. Family history is being lost. The family home rarely exists as a gathering place of the generations. The small family group is on its own. In time of crisis its members must often turn to less personal community agencies to secure advice and help.

Frequently the support of friends and neighbors is also denied, for *mobility* has become part of the pattern of modern life. In our own country about one fifth of our people move within a given year. Roots must be pulled up, friends and schools changed. No longer is this true only of the migrant worker or of the laborer who must go where there is work. Executives are transferred from one locality to another. Scientists and technicians are frequently sent to other plants. The personnel of government and the armed forces may travel, with their families, all over the earth.

Some children, in families that are secure within themselves, can gain an enrichment of experience through such moves. But for others, the constant mobility spells insecurity, loneliness, and a feeling of constant unrest and anxiety. The need to move may put an added strain on the family group at a time when the stability of the family unit, which is so essential for the children, is being threatened for other reasons. There are many boys and girls who have never experienced the stability that can come from growing up in a community where there is a feeling of belonging. Some have never had the opportunity to move through a well-planned educational program but have changed from school to school, sometimes several times a year.

Automation is a new and increasing problem for many families, as fathers are faced with the fact that the work for which they had prepared is no longer needed. This may be particularly hard for the fathers of adolescent boys and girls. They are reaching an age when learning a new skill or moving into a new field of work is no longer so easy as it might have been when they were younger. The normal tensions between adolescents and their parents may be heightened by the

9

very real strains under which the parents are living. Automation also may affect the plans of teen-agers, many of whom tend to become concerned for fear that they, too, may be preparing for jobs that will no longer be in demand or even exist when they leave high school or college.

Confusion of ethical values

In any period of change there is likely to be a confusion of ethical values. It is usually a time of questioning and of rejecting many previously accepted beliefs and standards. There is often a loosening of the moral code. Many grown-ups are no longer sure of their own beliefs. This adds to the confusion of boys and

girls, who must look toward their parents and other adults for guidance as they gradually learn the patterns of behavior and the ethical values which are essential in any society that is to survive.

Children today receive their impressions of the values of their society not only from parents, teachers, and other adults in their own immediate environment, but also from many sources far removed from the home. The *mass media,* which are so much a part of life today, touch the lives of even our very young children. They can extend the horizons and enrich the lives of boys and girls. But they also can, and often do, add to the confusion of youngsters as they bring an intensity of experience into the very living room of the home. Our children are constantly exposed to false concepts of success created by a materialistic society; to undesirable behavior on the part both of other boys and girls and of grown men and women; and often to experiences in human relationships that they are not yet ready to interpret or evaluate. Many of these unwholesome and false concepts are developed before our boys and girls have been helped to develop a sound basis of ethical values which they can use as a base from which to judge what they see and hear.

Children are not small adults. They do not think, feel, or react as adults do. They do not have the knowledge, judgment, or background to choose experiences that will be beneficial to them and reject those that may be harmful. At the same time we cannot judge or measure them by adult standards. Children need grown-ups who can thoughtfully lead the way through the confusion of our times. The first responsibility of those who sincerely want to help children to grow up ready to take their part in this changing world is to try to understand the world of children: the general pattern according to which all children grow and, within this framework, the individual needs and characteristics of each particular child for whom they are responsible.

chapter 2

All Children Are Alike—and Different

Basic influences on development—
heredity and environment

It is essential that we be aware of the differences among children that are due to their endowment, for these innate differences are the keystone on which a child's development will be built. Some people will always learn relatively slowly; others will learn rapidly and easily. Some will have an unusual capacity for understanding abstract concepts and working creatively with ideas.

Certain basic traits of temperament are apparent at birth. There are babies who are placid and others who are vigorous. Some are more sensitive to stimuli than others. Some have a quick reaction time while others respond more slowly. Some react to frustration with lusty crying and active body movements; others do not seem so deeply disturbed. Even in the first days of life, there are babies who have more energy and drive than others.

But whereas heredity determines the potentiality that can be developed, the environment determines *how* or even *whether* that potential is developed. Even before birth the environment is an important factor. From the day of conception, each child brings his own potential into an environment that is uniquely his own —different even from the environment of his brothers and sisters.

We are all aware of the tragic results of brain injury at or after birth. Such injury can make it impossible for a potentially fine mind to realize its original possibilities. We know that a crippling illness or accident can limit the use of a body that could have developed normal coordination; deafness can silence a musician; blindness can prevent an artist from expressing on canvas his great innate ability. An impoverished educational background can impede the development of a scientific genius.

In the same way, an unfortunate emotional environment can keep a child with normal potential from becoming a mature, emotionally healthy adult. The child who feels unloved and unwanted may grow into a discouraged, self-doubting individual or an aggressive bully. A child who has been dominated by an over-severe parent may be unable to make his own decisions when he grows up.

The influence of heredity and that of environment on the development of a child's personality cannot be separated. They are closely intertwined, one influencing the other. It is often difficult to decide whether a particular developing trait is due to initial endowment or to factors the child has experienced—or failed to experience—as he grew up. Mental retardation, for example, may result from limitations present in the original cells at conception, or from cultural deprivation, or from brain damage due to illness, accident, or biochemical deficiency. It is futile to argue whether heredity or environment, nature or nurture, has the greater significance for a child's development, because both affect the child's ability to grow into a mature adult.

Probably no one realizes all his potentialities. The child possesses at birth the capacity for far greater development than he will usually achieve. With understanding and help, even the mentally retarded, severely handicapped, or culturally deprived child can often develop far beyond the point he might otherwise have been able to reach.

Obviously, no matter what we as teachers and parents do, we cannot change the heredity of a child. Our sphere of influence is necessarily limited to the environment. But this limitation encompasses a wide variety of overlapping factors, often broadly classified for the sake of convenience as the *physical, mental, emotional,* and *social* growth and development of children.

The development of a child is a complex and individual matter, and the factors that interact to help or hinder this development are infinitely varied. It is impossible to control them all, nor should we even try. Learning to cope with problems and disappointments is one of the important tasks of growing up, and the ways a person works through his everyday problems are as much a part of his personality as are his unique abilities and interests. But we can—and must— try to protect children from situations that are completely beyond their ability to handle independently, such as the devastating effects of disease or malnutrition, lack of educational opportunities, or severe emotional setbacks.

An overall sequence of growth

It is difficult to help any child grow to his full potential without understanding the overall sequence and pattern of growth characteristic of all children. *These Are Your Children* is concerned with this foundation of knowledge and understanding. But although we talk about stages of development, we need to remember that there is no sharp cutting-off point at which one stage ends and another begins: one stage passes naturally into another. At any point in his development a child still evidences some of the needs of a previous stage of growth. Yet he shoots forward in other aspects of his development into a more advanced stage. The toddler occasionally behaves like an infant, though at times he carries out activities more typical of the run-about. The adolescent sometimes returns to the dependency of a grade-school youngster and at other times displays the responsible behavior of a young adult.

All normal children follow an essentially similar *sequence of growth,* yet because of great variations in endowment and experience, no two children, even in the same family, pass through this sequence in just the same way. Some meet life eagerly, head on; others are more phlegmatic, less easily interested or excited.

Some are easily guided; others are aggressively independent. Some have great vitality; others have less stamina. All these factors influence the point at which a child reaches any particular level in the sequence of growth.

Thus if we are to understand and help children as they grow, we must accept the fact that within a range termed "normal" some children will develop much more rapidly than the average, others much more slowly. In the total progress of growth they all will reach normal adulthood. But in every group of children some may be as much as several years ahead of their age group physically, mentally, emotionally, or socially, while others may be as far behind. So when we talk about "the six-year-old" or "the eight-year-old," we are talking of averages—the stage of development *most* children reach around six or eight. Some children will reach "six-year-oldness" at five or even four, others not until seven or eight or even later.

Individual rates of development

We must try to understand a child's *individual rate of development.* Is this child fast-maturing? If so, he may need opportunities to go ahead of his age group. Is he slow-maturing? Then caution must be exercised so that he isn't pushed too hard or overstimulated in an effort to keep him with his age group. We are usually aware of the need to allow the mentally retarded child to take things at a different pace from that of his age group; but we are not always so keenly aware of such special needs among children in the normal group who are maturing more slowly than the average. If a child is functioning well at his own level, his efforts should be accepted and respected.

Growth does not always go ahead smoothly. It is continuous, but not necessarily steady. Sometimes for weeks or even months the child's development seems to be at a standstill. At other times he appears to slip backwards in his behavior, seeming less independent today than he was last month. Sometimes, in both physical and psychological growth, these slower growth periods occur before a new spurt. There is slower physical growth, for instance, before the spurt preceding puberty.

Some children seem to grow at a relatively constant rate, so that at any given age they appear to achieve a level of development that is consistent for them physically, mentally, emotionally, and socially. For example, at the chronological age of twelve, these children display the physical, mental, emotional, and social characteristics more or less typical of a twelve-year-old. There are indications that such children may have less difficulty in growing up and adjusting. They may also show fewer behavior problems than do those children who grow at a more uneven rate.

Observing all areas of development

We must take into account all areas of a child's development if we are to understand him and meet his needs. For instance, if a child has developed rapidly mentally but remained immature socially, it would be unfair to judge him by the area in which he is advanced and scold him for not living up to the same level in all his other activities.

14

In order to evaluate a child's growth, we should avoid looking at the immediate present, comparing this week with last week or today with yesterday. We should *take the long view*—look back six months or one or two years and observe the growth that has taken place. The nine-year-old may baffle adults with his poor language usage and his untidy appearance, but he knows more about truthfulness and honesty than he did at six or seven; he is likely to be more cooperative in his work and play and more self-reliant. How fast and how evenly a child develops is significant, but more important still is the fact that he progresses from one stage to the next without being blocked along the way.

Although a child's personal pattern of physical maturing seems largely predetermined, his growth can be encouraged by an environment that provides ample physical and emotional care; it can also be hampered by sickness or malnutrition. A child will grow in some fashion whatever care is provided for him, but he cannot fulfill his optimum growth possibilities unless he receives adequate care suited to his individual needs.

Physical growth

Physical growth is easily observed. We can tell whether a child has gained weight, check his weight in proportion to his body type, and observe his nutritional state as shown by weight gains and skin and muscle tone. We can examine his teeth, find out the stage of his skeletal development, and test his coordination. In these ways we know whether a youngster is unusually mature or immature physically—that is, how he is growing in relation to the average for his age. Such knowledge can guide us in planning a program that will further develop the strong points and correct the deficiencies in the child's physical growth. Physical examinations can also help determine whether he can be expected to do his schoolwork at the pace of his age group. If he lags in physical development, he may be unable to keep up with others in handwriting, for instance, which demands fine coordination of the muscles of his fingers. Or he may be unable to climb and run as well as his schoolmates or to handle tools as skillfully as they do.

Every child needs ample physical observation and care; a fatigued, poorly nourished, or physically ill child cannot grow as fully as he might or accomplish the schoolwork that is expected of him. Knowledge of the child's level of physical development, good food, fresh air, protection from disease, correction of physical defects, plenty of exercise and outdoor play balanced by rest and relaxation—all these are essential for optimum growth, not only of a child's body but of his total personality.

Mental growth

A child's mental growth and capacities can be observed through standardized psychological tests, carefully given and interpreted by a trained person. We know through such tests and through observation that all children of a given age have not reached the same point in mental growth. In any first-grade class, we may find children with mental ages ranging from that of a four-year-old to that, in exceptional cases, of a ten-year-old. Parents and teachers must recognize these

15

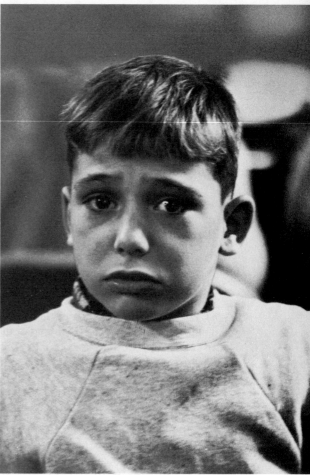

wide differences in intelligence and in capacity for mental growth if they are to give each child the opportunity to grow and achieve in terms of his own greatest capacity.

It is important that the experiences offered to the child fit his own maturity level. A child cannot learn either reading or independence until he has reached the stage in his growth at which he is ready to learn these things. If too much is expected of him before he is ready, he will fail, and his failures may seriously discourage him.

On the other hand, a child's growth may also be slowed if parents or teachers fail to recognize his readiness for the next step. If he is kept dependent when he is about to take some independent step, he may either rebel against restraints or yield to them and lose interest. The infant-child who reaches for his spoon is moving toward independence. If his mother refuses to give him the spoon for fear he will be messy, the child may later refuse to feed himself when his mother decides he should begin to do so. If a youngster is keen to take the next step in arithmetic but is held back until the slowest member of the class is ready, he may lose interest and just fool away his time.

16

Emotional growth

Emotional growth is not easy to understand or even observe scientifically. Growth—or the apparent lack of growth—in this area may be misinterpreted or overlooked. A child's behavior reflects his emotional development. If he seems generally interested in life, reasonably happy and relaxed, free from undue strain and tension, and able to meet situations appropriate to his age, his emotional needs are probably being cared for adequately.

Every child has certain basic emotional needs that must be met if he is to be emotionally stable. A child needs the security of knowing that he is loved, that he belongs and is wanted. He also needs the self-confidence that comes from being able to meet situations adequately. His successes must at least balance his failures as he tries to cope with the normal problems and frustrations of growing up.

If his needs are met, a child is able to develop through the stages of childhood into an adequately mature adult. If one or more of these needs is consistently overlooked, his emotional growth may be retarded, and he may have real difficulty in achieving emotional maturity. A baby who does not feel the security

of being loved may refuse food and show serious malnutrition, even though he is in a home in which excellent physical care is available. Or an older child, anxious because of a new baby in the family, may return to outgrown baby ways. The school child who cannot read is often one who is discouraged with himself because he feels unloved and unwanted at home. The bully is often the rejected or unsuccessful child who has been made to feel that he is a failure, that nobody likes him and nobody cares.

A knowledge of the stages through which we can expect children to pass will help us recognize behavior that indicates some problem in a child's emotional growth. A three-year-old may wake frequently from his sleep—this is normal for many three-year-olds. But if this waking continues over a period of time and is often accompanied by nightmares, we should begin to look for the cause or causes of tensions and anxiety. Perhaps too much is being expected of the child, making him overanxious and worried. Similarly, if the adolescent moodily shuts the door to his room or temporarily slumps in his schoolwork, it may be just a part of his growing up. But if he develops a *pattern* of withdrawing from his

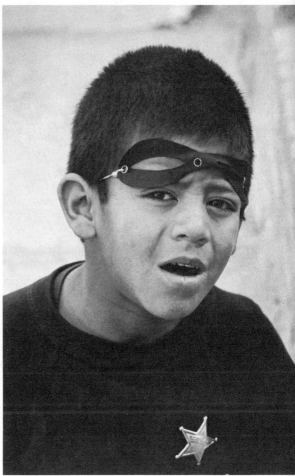

friends and family or of neglecting his studies, we should look for the causes. Behavior in excess of the normal reaction is the child's way of showing that for some reason his growth is being blocked or hampered.

Many environmental factors influence emotional growth. For this reason, if growth is to progress as well as possible, adults close to a child should be sensitive to behavior that suggests that the child's needs are not being adequately met. When a child is tense, anxious, unhappy, and out of harmony with his parents or his surroundings, his growth cannot proceed as well as if he were reasonably happy, secure, and self-confident. For example, a child experiencing too much competition with older brothers or sisters and discouraged by constant comparisons may simply stop trying to compete, or he may feel unloved in comparison to a brother or sister.

A child's self-image is built through the attitudes shown toward him by those with whom he is most intimately connected—his family, relatives, playmates, neighbors, and teachers. He sees himself as he thinks others see him. Those who work with children are increasingly aware of the significance of a child's concept

19

of himself in affecting his behavior, his motivation, and his ability to live up to his potential.

A child's opinion of himself largely determines his attitude toward the growing demands that are put upon him. If he is self-confident, he will have the initiative to move ahead, to explore his environment, to try new things, to meet and attempt to solve his problems. But if he doubts himself, if he has already met too much discouragement, too many defeats, too much adverse criticism, he may be so insecure that he will be afraid to meet the demands of growing up.

Even well-meaning parents or teachers sometimes damage a child's self-confidence by criticizing and scolding him for his mistakes and failures, without giving him balancing praise for his successes and assurance that he is liked in spite of his mistakes.

Social growth

Social growth closely parallels emotional growth, for it involves the child's feelings and relationships with the people among whom he is growing up. No child lives in a vacuum. He must learn to get along with others, to accept his growing responsibilities, and to live and work with other people at the same time that he keeps his own identity as an individual.

Children vary in the ease with which they develop socially. These variations in part reflect differences in personality: some children are naturally more outgoing than others. There are differences in environment: some children have had warmer family relationships and greater opportunities for satisfying contacts with other people. There are differences in ability and in training: some children have skills in games and sports that make other children enjoy their company; others are shy or less skilled and find it difficult to make friends with other children.

Any assessment of social growth is relative, because it may change according to the situation in which a child finds himself. A child may be comfortable and happy in his home life, but unhappy and uncomfortable in his relationship to a particular teacher. Sometimes a child does not fit in with the group of youngsters on the block, so that he temporarily feels left out and inadequate; yet the same child might get along well with other children who are more like himself in interests and abilities.

Group acceptance is seldom a safe criterion of social adjustment. It is essential to know more about the child and his total situation before judgments are attempted. If a child's growing social development is healthy, he will be able to relate to some other people. Whether he relates to a large group or a small one is not so significant as that he relates to his family and to some children his own age.

No child can develop normally as an isolate. All children need contact with and acceptance by other people. The child develops socially as he plays and works cooperatively with others and assumes increasing responsibility for his share of a group enterprise as well as for his own personal activities. The child who is a loner is a child who needs special help with his problems. But the label of social immaturity is one that must be used with the greatest care.

There are tests to assess social adjustment and to give insight into a child's feelings about other people. But such tests are not yet perfected. They can give some indication of a child's possible problems or anxieties in his relationships with others, but the results are not an accurate indication of a child's social adjustment.

Normal behavior and acceptable behavior

Unfortunately, much of the behavior typical of normal children is exasperating to adults who do not understand the stages of development through which children normally pass (and sometimes even to adults who *do* understand). Recognizing that some disruptive behavior is necessary to children's growth doesn't necessarily make the behavior less irritating, but it does enable parents and teachers to cope with it more calmly and intelligently.

The active, fifteen-month-old baby who touches, feels, and puts into his mouth everything about him is exploring an unfamiliar world, not just being a nuisance and "getting into everything." The restless six-year-old who is boisterous and who finds it difficult to sit still may annoy adults, but he is simply responding to his tremendous drive toward activity. The child who is passing through the growth spurt at the beginning of adolescence may be awkward and trip or drop things, not because he is careless but because his body is growing unevenly.

Often the child who is labeled naughty or badly behaved is a child who is misunderstood by the adults around him. They may be pushing him too hard and expecting too much from him, or they may know too little about children to realize that he is reacting as other children of his age would react in similar circumstances—that he is not deliberately naughty but is trying to assert himself as a person. If we can learn what may legitimately be expected of our children, we will save ourselves and them unnecessary heartache and bewilderment. We will not make the mistake of regarding as wrong or abnormal behavior that is perfectly normal for the child's age and development.

But even though we know what behavior is normal for the child, we cannot assume that all *normal* behavior will be *acceptable* behavior. Adults cannot assume a "do-nothing" attitude. They must curb, guide, and help the child grow toward behavior that is acceptable as well as normal. The noisy activity of a healthy group of boys may be permitted on the playground, for instance, but not in the classroom.

Approaches to understanding

Numerous clinics and research centers throughout the country contribute to our growing knowledge of children—their needs and development. Most of the studies conducted by these child study centers are of two types: *cross-sectional* studies and *longitudinal* studies. Cross-sectional studies compare and study large groups of children and isolate those characteristics that almost always seem to appear at certain age levels. Longitudinal studies follow individual children over a period of years, so that their patterns of growth can be observed and charted. Both types of study have made valuable contributions to our knowledge.

Another approach to understanding children's behavior is that of the psychiatrist, the clinical psychologist, and the social worker. Although the methods of these three professional groups are not identical, they all emphasize the under-standing of each child as an *individual* with personal needs, a personal growth pattern, and personal problems. This is in contrast to the normative approach of longitudinal and cross-sectional studies. Psychiatrists, clinical psychologists, and social workers are interested in child development not only theoretically but because they are often confronted with practical problems that need a solution. Through clinical experience and research, they have found that they must have all the information they can obtain about a child's heredity, his potential endow-ment, and the influence of his environment—what happened to him as he grew up that either helped him grow successfully or warped his personality and pre-vented the development of his potentialities. Largely through the influence of these clinicians and their increasing awareness of the effect of the child's total endowment and environment on his adjustment, our emphasis today is on *the whole child*—his individual problems and needs.

Clinical specialists have supplied valuable information concerning children's feelings about their relationships with parents, brothers and sisters, teachers, and children of their own age—and also about the effect of the child's self-concept on the development of his personality. Their interviews, in which the child is helped to talk about his feelings, his memories, and his reactions to the experiences of his life, have been useful in understanding children's basic needs and the way that tensions and anxieties can block or distort growth. Material gathered in this way is more subjective and less easily measured than that which has come from child study laboratories, but it is of great importance in appreciating our chil-dren's points of view and reactions. It also adds to our understanding of normal and abnormal emotional growth patterns.

We need both types of understanding—one to give us the general pattern of development and the individual variations that are normal within the pattern, and the other to give us insight into the child's emotional life and its interplay with the growth process.

Focus on the individual

Children are alike—and different. Alert teachers and parents will always keep the individual child foremost in their minds, seeing him against the background of the overall developmental picture. If a child's growth seems to differ greatly from that of most children of his age, it is wise to look for a reason. We need to be aware that some problems arise from a particular phase of development or a temporary environmental situation, but that others have a serious emotional basis. Children with the first type of problem can often be helped within an understanding home or school, but more seriously troubled children may need the more specialized help of community or state agencies or of a private psychol-ogist or psychiatrist.

From the day of his conception a child is constantly growing, developing, maturing. As he changes from year to year, his needs and his behavior patterns change, too. In growing up, a youngster needs the understanding guidance of both his parents and his teachers, together with the kind of environment in home, school, and community that makes the most healthful total growth possible.

Guiding All Our Children

FOR THOUGHT AND DISCUSSION

1. Give general definitions of the terms *heredity* and *environment*. Which of the two seems to you to pose the more immediate problem in educating children? Give reasons for your choice.

2. If a slow learner's mother described her child's problems in school as "definitely environmental," would you hesitate to believe her? If so, why?

3. Why should "the bomb" be of concern to today's adults when dealing with their children's problems?

4. How does the effect of the modern age on the family unit relate to children?

5. Discuss the meaning and causes of *vanishing childhood*. What kind of problems are parents and teachers faced with because of it?

6. Divide *total growth* into its four major areas and arrange the areas by number according to the ease with which you think they can be measured.

7. Can growth in any of the areas you have named be measured on an absolute scale?

8. "Children are alike—and different." Recall the two general types of child studies mentioned in Chapter 2 and match each type to the side it accounts for in this quote.

9. What is the difference between normal behavior and acceptable behavior? Give an example of a case where normal behavior may not be acceptable and of another where acceptable behavior may not be normal.

10. In a sixth-grade class, one child's academic average dropped from A to C in the month of May and another child's academic average dropped from B to D in the course of the whole year. Which of the two children do you feel would pose the more important problem to the teacher? Why?

11. Agree or disagree with the following statement and give reasons for your answer:
   "While normal children grow at different rates, they all have the same basic capacities. If they are given ample time to think things over, they will behave the way they should, and they will face their problems correctly in due time. The job of parents and teachers is to provide for them the environment in which they can mature normally, on their own."

12. Discuss the range of your own community's economic and cultural differences. For example, does your community have a wealthy residential district or a "wrong side of the tracks"? Give an example of a particular classroom problem that may occur as a result of your community's economic and cultural variations.

13. Briefly discuss how the geographic location and size of a community affect the social relationships of that community's children in school.

14. At what general age during a child's school years would you expect to find the most complex problems? Why?

FOR FURTHER READING

ALMY, MILLIE. *Ways of Studying Children.* New York: Teachers College Press, 1959. A comprehensive guide to specific techniques and approaches that all teachers can use in understanding the ways children think, feel, and behave.

BAYER, LEONA M., and BAYLEY, NANCY. *Growth Diagnosis.* Chicago: University of Chicago Press, 1959. A comprehensive growth study based on careful research.

BELL, NORMAN W., and VOGEL, EZRA F., eds. *A Modern Introduction to the Family.* New York: The Free Press of Glencoe, Inc., 1960. A sociological analysis of the American family, its relationship to society and its contribution to personality.

BLOOM, BENJAMIN S. *Stability and Change in Human Characteristics.* New York: John Wiley & Sons, Inc., 1964. Summarizes research based on longitudinal studies covering ten to thirty years and suggests that human characteristics are determined, in part, by environmental factors which can be measured. Stresses the importance of the early years.

BRECKENRIDGE, MARION E., and MURPHY, MARGARET N. *Growth and Development of the Young Child.* 7th ed. Philadelphia: W. B. Saunders Company, 1963. Refers to research data for factual material.

BUCK, PEARL S. *The Joy of Children.* New York: The John Day Company, Inc., 1964. Pictures from the photographic exhibit prepared for the 1960 White House Conference on Children and Youth, with a delightful text by Pearl Buck.

CARMICHAEL, LEONARD, ed. *Manual of Child Psychology.* New York: John Wiley & Sons, Inc., 1954. A thorough, systematic coverage of research in child development.

CHILD STUDY ASSOCIATION OF AMERICA. *Children and the Threat of Nuclear War.* New York: Duell, Sloan & Pearce, Inc., 1964. Discusses the extent to which today's children are disturbed by nuclear war and some ways in which adults can help them cope with their anxiety.

ELKIN, FREDERICK. *The Child and Society: The Process of Socialization.* New York: Random House, Inc., 1961. Discusses how a child learns the ways of the particular society in which he grows up.

GARDNER, JOHN W. *Excellence: Can We Be Equal and Excellent, Too?* New York: Harper and Row, Publishers, 1961. Suggests how excellence can be obtained at many levels of ability. A book not to be missed.

GINZBERG, ELI, ed. *The Nation's Children.* 3 Vols. Golden Anniversary, White House Conference on Children and Youth. New York: Columbia University Press, 1960. Articles about the major developments concerning children and youth during the fifties.

GORDON, IRA J., ed. *Human Development: Readings in Research.* Chicago: Scott, Foresman and Company, 1965. A collection of sixty-one articles concerning research and theory on human development from birth through adolescence.

HOFFMAN, MARTIN L., and HOFFMAN, LOIS W. *Review of Child Development Research.* Vol. I. New York: Russell Sage Foundation, 1964. First of a series of volumes to be compiled especially for the professional person in such areas as pediatrics, social work, education, and child psychiatry.

ISCOE, IRA, and STEVENSON, HAROLD W. *Personality Development in Children.* Austin: University of Texas Press, 1960. Points up factors entering into the development of personality as children grow.

JOHNSON, RONALD CHARLES, and MEDINNUS, G. R. *Child Psychology.* New York: John Wiley & Sons, Inc., 1965. Not only gives the basic facts of child development but explains the relationship of scientific methods to child psychology.

KAGAN, JEROME, and MOSS, HOWARD. *Birth to Maturity: A Study of Psychological Development.* New York: John Wiley & Sons, Inc., 1962. A significant report of a longitudinal study covering a thirty-year period.

MILLER, DANIEL R., and SWANSON, GUY E. *The Changing American Parent.* New York: John Wiley & Sons, Inc., 1958. Discusses the possible differences in personality that may result as bureaucratic orientations become increasingly characteristic of America. Based on research conducted in Detroit.

Murphy, Gardner. *Human Potentialities.* New York: Basic Books, Inc., Publishers, 1958. A stimulating discussion of the potentials of each human being and better ways of developing them.

Olson, Willard C. *Child Development.* Rev. ed. Boston: D. C. Heath & Company, 1959. Based on research relating to the school-age child.

Schramm, Wilbur Lang; Jack, Lyle; and Parker, Edwin B. *Television in the Lives of Our Children.* Stanford, Calif.: Stanford University Press, 1961. Material on children's use of television and their reaction to its content.

Shacter, Helen. *How Personalities Grow.* Bloomington, Ill.: McKnight & McKnight Publishing Co., 1949. Discusses how personalities change and develop as people attempt to satisfy their social and emotional needs. A guide to understanding oneself and others.

Solnit, Albert J., and Provence, Sally A., M.D., eds. *Modern Perspectives in Child Development.* New York: International Universities Press, Inc., 1963. A tribute to Dr. Milton Senn. Some of the articles are highly technical, but all will be interesting and significant, particularly to teachers.

Stendler, Celia Burns, ed. *Readings in Child Behavior and Development.* New York: Harcourt, Brace & World, Inc., 1964. A well-selected group of readings based on an interdisciplinary point of view.

Witmer, Helen L., and Kotinsky, Ruth, eds. *Personality in the Making.* Palo Alto, Calif.: Science and Behavior Books, 1964. Excellent material on family interrelationships and the development of healthy personality. Not to be missed.

The Earliest Years

The birthright of every child is to become fully the unique person he was meant to be. From the very first, the child has been an individual—separate and distinct from his mother in spite of his very close prenatal connection with her. After birth this separation will widen as the child takes each new step in independent living, though he will long continue to be both physically and emotionally dependent on his mother. Starting from conception, the child will pass through a period of rapid and spectacular growth, marked by the completion of the physical structure and the effective functioning of his body.

He will move out of the misty, undifferentiated grayness of his early consciousness into a world of color and movement.

He will gradually be able to explore the world about him by touching, tasting, looking, hearing, smelling—using all his senses as he begins to develop simple concepts that will enable him to think.

He will learn how to walk upright and to talk. Through these distinctive human characteristics of language and locomotion, the child will be enabled both to grow in independence and to participate with increasing adequacy in a world of people.

He will learn about human relationships through the feelings that he develops for his parents and others and through his interaction with them. If these interrelationships are warm and harmonious, he will have been given a good start toward learning how to love and live and work with other people.

This is also the period when a child begins to experience the pressures of the cultural pattern in which he will grow up. He must learn that there are limits to what he may do. He must learn that there are various and sometimes contradictory expectations of how he will behave. He will have to find his own way of living in relation to the myriad demands made of him by that process called *socialization*.

Let us see how a child grows from the infinitesimal cell from which he began life to the sturdy toddler of two, who is up and off and ready to go.

chapter 3

The Very Beginning

The beginning of life

The main concern of those who work with children is with the growing and developing child after his birth. Indeed, many people are accustomed to speaking as if life begins when a baby is born. Actually the individual life of every child begins at conception with the uniting of the sperm of the father and the ovum of the mother. These two minute cells contain all the potentials of a new personality. As soon as they unite, the miracle of growth begins. During the following nine months the child's development is progressing steadily, in just as vital a fashion as his development after birth. What happens to the growing organism within the uterus is highly significant in its effect on the possibilities for the child's normal growth and development after birth. We cannot ignore this period of intrauterine growth if we are fully to understand the continuity of development that begins nine months before a child is born.

Each child's potential characteristics are determined at the time of conception. Within the nucleus of each sperm and ovum are microscopic rods called chromosomes. These rods include tightly coiled spiral molecules of DNA (deoxyribonucleic acid) made up of ladder-like chains of atoms. It is now known that DNA in the chromosomes is the material basis of heredity. The actual carriers of heredity, or genes, are areas within the spiral molecules of DNA. These genes determine the characteristics that will be passed on to the child from his parents and from other ancestors through his parents. There are specific genes for such inherited characteristics as color of eyes, texture and color of hair, pigmentation of skin, length of fingers, shape of nose and ears, height, and body build. Complex factors such as intelligence and temperament seem to be influenced by a large number of different genes. There is also some indication that artistic, musical, and mathematical potentiality may be transmitted by the genes. The baby's sex is determined by a special chromosome from the father. No way has yet been found to influence or control the determination of sex, although there are indications that a way may be possible in the future.

The genes control the way in which the body grows and the development of particular body functions. This amazing process is carried out by "directions" which are given to the cells through a coding in the chemical structure of DNA. The discovery of DNA and its influence on the development of life and the

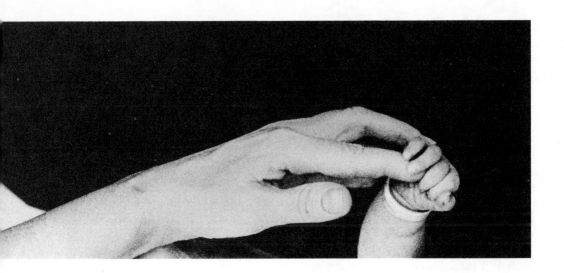

control of growth is bringing a new understanding of the functioning of the chromosomes. It is opening up new fields of exploration which, in the years ahead, will provide much more accurate knowledge of the passing on and selection of inherited characteristics and the whole process of life itself. It may be necessary to modify many of our present concepts of hereditary factors in the light of new findings.

Each parent has twenty-three pairs of chromosomes, but only one of each pair is passed on into any given sperm or ovum. Each man may have over eight million combinations of chromosomes in his sperm cells, and there are just as many different possibilities for a given ovum. Since pure chance seems to determine which member of each pair winds up in a single sperm or ovum, the heredity of each child (except identical twins) will be different. This is the reason why children in the same family can be so different from one another, although they may also have some characteristics in common. They have the same parents but they have not received the same chromosomes and, therefore, do not have entirely similar genes. Only identical (or monozygotic) twins have identical chromosomes, because only they develop from the same fertilized ovum.

The selection of the particular genes takes place when one sperm out of the many available thousands reaches, by chance, the mature ovum that is ready for fertilization. Within every woman's two ovaries, there are thought to be about one quarter of a million immature egg cells. Some of these were present even at birth. Once a month, midway between the menstrual periods, an egg becomes mature and leaves the ovary. It makes its way slowly through the fallopian tube toward the uterus, or womb. Usually only one egg is released each month, but occasionally two are released. If both should be fertilized, fraternal (or dizygotic) twins are born. Although only one egg is usually released, thousands of sperm from among the millions stored within a man's testicles may be released at any one time.

Both the mature ovum and sperm have short lives. Conception can only take place within about two days after each is released, and it is a fresh and vital sperm that is most likely to fertilize the ovum. This means that a child can only be conceived during approximately the two-day period of each month following the release of the ovum.

Orderly growth, suitable environment

Following conception growth follows an amazingly orderly course, as the fertilized egg cell develops to form a body pattern which will be ready for birth as an infant in about 265 days. There is a special timetable for the development of each part of the growing body. If development does not occur in its normal sequence at the appropriate time, the result will be seen at birth in defects such as a harelip, cleft palate, defective heart, or deformed limbs.

During these 265 days, called the prenatal period, the developing baby is known by several names. In the *germinal* period, which is the first two weeks of development, he is called a *zygote;* during the next six weeks, the *embryonic period,* an *embryo;* from eight weeks until birth, the *fetal period,* a *fetus;* at birth and for a few weeks afterwards, a *neonate.*

Nature has provided not only a plan for growth but also a suitable environment for growth. Within the uterus the developing baby is suspended in a membrane sac and immersed in amniotic fluid within the sac. The thickened, soft, spongy walls of the uterus provide further cushioning, while the mother's wide, supporting pelvic bones serve as a shield.

Although before birth the developing baby is completely dependent on the mother for survival, there is no direct connection between the blood stream of the mother and that of the baby. The connection, or exchange, is through the placenta. This is a spongy, complex tissue which develops after conception. It is composed of a mass of blood vessels and connecting tissues which are attached to the wall of the uterus. It is connected with the fetus by the umbilical cord, which is attached to the abdomen at the point that becomes the navel. Blood vessels of the fetus run through the cord into the placenta. The circulation exchange is through the membrane of the placenta, one side of which is bathed with maternal blood. This membrane permits oxygen and necessary nutriments from the mother's blood to reach the circulatory system of the fetus. It also enables carbon dioxide and other wastes from the fetal circulation to pass into the maternal blood stream.

There is no direct connection between the nervous system of the mother and that of the fetus. The old superstition that a mother's thoughts can harm or mark her child is untrue. What she sees, hears, thinks, or reads cannot directly influence her child before birth. The young mother-to-be who gazes at a beautiful picture may be enriching her own life so that later she can give more fully to her child, but she is not directly affecting either his personality or his future artistic sensibility.

The fetus does seem to respond, however, to vibrations from the outside world and sometimes appears to be more active if exposed to loud noises. Increased fetal activity may also be evidenced when the mother is tense, excited, or excessively fatigued. For example, there is some evidence that adrenalin, which is released into the mother's system when she is under extreme tension, may pass through the placenta into the baby's circulatory system, resulting in increased fetal activity.

Interruptions in orderly growth

In spite of nature's protective mechanisms, the fetus is not completely invulnerable. Even before birth the environment in which he grows can affect the developing baby and interfere with the optimum development of his capacities, even his ability to be born alive.

We do not know all the factors that may interrupt the sequence of normal growth, but we do know that there are specific environmental factors which, if they occur at a certain stage of development, may damage a particular organ as it develops. For instance, the otherwise benign infection of German measles, if contracted by the mother during the first three months of pregnancy, can have serious effects on the baby's eyes, ears, or heart, or even result in mental deficiency. Other virus and bacterial infections and toxemia during pregnancy also may affect the development of the embryo and fetus. Both the embryo and the fetus are more sensitive than the mother to large doses of X ray or atomic radiation. Such doses can produce defects, particularly in the nervous system. The widely publicized effects of the drug thalidomide on prenatal development adds to the evidence of the extreme vulnerability of the embryo during these early weeks. As a result, the possible effects of other drugs are being carefully studied. Doctors are warning mothers-to-be that other drugs may be harmful to the embryo and that all drugs should be avoided during pregnancy unless they are taken on the advice of a physician.

There is growing evidence that the mother's nutrition may affect the growth of the fetus. Babies born in a poverty-stricken environment are frequently smaller in all dimensions than those born in a more favorable environment. Inadequate maternal diet also appears to be related to stillbirths, some congenital defects, and some types of retarded development. Even a spontaneous abortion or a miscarriage may occur if the damage to the embryo or the fetus from the mother's malnutrition is great.

The Surgeon General's report on "Smoking and Health" indicates that women who smoke during pregnancy tend to have smaller babies and a significantly greater number of premature deliveries than non-smokers of a comparable social group. Whether the mother's smoking is detrimental to the child's development is not known.

A growing awareness of and alertness to environmental factors that can harm fetal development should eventually reduce the number of children born with handicaps. Fortunately, some congenital and hereditary defects can be at least partially corrected after birth.

The pattern of prenatal development

Even before the mother is aware that conception has taken place, the growth of the new individual is proceeding at a remarkable rate. During the weeks that pass before the first evidence of pregnancy (usually the cessation of menstruation), the new little being has already progressed from the first to the second stage of the prenatal period—from a zygote, smaller than the dot over this *i*, to an embryo ten thousand times larger, complete with rudimentary eyes, ears, mouth, and brain, simple kidneys, a liver, a digestive tract, a blood stream, and a

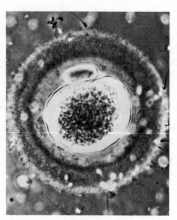

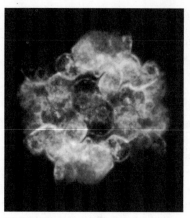

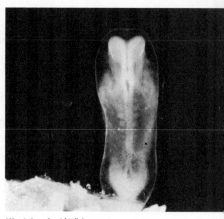

(1) *Microphotograph at conception.*
Courtesy, Landrum B. Shettles. Ovum Huma-
num. *Hafner Pub. Co., N.Y., and Urban &*
Schwarzenberg, Munich, Germany.

(2) *Microphotograph at 6 days.*
Courtesy, Landrum B. Shettles. Ovum Humanum.
Hafner Pub. Co., N.Y., and Urban & Schwarzen-
berg, Munich, Germany.

(3) *3rd week: 1/10″ long.*
Courtesy, the Carnegie Institution of Washington.

(1) *Male sperm cells, shaped like tadpoles, approach the female egg cell, or*
ovum, and attempt to penetrate it. Fertilization is completed in about thirty-five
hours, when a sperm reaches the nucleus of the ovum. The ovum is about the
size of a pinpoint, and the sperm cells are 85,000 times smaller. (2) *Six days*
after fertilization the zygote has about one hundred and fifty cells, already
differentiated for particular functions. The cells are beginning to form a hollow
cluster and are about to burrow into the spongy inner lining of the uterus, a
process called nesting. (3) *In the third week the two lobes of the brain and the*
developing spinal cord and vertebrae can be distinguished. (4) *At the end of a*
month many of the internal organs have developed in rudimentary form. The
folds of tissue that resemble gills will soon develop into chin, cheeks, jaw and outer

tube-like heart that begins to beat on about the twenty-fifth day. All this in a
body about one quarter inch long.

At the end of the first two months, when the embryo becomes a fetus, the body
structure begins to be recognizable as that of a human child. The ears and eyes
have begun to grow. The deciduous, or baby, teeth are forming. The blood is
circulating and the heart is beating, though it cannot yet be heard. By the end of
two and a half months, the fetus has a head, nose, mouth, fingers, and toes. His
other organs have started to develop and his bones are beginning to harden into
the skeleton that will later enable him to stand up and walk. The growing organization of his nervous and muscular systems is apparent to the mother a few
weeks later, when she begins to feel the baby move inside her. At first, activity is
in the muscles of the head, arms, body, and legs. A little later the eyes and hands
can move also; some fetuses even suck their thumbs.

In three and a half months the gums are developed, and there are signs of the
coming baby teeth. Fingernails and toenails are forming. From this time on, the
fetus begins to look somewhat like he will at birth. The doctor can hear the
baby's heartbeat at about the sixteenth to the eighteenth week, and the mother
begins to feel more activity and more strength in his movements.

The last three months of the prenatal period are marked by steady growth and

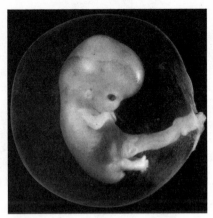

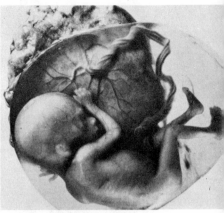

(4) *1 month: 1/4" to 1/2" long.*
Courtesy, Eugen Ludwig of the Anatomisches Institut der Universität, Basel, Switzerland.

(5) *7 weeks: about 1" long.*
Courtesy, the Carnegie Institution of Washington.

(6) *4th month: 8" to 10" long.*
From Fundamentals of Human Reproduction *by E. L. Potter. Copyright, 1948. McGraw-Hill Book Co. Used by permission.*

ears. The spinal cord is temporarily longer than the rest of the body and looks like a tail. The root-covered capsule shown here in cross-section houses the embryo during the first and second months; the roots provide nourishment as well as anchorage to the uterus. The balloon-shaped mass at the left is the yolk sac, which is by now nonfunctional and will diminish in size. (5) In the seventh week the embryo weighs only one thirtieth of an ounce, but he has facial features, all his internal organs, muscles, skin, and even fingers and toes. In about another week the physical structure of the baby will be essentially complete. (6) This photograph taken in the fourth month shows the fetus attached by the umbilical cord to the placenta, a versatile organ which performs for the fetus the functions of lungs, kidneys, intestines, and liver.

a continuing refinement of structure and function. In addition, the fetus receives during these final months a number of immunities that will protect him for about six months after birth. From his mother's blood, he will receive antibodies against all the diseases she has had to which she is now immune—for example, measles, chicken pox, scarlet fever, mumps, whooping cough, and the like. He will also secure protection against any diseases his mother has been effectively vaccinated against, such as smallpox and polio.

The baby receives another protective substance known as gamma globulin, most of which is produced by the placenta, although some comes directly from the mother. It is believed that gamma globulin immunizes the mother against certain diseases in the last three months of pregnancy, thus protecting both mother and child. The baby born prematurely misses out on this protection.

Even after seven months, when the child has a good chance of living in the outside world if born prematurely, he is still far from a "picture baby." As a matter of fact, he looks more like a tiny old man. He may weigh only two or three pounds, for the fat which will give him the more rounded baby look comes during the last month or so before normal birth. During these last two months he will grow rapidly, from about fourteen to about twenty-one inches in length, and his weight will increase to about seven pounds at birth. Even then he will

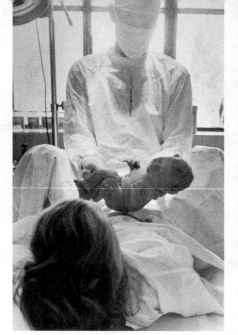

probably be wrinkled and red. He may, in fact, shock his parents if they are anticipating a smooth, pink-skinned, chubby baby at birth.

The birth process

When the fetus is ready for birth, the mother experiences contractions of the uterus, which are called labor pains. Through the pressure of these contractions, which begin gradually and increase in intensity and frequency, the membranes that have supported and protected the fetus are broken. The amniotic fluid leaves the mother's body at some time during this process. The baby (or the neonate as it should technically be called for the next two weeks) is gradually pushed by the contractions through the birth canal, which is enlarged at this time by its special capacity to stretch.

The birth process may be relatively easy or difficult, depending on the size and structure of mother and child, the elasticity of the mother's muscles, and the position of the child. The mental attitude of the mother may also influence the birth. Tension caused by fear and anxiety at the time of the birth may make the birth process longer and more difficult. Studies also have shown that a mother prepared through special exercises and an understanding of the birth process will usually have an easier time at the birth than a mother whose muscles have not undergone preparation and whose lack of understanding of the normal stages of the birth process causes her to approach the delivery of her child with fear. Consequently, there is increasing recognition of the importance of prenatal care to prepare the mother constructively for the birth process and also to prevent those complications of pregnancy that are likely to harm mother or child.

The period of birth usually varies from twelve to twenty-five hours for the first baby. With some babies, however, the process is much more rapid than this, and with others it is considerably slower. The duration of labor is typically shorter for subsequent babies than for the first one.

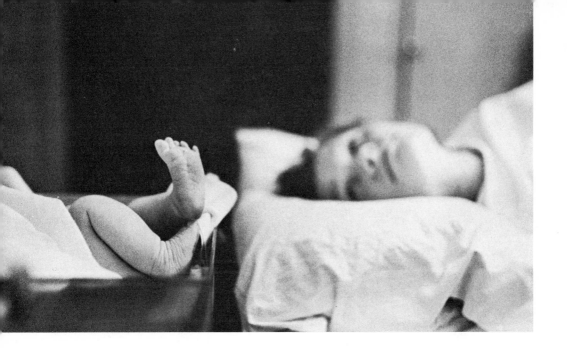

Entering a new world

The baby's environment changes dramatically at birth. In the uterus the temperature was stable; the baby was cushioned and protected; the mother supplied all of his needs for survival. But at birth this close connection with the mother is abruptly broken; the baby must breathe air if he is to survive, and he must make this adaptation quickly. Babies normally cry as they enter the world. This cry is an important signal that the lungs have inflated and begun to function. With the start of breathing, the valves of the heart alter the circulatory pattern and the blood flows no longer to the placenta but to the lungs.

The placenta, which is no longer needed, is expelled following the delivery of the baby. It is then called the after-birth. The umbilical cord, which is still attached to the baby, is tied and cut off. This is done without pain to the child, since the cord contains no nerves. Now the baby must take food, digest it, and excrete wastes. It must also respond to changes in body temperature and react to an environment which is no longer quiet and protected but contains many varieties of stimuli. From the moment a child is born, it must adapt to survive. This need for adaptation is present throughout life; indeed, without it life would cease. It is this necessity and capacity to adapt that has enabled man to conquer his environment and to meet life's problems.

We do not know much about the effect birth has on the child. Most babies come through in fine condition, but a few suffer brain damage in the process; such birth injury is one cause of cerebral palsy. Studies indicate that children whose birth was difficult are more likely than other children to develop symptoms that may include poor coordination, undue restlessness, hyperactivity, and distractibility—possibly as a result of slight, often undetected injuries to the brain. But birth is a normal process for which the mother's body usually is well prepared. Parents can expect that delivery will ordinarily take place without damage to their newborn child.

35

chapter 4

The Infant-Child

Physical development at birth

Many people think of a newborn baby as a complete miniature person, equipped with small replicas of adult organs, ready to function immediately and efficiently, as though all he has to do is grow in size. This is not quite so. At birth all the baby's organs are present, but many of them must develop further before they can function maturely. His heart has been beating since the first month of pregnancy, however, and is ready to carry on in the new environment. His lungs also will function as soon as he gives his first cry and begins to breathe.

Soon after birth the baby usually is able to suck. When the nipple is placed in his mouth, he automatically makes sucking movements, weak at first, but increasingly vigorous with practice. The ability to suck is necessary for his survival, since he can no longer obtain nourishment through the placenta. His digestive and excretory systems are ready to function within limits—he can digest only liquid food at birth and only semiliquid or soft foods for the next several weeks. His excretory system is not yet under voluntary control. Occasionally a baby will be born with a tooth, though usually he has tooth buds but no teeth. His bones are softer and more pliable than an adult's and the structure and proportion are different; they are not yet ready to support the baby. Nerve and muscle structures are still so incomplete that the infant cannot yet learn to do the simplest things such as hold his rattle or raise his head.

At birth there are a few things a baby *can* do. He can kick his legs and wave his arms, but his movements are random, unorganized; he can neither control nor direct them until further development occurs. Yet his grasp on a finger is surprisingly strong, and for a few weeks after birth many babies can support their weight for two minutes or longer by such grasping. The new baby hears well and will be startled by a loud noise. He responds more intensely to a high pitch than to a low one. He can be soothed by a gentle voice, but he cannot understand words nor even connect the voice with a person. He cries, but he doesn't know what he is crying about. He cannot see clearly. His eyes do not

focus at first, but soon after birth he is able to follow a moving light with his eyes. His senses of touch, taste, and smell are better developed than his sight. He reacts to changes of temperature and to discomfort in the position of his body, but he cannot change his position. Most of the time the new baby sleeps; he may even have difficulty staying awake long enough to take his milk.

The brain of the newborn baby has the same pattern as that of an adult; but the nerve fibers and nerve cells are unfinished, and not all the blood vessels have as yet developed. Furthermore, the baby has had no experience that would enable him to develop ideas, no memory on which to build. He cannot think; he can only feel. The four pieces of bone that make up the skull have not yet grown together so that there is a soft spot on the top of the baby's head known as the *fontanel*. This will close sometime between nine months and two years.

A warm relationship

As the newborn baby adjusts to his environment in the outer world, the tone of his feelings will be established through sensory experiences. A baby begins to relate to his world through his continued close relationship with his mother or the person who cares for him. At this time the basis for his later emotional and mental growth begins to be laid. A desirable environment for a baby is one in which he is not only cared for physically but is also kept comfortable and content, receiving enough stimulation by being held, talked to, and later played with. Even when given adequate physical care, a baby left lying in his crib without human response is deprived of the mental stimulation and emotional warmth that he needs to develop normally. His early feelings should be, so far as possible, satisfaction and pleasurable sensations rather than discomfort.

It is usually the mother who is able to establish this first warm relationship with her baby as she takes care of him, feeds, holds, and soothes him. The baby needs the continuity of a relationship with one mother figure. Studies show that he does not thrive to the same extent when he is cared for by many different individuals. The baby probably does not recognize his mother as a person, for he begins life in a world in which one thing is not clearly differentiated from another; but he does respond to the way she answers his cry, the gentleness or roughness of her touch, the way she holds and moves him, and the food she offers him. Studies have shown that if a mother is tense and anxious when she handles her baby, the baby may respond with greater restlessness and crying. The mother seems to communicate to the baby through her body. If she can be relaxed and at ease when she handles the baby, the baby usually responds positively, seeming more content, relaxed, and comfortable.

Nursing the baby

During the first month the baby begins to explore the world with his mouth, seemingly one of his most sensitive sensory areas. Nursing brings him comfort and contentment and is one of the ways through which his closeness to his mother is continued in the new environment of the world outside her womb. Later he will not only use his mouth in rooting for the nipple and receiving food but will also mouth his toys, his fingers, or whatever is within his reach. This is one of the ways in which he begins to explore the world through his senses.

If the baby's first experiences with nursing are difficult or frustrating, he may respond with restless crying and may experience greater difficulty in developing feelings of trust and security. Some babies do not learn to suck easily and must be helped with the suckling process; others may develop colic, which makes them uncomfortable and, as a result, irritable. These conditions can be so disturbing to both baby and mother that sometimes tension develops at the very beginning, making it more difficult for the mother to give the gentle, relaxed comfort and care a baby needs. This potential problem needs to be recognized, since the mother may need help in adjusting to a child who has feeding difficulties at the very beginning of life, if she is not to feel mounting irritation and frustration over the extra time, comfort, and care such a baby needs.

Whether or not bottle-fed babies receive sufficient gratification of their emotional needs has been a matter of considerable discussion. Equally competent pediatricians differ in their opinions on the subject. Physically, a baby seems to gain just as well when fed by bottle as by breast. Some pediatricians, clinical psychologists, and psychiatrists feel that breast feeding, however, has an advantage psychologically—that it brings about a closeness between mother and child that is valuable for the baby's emotional development. This would seem to be true only insofar as the mother wishes to nurse her baby: if a mother breast feeds without really wanting to, the feeling of harmony between mother and child, one of the most important benefits of nursing, is seemingly lost. A mother who bottle feeds her baby can establish much the same closeness and warmth by holding her baby when giving the bottle.

Self-demand feeding

Another step in laying the foundation for healthy emotional growth is adjusting the schedule to the baby rather than the baby to the schedule. This means that instead of feeding the baby at certain prescribed hours, which was the recommended practice for many years, one adjusts the baby's feeding schedule to his hunger needs. Such a plan is called *self-demand feeding*. It is now known that some babies are hungry in two hours, some in three hours, and others in four hours. Self-demand feeding recognizes these differences so a baby is fed according to his own pattern. Most babies soon find their own schedule and within a month or six weeks settle down to fairly regular feedings.

Again the feeling between mother and child becomes an important factor. If a mother is overly anxious or unable to differentiate between hunger cries and cries that may signal other needs, or if she is so tense about her baby that she puts him to the breast or runs for the bottle whenever he cries, it might be better for the relationship between mother and child if the baby were on a more definite schedule worked out by the mother and her doctor.

Studies made of babies on self-demand schedules seem to show that, on the whole, they are contented and responsive babies who cry less than many babies fed on a more rigid schedule. Self-demand babies also regulate the amount of food they need; consequently, the mother does not have to force a certain amount of breast milk or formula into the child, regardless of whether or not he wants it. This procedure takes into account individual differences in food needs, which are apparent even at this early age.

Crying, thumb-sucking, and smiling

Another means of helping a baby develop a feeling of well-being, trust, and confidence during the first three months is by answering his cries. The baby's cry is his first means of communication. It is his instinctive way of protecting himself, for it is his only way of indicating that he is hungry, wet, cold, uncomfortable, or disturbed in some other way. If the cry is answered and the baby is made more comfortable, tension is released and he feels secure again. If the cry is unanswered, the discomfort persists and tension mounts within the child. Such tension, if frequently repeated or prolonged, may block the gradual development of trust in those who care for him. The studies of the late Dr. Aldrich at the Mayo Clinic on the crying of the newborn were among the first to help us understand the automatic nature of the infant's crying and his response when the cry is answered. Contrary to popular belief, such attention will not spoil the baby or cause him to develop bad habits, for he is not yet capable of voluntarily planning to cry in order to attract attention.

During the second month, the baby becomes increasingly alert and aware of the world around him. His muscles are stronger. He begins to kick and exercise more than he did when he was a newborn. He fusses more if he is restrained. He is not as compliant when his mother is dressing or changing him. His arms, legs, and fingers are less curled up than when he was born. His head still looks too big for his body and is still wobbly when unsupported, but the baby is usually able to lift it. By the second month, because of the increased capacity of his stomach, he is able to take more milk or formula at a feeding. He may even sleep through the night without waking from hunger.

Many babies have already found their thumbs and suck them contentedly.

Often a crying spell stops as a baby slips his thumb into his mouth. Again there seem to be individual differences in the amount of sucking a baby needs; some babies suck their thumbs constantly, others rarely. The amount of a baby's sucking may be determined in part by the length of time he has at the breast or bottle; there is some indication that slow-nursing babies do not suck their thumbs as much as fast nursers. Thumb-sucking may also serve as a release for some inner tension or need for comfort, or it may merely provide a pleasurable sensation to the child's sensitive lip and mouth areas. We do not know just why many babies seek the comfort of a thumb, but during their first year such sucking is harmless, and usually it decreases gradually as the child becomes interested in other things around him. Parents' efforts do not seem to affect the amount of sucking that is done.

Sometime during the second or third month, the baby gives his first real smile of response. This always delights his parents, even though the smile is not really a recognition of them as individuals. Such recognition comes about the sixth to eighth month. At first the baby smiles at anyone who pays attention to him; it has even been reported that some babies will smile at a full-face mask that moves in front of them. Again there are individual differences, for some babies are much more responsive and smile more readily than others.

The infant's smile is not only delightful but important, for it is one of his first real responses to someone else. It shows, too, that he is beginning to focus his eyes and his interest on a specific object. But even though the baby's perceptive powers are increasing, he does not yet have enough experience or memory to separate people or objects from one another with any real meaning. That will come later.

Improved coordination

By the time the baby is three or four months old, the nerve cells of the brain are more efficiently related to the different muscle groups, so that voluntary action begins to be possible. This improvement in coordination follows a downward sequence, starting with the head and upper part of the body and ending with the legs. The baby is able to smile, turn his head, and reach out long before he can walk.

He opens his mouth now at sight of the breast or the bottle. By this time, his feeding usually follows a fairly regular pattern and he lets his mother know if she is late with his meal. He is beginning to take more soft foods, for the neuromuscular development of his tongue and throat now allow him to swallow foods other than liquids. If new foods are offered too soon, however, the baby may not be able to handle them and will push them out with his lips or his tongue.

His eyes are beginning to focus better and he is beginning to lose the cross-eyed look so disturbing to some parents of newborn babies. He still sleeps much of the time, usually falling asleep as soon as he has been fed. His cry is still his means of communicating a need, and it is still wise to answer it and supply the attention, comfort, or change of position that he needs. The baby is now able to change his own position in a limited way. He can hold his head more steadily and look around a bit when he is laid on his stomach. The muscles of his arms, legs, and trunk are larger and stronger. He can wriggle and twist around and possibly even roll over. His whole body is more active, with many random move-

ments of arms and legs. He may occasionally catch his toe with his hand, but he cannot yet plan to do so. His movements are still automatic rather than voluntary. His mind cannot yet guide his body.

Enjoying life

During the second three months it is exciting to watch the baby grow. He is awake much more of the time and is starting to enjoy being near people. He now responds not only to his mother but also to his father and to the other children in the family. He babbles and coos and smiles and may even begin to laugh. It is possible to carry on "conversations" with him. This is another step in communication (his cry was the first), and his burbling is important for later language development, for he is beginning to master sounds that will later be used in forming words.

If his needs are being satisfied, the baby cries less for immediate attention and often lies happily in his crib, looking at his hands and watching the sunlight and shadows in motion on the ceiling or the movement of the branches of a tree. Around the fourth month, as his coordination improves, he plays with his fingers and his toes, tries to grasp a rattle, or clasps his hand around his bottle. His arms and legs are almost straightened out by now and his body proportions are better. He no longer appears top-heavy.

The four-month-old baby is not content just to lie on his back when he is awake, but tries to turn over, and sometime during his fifth month he may succeed. It is a big step toward independence when he learns to change his own position by rolling from his back to his stomach. By this time he also enjoys being held in a sitting position on his mother's lap for a short time. When supported in her lap or against her shoulder, he can hold his head erect and fairly steady and enjoy watching what is going on.

By five months the baby laughs aloud and responds gaily when played with. He enjoys a little time with his toys in a padded playpen or on a blanket on the floor. He is beginning to reach for a toy and often succeeds in grasping and holding it. He enjoys trying to roll from his back to his stomach and is soon able to get there. If propped up, he will sit like a frog with his head pushed out. Some babies cut their first tooth during this month. Most babies begin teething and some are irritable because their gums are sore, although the extent of such irritability varies greatly with individual babies. It is during this month that most

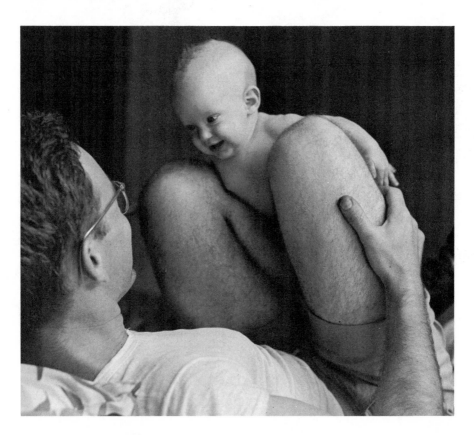

babies begin to chew on anything they can put into their mouths. They may also drool, because they cannot yet manage an increasing amount of saliva.

Six months—a midpoint

Six months is a real midpoint in the development of the first year. From this point, the baby rapidly leaves behind the helplessness of his first months and grows in functions that lead toward greater independence of action. He may try to sit alone; when he succeeds, he will be able to see the world from a completely new position whenever he wishes to do so. He takes increasing delight in watching activities around him. Now he can enjoy his playpen for a longer period and can usually sit for a short time in his high chair or in a small, low chair. His neuromuscular development has reached the point where he can not only hold things but also have fun banging them on the ground and on his chair, or shaking them and dropping them over the edge of his pen. He seems absorbed for a minute or two as he looks at something. He is beginning to take sizable steps forward in amusing himself. He gets up on all fours and rocks back and forth as if he were all ready to be off and creeping. Occasionally a baby does begin to creep at this age.

He knows his mother well and sometimes cries if she goes out of the room and leaves him. He notices the difference between familiar people and strangers. He may experience a period of shyness, showing fear or crying when a stranger

approaches him, or perhaps turning away and burying his head in his mother's neck. Some observers place this period of shyness at five or six months, others at as late as eight months. But sometime during the middle part of this first year, the baby will "freeze" and then burst out crying at the sight of a stranger, perhaps even at the sight of his mother in a hat or coat that makes her unrecognizable to him. During this period of being shy he should not be forced to go to strangers but rather should be allowed the security of nearness to his mother. If he must be left with someone else, it should be someone who has spent at least a little time with him and so is not totally strange.

At six months the baby enjoys going out and, if propped up, looks with interest at people and dogs and cars or whatever catches his attention, although his span of interest remains short. He soons tires and still often drops off to sleep in his buggy.

By this time he is able to take food off a spoon with his tongue and lips instead of having it put into his mouth by his mother. In fact, he often opens his mouth and reaches eagerly toward the spoon. He can swallow better and take foods of much more varied consistency. He is also beginning to show food likes and dislikes, turning his head away or fussing if his mother tries to make him eat when he doesn't want to. During this month the baby is likely to cut his two lower front teeth, the lower central incisors, indicating that he is moving out of the suckling stage into the biting stage.

On the move

At about seven months the baby's back has become flat and strong and his back and abdominal muscles are much better developed. He will soon be able to sit up without help. He is also starting to get around more, and many seven-month-old babies even try to crawl.

There are many different ways of crawling. Sometimes a baby begins by just rocking back and forth on his knees before he finds that he can move. Some babies hitch themselves along on the floor, some roll over and over, others arch along on their backs. Some go backward at first instead of forward. But whatever means they use, seven-month-olds are usually eager to try to get around. Many babies of this age also try to stand by grasping the bars of their playpens and attempting to pull themselves up from a kneeling or sitting position. Some seven-month-olds are successful, and very occasionally a child this age will even start to walk.

The seven-month-old wants to touch and handle and taste everything within his reach. He puts his toy in his mouth, feels it, bangs it on the floor or on the tray of his high chair. This is just the beginning of his interest in touching, feeling, and mouthing everything within reach, an important stage in learning.

While the seven-month-old still picks things up with his whole hand and holds them tightly in his fist, the eight- to ten-month-old baby learns to bring his thumb and his index finger together to pick up a small object. At this stage, his mother must be careful to see that there are no buttons, pins, or other small objects within his reach, because whatever he can pick up he will probably put into his mouth. He now feeds himself by taking up small pieces of food from his tray. He uses his index finger to point and poke. From now on the infant will

The baby's new independence in being able to move about by crawling brings him problems as well as pleasures. He finds that doors prevent his going where he likes, that his mother will take away some of the appealing objects he works so hard to pick up, and that some places are too small to crawl through. Here the infant is doubly frustrated—he can neither crawl between the furniture legs nor pull his overalls out from under them.

use his fingers and hands more and more skillfully, manipulating everything eagerly, using both hands to reach, hold, and bang, and using his fingers to pick up or explore cups and boxes.

During the eighth and ninth months, growth begins to slow down. The baby's movements are no longer random. He spends more and more time practicing sitting, creeping, pulling himself up, and getting ready to walk. He is very active, often creeps rapidly, and gets into all sorts of mischief if he is not carefully watched. Scoldings are useless, for he is not yet ready to understand what he may or may not do. He probably needs less sleep and oftens wants only one nap a day. The child's appearance often changes greatly in these two months. He is getting more hair, and his face is beginning to lose its baby expression and take on the more individual characteristics of later childhood. These two months might be called the transition period between being a baby and a toddler.

Progress toward childhood

The baby at ten months seems more a child than he did at eight months. Now he can sit up alone whenever he wants. He can usually stand with support, but should not be urged to do so until he shows that he is ready and wants to stand. He may be able to pull himself up to a standing position, but he has difficulty getting down again. Sometimes he stands holding on to a chair or to the edge of his playpen and cries for someone to come and put him down; if no one does, he just topples over. A few babies even begin to walk at ten months, although most are not ready for this development until several months later.

A baby ten months old shows how grown-up he is in still another way. He starts to notice the different tones in his mother's voice and to know when she approves or disapproves of what he has done. He begins to respond to his mother's "No, no" and may even pull back his hand and look at her if he is reaching for something he knows is forbidden. This is the time for his mother to start teaching the baby some of the things he must learn if he is to live with other people. But even though he may seem to understand at the moment, he cannot yet be expected to remember very well from one time to the next. He cannot yet take responsibility for his actions. The "no" will have to be patiently repeated in each situation.

At ten months a baby will respond and stop what he is doing if he is scolded and punished, but harsh tones frighten him and develop anxiety and tension. Such teaching through fear, though sometimes effective, can block rather than encourage learning. The change from the permissiveness shown toward a younger baby must come only gradually, or the child may become overly disturbed by the "do's" and the "don't's" which seem to color his life as he gets a bit older. At this age the baby is easily distracted, and his attention can generally be turned quite easily from something forbidden to something that he is allowed to have or do. This is a better way of teaching.

Gradual weaning

By ten months most babies are able to bite and chew well enough to eat solid food and can drink milk from a cup instead of a bottle, so that the gradual weaning process, which was probably started several months earlier, can soon be completed. Some babies, however, still want a bottle, especially at bedtime, well on into the next year. There is no "right time" to completely do away with the bottle, and, in most instances, a child should not be forced to give it up until he is emotionally ready. Most ten-month-old babies have reached this point, but many normal children still cling to the bedtime bottle at seventeen or eighteen months, seeming to need the comfort and security that it implies.

Weaning is one of the major adjustments a baby must make. It not only involves a change in the way he gets his food and the kind of food he will be offered, but it also makes a change in his relationship with his mother. The younger baby associated eating with emotional satisfaction and closeness to his mother. Later, when he is physically able to sit up in his chair and receive food entirely from a cup and spoon, with perhaps a bottle of milk at bedtime, the physical closeness to his mother that he experienced as he nursed or took his bottle in her arms, and the comfort he derived from this closeness, are taken away from him.

If this step away from physical closeness is taken too suddenly or too soon, the baby may be greatly disturbed. This is why it is wise to take weaning slowly and in many steps. Even with the preparation that most babies today receive—being offered food by spoon as early as four or six weeks, and later being given occasional sips of juice and milk from a cup—doing away entirely with the breast or the bottle is often disturbing. A baby's emotional readiness for the final weaning needs to be taken into account. Some babies seem to need both the suckling and the closeness of their mother's body longer than others; some push the bottle or breast aside, preferring to drink from a cup, even before the mother is ready to complete weaning; some go through a period of clinging closely to the mother and not letting her out of their sight. Extra holding and cuddling at times other than meals may help the child's emotional adjustment. If the child is shown his mother's affection in other areas of his life, weaning may be distressing to him but not unduly disturbing. The child's overall relationship with his mother is the most important factor in his emotional growth, not the effect of one experience, even if that experience is disturbing.

The baby may now reach for his spoon and try to feed himself. If he is given a spoon he can grasp, he may be able to get some spoonfuls into his mouth, doing a messy job but one that often delights and absorbs him. He will also try to eat with his fingers. This attempt to feed himself, although perhaps not very satisfactory in the eyes of adults, is another important step toward independence. It is always a little sad if his mother is so concerned with cleanliness that she takes the spoon from him because she can do a quicker and neater job.

As with all growth steps, independence in eating comes gradually. The child cannot always be expected to feed himself just because he has shown an interest in trying and has had some success. He should be allowed to feed himself as long as he is eager to do so; when his interest lags, his mother should take over. Insistence on continuing first efforts will often discourage a child and make it harder for him to try later.

New pleasures and accomplishments

The ten- or eleven-month-old baby usually responds to people whom he knows, but he is sometimes still hesitant about strangers, although not quite as shy as he was a few months ago. He is very responsive to his mother and wants to be near her. He often holds out his arms to be picked up. He likes to sit on someone's lap, to romp and be played with. He enjoys watching other children. He throws his toys over the edge of his buggy or high chair or pen and laughs gleefully. If allowed to explore the kitchen floor, he loves to get into his mother's cupboards and take out all the pots and pans. Now that he can use his hands more skillfully, he especially enjoys putting things into a container and taking them out again over and over—a spoon into a cup, clothespin into a box. He now frequently amuses himself happily while his mother goes about her work, as long as he can watch her or can see other children when he is outdoors in his pen or play yard. Cats, dogs, and birds fascinate him; he watches them with interest and tries to reach and play with them. Passing cars and people also hold his attention. However, he will no longer stay contentedly in his pen for long periods. He needs to explore and can safely be allowed considerable leeway if he has a play space in which dangerous objects are out of reach.

He now loves to play games and will display his abilities on request. This is the time to teach him pat-a-cake and peekaboo. He loves rhymes when they are chanted or sung to him and often enjoys listening to music. He is imitative and will repeat sounds like "da-da." Perhaps he may begin to wave "bye-bye." The child who is deprived of this kind of play may not develop as rapidly as he otherwise could. Care, of course, must be taken not to overstimulate or tire the child. Neither should responses be demanded of him.

A child's early accomplishments will depend partly on adult encouragement and partly on the maturity of his growth. It is particularly important for adults to be constantly aware of the great variation between children in timing and achievement that may be expected even in this first year. There is a wide range of the normal, particularly in walking and in language development. Some normal children walk as early as ten months; others, equally intelligent, walk as late as sixteen or seventeen months. Some normal children begin to say words before they are a year old, while others use no words until they are eighteen months or older.

The first year—laying emotional foundations

During these first twelve months the baby has grown more rapidly than he will at any other time in his life. Usually he has tripled his birth weight, and he has grown from a new-born infant—completely dependent on his parents for care, even for a change in position—into a child who has learned to recognize himself as an entity apart from his mother. He has a definite personality of his own. By the end of the first year he is able to move around by himself, explore his environment, and assert himself within that environment. The year-old child expresses his wants through his actions. He shows his anger when frustrated in obtaining what he wants, or his pleasure when happy. He responds to other people and usually likes to be with them, although he may still have periods of shyness or fear if a stranger approaches him too quickly or noisily. He has changed so rapidly during this year that it is no wonder his parents have found it difficult to keep up with his varying needs.

The first year has been the "receiving" year in which the baby has been almost totally dependent on his parents; he has been expected to give very little in return. Yet even in this year the parent and child have interacted. The child has not received passively but has had to cooperate as he received. His mother offered milk, the baby had to suck to take it. This is the beginning of cooperation. During this first year the parents and the child have been learning to work together to establish a relationship in which they can cooperate with growth. And during the time that the parents have been learning about the baby, he has been learning about them.

During his first year the baby has not only been passing through a period of rapid and spectacular growth but also has been laying the foundation for his relationships with other people. If his parents have given him the kind of affection, attention, and stimulation a baby requires—if they have answered his cries and met his needs to be fed and dry, warm, comfortable, and loved—they will have built a warm and harmonious relationship with their child, and the child's trust in his parents will help him become a capable, friendly, happy, self-reliant child.

By the end of the first year the once almost helpless baby has come a long way. His parents will need to realize increasingly that they no longer have a tiny infant, willing to lie safely in his crib, buggy, or playpen, but a young explorer who needs scope and equipment for his activities.

study of a child

A Baby Is a Person

No two are ever alike

The concept of individual differences is today an accepted fact: we know that no two children are ever entirely alike. Their differences may encompass all areas of growth and development. Physical appearance and body build, mental alertness and potential, emotional qualities and responses, social attitudes and reactions—in his combination of characteristics each child is uniquely himself. As a total personality he has no duplicate. Frequently, however, parents ignore this

49

knowledge in caring for their children. As a result, they are likely to be concerned and dismayed when ways that they followed easily and satisfyingly with one youngster seem not to work well with another.

When their second baby girl arrived, the Aldens were delighted. They had enjoyed their first little girl, now a healthy, good-natured, alert three-year-old. They eagerly expected that Deborah would be just as fascinating and as responsive to their love and care.

"And everything will be so much easier with this one," Mrs. Alden said confidently to her husband. "When I think how awkward and jittery I used to be with Ellen, it almost makes me laugh. I won't have to worry about things now. I'll know just what to expect and what to do."

Mr. Alden's memories of the first months of Ellen's babyhood were somewhat vague. But he knew that she had been a good baby who seldom cried and who seemed to be obligingly willing to do whatever was expected of her. He supposed that her mother's training had had a great deal to do with this, and complacently agreed that all would go smoothly in caring for the new baby.

The first surprise came when Deborah was only a few weeks old. Coming home one evening in an especially jovial mood, Mr. Alden opened the door somewhat noisily, whistling and tossing his hat at the terrier pup who came eagerly to greet him. There were several reactions—the dog barked with delight, the baby cried, and his wife protested in an annoyed tone of voice that he rarely heard from her.

"Oh, you woke the baby! And I've had such a time getting her to sleep! Couldn't you be more quiet?"

"You don't mean a little whistling and a bark woke her up! Why, Ellen slept through records playing and the telephone ringing and even a couple of tables of bridge. The baby was probably just waiting to say 'Hello' to her daddy," he added, striving for a light tone as he noted his wife's woeful expression.

"I had just managed to get her to sleep," Mrs. Alden said wearily. "She frets and cries more in one day than Ellen ever did in a week at her age. She's awake when I expect her to sleep, and when she finally does drop off, the least little thing wakes her up again."

As the days went by, the Aldens were increasingly aware of differences between Ellen and the new baby. Ellen had been a placid infant who drifted off to sleep between feedings. Debbie was restless and easily startled; she often awoke crying. Ellen had generally accepted her bottle and emptied it in the expected time. But, evidently quite content with her schedule, she had rarely shown any impatience to be fed. Debbie, on the other hand, usually cried demandingly and lustily long before her bottle was due. Then, after emptying it thirstily, she showed none of the satisfied readiness for a nap that had been customary with Ellen. Instead, she puckered her face, mouthed her lips and tongue, and, with clenched fists waving, often cried until her mother felt exhausted listening and wondering what she should do. More and more Debbie sucked her thumb as solace before she finally fell asleep. Thumb-sucking had very rarely been Ellen's way of going to sleep.

When cereal had first been offered to Ellen, she had tasted it tentatively, almost wonderingly. But she had not objected to it. Just as with her bottle, she took what was given to her at the time it was given. Not so Deborah. She spit out her first cereal, turning her head and crying when her mother attempted to give her more. A number of days passed before she would accept the new taste and texture.

But although the new baby proved difficult to manage in many situations, in other ways she pleased her parents greatly. She reached for and held a rattle, she turned over, and she held her head erect at a considerably earlier age than had Ellen. A bigger, stronger infant, she reacted quickly and was aware of many stimuli to which Ellen had given scant attention. Her behavior with people was a bit puzzling. Ellen had smiled happily and calmly at every face she saw and had often cried a bit when left alone again. Debbie reserved her smiles for her parents and gave an amusing impression of aloofness as she stared gravely at an unfamiliar adult. She made no protest, either, when she was again left alone. But she was more restless and kicked and tossed more vigorously after the visitor had gone.

Interested as they were in such reactions, her parents' primary concern was with Debbie's sleeping and feeding behavior. Mrs. Alden particularly felt disconcerted that she no longer knew "just what to do." Indeed, she was finding that she no longer even knew what to expect.

A long interview with the pediatrician brought several revelations. Mrs. Alden had had less contact with the doctor than when Ellen was an infant because, with her experience, she felt sure she knew how to handle a baby.

"Maybe I'm imagining things, but I'm worried," Mrs. Alden confessed to the doctor, after recounting some of the episodes that had been troubling her.

"I don't think it's imagination," said Dr. Thomas. "Your two babies are two individuals. You've been setting up standards for one on the basis of your experience with the other. And obviously the two are very different. Think of the new baby as herself, not in terms of her sister. Don't try to compare them, because no two babies are really alike. And as they grow older, the differences are still there.

"It seems to me first of all that the baby should have a larger feeding each time. I know you say Ellen was satisfied with what you gave her and the baby has been getting just as much and has, as a matter of fact, been gaining weight. But she is Debbie, not Ellen. The way she acts shows that she wants more to eat. Certainly she wants to suck more! Let's try increasing the formula as a first measure. That thumb-sucking you're so worried about will probably be less in evidence—may even disappear—when she gets more sucking activity. Thumb-sucking in a baby can mean a need for more milk or a need for more sucking or a need for a little more loving and comforting.

"All behavior has a reason, you know. A certain amount of crying is to be expected from every baby. But when one cries as much as yours has been doing, it's a pretty sure sign that something in the picture should be changed—perhaps the baby's schedule as well as the amount of her feedings. Remember how we talked some time ago about not being too rigid in planning a baby's day? Maybe you're watching the clock instead of watching the baby. Forget the clock. Let *her* tell you when she's hungry. It certainly sounds as if she uses a lot of energy trying to tell you when she wants to be fed. Then when she finally gets her bottle, she's not only upset at having had to wait—and I think also at feeling neglected—but she's tired out with all the crying she's done. And to make matters worse, she's still hungry when the milk is all gone."

"It would be easy enough to give her larger feedings," said Mrs. Alden. "But if I don't schedule my day, I'll never get through with the house and the children. Ellen never had any difficulty getting used to regularity. I can see the sense of giving one child more milk than another has needed. But if I give the baby more, surely she'll not need to get it when it's not *time*."

"The time to feed her," said Dr. Thomas, "is when she tells you it is. She'll tell you by crying and by being restless. She'll get very fretful and upset if you make her wait too long. All babies need the same general care and attention, Mrs. Alden. But every child has his own rhythms, which mothers have to learn to watch for and to respect if they want to have a happy baby as well as a healthy one."

"You can't say Ellen isn't a happy child!" Mrs. Alden quickly protested. "Why, she's so good and cheerful. I don't think she's done as much crying in all her life as Debbie has in this little while."

"Of course no one can say positively, but I would guess that your schedule and Ellen's own feeding rhythm were about the same, whereas Deborah's system seems to require shorter periods between feedings," replied the doctor. "Then, too, Ellen seems to have a different temperament as well as different body needs. It seems she can be satisfied more easily, isn't upset as quickly, and in general accepts circumstances more placidly.

"Really there are a great many differences between your two children. This baby is developing muscular control earlier than your first child did. She reacts more positively to stimuli, too. And it seems she's showing signs of differences in social behavior.

"Don't try to make her over into Ellen's pattern, just because you found Ellen easy to take care of. And don't resent the fact that she doesn't do the same things Ellen did. She's a different person, an individual, and parents have to learn to accept individuality, unless they want to worry needlessly—and unless they want to risk making their children less relaxed and happy than they'd like to have them. Babies whose own rhythms happen to match pretty closely the schedules their mothers set follow regular schedules easily. But others won't let routines be imposed on them without some noisy protesting. That's hard on their mothers, but it's hard on them, too."

Mrs. Alden was skeptical. "I know there's been a great deal said about former ways not being good for children—like keeping rigidly to routines, and expecting all children of the same age to do the same things in the same way. But what's the use of trying to find out how children develop," she protested, "if you can't learn about one baby from having taken care of another?"

"It isn't comparing *one* baby with another that tells us how they grow and develop or tells us the best ways to handle them," the doctor responded. "It's work with hundreds and hundreds of babies that counts. Studying a large number of children over a long period of time tells us what to expect and what not to expect. It corrects some things we've taken for granted. It suggests better ways to help children grow and develop. But with all our general knowledge, we need to adjust considerably in planning for a particular baby, to meet his particular needs. I'm not suggesting that you feed Debbie every time she cries, but that you adjust your schedule to *her* rather than try to force her to adjust to an arbitrary schedule.

"Don't get worried about different methods being advocated from time to time. If we didn't learn new ways and better ways, we'd keep repeating many mistakes. The experienced person knows that each baby is likely to respond in his individual fashion to whatever way he is handled. One gets along well because of the procedures followed. But another gets along in spite of what's done. And some others won't get on satisfactorily at all unless the approach is varied to meet their special needs."

"Is anything the same for all babies?" Mrs. Alden sounded a little dismayed. "Isn't there any general advice a mother can always follow safely? I feel more helpless now than before I had any babies at all."

Dr. Thomas smiled. "You feel confused, I know, but I don't think you will be when you've thought over all we've talked about," he said consolingly. "And there *is* one thing you can bank on with every baby—he needs to feel secure, important to his parents, and sure of their love. That need is the same for all, for both Ellen and Debbie. Make Debbie feel that you love her and want her very much. Let her always have the comfortable assurance of being loved. Later, when you must criticize and sometimes even punish her for unacceptable behavior, let her still sense that you love and accept *her,* although you can't accept her behavior. If every child could grow up feeling that way, there would be fewer problems in the schools and the courts. There would be happier boys and girls, and happier grown-ups, too.

"All normal children within any age range show many similarities. But no two in a group are entirely alike. Every procedure suggested for caring for children will have to be changed here and there, altered this way or that, perhaps even entirely discarded to fit the individual needs of an individual child. New ways in child care will be advocated as we gain new information about child development and adjustment. But there's no substitute for the emotional security which must be given a child if he is to feel the assurance, the sense of belonging, the contentment that spell for him happy, healthful growth. And such feelings come from the feeling tone between parents and children.

"When your baby cries because she is frustrated by her schedule, that frustrates you and destroys the pleasantness of the feeling tone. Making the schedule fit the baby rather than forcing the baby to fit the schedule is important. And, as a matter of fact, it will help both of you. You'll feel easier, so you'll find your baby easier to handle."

Mrs. Alden smiled as Dr. Thomas finished. "It's a lot easier to cuddle and love a baby when you aren't worn out by her crying and fretting. Yes, I think I see now what's been happening. Debbie's eternal crying has made me impatient with her, and I suppose she senses it. I love her just as much as I do Ellen, but Ellen was such a *good* baby that I cuddled her more, I know, than I've cuddled Debbie. It *is* something of a circle, isn't it? Thank you for showing me a possible way out."

chapter 5

The Toddler

Part baby, part child

There is no exact day or month when a baby becomes a toddler. Some children get up on their feet before their first birthday, others not until they have reached seventeen or eighteen months. The toddler age usually begins somewhere between fifteen and eighteen months and ends between two and two-and-a-half years. It is an in-between stage. The child no longer crawls on the floor, but neither has he attained the maturity or the growing self-sufficiency of the runabout. He is still part baby although already part child.

During the toddler period the child learns not only how to walk upright but also how to talk. Both are of the utmost importance, for they enable the child to participate adequately and independently in the activities he will encounter as he grows up. The child who cannot walk and the child who cannot hear and so imitate the sounds of speech are both severely handicapped and must have skillful assistance if they are to survive in a world of mobility and speech.

This is also the period when a child first feels the pressures of the cultural pattern that he will be expected to follow. Most parents in most cultures seem to accept the necessity and advisability of protecting, loving, and caring for a baby. However, they differ over the age at which constant and immediate responsiveness to the baby's demands for attention should be gradually modified toward guidance in the kind of behavior that will be expected of him as he grows up. Although many parents begin gentle teaching toward the end of the first year, in our culture this process of socialization usually starts during the toddler period. During the second year a child is first asked to give up doing some of the things he wants to do and to begin learning to conform to some of his parents' expectations. He must begin to learn that there are things he may not touch, taste, hold, or take apart; that there are places he may not go; that there are actions, such as learning to use the toilet, he will be expected to perform; and that there are kinds of behavior that will be unacceptable to other children or grown-ups. The almost complete permissiveness of the first year must give way very gradually to necessary teaching of what the child may or may not do. But these limitations of

freedom should be balanced, whenever possible, by allowing the child to do things his own way.

The toddler's willingness to cooperate and his desire to learn are dependent on a happy, loving relationship with his parents. Battles between parent and child, scoldings and slappings, far from making the child learn acceptable behavior, make him more difficult to teach and may retard his growth toward independence by making him insecure and anxious. Part baby and part child, the toddler will take steps toward maturity if his mother and father will love him along, have fun with him, patiently teach him as he seems ready to learn, and encourage independent behavior without forcing him out of his baby ways too rapidly.

Guidance—not punishment

The way guidance is begun and the way it is enforced as the child grows older and more capable have an important influence on his development. If those who teach him are oversevere or if their expectations are beyond his level of achievement, the child may become tense and negative, rebellious, timid, or afraid. If this happens, he will be continually more difficult to guide and teach.

Because the toddler sometimes proves difficult to manage, many parents feel that the time has come to use "discipline" with their child for fear he will get out of hand. But the toddler is not ready for punishment. He is not old enough to understand much about cause and effect or remember a lesson very successfully from one time to another. Although a child can be taught by fear and punishment, the anxiety he feels from his parents' seeming hostility when such forms of teaching are employed is often destructive. This does not mean that a toddler never should be frustrated or denied, for encountering limits and consequent frustration are unavoidable parts of growing up. It *does* mean that frustration and denial should be kept at a minimum and balanced by the satisfactions of achievement even in the second year of life.

The little child wants the approval of his parents. He feels better when they approve what he is doing, and if he is in harmony with them he will usually try to do the things they want him to do. But guiding a child and teaching him desired behavior naturally involve denial and frustration. He has to give up doing some things his way in order to do them the way adults expect. Such lessons are hard for a toddler, since he is not yet capable of understanding why things should be done in a certain way. Often he is unwilling to give up his own way and hits out against adults. He may bite or kick or hold his breath or bang his head on the floor in a temper tantrum. As one mother described it, "She expresses anger by banging her head right on the floor. Sometimes, when she gets mad, she just slaps me right on my face." Another mother described her angry toddler as throwing a block across the floor and banging a peg in obvious anger. Displaying his anger is a young child's natural response to frustration. If it becomes a continuous and marked response, however, it is a signal to his parents that they are expecting too much too soon or are trying to teach too much at once.

It is easy for adults to make the mistake of trying to teach a toddler too many things at once, overburdening the child with learning before he is able to assimilate all that they feel he must know. Other cultures are perhaps wiser than ours in this respect.

These are the months when parents learn that it is often best to use a light touch with their child. He responds to humor, fun, and games better than to direct interference with his activities. Reasoning is not very effective at this age. If the child refuses to do something, or seems tired and cross and cannot be distracted, it is usually best for his mother or father to go ahead with what must be done as quickly and gently as possible, without scolding or argument.

Although at times a direct "No" or "Don't touch" must be used, toddlers respond best to a positive approach: "You may have this" rather than "You can't have that." There is no reason why learning should not be fun. A game is more effective in teaching the toddler that he must wash his hands before eating than a cross or irritable command. A child comes in from play much more readily with a ride on the shoulder if he is tired. By using a light touch in teaching the child what he is expected to do, parents are cooperating with growth, for they are making it easy for the child to understand and pleasant for him to respond.

Discovering himself and asserting himself

The way adults guide children has another important influence on the child's emotional growth. During the second year, the toddler is continuing to build up experiences that will either help him to develop feelings of trust and confidence in his environment or to draw back from those who care for him without love and warmth. He is also passing into the second stage of emotional development

56

—he is beginning to discover himself. He wants to try himself out, to make choices, to decide whether he will do things his parents' way or not. If his parents encourage his independence but set the necessary limits, if they show him the desired pattern of behavior gently and understand his need for some success in what he does, the child begins to build the confidence that will make it possible for him to reach out into his world and take part in it with growing self-reliance. If he is continually scolded and restrained, on the other hand, he begins to doubt himself and his own abilities. He becomes timid and afraid. He holds back instead of reaching out. Growing up becomes too difficult. It is safer to be a baby.

At the same time that the child is feeling the pressure of adult demands, he is also realizing that he is a person in his own right and that he has the power to reject or accept his parents' demands. He finds that he can run the other way when his mother calls him; he can refuse to go to the toilet at the proper time or place; he can push his food aside if he does not want it. He can say "No" when his mother wants him to do something. He can drag a chair over to a shelf and climb up to get what he wants.

In short, the toddler begins to assert himself and to resist attempts to distract him—attempts that were successful a few months ago. Because he does not yet understand the reason for doing things his parents' way, he often becomes angry and has a tantrum or hits out at them if they interrupt his activities or interfere with his attempts to help himself. At the same time, he is still too young to take responsibility for himself or to be held responsible for what he does. He may seem to have learned not to touch the hot water faucet or the burner of the stove, and to stop at the curb when he toddles toward the street, but he is not yet sufficiently mature to really understand what he may or may not do. His mother and father must still take full responsibility for his safety, while they patiently continue their teaching and repeat it as the situations arise.

By eighteen months a youngster may have a temper tantrum if he fails to make some object do what he wants it to do. He may kick the box or the doll or the truck that he cannot manipulate and perhaps throw himself on the floor, kicking and screaming. Within another month or two he may also cry or become upset because he doesn't know enough words to say what he wants to say. After two and a half, he will probably be able to handle himself better, and tantrums should occur less frequently.

The toddler needs help to become an individual—independent, yet able to recognize and accept the impossibility of having everything his own way. This is difficult, yet it is essential if the child is to grow into a self-reliant person, able to meet life situations with initiative, and able to cooperate with and respect the rights of other people. A child does not know these things from birth. He learns them gradually by trying to please the adults who teach him and by imitating the pattern of behavior he sees around him.

A difficult year

Many parents consider this second year of life the most difficult in their relationship with their child. It is during this year, as the parent tries to teach and the child tries to assert himself, that disharmony and a battle of wills often begin

between parent and child. Sometimes parents begin to lose confidence at this point and wonder whether they know how to bring up a child. Their self-doubt may result in increased tension and anxiety, readily sensed by the child. This may result in problem situations, a cycle of interaction between parent and child that can slow up and interfere with the child's emotional growth.

During the child's first year, the parents usually controlled the situation. The baby could be placed in a safe spot in his crib, high chair, buggy, or playpen. If he cried, he could be picked up, and with a little ingenuity his attention could usually be diverted and his tears stopped. The baby could not get about by himself, neither could he use words to express his wants or his feelings. His needs were few, his tears quickly showed his discomfort, and his mother could meet his needs with a feeling of comparative success. But during his second year, the child discovers his environment. The toddler notices and wants to touch, taste, and feel the many appealing objects everywhere about him. He can open doors, turn faucets, and pull things down within his reach. As the year goes on, little is safe from his curiosity and zest for exploring. Knowing how much freedom to allow the young explorer and when to curb him for his own safety and for the sake of the rest of the family is a real puzzle to parents.

Activity—the keynote

Activity is the keynote of the toddler period. Now that the youngster is able to get around by himself, he is off in every direction, as any mother who has tried to watch and keep up with her eighteen-month-old child well knows. The child's attention span is usually short. He goes from one pastime to another and is usually easily distracted by new sights or sounds, although at times a particularly fascinating activity, such as exploring a hole with his finger or looking at color-

ful pictures, absorbs him completely. He is learning to throw and he tosses things indiscriminately—a ball, a bean bag, a spoon, or a dish. He enjoys playing throwing games. He does not throw a ball as older children do but uses his whole body, letting the ball go in any direction whatsoever and usually laughing with glee as he tosses it. He cannot yet throw with any sense of direction.

This has been called the "dart-and-dash-and-fling" age. To his mother the child seems to be in constant motion, for he rarely stays still when he is awake. He likes to open drawers and pull all the contents out onto the floor. He overturns wastebaskets and rummages through them. He tries to climb the stairs. He clambers onto tables and even the piano. At first, if he succeeds in getting up on the couch or bed, he is apt to roll off or come down again headfirst. Soon, however, he learns to turn around and slide off backwards. His mother still needs to be constantly watchful, even when she has moved as many dangers as possible out of his way, because the child shows no discretion in where he goes or what he does.

The toddler is full of curiosity. He still learns by touching, feeling, and mouthing everything within his reach; but now that he is on his feet, he can explore his world more fully. He no longer enjoys his playpen but prefers to range through the house or yard.

Leaving babyhood behind

More and more the toddler is losing his baby appearance. His hair has become much thicker and his features are taking on their own individuality. One can begin to see what he will look like as he grows older. His face is taking form and his jaw is shaping for his teeth. By the last part of the second year, he will have his complete set of deciduous, or baby, teeth.

The child can stand erect now. At first he walks with his feet wide apart, his stomach sticking out, sometimes with his arms held up for balance. He cannot run or turn corners, and often stumbles and falls. But by the end of his toddler year, he has a much more grown-up walk. He is steady on his feet and has learned to walk backward, to run, and even to turn corners without falling down.

As a youngster nears two, he also begins to show much better coordination in using his fingers. He is usually able to put the big pegs into his peg board, and a little later he can slip a ring over them. He places one block on top of another and often manages a tower of five or six blocks. He can turn the pages of a book, if it is made of heavy material, and he likes to look at pictures and feel and pat them. But a toddler does not use his small finger muscles nearly as often or as well as his large muscles. Some of his greatest fun lies in pulling, pushing, lifting, and dragging things around. He enjoys sand and water, and delights in dumping and pouring them. For the most part his attention span remains short, although sometimes his mother may be surprised at his temporary absorption in what he is doing.

Music often calls out an alert response in the toddler—he may even try to dance to a marked rhythm that appeals to him. He often tries to turn the radio on for himself. He likes to have someone sing to him and play rhythmic games. Although peekaboo and pat-a-cake are still fun, he revels in the more boisterous play of being picked up and carried over a shoulder or of rolling on the floor and roughhousing with his daddy. He laughs uproariously and has such great fun that his excitement sometimes gets out of hand. Adults should take care not to overstimulate him, especially before meals and at bedtime.

Time—the here and now

One source of frustration the toddler constantly experiences is the difference between his concept of time and that of adults. During this period, the child lives in the "here-and-now." He has no conception of past or future time, and no capacity to wait for something he wants *now*. He does not understand about waiting and will be quite disturbed if it is necessary. If his mother says "outdoors," the toddler may head for the door. Further, the toddler does not understand the pressures time imposes. If he is engrossed in what he is doing, the fact that his mother must get to the grocery store means nothing. Here may begin another cycle of battles between parents and their children. The mother moves quickly—time is of the essence to her. She has many things to do and wants to get the next thing done. The toddler moves slowly, absorbed in the moment— perhaps trying to put the lace through the hole in his shoe, perhaps looking at something in the crack in the sidewalk. The mother wants the youngster to ride in the buggy so that she can get to the store and back before the older children get home from school, but he wants to toddle along and explore. He wants to climb up every step or to pick up little objects from the sidewalk. This puts a strain on the patience of the parent, who in desperation may pick up the child and put him screaming into his buggy.

When possible, it is best to cooperate with the child's exploring. When that is impossible, diversion may work, since his attention can usually be drawn toward some other equally fascinating object. When the mother's schedule necessitates moving the child along faster than he is prepared to go, and diversion no longer works, picking him up from behind seems more effective than a head-on approach. If the interruption is too abrupt, however, the child often responds by hurling himself down and screaming and kicking a direct protest. The toddler has little capacity for self-control.

The wise mother recognizes and makes allowances for this difference between her sense of time and her child's. She also recognizes the importance of his attempts to do things for himself, even though he may be slow and inept; these attempts are necessary for the growth of independence.

Independence—in spurts

Sometimes a child of this age shows great interest in trying to do things for himself; at other times he wants his mother to do everything for him. Parents should never *insist* on self-help. If a youngster is encouraged and praised for what he does, he will try of his own accord to become increasingly independent as he grows more capable in using his fingers and hands.

Most toddlers try to undress themselves and have some success in getting off their shoes and socks, and perhaps their shirts and pants. Dresses and suits present greater difficulties, and slipover sweaters and most snowsuits are almost impossible to manage. Some toddlers can put on their shirts; they may even manage to put on a sock after a fashion, but the heel is likely to be on top. If they struggle into their pants or pajamas, both legs are often in the same opening. But they are trying and should be allowed and encouraged to do so whenever possible, even though their efforts are not a complete success by adult standards.

The toddler makes a mess when he tries to feed himself, for his eye-and-finger coordination is still imperfect. There is often more food in his hair and on the

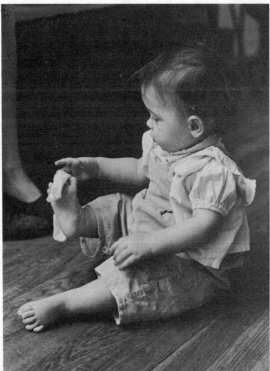

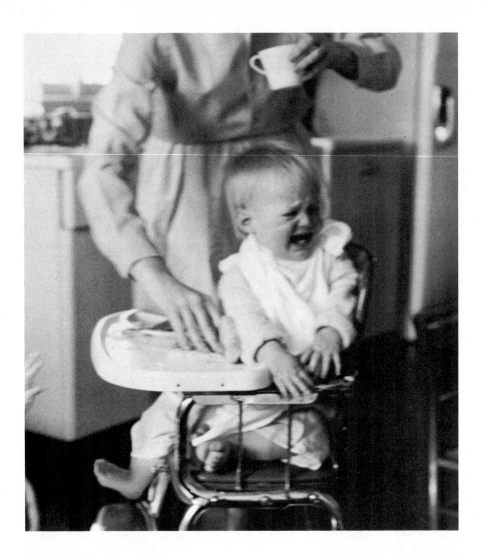

floor than in his mouth. By the time he is between two and two and a half, however, he may have learned to manage his spoon and cup quite efficiently.

Fasts and feasts

Feeding problems often develop during this period. The first year the baby triples his birth weight; the second he gains only three to five pounds. Obviously, he neither needs nor wants the quantities of food in proportion to his size that he did as a baby. This drop in appetite often worries the mother, who begins trying to make her child eat more than he wants, with the result that he rebels and a problem is created. For instance, a mother who still insists on a quart of milk a day for her child leaves little space for the solid foods she also wishes him to eat.

The toddler accepts and enjoys a much wider variety of food and can eat many of the simpler foods from the adults' table. But he is also showing preferences; by two he expresses his likes and dislikes and pushes his plate away if it contains something he does not want to eat. Most toddlers do not seem to relish foods mixed together, as in creamed or casserole dishes. They are conservative and want to see the meat, potatoes, and vegetables as separate items on a plate. Often they finish one food before they start the next.

Children of this age often go on food jags that are disturbing to their mothers. They refuse certain foods and want large quantities of others. Mothers who have been taught to believe in the clean plate—the eat-everything theory—sometimes find a feeding problem developing when they make an issue of the child's eating everything. The toddler does not understand his mother's concern, but he does sense her anxiety. Often he refuses to eat and begins to associate unpleasant feelings with mealtime. Offering foods that the child enjoys eating within a reasonably balanced diet is emotionally healthier than battling with the child, whose understanding necessarily is limited. The most important thing during this period is the child's attitude toward eating. When possible he should be given food he will enjoy and eat heartily; forcing disliked foods on a child is usually unwise.

Naps and bedtimes

Toddlers still need a great deal of rest. Most of them take a nap right after their midday meal and sleep around the clock at night. If a child will not take a nap without a struggle, he should go to bed earlier at night. Such a child should also have a quiet period in the afternoon, playing with toys on his bed or in his room, listening to records, or just resting cuddled in his mother's arms. A toddler who does not take some time out in the middle of the day is usually fussy by suppertime.

Bedtime, too, may begin to present difficulties, for the child may not go to bed as readily as he did a few months earlier. If he has taken a long afternoon nap, he may not be ready to sleep again until eight or nine o'clock. If he is put back to bed too soon, he may be restless and demanding. Mothers often find it necessary to change their schedule to better accommodate the child's changing needs. The toddler usually wants bedtime to follow a certain routine, and even then makes many demands for drinks of water or trips to the toilet. Often he is attached to a particular toy or blanket and will not go to bed without it.

Fears of the world around him

Because the toddler is aware of the world around him before he is quite able to understand it, he seems to develop many fears. Noises frighten him: he may cry or cling to his mother at the sound of a loud train whistle or at the sudden whir of the vacuum cleaner. Wind, heavy rain, thunder, fire engines, or even the flushing of a toilet may be frightening to him. Sometimes he seems afraid at bedtime and clings to his mother when she tries to leave him; or he may wake up as if he had been dreaming, and still be afraid even after his mother has come to him. He may begin to be afraid of the dark and insist that the door be left open with a light in the hall at bedtime. Large, unfamiliar objects may make a toddler run to his mother's side. He has no conception of size and sometimes will refuse to get into the bathtub for fear he may slip down the drain. Nor does he like things to be changed. He may resist going to bed if his crib has been moved or if he is in a new room or a new house.

The child should not be laughed at or scolded for these fears. When he is afraid, he needs the reassurance and comfort of being near his mother. As she soothes him, she may be able to explain to him or, better still, show him what made the noise or what frightened him. When he understands more clearly, some of his fears will disappear. But nearness to his mother does much more to quiet and relax a toddler than her explanations. He is still very dependent on her for his feelings of well-being and security.

Toddlers sometimes evidence another kind of apprehensiveness—a timidity, anxiousness, and general fearfulness. This type of fear is not likely to be cured by explanations or reasons. Usually it suggests that parents may be putting too many demands on the youngster, expecting too many achievements for his level of development or too much self-control. They may not know what can reasonably be expected of a toddler. They may be using too many "do's" and "don'ts" or expecting that because their child now understands what they say, he should be able to conform to their demands and invariably remember their admonitions from one time to the next.

Sometimes apprehensiveness appears when toilet training is begun too soon or with too much emphasis. And sometimes it results from parents giving their child the impression that they find him a nuisance and don't really want him. Or again they may not realize that he needs cuddling and other clear evidences of affection if he is to be a secure, happy, and responsive child.

Demands made of the child are multiplying also and he is sometimes unsure of what he should do. His uneasiness is increased if he has been unsuccessful in meeting his parents' expectations, with the result that their scoldings and signs of disapproval have also increased. Little children are often worried and anxious for fear that if they fail to please their parents, their parents will no longer love them and may leave them. This fear is sometimes behind the two-year-old's restlessness at bedtime, particularly if he has been scolded or punished during the day. He may climb out of bed repeatedly to reassure himself that his parents are still there—that they have not gone away.

Toilet training

Toilet training is one of the major demands put upon the toddler to conform to the ways of our culture. In other cultures, such as the Chinese and the Philippine, this particular type of conformity is not given the importance it is accorded in most of the United States. Sometimes adults, in their desire to make the young child conform, forget that two considerations must be taken into account if toilet training is to be successful. First, the child must be ready for training. He not only must understand what is expected but must also have the muscular coordination necessary to control the bowel and bladder muscles and to release them voluntarily at a given time and place. Second, successful training depends on the child's willingness and interest in cooperating. Until he seems physically and emotionally ready to cooperate, toilet training should not be begun.

Twenty-five years ago training was started early in the first year, but the child today is not usually trained until the middle of the second year, and it is sometimes during the third or occasionally even later that training is completed. This shift in the cultural pattern has occurred as a result of our recent understanding that the child is not ready for training before this second year. Success in toilet training usually depends on the child's relationship with his parents and on their ability to accept accidents casually, to express encouragement, and to praise success. A tense, anxious mother who communicates to her child her tension over toilet training can begin a cycle of difficulties in guiding the child in other areas. Rebellion or anxiety over too severely enforced toilet training may cause a child to be defiant or overanxious in any situation where an adult makes demands. Consequently, the toddler's relationship with his mother is very important at this time. If it is harmonious and happy, the youngster, once ready physically, can usually learn to use the toilet without too much effort on his or his mother's part. But if tension already exists between mother and child, or if anxiety, severity, or overinsistence characterize training, the process may be very upsetting to the child.

Bowel training before bladder training

The toddler is usually ready to start bowel training a good many months before he can be expected to control his urination, because the stool, when it is ready to leave the body, causes a more definite pressure and generally comes at regular times. Many toddlers have only an occasional bowel movement in their diapers after eighteen months, though it may be several months longer before they can tell their mother when they need to go to the toilet or go alone. Bowel training may not proceed smoothly, however, and there may be relapses, just as in other forms of learning. This seems to be especially true at about fifteen months.

Learning to keep dry is much more difficult. Urination does not always occur regularly and is easily affected by the quantity of liquid drunk, by temperature, by excitement, by an approaching illness, or by the size of the bladder. At some time during the second year, children become interested in the puddles they make and will show them to their mother or get a cloth and busily try to mop them up. This is an important step in the baby's awareness of his urinary function—even though it may irritate his mother, who feels that he should have told her ahead of time instead of waiting until he has made the puddle.

When a youngster starts walking, he is usually ready to begin learning to keep dry (though, of course, if he is an early walker, he may not yet be ready for control). Children differ greatly. Some tiny children seldom have accidents; others soak many diapers a day. Parents can best cooperate with nature by noticing at what intervals the child usually urinates and then placing him on the toilet seat near those times. This is apt to be about a two-hour interval, although the time varies with different children and even with an individual child from day to day. Toilet training may be achieved quickly, or it may be a very slow process. A child should never be forced, scolded, or punished for lack of success. If he does not seem to get the idea when his mother tries to teach him, she should wait and try again a little later. Many mothers find the last part of the second year best for starting toilet training.

By two years accidents are usually becoming less frequent. The child can sometimes tell his mother when he wants to go to the toilet or may even go of his own accord. He should not be expected to keep dry at night until after he has learned to stay dry during the day, and occasional accidents, both night and day, must be expected throughout the preschool years. If a child who has been rather consistently dry begins to have lapses over any considerable period, however, it is well to look for the reason behind his need to return to baby ways.

Language development

During the toddler year the baby's babbling sounds start to form into words. He not only is learning to master his body through walking, climbing, pushing, pulling, and using his hands, but he also is learning to form words and to use these words for objects he wants or sees.

It is interesting to notice that both these efforts—walking and talking—seem to require tremendous energy and concentration, for studies show that most children do not acquire these skills simultaneously. The child who talks early and well often walks at a later date, whereas the child who is an active, early walker is often slower in learning to talk. Children vary as to which they learn first. Some children walk first and talk very little; others talk first and then walk. It appears that youngsters need to expend their energy in one direction or the other, but that typically they cannot master both feats at once.

Language skill, like other accomplishments, is an individual matter, and wide variations are to be expected among normal children. Some eighteen-month-old youngsters can say as few as four words, others ten or eleven; some have been reported as using "too many words to count." Some normal two-year-olds use only six words; others over two hundred fifty.

But real speech begins only when the child has meaningful associations for the words he uses. One mother did not feel that her toddler was talking until he held up his duck and said, "Uck." The repetition of words as sounds is a step toward the mastery of language. A little child may say "ma-ma" long before he makes the sound in response to seeing her or wanting her. Many children make chains of sounds in rhythmic patterns when they are tiny, as if they are copying the rhythm of the speech they hear.

The words a child uses are determined by the culture in which he grows up. All babies, wherever they are born, seem to make the same basic speech sounds. But the sounds the child will continue to use as words or will combine to form words will be those he hears in his environment. For example, a child of American parents brought up in a Japanese family will speak Japanese if that is the language he consistently hears.

Many toddlers experience considerable frustration during their second year as they try to make themselves understood through words. A child who is trying to express himself verbally with indifferent success may work himself into a tantrum because he is not understood.

Many factors enter into language development. Some children seem to have their wants met so thoroughly that they apparently feel no need to use words at an early age. Some, growing up in highly verbal families, talk more readily than most children. Others, growing up in families that speak rapidly or indistinctly, or in families that pay little attention to the child, may be slow in speaking.

Parents can help their children to master language by speaking clearly and simply. Either baby talk or speech that is too involved may impede the child's learning to talk. Parents can also help by chanting rhymes and reading simple stories aloud and by naming objects as they give them to the toddler, though they should never force him to say the word for what he wants.

The toddler's devotion to the person who cares for him is important in helping him develop proper motivation for speech learning. Clinically, we see children blocked in language growth because of tensions that exist between them and their parents. Parental acceptance and encouragement of the baby's babbling and cooing is an important step in the child's speech development. Support is even more vital when the child is trying to form the sounds he hears into words.

Reaching toward social relationship

The toddler is still a baby. His instinctive drive is toward growing up, but growth must come naturally if the child's confidence in himself is to be gradually built. He still needs a baby's care, but he also needs encouragement and opportunities to grow up that are within his capacity for success.

One of the steps toward growing up that the toddler hesitatingly tries to take is reaching out toward other children. He does not know how to play with them, but he is beginning to like to be near them when he plays. By the age of two, most youngsters enjoy *parallel play* with another child—the two sitting contentedly side by side in the sandbox, each one doing what he likes. They enjoy each other's companionship even though they don't actually play together. But though the two children like being together, they will still snatch one another's toys whenever they have a chance.

The toddler's social relationships are awkward, and he cannot safely be left alone with others his own age, for youngsters of this age may push, hit, hurt one another, or even bite. The toddler can rarely share or take turns. This is the period of "mine," with everything still related to the self. The child clutches his teddy bear or toy tightly to him if someone else wants it. He has not yet reached the age when he can understand that there will still be something for him if he lets go of what he has or shares it with another. Occasionally, he may make a gesture away from himself—reaching out toward the other child by offering a toy or a cookie to bite. But often he quickly snatches back his toy if the other child takes it, or cries if the other child eats his cookie. The toddler still needs to have a substitute placed in his hands if he is to relinquish what he holds.

During this year, the toddler seems to feel safe only when he is close to his mother or some other accepted adult. Around eighteen months and again at the end of the year he goes through a period of accentuated clinging. At two this is particularly noticeable, perhaps because he seems so much more grown-up that his parents expect greater independence of him. But far from showing more independence, he clings to his mother and often cries when she leaves him. His mother is all-important to the child at this stage, and he frequently goes through a period when he will rarely let her out of his sight. He follows her around while she is at work and tries to help her. If a mother has patience enough to accept her toddler's need to be close to her at this stage, she will usually find that within another year he will begin to be drawn to other children and will be not only willing but often eager to leave her side.

The toddler enjoys the members of his family, but few children at this age respond to strangers or are willing to go to them or stay with them. The toddler needs his father or some other familiar adult to help in his social weaning from his mother. If during the second year his father or some other adult can sometimes feed him, play with him, put him to bed, take him out, or stay with him while his mother is out, he will learn gradually to tolerate longer times away from his mother and to feel safe with other people. When the toddler has learned to leave his mother's side, he is ready to learn to play with and get along with children of his own age.

living with a child

The Light Touch

Sometimes parents try too hard

At a Child Study Group meeting young Mrs. Bartlett, mother of not-yet-two Connie, raised the question of how to manage a busy, active, investigating, protesting toddler and still carry on necessary household routines. Half apologetic and half defensive, she told of constant turmoil—prolonged mealtimes, delayed bedtimes, temper outbursts, tears, spankings, and strewn-about toys, picture-books, and kitchen utensils.

She was somewhat consoled when others in the group instantly chimed in to tell of similar experiences and similar concerns. A few of them, however, were a little disconcerted when the mother of a somewhat older child agreed blandly that not-yet-two is certainly a trying age but that mothers do live through it.

"But how do I handle *now, today?*" persisted Mrs. Bartlett. "I don't want to discourage healthy curiosity by constantly frustrating it, but I seem to be saying 'No, no' and 'Mustn't touch' mighty often. I'd like to know if I could manage better."

Mrs. Morton, a former nursery school teacher and the leader of the group, suggested, "When they pick up something they shouldn't, generally it isn't too hard to distract them from it by offering something else. They want to look and feel because they're curious about everything. Give them something that they can safely squeeze or shake or poke. The beginnings of their self-assertion, the early evidences of trying to be a bit independent, are what must be handled appropriately. Toddlers aren't always being naughty, you know. Being inquisitive and investigating things are good signs. Toddlers want to know; their ways are part of their growing, and we need to see them in relation to their total growth picture.

"Let's talk about some of the situations that are troublesome at this age and that worry you. Who'll give us a specific example?"

Mrs. Bartlett was quick to respond. "Take just this morning," she said. "Connie was good for a change while she was being washed and dressed. Then she played in her high chair while I got her milk and cereal ready. She took her milk right away, and the cup was half empty when she put it down. I guess she was thirsty. The first few spoonfuls of cereal went down nicely, too.

"Then suddenly she—well, she just revolted. She tossed her head from side to side and pressed her lips together tight. I couldn't get another bit inside her mouth. Well, I didn't think she should get away with that, so I just took everything off her tray and started to lift her down. She stiffened—you know how they do—and shrieked, 'Milk! Milk!' I said, 'Be a good girl and finish your cereal. Then you can have more milk.' But she went on screaming. I held out a spoonful and she knocked it out of my hand. I'm afraid I slapped her. I know I shouldn't have, but what do you suppose made her act like that? It was an awful session."

"I can't say exactly what caused the trouble this morning," said Mrs. Morton, "but there are a number of possibilities. Of course, as soon as you found *yourself* hard to control, Connie became that much harder to control, too. It's not unusual. I'm sure most of us here have had something of the sort happen at one time or another. Will anyone suggest a possible cause? If we know why something happens, we can be more certain of what to do about it."

A chorus of voices contributed suggestions. "Did you give her more than she could eat?" "Did you feed her too fast?" "Maybe she's just tired of cereal." "Did she want to feed herself?" "You scolded and hurt her feelings."

Mrs. Morton turned to Connie's mother. "You might find your reason in one of those," she said. "Suppose I list a few general suggestions on the positive side. There are things to do that we know contribute to good eating habits and help avoid problem habits. For example, it's wise to serve a small portion of food and offer more when that's all gone. 'All gone!' can be a satisfying game instead of almost a threat. A colored dish or a dish with a picture at the bottom is a help, too. And you can vary the child's foods now and then, though with some children familiarity with taste and texture seems important. When you start on a new food, give only a taste or two at first. Let him get used to it gradually.

"And you know toddlers can't be expected to concentrate on anything for more than a little while. Let a child hold a toy to turn or examine or press, and often mouthful after mouthful goes down without any objection. Sometimes little ones like to listen to a nursery rhyme or a very simple story while they eat. One with rhythm, repeated over and over, has a great appeal.

"Then, of course, remember that appetite varies. You aren't always very hungry—and neither is your child. The old clean-your-plate edict needs rethinking. A scant meal, even a missed meal now and then, won't hurt a child. It's far better than a hectic, stormy session. Only be careful then about cookies between meals. Better advance the next meal than take the edge off hunger.

"Perhaps the greatest interference with good eating habits comes from upset feelings," Mrs. Morton went on. "Being scolded or just sensing from his mother's face or voice that she is worried or angry may frighten a child. It makes him anxious. It threatens his feeling of security. Upset feelings interfere with any activity, including eating and digesting, so scolding has no place during mealtimes.

"Actually, scolding a little one isn't nearly as effective as getting down to his level of activity and understanding and enjoyment. Making a game of necessary routines seems more sensible than unimaginatively forcing a child to complete them. Try for a light touch. So many mothers are too tense, far too serious and determined. Take things easy. Look pleasant and sound pleasant, and you'll have a pleasanter child, easier to handle.

"The game approach works in lots of ways. When you want to dress your child and he wants to play, why *not* play—by making a game of getting dressed? You know what I mean. 'Where's Tommy's head? There it is!' and on goes his shirt. 'What's wiggling in there? Why, it's a foot!' and off comes the sleeper. 'First one foot, and then the other,' is a chant little children enjoy when you put on their socks and shoes. 'Where's that hand?'—and an imaginary search for it helps get a snug sweater sleeve down. Have a good time yourself! You'll get chuckles and grins from your youngster rather than having him pull away and fight you off. The more matter-of-fact you are and the more cheerful you sound, the easier you'll find the whole daily process of child care."

There was silence for a moment. Then Mrs. Mahler ventured, "You can't *always* be matter-of-fact and cheerful. Teddy has his own room and after breakfast I usually take him there to play while I make the beds and straighten up the house. Yesterday the back doorbell rang, and going through the kitchen I found him in front of the refrigerator—and in front of him, on the floor, was everything he could reach from the shelves. While I thought he was quietly playing in his room, he was busy tearing labels off cans and putting the bits of paper in a row of pots and pans. He had taken the cans out of the cupboard and lined them up. He said, 'Look at my train!' *He* was cheerful but *I* certainly wasn't. I took him back to his room and left him howling behind the locked door while I cleaned up the mess. When I went back to him later, he had taken everything out of a drawer in his chest and was rubbing away inside with a wad of Kleenex. 'Teddy cleaning, too,' he informed me. Who'd keep calm and matter-of-fact with that going on?"

Lively and at times controversial discussion followed. It was finally summed up by the group leader:

"Little children can't be left for long to their own devices. When they are left alone at this age, a gate across a doorway provides the reassuring sight or at least sound of mother's presence nearby. That avoids the feeling of loneliness or fear which isolation behind a closed door so often brings. And it keeps the child where he is supposed to be. But behind the gate where the child is to play, the stage must have been set. A favorite toy, a box of building blocks within easy reach, a simple puzzle, a well-liked picture-book—these can fill contented minutes.

"When your work keeps you in one room for some time, a happy solution is to have the child with you in the room with the door safely closed. Then provide him with a rag, perhaps, so that he can dust the window sills while you work. Or give him play materials appropriate to the space available. A friendly glance and a few words now and then keep a child from feeling left out. With some youngsters, saying rhymes together or telling a simple short story helps enormously to keep things running smoothly. But language development varies so widely at this period of growth that you'll have to be the judge of whether this scheme will entertain your child.

"Lack of language comprehension often explains apparent stubborn or disobedient behavior. Wordy directions or reproofs often aren't understood. A child may listen without really comprehending what it's all about, but he gathers from his mother's manner and voice that she is irritated or displeased. This may trouble a child more than anyone realizes at the time.

"But it is not always lack of understanding that makes a youngster do again and again something he's been scolded for. Sometimes it seems to him the only way of getting his mother's attention away from her engrossing work. It's good to stop every once in a while and give him a few minutes' undivided attention."

The group agreed that it takes enormous patience and great ingenuity to dovetail housework with the care of a child. Few of them had really tried to think through their particular situations, and most felt there were things they might try that would contribute to easier and pleasanter mornings at home.

"But we don't stay in the house all the time," protested a mother who had not yet joined the discussion. "I don't have as much trouble indoors as I do when we go out for a walk. The stroller has lost its appeal entirely—Susie wants to walk. Going around the block seems miles, sometimes. She goes up and down steps in front of houses, and in and around walks that take her fancy. She has to feel everything—fence pickets, and tree trunks, and lamp posts, and grass, and twigs, and even cigarette butts, if she can get to one before I spot it and hold her back. A walk just about exhausts me."

This, too, the mothers agreed, was a common experience. But Mrs. Morton was encouraging. "Just remember, when it seems too much, that all the stopping and feeling and touching are part of a child's learning experience. Children want to know, if they're normal! We should really be much more concerned when a child almost two or older is *not* curious. The always passive, unobservant, incurious, content-to-sit-quietly-in-his-stroller toddler, if he is physically well, is not showing signs of normal mental development.

"The actively looking, probing, questioning toddler is learning to identify things, finding out if they are hard or soft, rough or smooth, warm or cold to the touch, and so on. We take many concepts for granted—up and down, in and out, around and straight ahead—forgetting that a child learns them by experiencing them time and again and by having you further his store of information with your verbal explanations.

"Don't dread your walks. If you expect typical behavior—and keep in mind its great importance for development—you're likely to be more patient with it. When outdoors, toddlers like to get close to things. They want to examine a stone, a leaf, a bur, a hedge. Being restrained in a stroller keeps them from the fun of learning what is smooth and what is prickly. Small children must have some opportunity for investigating. And when freedom to explore is substituted for, 'Hold my hand, now!' or, 'How many times must I tell you not to pick up those dirty things?' everyone is happier.

"Obviously there are times when it is not feasible to let a child go exploring freely. Safety or lack of time may interfere. Then a bit of socializing helps—for instance, a rhyme or a song. Children usually enjoy that. Or if your child's language development makes it practical, call attention to a big green car or a funny little white dog or a group of older children playing with a red ball. Sometimes even though he may not understand the words, the child responds to your voice and feels a shared activity.

"Often what seems like interminable dawdling is actually intense interest. And what seems like rebellion and refusal to comply—when a child shouts, 'No! No!' —is not resistance at all, but simply the child's way of asking you (with great limitations of speech) to wait just a minute to see how this goes, or how heavy that is, or if this feels the way it looks. It helps considerably to remember that such behavior is part of normal developing and an important phase of growth."

"We haven't said a word about temper tantrums," mentioned one of the mothers. "I get so uncomfortable when Timmy yells and yells. The neighbors must hate us when we're in, and I'm terribly embarrassed when we're out and he makes a scene."

"It's a fairly safe rule to pay no attention to a child in a temper outburst," said Mrs. Morton. "He'll stop sooner if he's ignored. But if fatigue is behind the outburst, it's better to distract him with something he likes."

"It sounds so simple when you tell it," the mother said uncertainly. "I get so on edge. I feel so upset and—well, inadequate."

"I think all mothers have that feeling at times," Mrs. Morton replied. "They're better off if they can accept the fact that households with small children can't always run smoothly and quietly, and that things can't always be in apple-pie order. The less anxiety a mother feels about neatness or about a schedule, the easier it becomes for her to handle her child. Part of it is handling herself."

"It's certainly a relief to realize what's normal," Mrs. Bartlett said. "I can see how I can manage better, in the light of all we've talked about. Going over a child's day, point by point, gives the perspective you said we needed."

To understand an individual child and meet his needs wisely we need to have in perspective *how children grow*. If we understand how development progresses in general, never forgetting that each child develops in his individual fashion, and if we can use the light touch in living with our children, the way toward their growing up will be immeasurably smoothed.

living with a child

Habits and Attitudes Are Learned Together

Both are long-lasting and important

For many mothers, one of the most troublesome aspects of early childhood is toilet training. Current opinion deplores too early or too insistent an approach in helping a child learn bladder and bowel control. Yet even while accepting this opinion, few parents quite know what is meant by "too early" and not many are likely to feel that *their* method is "too insistent." Very often a young mother of a first baby has only the vaguest idea of how to go about the whole procedure and what to expect of her child.

Ronny's parents had been looking forward to the time when he could get about by himself, say at least a few words, eat without being fed, and keep dry. He had finally fulfilled their anticipations in all but the last of these, and Mrs. Hyde was commenting ruefully about it to her husband one morning.

"He's always so wet when he wakes up!" she said. "His diaper and his sleepers and even the bedclothes are just soaked. And during the day he has so many accidents. He doesn't seem to get the idea of what the bathroom is for, even when I get him there in time. Little Mary Elroy, down the block, is almost always dry, and her mother says that she never has a bowel movement except on the toilet. Ronny soils a diaper every day. Do you suppose there's something wrong with him?" She was genuinely concerned, so much so that she passed on some of her feeling to her husband.

"Mary's a couple of months younger, too," he said thoughtfully. "What does the doctor say? Did you ask him? Does he think there's anything wrong with Ronny?"

"Yes, I've asked him, and he said to stop worrying. He said there's not a thing wrong with Ronny—that most girls learn to stay dry several months before most boys do and that what may be right for Mary isn't necessarily right for Ronny. But I'm not convinced."

And she was not. She was quite sure that her baby was not responding adequately to her method of training, and this she found most disturbing. Now that Ronny was almost two, she felt he should be able to keep dry.

As a matter of fact, many two-year-olds have been toilet trained. But very often this early learning has been accompanied by such stern and strict and insistent adult procedures and attitudes that the baby, while he manages to need fewer and finally no diapers, acquires a feeling about the total process that is emotionally unhealthy.

Without realizing it, young Mrs. Hyde had surrounded the maternal task of toilet training with an aura of unpleasantness. It had become her custom to place her baby on the toilet seat firmly and none too gently, saying, "Get through quickly now, Ronny. No fooling around." And a few minutes later she was likely to add that Ronny was holding her up in her housework and keeping her from important tasks.

Ronny, not quite two, probably did not entirely understand his mother's words, but no doubt he understood her attitude: "This is certainly a nuisance, a bother, this business of a baby's bowel movement." When he would have no success in following her admonition, she would take him off the toilet seat with a little shake and sometimes even a slap to emphasize her displeasure. Often only a short time later his mother had to change his soiled diaper. Was this perhaps Ronny's unconscious way of retaliating?

One morning Ronny *was* successful, much more quickly than ever before. His mother was not in the bathroom when he finished, and he managed to slide down from the seat. He leaned over the bowl and examined with interest this product of his which his mother seemed so concerned about. After a moment, he reached in and was smearing the lid when Mrs. Hyde appeared. She pulled him away, shook him hard, and with a look of disgust scrubbed his hands thoroughly. Throughout this process she kept up a running comment about how naughty he was, how much work he made for her, how slow he was in learning to behave properly. Her voice was sharp and displeased.

Ronny was frightened and cried, confused by his mother's reaction to what had happened. He had accomplished what she had always urged him to do, and now he was being punished for it. He was upset and worried. For some time after that episode, Mrs. Hyde had another problem: Ronny became constipated. Was it perhaps his unconscious fear of further punishment that made Ronny retain his stool? That is not inconceivable.

Mrs. Hyde might have managed more wisely if she had been less tense and felt less inadequate about the toilet training procedure. She might well have said a word in praise of Ronny's successful movement, then cleaned him and the toilet lid with the firm but not scolding comment that "Big boys don't play with a BM. They just flush the toilet." Later, play with plasticine or finger paints or sand and water would have provided satisfaction for Ronny's desire to squeeze and smear a soft substance.

Bladder training, after a time, was proceeding fairly successfully, and Ronny had become quite dependable. "I wear big boy pants," he said proudly.

Mrs. Hyde was expecting a few friends over one afternoon, and the rooms had been put in order. Ronny had been freshened up, too, so his mother was annoyed at seeing a large damp spot on his clean pants.

"Oh, Ronny, not again!" she protested. "It hasn't been ten minutes since you were in the bathroom! You're a naughty, naughty boy!" In her exasperation at seeing the first guests coming up the steps at that moment, she slapped the youngster. He burst into tears, and she was chagrined to have her friends find her red and cross and the baby wet and sobbing. "It was an accident," soothed one of the guests, herself the mother of three. "Don't punish him." But Mrs. Hyde could not believe that such a lapse was really an accident. Surely it was either carelessness or a deliberate attempt to plague her—Ronny could certainly have kept dry if he had really tried.

Mrs. Hyde was expecting too much of her child. Had she stopped to think, she would have realized that Ronny would sense her excitement about entertaining —something she could now do only infrequently—and that he would be stirred up also by the bustle and hurry of preparing for the visitors. She would have been wise to have put rubber pants on him as a precaution that particular afternoon, even though training pants had definitely been in order for some days.

Normally the bladder grows to sufficient size during the first two years of life, so that voiding approximately half a dozen times daily becomes routine. But this will vary under excitement or stress, when irregular and more frequent urination is very likely to occur. Indeed, such a reaction may be experienced at any age, throughout life.

There is really no *right* time for a child to learn control of the eliminative functions. This varies with individual children. Some develop earlier than do others the voluntary control of the muscles involved in urination and defecation, and the essential coordination of the nerves and muscles governing these functions. A child who walks and talks early is likely to indicate his elimination needs at an earlier age, too. A tense, restless child generally achieves the dry habit later than does a calm, placid one.

Even the most conscientious training will be ineffective until the child is physiologically and psychologically ready for it. And since it is the child himself who must learn to control his eliminative processes, it is futile and unwise for his mother to expect him to do so before he has reached the level of development where he *is* ready. Infinite patience is greatly to be desired.

"A child must have control of the sphincter muscles at the outlet of the bladder and of the rectum," the doctor said to Mrs. Hyde, "before he is ready to respond to any training to keep clean and dry. Be patient until then, and until Ronny can verbalize well enough to tell you in his own way when he needs to go to the toilet. For quite a while any success in training him will be *your* success in judging just when to take him to the bathroom, because he won't be able to let you know soon enough for you to get him there in time."

"It's all very well for *him* to be so casual about it," Mrs. Hyde had thought at the time. "He doesn't have the trouble and worry that a mother does!" She had felt almost indignant. The wisdom of the physician's counsel went unappreciated in the turmoil of her emotional reaction to what she considered Ronny's lack of cooperation and her own inadequacy in gaining it.

Casual, easygoing mothers often have much less trouble with toilet training their children than tense, determined, worried mothers. Mrs. Hyde's unfortunate attitudes were not only making her unhappy but were threatening her baby's happiest development, for they were making him uncertain of being able to do what was clearly expected of him.

Many individuals who lack self-confidence and self-assurance—and for this reason are ineffective in what they do, and fail to live up to their capacities—are found, on psychologic study, to have had unfortunate toilet training in their very early years. The far-reaching effects of difficulties during this stage of development are many and varied. Where there is too much pressure or where the insistence comes too soon, the child becomes fearful as well as hostile toward the demanding mother. Partially repressed reactions often reappear later, showing themselves sometimes in excessive playing with mud or dirt, sometimes in extreme anxiety over getting clothing or hands dirty. In his adult years the individual may be compulsively meticulous about order or routines. He may be uncertain or insecure in his feelings about himself and others. These kinds of behavior are not infrequently found to be closely related to the attitudes and procedures of the mother in her efforts toward bowel-control training.

Mothers' reactions during toilet training also influence other attitudes in their children. In our society there is all too often a feeling of shame or of disgust connected with the excretory functioning of the body. Inevitably the child acquires such feelings if the mother makes it evident that that is the way *she* feels. "Dirty!" a mother may exclaim when her baby has a soiled diaper. Or "Nasty!" when he examines his stool. And her facial expression and tone of voice will convey meaning even more exaggerated than her words. Yet the functioning of the organs of elimination is necessary for the child's good health and is a normal bodily activity to be experienced daily all his life. It is neither a dirty, nor a nasty, nor a shameful activity. Nor is the product of the body, excreted because not needed, dirty or nasty or shameful.

A very real complication often arises from the fact that the organs of elimination are located adjacent to the sexual organs. The feeling that the child learns to associate with the former may become associated with the latter, bringing still another difficulty from faulty attitudes toward excretory functioning. Sexual functioning, too, may be drawn into the feeling of shame or disgust, of dirtiness or nastiness. Even in adolescent and adult years, these feelings of early childhood are likely to persist. Later maladjustment frequently results when early training to be "clean" has incorporated a kind of "training" wholly unplanned and unrecognized by the mother.

The mother who is willing to wait, who is patient enough to be casual about toilet activities, who praises successes and underplays lapses, helps both herself and her child to avoid distressing feelings of failure. Babies rarely learn toilet habits in as short a time as mothers hope or expect. Indeed, once training is undertaken, it is not at all unusual for six months or more to be required. Since often the adult in charge has a vague feeling that six weeks ought certainly to be long enough, she may tend to burden the whole procedure with reproaches or scoldings or other evidences of disapproval. This all interferes with the learning so eagerly awaited.

When training has been started, it is important that the child's own rhythm be allowed to dictate the time when he goes to the bathroom. Directing a child to urinate or defecate to suit adult convenience is pointless. Indeed, such a procedure often results in an emotional reaction which brings about involuntary urination soon after the opportunity to use the bathroom has passed, or a need to return hastily to have the bowel movement that was impossible only shortly before.

The concern of the Hydes about their child could have been lessened if they had known more about how toddlers grow and develop, and what they could wisely anticipate and expect. They failed to realize that parental patience—in terms of recognizing individual readiness for new learning—is reflected in the child, and that the interpersonal relationship of mother and child influences not only the immediate present but much future activity as well.

Ronny Hyde was doing all right for Ronny Hyde. How the child on the next block reacted was inconsequential. Each child needs to be allowed to follow his own timing in mastering various aspects of bodily control, whether moving his bowels or learning to skip, whether building a tower or learning to control his bladder. Children are anxious to learn new skills, and take pride in achievement. Like their elders, they learn better with encouragement than with pressure or condemnation for failure. They will be quicker to take responsibility for conforming to social ways if they are made to feel that their mother knows they want to do the right thing, and that soon they will be able to do what is expected.

The Earliest Years

FOR THOUGHT AND DISCUSSION

1.   How is the discovery and understanding of the function of DNA important to the general study of child development?

2.   Briefly describe the different kinds of physical connections between mother and child during pregnancy. Give examples of cases in which a child can be affected physically by factors in the mother's environment.

3.   Define orderly prenatal growth and mention a few of the common environmental interferences in orderly prenatal growth.

4.   Recall the four areas of *total growth* from Part One and try to arrange them chronologically according to their earliest prominent manifestations between birth and the second year.

5.   What is self-demand feeding? Would you use it with one of your own children? If so, why?

6.   Why is the second year of a child's life considered by many parents the most difficult year? What are the main contrasting drives of parent and child during this time?

7.   Why is a toddler's relationship with his mother during toilet training important?

8.   What are the "pressures of the cultural pattern" that a baby feels when he becomes a toddler?

9.   Discuss the behavior of Ronnie Hyde in the case story entitled "Habits and Attitudes Are Learned Together." Do you feel that Ronnie's behavior is normal for a child of his age? Can you think of a few problems Mrs. Hyde might have had later with Ronnie if she had not consulted her doctor?

10.   What can parents do to help their child's language development? Can you think of any methods other than the ones mentioned in this section that would be helpful to language development?

11.   Observe three children at the ages of six months, one year, and two years. Note in each child's activities what you would consider typical behavior for his age.

FOR FURTHER READING

ALDRICH, CHARLES ANDERSON, and ALDRICH, MARY M. *Babies Are Human Beings.* New York: Collier Books, 1962. A classic presentation of the development and care of babies during the first two years.

BOWLBY, JOHN. *Child Care and the Growth of Love.* Baltimore: Penguin Books, Inc., 1954. Summary of a report presented to the World Health Organization concerning the effect on little children of too early separation from their mothers.

DRILLIEN, CECIL. *Growth and Development of the Prematurely Born Infant.* Baltimore: Williams & Wilkins, 1964. A technical but helpful book on the needs and problems of the premature baby.

ESCALONA, SIBYLLE; ESCALONA, HEIDER; and MOORE, GRACE. *Prediction and Outcome.* Menninger Clinic Monograph Series, No. 14. New York: Basic Books, Inc., Publishers, 1959. Describes a series of predictions made for a group of thirty-one children and the degree to which final data confirmed or negated these predictions.

FLANAGAN, GERALDINE L. *The First Nine Months of Life.* New York: Simon and Schuster, Inc., 1962. A complete, beautifully written and illustrated study of prenatal development. An unusual book.

FOSS, BRIAN. *Determinants of Infant Behavior.* New York: John Wiley & Sons, Inc., 1962. A record of the proceedings of the Tavistock Child Development Research Unit, London, 1959. Includes reports by thirty international authorities.

GESELL, ARNOLD, and ILG, FRANCES L. *Infant and Child in the Culture of Today.* New York: Harper & Row, Publishers, 1943. The classical presentation of the developmental stages of early childhood.

HAIMOWITZ, MORRIS L., and HAIMOWITZ, NATALIE READER, eds. *Human Development: Selected Readings.* New York: Thomas Y. Crowell Company, 1960. A collection of outstanding articles on infancy, childhood, and adolescence. An interesting and sometimes provocative selection.

LEWIS, M. M. *How Children Learn to Speak.* New York: Basic Books, Inc., Publishers, 1959. Traces the pattern of speech development from birth to early childhood. Based on carefully recorded observation. Both readable and understandable.

LEWIS, M. M. *Language, Thought, and Personality in Infancy and Childhood.* New York: Basic Books, Inc., Publishers, 1964. Discusses the role of language in child development.

MONTAGUE, ASHLEY. *Human Heredity.* New York: New American Library of World Literature, 1960. A study of genetic inheritance and how environment affects it, even before birth.

MUSSEN, P. H.; CONGER, J. J.; and KAGAN, J. *Child Development and Personality.* New York: Harper & Row, Publishers, 1963. Cites research on personality development of children. Discusses the early mother-child relationship and the results of good mothering.

PATTON, ROBERT GRAY, M.D.; GARDNER, LYTT I., M.D.; and RICHMOND, JULIUS, M.D. *Growth Failure in Maternal Deprivation.* Springfield, Ill.: Charles C. Thomas, Publisher, 1963. A study of the effects of early environment on children's psychological and biological development.

PROVENCE, SALLY, M.D., and LIPTON, ROSE C., M.D. *Infants in Institutions.* New York: International Universities Press, Inc., 1963. Compares the development of infants raised in institutions with infants raised within a family during the first year of life and documents the importance of mothering. Preface by Milton Senn, M.D.

REES, ELIZABETH LODGE, M.D. *A Doctor Looks at Toys.* Springfield, Ill.: Charles C. Thomas, Publisher, 1961. Discusses the relationship of toys to a child's development. A helpful book for both parents and teachers.

SCHEINFELD, AMRAM. *The Human Heredity Handbook.* Philadelphia: J. B. Lippincott Co., 1956. Popularly written but factually correct.

THOMAS, ALEXANDER, and others. *Behavioral Individuality in Early Childhood.* New York, New York University Press, 1963. Explores the relation of the child's reaction patterning to his personality development.

WEIR, RUTH. *Language in the Crib.* The Hague: Mouton and Co., 1963. A Dutch publication written in English. Delightful and interesting reading.

WHITING, BEATRICE B., ed. *Six Cultures.* New York: John Wiley & Sons, Inc., 1963. Compares the experiences of infants and children in six cultures.

The Preschool Years

The dividing border line between toddler and runabout child is a shadowy one. Once a child has crossed it, his parents may suddenly realize that he is growing up. In these short years children lose their baby characteristics and become able to take their place in the larger world of the school.

Growth in the runabout years is exciting to watch. The first two years of a child's life seem amazing because of the constant change and development, but the years from two and a half through five are equally amazing because of the youngster's growth in knowledge, independence, and ability to do things for himself. It is a period of development when the growing child is beginning to form basic attitudes about himself, the people around him, and the world in which he will live. The attitudes he develops about himself and about other people will color his behavior not only during these three years but later on as well.

The runabout child is gradually moving away from the self-centeredness of the baby. He is beginning to learn to share and to understand that other people's personal and property rights must be considered—that he must sometimes give up his own way to fit into a pattern more comfortable for everyone. These are complicated learnings that will continue throughout life. They are just beginning during these years.

The preschool child also must master concepts of the world about him. What are stars and flowers? Where does water come from? What is hot and cold? There are hosts of ideas we take for granted that the child must question and understand before he enters school. The beginnings of his concepts of time— today, yesterday, tomorrow, weeks, months, and years—are developing. The child must begin learning numbers and letters as symbols. He must master concepts of what is big, what is little, and what is real rather than make-believe.

In his social growth, he has to learn what it means to be a boy or a girl, a man or a woman, how to share and take turns, how to play with other children, how to leave his mother's side without being afraid, and how to meet problems when his mother isn't around. He must learn to listen and not always interrupt, to wait for attention, and to ask instead of snatching. He needs to learn, too, a few manners that make getting along with other people pleasanter and easier. And he has to develop concepts of relationship. What sorts of relationships exist between fathers and mothers and children, neighbors, teachers, storekeepers, mailmen, doctors and nurses? Often he acts out these relationships in his imaginative play. He must master the ability to live in a family and share his mother and father with other children and adults. Later he will need to learn to share his teacher with other children.

Probably more learning takes place during these years than in any other three years of a child's life. This is not the formal learning that we associate with the school years, but rather the accumulation through experience of a child's first knowledge of the world about him. This is a time of learning through all his senses—of actually touching, seeing, hearing, smelling, and tasting—a time of absorbed watching, questioning, and exploring. The preschool child is alive with curiosity. *How, why, what, where* are constantly in his vocabulary. Yet he still lives in a magical world—anything seems possible. Through his gradually increasing knowledge and experience he will move closer to the world of reality, becoming better able to distinguish that which is fantasy and imagination from that which is real.

There is no time in life when the world is as fresh and wonderful as it is to the child during his runabout years. He is fortunate indeed if he grows up among adults who treasure for him this period of childhood and provide for him the opportunities to explore his world widely and safely—adults who give him time to grow without pushing him ahead into experiences that he is not yet ready to assimilate.

chapter 6

The Runabout Years

Two and a half through four

Although he has lost his baby straddle and walks and looks like a child, the two-and-a-half-year-old has still a bit of the baby left in him. He still likes to be cuddled and his parents still enjoy picking him up and cuddling him. But now he is learning to assert himself by insisting that things be done his way, and he tells his mother so with his constant "No!" and his refusal to come when she calls him. He tries to boss her around and informs her of just how he wants things done.

He still resents interference with either his physical activity or his possessions. He may scream and bite or kick and hit his mother if she disturbs him. Sometimes he throws himself on the floor in a rage. At times he changes his mind quickly, for he has discovered that there are choices to be made. He may push away his soup and demand cereal, or take out blue socks and then insist on red ones. If his mother gives in to all his constantly shifting demands, she will be in constant turmoil. It is best to present a child of this age with few choices and to keep his routines as simple and as clear as possible. Statements made with an air of casual expectancy work best: "It's time for lunch now," or, "I'll help you put away your toys." The two-and-a-half-year-old will not always conform, to be sure, because he has a mind of his own, but reasoning or arguing with him usually only makes him more confused and unable to decide just what he wants to do. This does not mean that his mother should be severe or rigid. Teaching with a light touch holds for the two-and-a-half-year-old just as it does throughout childhood.

By the time he is about three, a child usually goes through a period in which he is less negative and much easier to take care of. He even seems to want to do things the right way and often asks, "Is this the way?" He understands words so well that he can be given simple reasons and explanations. He is less resentful of interference and can be more easily interested in a new activity. He may still be upset when things fail to go his way, but his temper tantrums are likely to be less frequent. Instead of hitting out when he is angry, he may begin to call names or say, "I don't like you!"

By the time he is four, the runabout has lost that last bit of baby softness and roundness. He is a great deal larger, sturdier, and more self-reliant. He is well aware of himself as a person and responds best when he is treated as an individual by those around him. At four, a child is often not nearly so pleasant to live with as he was at three. He is going through a noisier, stormier, more active year. He is often "out-of-bounds" in his behavior. Many family problems begin at this point. The four-year-old seems so grown-up that his parents are apt to expect too much of him and be less patient with him. They may try to clamp down on his noisiness, his manners, his language, and his personal care. Life often becomes filled with "do's" and "don'ts," with the child's resultant aggressiveness often turned toward his parents. The child becomes difficult to teach. He calls names and says, "I hate you!" "You're a mean mummy!" "I'll get you!"

Some four-year-olds are sufficiently adventurous to run away from home. This is usually not deliberate naughtiness or disobedience but simply a desire to see something going on a few blocks away, or boredom with what is happening in the yard. Sometimes a little girl, carried away by her play, will take her doll buggy and go to market.

The four-year-old's boundaries need to be widened a bit. His own yard is no longer enough to hold his interest. He may need freedom to visit a nearby friend. He is beginning to understand about crossing streets carefully and can often be trusted to cross a quiet street to play at a friend's house. Parents need to meet the four-year-old's growing independence rather than create problems by continuing to treat him as though he were a baby.

Vigorous outdoor play

The runabout years are years of bodily activity and vigorous outdoor play. Youngsters of this age would like to live outdoors, and they become restless and even irritable if they must stay indoors for too long a time. During this period the child makes great physical progress. The coordination of his large muscles improves strikingly, and he needs ample opportunity to use and develop them.

All runabout youngsters like boxes and barrels to clamber over, ladders or jungle gyms to climb, and slides to scoot down. The littlest ones enjoy climbing up the ladder to the slide almost as much as coming down, while four-year-olds experiment coming down headfirst or backwards or even try climbing up the slide. Three-year-olds usually discover the trapeze, and by the time they are four many youngsters can hang by their feet and do stunts. Swings are often used during these years; even two-and-a-half-year-olds begin to learn how to pump, and four-year-olds go "high in the sky." Although some youngsters have a good deal of difficulty when they first try to ride a tricycle, they soon find it a favorite and use it constantly. They would even bring it into the house, if their mothers would permit it. Until they are about four, children enjoy sand and water play and spend a great deal of time dumping and hauling and pouring sand. But many four-year-olds have outgrown the sandpile; they want to rush about in more active, noisy play.

During these years the child's small muscles are still not so well coordinated as his larger ones. Eye-hand coordination is also imperfect, and it is a strain for the child to perform small tasks requiring close concentration. Two-and-a-half-year-olds may be able to thread large beads and three-year-olds to enjoy a small peg board; four-year-olds often like cutting and using sewing cards with large holes. For the most part, however, nursery-school teachers and parents should encourage the use of the large muscles rather than putting too much emphasis on the use of the smaller ones.

Creative play

The runabout child is creative. He likes to use his body in rhythmic games. Even the two-and-a-half-year-old can run and jump and walk on tiptoe, gallop like a pony, or clap his hands to rhythm. Older runabouts also enjoy simple singing games and using rhythm instruments.

Imaginative dramatic play takes up much time each day. At first the child may play house with a doll, or be a train or a horse, but by the time he is four he and his friends will be inventing wonderful games of cowboy, spaceman, pirate, or doctor. These games may even carry over from day to day. Older children often assign roles—"You be the doctor, I'll be the nurse" or "I'll be the cowboy, you be the badman!"

85

Blocks are fun, too. At first the youngster builds simple towers or houses, later towns or a farm or a zoo, combining the blocks with other toys such as dolls, farm animals, cars, trucks, or airplanes. Crayons, paints, clay, and finger paints also provide opportunities for creativity during these years. It is fascinating to watch the two-and-a-half-year-old absorbed in crayoning or painting on large sheets of paper with big lines and splashes of color, smearing his finger paints with bold strokes and sweeps, or energetically kneading, rolling, and pounding his clay. By three, the youngster may be able to draw a recognizable man or house or to make a crude object out of clay. A four-year-old often chatters as he works, describing what he is doing, admiring his work, and expecting others to admire it.

During these years, children need a variety of creative mediums—paints, crayons, pencils, finger paints, clay, records, rhythm instruments, costumes, wood, a hammer, and nails. Using these things should be fun. At this age completion of a project is not as important as the satisfaction of creativity. Completion of a task will come later. A child's ability to begin creative play spontaneously is often killed by well-meaning adults who make him self-conscious or who impose on him their own adult standards of neatness, accuracy, and completion. This is a period of experimentation, not of finished or perfect results.

The need for adequate rest

Although runabout children, as their activity increases, are apt to resist having to stop their play for a nap, they still need a midday rest. It is not wise or possible to insist on sleep, but children can learn to have a quiet playtime, preferably on their beds after lunch. Records, stories, coloring books, puzzles, and peg toys are all useful in keeping the child quiet while he rests. Some mothers find that a special box or shelf of toys for resting time is helpful. If the mother rests, too, so that the pattern of the house is one of quietness and relaxation, the child is more likely to rest willingly. The neighborhood mothers can help one another by agreeing to keep their children at home for a time after lunch each day.

Bedtime is an individual matter, depending on the child and the situation, but most runabouts will be ready for bed between seven and eight o'clock and will sleep around the clock. Two-and-a-half- and three-year-old youngsters will want a bedtime ritual, but four-year-olds are usually a bit more flexible and often go to bed quite willingly, even though things are not done in just the same way each night. They still want a playtime with their mother or father, but are able to accept any one of a variety of activities. It may be riding in the car, making puzzles, building with blocks, playing a simple game, or listening to a story or a record. It is the closeness to their parents that counts, rather than the activity itself.

It is not unusual for a three-year-old to get up and wander about the house, or want to get into his parents' bed, or just lie in his crib and talk to himself in the middle of the night. By four, a child is apt to be less restless at night. If the four-year-old does wake, it is usually because he has had a bad dream or is disturbed about something. He now needs only a small amount of help in going to the toilet at night; he may even be able to go alone. He also usually amuses himself when he wakes up in the morning instead of calling for his mother.

The runabout child likes to try to do things for himself. Even the two-and-a-half-year-old may try to wash himself when he is in the tub or struggle to put on his socks or pull his shirt over his head. By the time he is four, the child is fairly efficient at dressing and undressing himself; sometimes he takes over and "surprises" his parents by appearing in their room fully dressed. True, shoelaces will be untied, and clothes or hair may not always be neat, but on the whole he does a good job.

During these years the child is also learning to feed himself more skillfully. At two-and-a-half he may still need some help with his meals, but by the time he is four he is usually capable of eating most food without help. His table manners are far from perfect, of course, but parents need to retain a light touch in teaching conduct at the table, since an overemphasis on table manners or eating correctly can make a child dislike mealtimes. It is better to let him eat in his own way, still using his fingers if he wants to. The child is highly imitative, and if he sees good manners at the table, he will gradually try to copy them. When he behaves particularly well at the table or says "Please" or "Thank you" or "Excuse me," a word of praise will help him feel proud that he has done something admirable, and he will try it again someday.

The runabout child also likes to "help" his mother. Even the two-and-a-half-year-old may try to set the table or help his mother dust or make a bed, while the four-year-old can empty wastebaskets or dry silver. But a child at this age cannot yet take responsibility for doing "chores" or even for completing those he has started. But though his interest may fade quickly, his desire to help is real and can be encouraged. Even if he does put the forks on the table upside down or runs away after he has emptied just one wastebasket, he will try to help again

if his mother rewards him with a "Thank you for helping me" or "That was a big help!"

Grown-ups need to be careful not to judge a child's early attempts to be helpful by adult standards. Demands that a job be finished or done just right may destroy a child's desire to help—a desire that is not easily re-created. Let the child do what he will to help, then run off, and help again some other time.

Although he is steadily becoming more independent, the runabout child will sometimes want his mother or father to take over or to give him considerable help in doing things he is able to do for himself. This is especially true when he is tired, out of sorts, emotionally upset, or ill. Understanding parents will help their child when he wants it, but will praise and encourage him when he does things for himself. Too much insistence on complete self-help discourages the runabout child just as it does the toddler.

Language development

Language develops rapidly during the runabout years. Most children add from five to six hundred words a year to their vocabulary between the ages of two and five, and they probably understand a great many more. Occasionally, a

A close parent-child relationship contributes greatly to early language growth. Studies have shown, for example, that children who lack warm emotional attachments with adults tend to be slow in learning to talk and may even remain retarded in speech throughout life. Language development, like other kinds of learning, depends upon there being a stimulus as well as an opportunity to learn.

child may begin to stutter because he has so much to say and cannot find the right words or get them out quickly enough. This type of stuttering is not so serious as another kind that may also appear during the preschool years—stuttering caused by adults' putting too much pressure on the child.

It is often difficult to understand the speech of a two-and-a-half-year-old, but by the time a youngster is four he usually talks clearly. Some normal youngsters use poor speech even into their school years. These children may need help in overcoming their speech difficulties or incorrect speech habits.

Four-year-olds not only use language well but seem to be fascinated by words. A group of four-year-olds can often be heard using all sorts of silly words and sounds and then bursting into gales of laughter. Many children of this age begin to acquire words their mothers do not like. They may discuss their toilet functions openly and chant toilet words. Usually it is best to ignore what the child is saying and turn his attention to some other activity that will interest him. This phase, though distressing to parents, generally does not last long. If a child has picked up words that are really disturbing, it sometimes helps to explain their meaning and matter-of-factly discourage their use. But if too much is made of a youngster's interest and play with "naughty" words, he is likely to discover that these words upset his mother and so use them when he wants to make her angry.

By the time a child is four, he is learning to use words to express ideas and feelings. This is an important step in socialization. Sometimes he can settle disputes by words rather than by the more primitive methods of hitting and snatching that he used when he was younger. He also finds words useful in helping to control his impulses. Since he can now verbalize his feelings and his needs, he no longer needs to throw himself down in a temper tantrum when he is angry or frustrated, although he may continue to do so for some time.

Clear and simple speech on the part of parents remains valuable for the child's language development, and stories—both read and told—assume increasing importance. Most runabout youngsters listen eagerly to stories and enjoy books filled with pictures. They should be given time to pore over books and to turn the pages slowly, not be hurried from one page to another.

Fantasy and fairy tales, except of a simple variety, do not belong in the library of most runabout children. The child is learning to know the real world about him. He has not yet mastered it and is not ready to cope with stories of the supernatural, the fairy world, or the world of magic. That will come somewhat later. The runabout does, however, enjoy make-believe stories of animals who talk and play like children. He never wearies of being told tales about himself or his playmates. He listens attentively to the running story his parents can make up of what he did and what he is going to do. (Parents must realize, however, that the child may interpret stories of his future adventures as promises of tomorrow's or next week's activities.) He likes stories about other children with whom he can identify, who are doing things he can understand. Some nonsense rhymes and jingles, as well as simple poems and songs, appeal to him.

Learning by seeing, hearing, tasting, and touching

As a toddler the child tasted, felt, touched everything within his reach. Now he wants to *find out* about the things he touches and about the things he sees and hears as well. As he grows up, he may not continue putting unfamiliar objects into his mouth, but he will want to touch and examine them and will ask questions many times over. He needs time to look at whatever interests him, whether it be in pictures or in reality. Because he needs time to absorb what he sees and hears, grown-ups should avoid rushing him along. Having his parents continually point things out to him is often distracting to the child, who wants to see for himself and ask his own questions.

Before a child can develop concepts or ideas, he must have had opportunities to get to know the things around him by actually touching, seeing, hearing. He learns first through his senses. Gradually, through his widening experiences, he learns how to bring together his impressions of things seen and heard and touched to begin forming ideas or concepts. These become the tools with which he will think and enlarge his knowledge. But a child cannot learn how to use the symbols that are words until he has had some experience with the objects those words represent. The word *b-a-l-l* can mean nothing to a child, for example, until he has felt and touched and used a ball.

It is easy to overstimulate a runabout child by offering him experiences that are beyond him. For this reason, most movies and most programs on radio and television are of doubtful value to the small child. The ones he is permitted to see or hear should be carefully selected, because most so-called children's movies and programs contain elements that the small child can't understand and that sometimes frighten him. "But I saw it!" said one three-year-old, afraid of a dragon on the television screen. Older children have the background of experience to know that dragons, even on television screens, do not exist, but most runabouts still feel that what they see is real.

Making the most of curiosity

Curiosity is an outstanding trait of a runabout and one of the most interesting sides of his personality. He wants to know about everything. If adults are willing to answer his questions and provide him with opportunities to find out about things himself, they will be amazed at how much he is able to learn. From the time a youngster arrives at this "What-is-it?" and "How-does-it-work?" stage, adults will be kept busy answering his questions. They should encourage this wonderful and useful curiosity. The questioning mind may be a nuisance at the moment, but it is a valuable asset later on. When an adult answers a child's questions, he should answer them simply, clearly, and without elaboration. He should not try to explain too much. If a child wants more information, he will ask. Sometimes a youngster asks questions to reassure himself that he is right: "That's a big building, isn't it?" Sometimes a youngster repeats a question over and over, making it a part of himself, or he may come back to the same question many times. If a nursery-school teacher or parent cannot answer a question he should say, "Let's find out." This is a useful approach to develop, in anticipation of the many times in the child's life when he will ask and will need to find out. If the question is one that can be answered by seeing or doing, this is the best way to explain, since children learn much from simple, close-to-home experiences. Climbing into a small boat, going to a farm to see the cows being milked, taking a trip to the airport, visiting the place where his father works, watching a

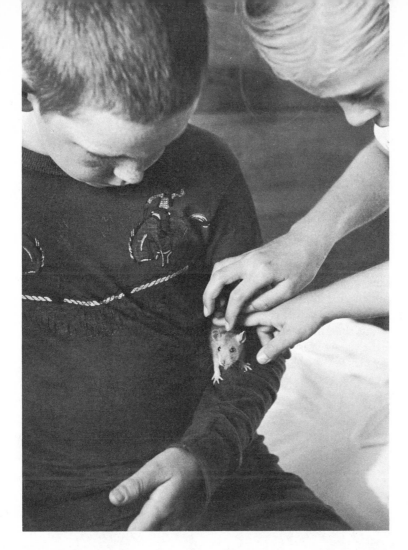

steam shovel at work—all these are rich experiences through which a child can find out about his world.

If parents are to help the child make the most of his curiosity, they must first help him cultivate the attitude of wanting to know. This attitude is of great importance in the preschool years. If the child finds that it is all right to explore, that his questions will be answered, he develops an inquisitive, adventurous approach to life that will be invaluable to him. Parents must also let the child try things out for himself as much as possible. "Can you do it yourself?" is a good key to follow. Let him try to ride the tricycle before showing him how to do it. Let him experiment with taking appropriate things apart. Don't help him unless he asks for help or shows that he is getting too frustrated.

Preschool youngsters are capable of absorbing much more information than most adults realize, if the information is given to them in terms they can understand and at a time when their own interest is awakened and they are ready and eager for it. Many adults do not take children's interests and questions as seriously as they should. They are apt to push the eager question aside or answer it carelessly, even incorrectly. But it is important that questions be answered as accurately as possible within the limits of the child's understanding. The concepts that he builds should be correct from the very beginning. Whenever possible he should be helped to see the reason behind things; this is the start of his understanding of cause and effect, an important part of his growing knowledge.

Parallel play to cooperative play

The runabout child learns to leave his mother's side to play with other children. At first he does not know how. He likes to be with other children, but he has to learn how to share and take turns, to ask for what he wants instead of using the more direct tactics of his toddler days. The two-and-a-half-year-old is only beginning to be able to share. He may want to show his new toy to another child, but he will still probably clutch it to himself if he is asked to let the other child hold or use it. He is experimenting with friendship, but he is not yet ready to manage many situations between himself and other youngsters; thus he may get into difficulties if an adult is not nearby to help out when he cannot solve his own problem. At first he plays very little with another youngster—parallel play is still the pattern. But the other child is now definitely in the picture.

By the time the runabout is three, cooperative play is usually beginning. Several children may play house or bus together. Even the three-year-old, however, has no real understanding of cooperation. Whenever his interest changes, he goes his way and does what he wants regardless of the wishes of the others. But he is

beginning to understand about sharing and taking turns. He may be seen waiting for his turn at the swing or drinking fountain.

He is also learning to ask for what he wants instead of just taking it. It still is hard for him to be really generous or to give up something he wants, but he may offer a playmate something other than the toy he is using, "Here, you take this." Although he still needs an adult in the background to help him learn how to play with other children, how to share and take turns, he is better able to take care of some of his quarrels and disputes himself.

The three-year-old sometimes selects a special friend and plays happily with this youngster, ignoring other children or even pushing them away. The special friendship may not be of long duration—it may be Mary today and Timmie tomorrow. It makes no difference to the three-year-old whether his friend is a girl or a boy. He enjoys children of both sexes equally, and both boys and girls play the same games. Girls are already showing increased interest in dolls, however, whereas the boys turn more frequently to cars, blocks, and trucks.

By the time he is four, a youngster usually wants to dash out of the house the first thing in the morning. His friends are now becoming more interesting to him than grown-ups, and he has special friends with whom he likes to play. Although he plays with either boys or girls, his best friend is apt to be of the same sex. Four-year-olds enjoy each other. They boast and brag, make noise, talk at great length, and are full of wonderful plans.

At the same time there is a lot of name-calling and quarreling, sometimes with words and sometimes with hitting and fighting. They often say, "Go away, I don't want to play with you!" or "You can't play here!" Sometimes they run to their parents with bitter complaints. They tattle a great deal, partly for reassurance that they are right about something. It is a form of checking up on what they are learning about right and wrong. On the other hand, they do not need nearly as much adult supervision, nor do they run to their mother quite as readily when things go wrong as they used to do.

Play as a means of learning and an emotional outlet

During the preschool years, play is an essential means of learning. Through such activities as running, climbing, swinging, and riding his tricycle, the child exercises and develops the large muscles of his body. By playing with peg toys and blocks, by cutting and pasting and threading big beads, he is helping to develop his coordination. Through his dramatic play, he is relating himself to and testing his world, trying out his role, and expressing his feelings about his relationships with other people. By working with clay, paints, and finger paints, he is discovering additional ways of expressing himself and his feelings. He is learning to solve problems as he meets them in his play. In mixing with other children, he is learning how to share, cooperate, take turns with, and listen to others. He is learning, too, that other people have rights just as he does. This kind of learning is of major importance in a child's life. It is a necessary preliminary to his success in school. Many a child who is intellectually capable of mastering his schoolwork has failed during his primary-school years because of his emotional, social, or physical immaturity. The child who has had little experience in playing with other children and little opportunity to try himself out and develop some self-confidence during his runabout years is ill-prepared to meet the demands of the schoolroom.

As far as possible within the limits of safety, common sense, and the rights of others, play should be spontaneous. The child should play what he wants to play. Telling him how and what to play tends to destroy his initiative and imagination, reducing the value of play as a learning situation. Children learn best when they are doing things they like to do and feel a need to do, rather than things that are forced on them.

Another important element that comes out of a child's play is the release it offers for his feelings as he learns to adjust to the demands of the world he must live in. We sometimes forget that it is not easy for a child to become socialized, to give up his free and comfortable ways of doing things, and to conform instead to such requirements as going to the bathroom, eating certain foods in certain ways, and sharing his parents and toys. He needs opportunities to release his feelings, and because he does not always know the words for expressing his feelings, he often unconsciously uses active, creative play to find this release. Although adults sometimes look upon play as a waste of time, play is essential to the all-round growth of children.

Nursery school

Many runabout children profit from going to nursery school. The nursery school is a children's world rather than an adult one. In it the child can find learning materials that individual parents may be unable to provide. He has an opportunity to learn to give and take and to interact happily in a group of other youngsters his own age. In the story period or at "telling time," the child learns to listen to what someone else is saying. At juice and nap time and in taking turns, he learns cooperation and consideration for others.

The nursery school provides new opportunities for growth by setting the stage for constructive play. The equipment, the toys, the opportunities to use clay and finger paints freely and to pound nails and build with the large nursery-school blocks, and—most important—the opportunity to share these experiences with others add to the value of play, as youngsters learn to express themselves and to try out their newly developing abilities. Many of these activities can be carried out at home, too, and should be encouraged, but rarely does a mother have the time to permit a child the same degree of freedom to explore and to try out many ways of expressing himself that the nursery-school teacher can provide.

The nursery-school teacher ideally maintains a healthy balance between free play and the kind of activities that offer a child an opportunity to explore his world more fully. She often succeeds in arousing the children's interest in nature, in simple scientific experiments, in beginning experiences with form and number, and in the symbols that will soon take shape as words. This kind of learning prepares the child for the more formal learning of the school years. Although usually he is not yet ready for formal lessons in reading or numbers, he is being helped to build basic understandings that will prepare him for his later school experiences.

A few children are ready for nursery school when they are two and a half; most are not ready until three. Not all children need nursery school, for some have neighborhood groups that satisfactorily provide freedom to play under the wise guidance a child needs. But when a child is ready and able to enjoy other children and to leave his mother's side nursery school may be a rich experience for him, providing a stimulating environment in which to grow and learn. The best nursery schools are flexible and friendly. The teachers keep in close touch with the mothers and work together with them in understanding and meeting the needs of the runabout child. Nursery schools also bridge the gap between home and school, so that there is no sudden break when the child first leaves the family circle. The mother often comes to school with her child until he is at ease in the new surroundings, and in many nursery schools the mothers are participants in the daily program.

The nursery school has special benefits to offer children who have a physical handicap or come from culturally disadvantaged homes. For the handicapped child the nursery school provides special learning experiences which can further his development and which might otherwise be outside his limited reach. It can also provide him opportunities for play with other boys and girls, something which cannot always be arranged at home. For the disadvantaged child whose own home cannot provide the stimulation and opportunities for creative play and learning of the more advantaged home, the nursery school can make the difference between readiness and lack of readiness to accomplish first-grade work. A child in an educationally starved environment starts with a severe handicap, and unless help is provided for him he may never come close to fulfilling his full potential. The nursery school can begin to provide this help.

Changing family relationships

Although he is ready to step beyond his home into the world of playmates and even nursery school, the runabout still remains deeply attached to his mother. She is the one he turns to spontaneously for comfort and care. He does not want her to be far away from him even when he grows more adventurous and independent. He likes to tag around after her while she works, bring his toys and play near her, or see her every little while as he plays.

Although his mother remains the central figure, his father is becoming increasingly important in the youngster's life. The runabout waits eagerly for his father to come home and runs to meet him as he comes up the street, or shouts, "Daddy's here!" as soon as the front door opens. Sometimes his father can get him to do things more readily than his mother can. During these years, a father may come to be seen as a rather special person. This is important, for a child needs the active interest and affection of both parents for his best development.

The child is confronted with the task of learning how to share his mother and his father with other people during the runabout period. He must permit the triangle of mother, father, and child to expand and include first brothers and sisters and members of the family group, then the various adults in his environment. He must feel secure enough with his parents to be able to go out toward other people and to be willing to include them. This is not easy at all for a child to do.

A child learns to love through his closeness to his mother and then to his father. He feels possessive about his parents, particularly his mother. During his

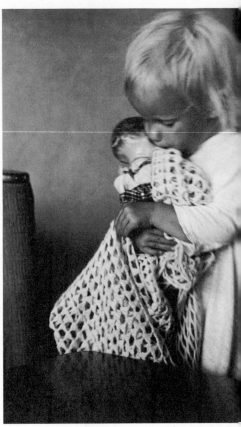

preschool years, the little boy sometimes resents his father's intrusion into his relationship with his mother; yet he is ambivalent because he wants his father's affection, too. Parents often notice the child's seeming jealousy when the father joins the group of mother and child. A boy has to learn to accept the relationship of his father with his mother and to supplement his own feelings for his mother by identifying with his father. And just as a boy must learn to identify with his father during these preschool years, so a girl must gradually learn to identify her feminine role with that of her mother. If this feminine identification is established in the preschool years, it is much easier for the child to assume the appropriate adult role at adolescence.

One of the runabout child's greatest tasks is developing an increasing ability to share his parents with his brothers and sisters. He needs to realize that his parents will continue to care for him even though a new baby comes, and that they have sufficient love to go around. Sibling rivalry is never completely overcome, and much of the quarreling and tensions that begin during these preschool years are due to this basic and fundamental rivalry of children for the love of their parents. If parents understand this, they will feel less guilt and sense of failure as their children quarrel. They will then be free to meet rivalry situations more constructively.

The runabout child has much to learn, and often he has to learn in an adult world under adult pressures. It is no wonder that many problems begin during these years. The child must have guidance. He must learn what is acceptable behavior and what is not. He needs a pattern to follow. But this pattern should be presented gently, consistently, without undue pressure to conform to adult ways, and with an understanding of the child's ability to learn. Scolding, force, threats, shouting, and in most cases spanking do not belong in the teaching of the runabout child.

He is gradually learning how to take some responsibility, and he is growing away from the concept of himself as the center of the group to himself as a part of the group. He is learning to love through his experiences with other people. He is developing a feeling of trust and, through trust, self-confidence. His self-confidence then enables him to develop initiative and to go ahead on his own.

Emotionally, the preschool child is still unstable. When he's tired, he is irritable and restless, but he is beginning to be able to handle situations better and sometimes tries to work them out by himself. He is easily discouraged and also as easily encouraged. Emotionally he is only beginning to grow up. He cannot yet be expected always to be independent or even always to do those things of which he is capable.

Unless he has been under too much pressure from adult demands, the runabout has also developed the ability to stand some frustration. The two- or three-year-old throws himself down in a temper tantrum, but by five the child has learned to control his temper to some extent. His tantrums are less frequent and he no longer says "No" all the time. He will listen to explanations and settle for a compromise. He is more reasonable. This is growth, indeed, from the days when he was two. But growth is a slow process and the child will still need a great deal of help.

If the parents are too stern and dominating during this period, the child may become too concerned about his behavior and may be overinhibited when he grows up. Such a child is unable to meet life with the initiative required to master skills and to meet new situations without undue strain and without ultimate rebellion or timidity.

If, because they were busy or unwilling to be bothered, parents have been inconsistent in their guidance—strict today and permissive concerning the same behavior tomorrow—the child may not know what is expected of him. He will be likely to constantly test the limits imposed on him to see what he can get away with: Is Mother going to be strict today, or is she too busy? Does she mean what she says, or is she just threatening again? This is a poor beginning for any child.

If a child's parents have been aware of his growing independence, helping him learn acceptable behavior gradually through kindly and affectionate guidance, then the child feels it is safe to grow up. Experiencing the security of his parents' love, he can go ahead, knowing that his parents will be backing him up with their support. When these early years are over, the child will be ready to leave his mother and the shelter and familiarity of the family and the block. He will be eager to take his place with other children in kindergarten.

Another Baby in the Family

A new experience for the older child

When a family's second child is born, everyone concerned must make new adjustments. For the older child, the appearance of a new baby in the family usually requires the first major adjustment of his life. To be expected to relinquish his starring role in the family group can be very disconcerting. To be willing to share his mother's time, attention, and love with a tiny brother or sister is infinitely difficult.

Mrs. Stern had seen many unhappy situations when she visited friends or relatives who had a new baby and an older child. She was anxious to avoid what she knew many mothers had had to overcome, the problem of a cheerful, cooperative, playful child turning cross, tearful, rebellious, or perhaps withdrawn and uncertain—or of a fairly competent and independent youngster becoming almost infantile in his return to babyish ways that he had outgrown before the new baby came. Wondering during her pregnancy about possible similar reactions in three-year-old Everett, Mrs. Stern arranged for a consultation with the pediatrician.

"Sometimes young mothers feel worried and guilty when they can no longer give all their time and attention to their first child," the doctor noted. "But a child will learn to share time and attention and even love, provided there is no situation that he interprets as a threat to that love."

"I had thought," said Mrs. Stern, tentatively, "that for a while I might have a practical nurse for the baby. That would give Everett a feeling of real security, don't you think?"

"But what about giving the *new* baby real security? Of course a nurse or someone else living with you can help you enormously, so you will have more energy and time for both your children. But Everett will very likely be jealous of the baby whether you have a nurse or not. You can help him most by trying to lessen his natural jealousy."

Although his parents' eager and busy preparations for a new baby held little meaning for him, Everett had shown some interest in "helping" to repaint his first crib and had asked many questions about who would use it. Bringing his vague and confused thoughts to the surface was a help to him; expressing his fantasies about a new baby was a satisfaction. This would not have been so had his parents laughed at him or teased him. But his mother was careful not to show her amusement, which she realized might be disconcerting at such a time. Instead, she offered Everett the reassuring information that he, too, had once been "carried near her heart" until he was born, just as the new baby was now being carried, and that the new baby would after a while be born and would grow as he had been growing.

When Everett's mother told him about how she was keeping the unborn baby safe and warm, he would ask with interest, "Just like me?" "Just like you," his mother would reply. Everett accepted the idea of the baby because he knew that he himself had once had the same place, the same protection, which he was now hearing about, and that the same preparations in which he was now taking part had once been made for him. He was told how tiny the new baby would be and that it would need to be held carefully and be nursed and changed and allowed to sleep a great deal of the time, so that it would grow as he had done. "Just like me?" he would repeat, wonderingly, and would hear again the reassuring "Just like you" from his mother.

These talks with his mother helped to give Everett some notion of what to anticipate and what he would need to accept. But of course the baby was still probably no more than a storybook baby to him; he surely did not realize the many changes it would bring about in his home.

Once the new baby became a matter of casual comment instead of exciting news, Everett's mother brought forward the next bit of preparation. "Grandma is coming to stay with us for a visit," she said one morning. "I think we'd better get things ready for her. Then when I go to the hospital she'll be all settled, and you and she can keep house together and have lots of fun."

So there was time for Everett to accept the idea of another bed and chest of drawers being moved into his room for his grandmother. Children are often suspicious and disturbed when their accustomed surroundings are changed. A gradual introduction to anything new is much easier for them to accept. On the day his grandmother was to arrive, Everett went with his father to meet her at the station and suddenly burst out with the statement, "A baby's coming, too. But not on a train."

Since her mother was in the house for a number of days before the time came for Mrs. Stern to leave for the hospital, it was an easy transition for Everett to learn that his grandmother, like his mother, would help him when he needed help. Even more important, his grandmother had time to learn the details of Everett's daily care which had become routine for him and which he, like so many children of his age, liked to have carried out in the same way and in the same order each time. Often the most kindly adult, unfamiliar with a child's routine, will be baffled by the cross resistance a youngster suddenly shows toward a procedure different from the one that has become for him comfortable evidence of a kind of security. Without a period of preparation, both Everett and his grandmother could well have experienced many uncomfortable and uncertain moments.

"You're far more concerned than I ever was," Mrs. Stern's mother said to her one evening after Everett was asleep. "I don't think I worried about you when Grace was on the way, and you were four."

Mrs. Stern recalled her feelings of resentment for her younger sister, feelings which apparently had not been recognized by her mother. She had learned from her talk with the pediatrician how childish feelings can continue to color one's reactions for many years afterward. She had come to appreciate why even now she experienced momentary irritation and even anger when her sister told of getting a new car, or when people admired Grace's newly decorated home and the garden she planned and cared for. Mrs. Stern felt uncomfortable about such feelings and hoped Everett might be spared this kind of resentment.

When Mrs. Stern selected the layette for the new baby, she added a few extras. Not at all appropriate for an infant, they were just right for a boy half past three. There was a blue sweater with a gay yellow duck embroidered on the front. There were furry slippers. There was a sturdy pair of coveralls wrapped with several jars of finger paints. Some small trucks and trains jingled in an attractive plaid box, and there were bright, new plastic blocks. Everett's mother hoped each of these would, at different times, forestall hurt or angry feelings. A three year old cannot be expected to feel unselfish joy in another's gifts if he has nothing new himself. And since almost everyone who comes to see a new baby comes bringing a gift, and other friends are very likely to send some remembrance, it is helpful for the child who himself was so recently the family baby to find that he, too, is given something new and interesting.

"But don't think it will be enough to provide just toys and trinkets," Dr. Brandon cautioned. "Remember that you must provide praise and flattery, too! When your friends exclaim over the baby's big eyes or chubby knees or sweet smile, if no one has anything to say about Everett—and he's around—you mention how high a tower he built or how quickly he finished up his lunch or how nice he looks in his new sweater. That will help him as much as the toys. Tangible evidence of not being forgotten is very necessary, but approving and admiring attention is also important."

A runabout has learned to do a great many things for himself. If his mother takes undue advantage of this capability when a new baby comes, she may find that habits apparently well established no longer function. When Mrs. Stern brought her new baby girl home from the hospital, however, Grandma's presence made it possible for Everett to continue having almost as much attention as he had previously. He had no more accidents with wet pants than before. He didn't cry or fuss any more than when he was the only child. Nevertheless, in some instances he did react negatively. Happily, the Sterns understood and accepted these incidents with a friendly, permissive attitude. They felt that such reactions would probably disappear as Everett gained reassurance that he really had not been displaced by the baby. The reactions were, in a sense, his testing of his parents' continued love for him.

One morning Everett announced firmly that he did not like his little table and chair. He climbed up into his old high chair, which had already been repainted for the baby. "Here!" he said decisively. "I want to sit here."

"All right," his mother said. "Shall I feed you, or do you want to eat by yourself?"

"You," pronounced Everett. "You feed me." He looked very solemn.

Without further question or comment, his mother gave him his breakfast, spoonful by spoonful, even holding his glass of milk for him. With the last swallow he smiled happily at her. "Get down now," he said contentedly. Everett repeated the same performance at noon, and when naptime came he asked his mother to carry him to his bed. He was being a baby again. That evening Everett suggested that he'd like to have his bath in the bathinette, and he was persuaded otherwise with some difficulty. Yet obviously he liked hearing his mother's admiring comments about how a big, heavy boy needed a big, steady tub. He ended the incident laughing at the picture of how he would look in the bathinette.

For several days Everett tried other things of this sort. He asked to be carried. He stood inert while being dressed. He spoke less often and less clearly. But when all his requests were met with a friendly casualness and nothing he did brought scolding or shaming or impatience from his parents, he seemed to feel less need to enlist adult help. Gradually he asked for no unnecessary aid in his daily dressing, eating, and toilet routines. He showed an increasing interest in the baby and in helping his mother to care for her. And he took keen delight in hearing his mother recount to his father what he had done during the day: "Everett brought me the baby's blue blanket when it turned chilly this afternoon. He picked out just the one I asked him to bring," she would say. Or, "The baby was so cross today. The only thing that seemed to quiet her was Everett's playing with her. He was such a help."

Mrs. Stern often mentioned the many things a big boy could do that were not to be expected from a tiny baby. Often, too, she arranged to take a walk alone with Everett or to visit the nearby park playground with him or to read to him from a favorite book. She frequently commented how much she enjoyed the company of her big boy, how much he knew, and how much he could do, now that he was past three.

Of course there were times when Everett evidenced difficult feelings about his new sister. Eying the sleeping infant one afternoon, he suddenly let out a piercing shriek. The baby, of course, awoke crying, startled and uneasy. Another time he leaned over his sister's carriage as she was about to be taken for an airing, and what began as a pat evidently ended as a pinch. The baby cried long and loudly. On such occasions Mrs. Stern refrained from the spontaneous reaction that so often follows episodes of this kind. Instead of slapping his hand or reproaching or shaming him, she would lead the boy aside, take him on her lap, and talk to him quietly about how necessary it was to be gentle with a little baby. She said she knew that sometimes he did not feel gentle.

"Sometimes you want Mother when she has to bathe the baby or nurse her or do something else for her. And that makes you angry at the baby. I know how you feel. All little boys feel that way sometimes. But when you were little I did all those things for you. Pretty soon your sister won't need so much done for her, because she'll grow up the way you're doing. And then you and she can have fun together, if you like. But now I must take care of her just as I took care of you when you were as little as she is. Only, of course, I always like the time I do things with you, too, because I wouldn't want to miss the fun of being with my big boy."

When an older child makes some attack on the baby—pinching or hitting, making a loud and frightening noise, or bumping the crib or carriage so that it sways threateningly with the baby in it—the parents must be firm with him and make him understand that such behavior is not allowed. This obviously is for the protection of the infant. But, interestingly, it serves too as psychological protection for the older child. For his childish logic may suggest that if his mother permits him to harm the baby, who is not nearly so big as he is, she might also permit someone bigger than *he* is to harm *him*.

The reassurance that he still holds an important place in his parents' love will help an older child to accept the new baby and to feel better about his own reactions. His parents can handle his occasional and entirely natural resentment as Mrs. Stern did, in ways that will lessen his stirrings of jealousy and his subsequent feelings of guilt. As a result, the older child will get along more amicably with his baby sister or brother, and he will later be able to get along better with his playmates and schoolmates, too. Indeed, his ability much later in life to build and maintain good relationships with co-workers and colleagues will stem from the successful learning of these early lessons.

Adjusting to another child's sharing his home and his belongings and, particularly, his parents may bring a youngster difficult moments and jealous feelings. The proverbial ounce of prevention is especially effective when a new baby is expected in a home where there is already a child. The older child will still crave attention. But if he is handled gently and wisely, crises and unhappiness and insecurity will not usually develop.

study of a child

Nancy Goes to Nursery School

Wider experiences broaden learning

Most children go to school by the time they are six years old; many go to kindergarten when they are five. But increasing numbers of communities are offering the advantages of nursery school, and more and more youngsters are starting to school at four or three or even earlier.

Mrs. Travis wondered about entering her little girl in nursery school. At times Nancy seemed entirely content at home with her mother and father and grandmother, accepting routines in a docile manner. But at other times she would burst into noisy, boisterous play, vigorously objecting to any less disturbing activity which an adult might suggest. And at still other times the child would sit passively, doing nothing, clearly lost in daydreams.

There were no children of her age in the neighborhood, and Nancy usually played by herself. But when she was with other children, there was almost always turmoil. And when Nancy could not carry through what she was attempting to do, whether taking off a snug sweater or manipulating a toy, she was likely to burst into angry tears. All this troubled the entire family, but only her mother thought seriously about it.

One day Mr. Travis, on coming down to breakfast, heard angry screams of protest from his little girl. "What's all the rumpus about?" he asked.

Nancy's grandmother looked aggrieved. "Nancy insisted on getting her own cereal," she said. "She spilled more than she poured in her bowl, and then she cried and cried. But she wouldn't let me help her."

"She'll learn," was Mr. Travis' vague reply.

On an afternoon when Grandmother finished dressing the little girl for a walk, Mrs. Travis remarked, "Seems to me Nancy should be doing that for herself."

"I like to help her," her grandmother quickly replied, with an affectionate pat on Nancy's head. "She's a good, quiet, little lady today. No trouble at all."

Nancy skipped out of the room and Mrs. Travis looked after her ruefully. "You wouldn't have thought so this morning," she said. "We stopped at Mrs. Dale's for not more than ten minutes to settle some details for the club party. That was long enough for Nancy to knock over Freddy's fort and have a battle royal when he objected to her taking his new ball. I'm sure Mrs. Dale was glad to see us go!"

That evening after supper, Nancy was happily engaged in drawing on a large sheet of paper when her father came into the room. He studied her efforts a moment, then said with interest, "Look, Nancy, this should be this way. And see, the head is too big. And who ever saw a blue dog!" With a few strokes and a little erasing, he transformed the dog to his liking, filling it in with brown crayon. "There you are! Here's your dog," and he held out the picture.

But Nancy struck at it. It was no longer *her* dog. "I don't like it!" she wailed, and ran out of the room crying.

"What's gotten into her?" her father wondered, uncomfortable at this tearful scene.

Shortly afterwards Nancy was invited to a birthday party. She didn't share the grown-ups' interest in the event but permitted herself to be dressed in her best. Obediently she picked up the large, tissue-wrapped package. "For Mary's happy birthday," approved Grandmother, standing at the front door to see Mrs. Travis and Nancy off to the party. When they arrived, ribbons and gay papers were strewn about. Mary, with more curiosity than care, was promptly opening each gift as it arrived.

"Say 'Happy Birthday' to Mary, dear," coached Mrs. Travis. Nancy repeated the phrase but still held the box, eying the birthday child warily. "And give her the gift," Mrs. Travis continued, a little discomfited that Nancy did not enter more readily into the spirit of the occasion.

Before Nancy could make up her mind to part with the package, Mary had taken hold of it. Immediately Nancy wrapped both arms around it. A momentary, wordless struggle ended with a hard push by Nancy and a shriek from Mary. Mary's mother flew to her child, distressed that today there should be tears, while Nancy's mother, dismayed, sought vainly to make Nancy understand the situation and relinquish the box. The bell, announcing another child's arrival, finally afforded a welcome interruption.

Later a film cartoon was shown, and all the children settled down happily on the floor. But around Nancy there arose a succession of small disturbances.

"Get outa my way," Michael complained as Nancy, ignoring him, moved over for an unobstructed view.

"Mommie, she poked me!" wailed Janet, when Nancy shifted to a more comfortable and advantageous position.

But such problems were forgotten when the lights were on again and the children were ushered to the table. Now, most of them thought, came the real party. They were riotous in their excitement over the little packages which came out of the "pie" in the center of the table. Whatever manners they had learned were now forgotten as ice cream in animal shapes was placed before them. Again Nancy was a storm center.

"I want the elephant," she announced, and tried to change her chocolate bear for Teddy's strawberry elephant. Teddy, of course, objected vigorously.

"Here, you give me that!" yelled Charles, grabbing his cookie away from Nancy's slyly reaching hand.

"That's mine! You snapped yours!" Barbara objected loudly when Nancy tried to pull another snapper after demolishing her own.

A little while later a father arrived for his child. Noisy youngsters, engaged in an energetic game, blocked his passage at the doorway. He appealed to Nancy, who was the nearest child. "Do you know Gloria? Do you know where she is?" he asked hopefully.

"I'll show you," Nancy offered brightly, recognizing the name. She led the way to where Gloria was playing with another group. Casually pushing a child out of her path, Nancy pulled Gloria forcibly away. "Here!" she said triumphantly. But, "You let me alone!" shrieked Gloria, while the boy Nancy had pushed struck out at her. Nancy hit back, and over went a lamp. "I was just bringing her to her daddy," Nancy sobbed, upset at sudden commotion as her mother and Mary's mother converged on the scene.

Describing the party to her husband that night, Mrs. Travis said, "We must do something. Nancy seems sweet and good most of the time, but when she's with other children, she's a different child. I wonder if that nursery school that opened last year wouldn't be good for her. I think she needs to be with children more."

"School!" scoffed Mr. Travis, laughing. "Come now, for that baby?"

"She's really not a baby, you know," said Mrs. Travis. "She's four years old. She has to begin learning how to get along with other children."

"She'll learn in plenty of time," said Grandmother. "School means germs. She'll pick up a cold or something worse. She's better off here, with us."

But Mrs. Travis did go to the nursery school and had a long talk with the principal, Miss Adams. She indicated her worry over four-year-old Nancy— usually so tractable and polite with grown-ups but so rough and belligerent with other children.

"And at still other times," said Nancy's mother, determined to tell the whole story, "she sits and gazes into space or talks to herself as if she's two children. And the stories she makes up! Have you ever heard of a child acting like that?"

Miss Adams was reassuring. "Nancy is like a great many children who are with grown-ups most of the time. They get along nicely when most of their wants are met without argument. They seem to be conforming to the household routine, but really the household is conforming to *them*. Then when not everyone acts the same way, they are upset. Nancy needs to learn that she has to give in sometimes. She hasn't had to at home. She should be learning to do more for herself, too. And she needs a chance to learn certain things her home can't teach her. Playing with children, learning group social skills, takes practice. That can't be provided by her grandmother or by you and her father. I think you're right. Nancy not only seems ready for nursery school. I believe it would be very helpful for her to have the experiences the group offers."

"Miss Adams says," quoted Mrs. Travis upon returning home, "that Nancy needs help to learn to get along with other children—and I agree with her. You would, too, if you saw the way Nancy 'plays' with them. And that funny smiling to herself, and talking—as if she were somebody else. Miss Adams thinks she probably has an imaginary playmate. She says a lonesome child very often resorts to that sort of thing."

That was too much for Grandmother. "Lonesome!" she scoffed. "I never heard such nonsense. Why, there's always one of us with her. Lonesome, indeed!"

"But we're all grown-ups," Mrs. Travis reminded her. "Nancy needs playmates her own age. She needs to be with other children, to find out that they have ideas and feelings, too. Learning to get along with other people takes practice, just like any other new skill. And she needs practice in other things, too.

"You should have been there today to see the way the children took off their own wraps and put them back on again later. And they managed practically without help in the bathroom, and when they had milk or orange juice. They chose whatever they wanted to play, and they shifted to something else when they felt like it. They were having such a good time—and it all seemed so good for them."

Nancy was more curious than hesitant about starting to school. And the family was both relieved and surprised that the new situation offered no problem about leaving home each morning. Indeed, the family was almost chagrined at not being missed. Skeptical as she was at first, Grandmother agreed after a time that nursery school provided for Nancy in some ways that were impossible at home. She finally even cooperated by ceasing to stress the desirability of Nancy's always being "a quiet little lady."

The noisy and boisterous Nancy was really no different from the other run-abouts in the nursery-school group. At four—a time of loud, strenuous activity—children need periods of vigorous group play as a wholesome release of energy. This helps them be content at other times to listen to stories or music, or to participate in quiet table play with crayons, clay, or scissors.

It was not in being boisterous that Nancy was unlike other four-year-olds, but rather in being overly dependent—in allowing herself to be dressed, washed, and even fed much of the time. Very soon after entering nursery school, as she saw how much more self-sufficient the other children were, she began showing not only a desire to help herself but an eagerness to learn how to do so. She became more patient with her limitations, too. There were some things she still couldn't do for herself—fasten the top button of her coat, manage the boots that just wouldn't come off—but her vain efforts no longer brought angry tears of frustration. Instead, Nancy was willing to accept help so that she could learn to do these things alone, too.

Progress was soon apparent, also, in her relations with other children. During her very first days at nursery school Nancy shoved and pushed vigorously to lead the line or to get to the table first for milk. She seemed surprised that the teacher discouraged this. And she was disconcerted when one of the children stared at her disapprovingly, or when another, just as eager to be first, shoved her even harder.

One day Nancy impatiently pushed away a child who came to join her in clay modeling. She wanted all the clay for herself. But she soon found that she had more than enough, and that there would be more "cakes" for her "bakery" if Ruthie shared the activity. Later she beamed with pleasure at the smiles she received when she pulled her clay apart and gave some to two other children There were now fewer squabbles about possessions and less snatching and clutching.

When she first came home from school, Nancy replied only briefly to her parents' questions. But soon she had a great deal to tell about. "Guess what! We made a garden!" "You know where we went? To the zoo!" The exaggerated tales of former months were no longer heard. Real playmates and real experiences were more satisfying than imaginary ones. She had scant time for daydreaming.

Some activities generally frowned on in Nancy's home were readily allowed at nursery school. When marching and stamping her feet appealed to her, school had a place for it. When she wanted to bang, there was a workbench with real tools. When a sound delighted her, there were others to join in chanting repetition. "Woozy doozy!" she might sing out, and Amy would laughingly reply, "Woozy soozy!" This would go on with more rhyming nonsense syllables. No one said to be quiet or to stop the silliness when child after child picked up the rhythmic pattern. After a few minutes of loud laughter, they would forget it all in another shared interest.

If the children were engaged in a group activity and one of them wandered off, Nancy learned not to shout accusingly, "Dorothy's gone away!" Time after time the teacher either called the wanderer back quietly or left her alone to find that she was missing the fun. Nancy, learning from her teacher's ways, discovered that other behavior than aggressiveness could be effective in persuading others.

When a child misbehaved, Nancy at first would say, "He's a bad boy" or, "She's naughty, isn't she?" But her teacher would calmly remark, "Tommy hasn't learned how yet" or, "I'm sure Cora will try not to do that again." Nancy's condemning, critical comments gradually stopped.

Most small children profit greatly from the experiences provided by a good nursery school. Their horizons expand as they encounter new ideas and learn new skills, social skills among them. For nursery schools provide opportunities to practice working and playing with other children while friendly adults guide and help and encourage.

Nancy needed these experiences particularly, and through them she learned to meet many kinds of situations. She recognized group standards and, accepting them, learned to adapt with a more even temper. She learned to do what she could for herself and to accept aid with good grace when she really needed it.

She showed increasing good nature as well as skill in working out disagreements and disappointments. In short, she acquired appropriate four-year-old maturity.

Habits and attitudes as well as facts and skills are important acquisitions for young children. The nursery school, an excellent place to acquire them and to practice them, broadens the life of a small child and helps the home meet its responsibility for the child's growth and development.

chapter 7

Starting Kindergarten

How different the five-year-old

Probably at no period of life does a child accomplish as much as during the runabout years. The distance he travels in growth and development, in learning and absorbing, becomes readily apparent when we look back over the years from two to five. As a toddler of two, he was barely beginning to talk; he uttered words, but only rarely a sentence. He could walk, but still fell down if he ran or turned quickly. He needed his parents to take almost complete responsibility for his physical care. His concepts of good and bad did not yet exist. He lived in the immediate present, relating himself to neither past nor future. He had not learned how to play with other children and could not yet really cooperate or even share. He knew nothing about the world outside his immediate environment; without his mother or some other responsible person, he would have been utterly lost.

How different the five-year-old when he starts off for kindergarten. In three years he has developed a definite personality. The person he will be is beginning to show, not only in his appearance but in his way of meeting situations and in his approach to life. His speed of learning, his potentialities of intelligence, some of his special skills and talents are beginning to be noticeable. Some of those individual characteristics that make him different from everyone else are already evident.

A child usually goes to kindergarten eagerly, looking forward to the new experience. He may hold his mother's hand tightly as he approaches the building the first day, but rarely does he try to turn back. Not only does he want to know what kindergarten is like, but he enjoys other children and wants to be with them. He is relating what he sees to his past experience and is anticipating the future. The five-year-old is no longer a baby but a child who is ready to be away from home for two or three hours a day as an independent person.

A period of slow growth

The five-year-old has entered a period of slow growth, very different from the rapid growth of his first eighteen months. If he is a boy, he will be between 37

and 45 inches in height and will usually weigh from 33 to 45 pounds. A girl will be from 36 to 44 inches in height and will weigh from 31 to 42 pounds. The five-year-old may be expected to grow two or three inches during the year and to gain from three to six pounds. Children vary greatly in the amount they gain, depending partly on their total body size.

Although boys are often slightly taller and heavier than girls during the years from five to ten, girls are usually about a year ahead of boys in their physiological development. The skeletal development of a five-year-old girl approximates that of a six-year-old boy. At puberty, girls are about two years ahead of boys physiologically and often socially, too.

The five-year-old is beginning to be able to control and use his body purposefully and skillfully. He can run, skip, and dance; he can climb and jump. Individual differences may be marked, however, for some children will always have better coordination than others. These differences must be taken into account when plans are made for kindergarten children.

The five-year-old's physical growth is uneven, and his posture may need watching. His legs are lengthening more rapidly than other parts of his body. His lungs are still relatively small, and his heart is growing rapidly. His large muscles are much better developed than the small muscles controlling the fingers and hands, so that he should still be encouraged in activities that strengthen the large muscles of arms, legs, and trunk. Many children are not yet ready for such activities as writing. They may enjoy painting with a large brush on a large surface, but holding and manipulating a pencil and trying to make small letters will sometimes cause undesirable strain.

A child's handedness is usually determined by the time he is five and should not be changed. Ninety per cent of youngsters are right-handed. The left-handed child may need special help in learning to write. He will need to be shown how to hold his pencil and the angle at which to place his paper.

The five-year-old's hand and eye do not yet work with complete coordination. He may still have difficulty when he tries to reach for things beyond arm's length and may sometimes spill or knock them over. His eyeball is still growing in size and will not be fully developed for several years. The kindergarten child is normally far-sighted and should not be expected to spend much time looking closely at small things. If he reads, he should not read print of less than 24-point size (24-point type is roughly 3/8 inch in height). When he looks at picture books, he should sit in a good light and hold the book upright or at a slant rather than flat on his desk or lap.

Active but less restless

The five-year-old is an active child, but he is less restless than he probably was at four. Though noisy and vigorous, his activity has definite direction. He runs and climbs, shouts and jumps, and enjoys games in which there is plenty of movement. He needs equipment that gives him an opportunity for purposeful, planned activity—a tricycle or small two-wheel bicycle that he can handle, a wagon to pull or push or to use in hauling his playmates around, plenty of large planks and boxes to build bridges, boats for sailing, or just something to jump from. He needs ladders or a jungle gym to climb, unless he lives near a tree of just the right height with large, spreading branches.

The five-year-old is learning to throw and catch a ball and may greatly enjoy trying to toss it through a low basketball hoop. The more adventurous five-year-olds experiment with roller skates and perhaps stilts. Little girls enjoy trying to jump rope, though their efforts are often less than successful. By recognizing this developmental need for activity and cooperating with it, both parents and teachers can encourage activities that will strengthen the large muscles and develop body control as well as give the child constructive channels for expression.

Quiet activity

Periods of strenuous activity need to be balanced by periods of quiet activity and by periods of rest, for the five-year-old gets tired easily in spite of his vigor and his eagerness to use his body—or perhaps because of it. A five-year-old will often withdraw from play of his own accord and either just watch or seek a quieter activity; occasionally he will even lie down. Often he shows fatigue by being cross or irritable.

Most five-year-olds sleep about eleven hours at night. Few children at this age take regular afternoon naps, but many of them will take a nap one or two days a week, as weariness seems to accumulate. In a kindergarten program one or several rest periods are advisable, depending on the length of the kindergarten day. If the child attends morning kindergarten and is at home during the afternoon, he should have a "quiet-play" rest time even if he is unable to sleep. If he attends afternoon kindergarten, it is usually wise to bring him in from play at about eleven in the morning for a quiet period or a rest before lunch and school.

During these periods of quiet activity, the child needs to feel free to move from one activity to another. He cannot yet be expected to sit still for a long time, although his attention span is increasing rapidly, so that he may remain interested and absorbed in the same project for twenty minutes or even longer. The five-year-old finds blocks, paints, clay, "work-with" tools, and puzzles all satisfying to his growing interests. He may work for a period of time at the easel or settle down at the puzzle table; he may make a clay bowl or spend time with blocks, working out a plan he has in mind. He no longer runs from one activity to another, experimenting with this and that. He knows more fully what he wants to do today and will even carry over a project until tomorrow.

The five-year-old usually has an idea of what he wants to do before he goes to work. In painting he may begin by announcing what he is going to paint. Often he will be very critical of his own work, expressing dissatisfaction with it or asking for directions. Many five-year-olds have passed the stage of just smearing and dabbing paint; they want to create something and have a definite feeling of accomplishment when the picture is finished. They enjoy showing the product to their teacher for her praise and taking it home for their parents to admire.

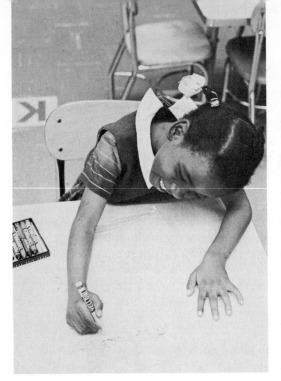

Preparation for reading

Whether at home or at school, the child of five will respond eagerly to "Let's have a story." He enjoys stories that answer his questions about things he sees around him—steam shovels and engines, airplanes and boats. He also likes stories about the activities of children and about family life. He is ready to broaden his horizons with tales about other lands, for television has already transported the five-year-old far beyond his own block and neighborhood. Many children have traveled extensively by the time they are five and can share their experiences, from camping out to crossing the ocean by plane or boat.

In this space age many five-year-olds are ready also for simple, basic principles of science and mathematics, which they can learn through hearing stories or through watching or taking part in simple experiments. They love nature stories, particularly if these are supplemented by such activities as watching or caring for animals and plants, taking nature walks, and collecting natural objects.

The five-year-old still delights in some imaginative stories, especially those about animals, but he isn't yet old enough to enjoy the more fantastic and unreal fairy tales. He listens to poems with pleasure, the rhythm adding to his joy in listening. The youngster typically becomes quite absorbed in a story or poem and resents interruptions. He wants to see the pictures in a book and is disappointed if there are none.

112

Many children in this age-group are able to take part in activities that lead to reading. In vocabulary alone, the child of today who has watched television is usually about a year ahead of kindergarten children of pretelevision days. A small number of five-year-olds are ready to read, and some do read; others pretend that they can do so, telling a story as they turn the pages of a picture book. If the desire to read comes from the child, he should not be denied the opportunity to learn; neither should he be discouraged from making the progress he is ready to make in reading. However, many kindergarten children will not be ready and may become overanxious if they are pushed before they are physically and psychologically ready to master the complex use of symbols.

A good kindergarten program will always try to meet the needs of the individual child. It will avoid a formal program that pressures children to learn to read and thus discourages the many who are not yet ready for reading. Much valuable learning can be accomplished without the use of the printed word. Informal reading may be a valuable addition to the kindergarten for a few children, but it is not necessary for the development of a vital program for all children.

Physical development as well as mental ability must be taken into account before a formal reading program is started. This may be particularly true for boys, many of whom have trouble learning to read in the elementary school. In general, boys are more active than girls and have a harder time sitting still and listening and applying themselves to formal schoolwork. They seem to learn better in an active program in which they can learn by doing. Because boys often are as much as a year behind girls in their physical development, many may not be ready for reading as soon.

Physical development must also be considered in using workbooks for the kindergarten. Some children may be ready for the experience, but others may become so discouraged that their future confidence in themselves as learners is impaired.

Music, dramatic play, and sociability

Five-year-olds enjoy rhythms and songs. They like to make up dances to music and enter enthusiastically into singing and rhythmic games. They also enjoy taking part in a rhythm band. Many of the children are beginning to follow a tune and will even correct a child who does not know it. Often a five-year-old chants a short rhythmic song of his own as he goes about his play.

The five-year-old loves dramatic play. He is ready to act out the story he has heard—very simply and with plenty of action and spontaneity. His love of dramatic play is the keynote to many of his activities. He acts out his interest in his home and the places he goes by playing house, being mother or father, playing doctor, or playing store. Both boys and girls enter into this home-centered dramatic play. They also show their interest in the exciting world in which they live by playing spaceman, jet pilot, and airline hostess. Planes and rockets enter their play much more frequently today than trains.

The kindergarten child is greatly interested in group activities and group play. He likes to play with other children, but he is still not very good about really cooperating with others. He stays in the group as long as he enjoys it, but his interests are self-centered. If he tires of the group activity, he becomes restless or seeks something else that pleases him more, even if it means leaving the group without a father in the home or a delivery truck for the supermarket.

The kindergarten child is capable of taking part in large group activities if they are well supervised, but he gets along better in small groups of five or six children, or with just one other child. At this age, three is often a crowd; a child can adjust to one playmate or the other but often not to both. Thus on a rainy day a mother is wise to invite one other child over rather than two.

The five-year-old is improving in taking turns, in respecting other people's belongings, and in asking to use things rather than snatching or hitting. His sense of property is developing. He will still quarrel and fight, but he is learning better ways of getting along and is increasing in his ability to handle situations himself. His mother and teacher can usually remain in the background while children of this age work through their own problems as they play together.

Putting needs into words

A five-year-old is beginning to use language fluently and correctly. He usually pronounces words clearly and is easily understood. He talks freely, carrying on conversations and expressing ideas. He loves to tell a story, and he will recount an incident that happened at home to his teacher or will tell his mother about the happenings of the day at school. He has learned to put his needs into words. Parents can help by listening to their youngsters when they try to tell about incidents or personalities or objects, by encouraging conversation in the family, and by avoiding overemphasis on correct speech. That will come later and large-ly from example. Speech at five should be spontaneous.

The five-year-old is becoming able to put his fears and his anxieties into words. He sometimes will spontaneously tell his parents what is bothering him; or a parent or teacher, seeing or sensing that the child is disturbed, may be able to help him talk about the things that are bothering him. Adult assistance in under-standing and solving problems is particularly important to the child today, when the whole world is brought into the living room. The kindergarten child, with his growing awareness of reality, may be confused by the behavior of adults he sees on the television screen. At an age when his conscience is developing, when he is trying to learn to control his own impulses and to behave as his parents have taught him, he sees grown-ups on TV fighting with and screaming at each other and generally behaving in ways that he has been told are unacceptable. Documentaries and news reports of current events are often bewildering to a small child, and sometimes they provide real cause for his concern and anxiety.

Parents in the past were able to protect their children from the impact of anx-iety-producing reality while they were very young, but today's child must meet life head on and needs the support of adults as interpreters and protectors; he must be sure they will take care of him. Most children can absorb most of their concern over bewildering or distressing events if they receive adequate answers to their questions, so that what they see and hear is not distorted. But a child who is already disturbed or insecure will need special help and understanding. The questions of the observing child today may have much more serious import and need more thoughtful answers than those of most children who grew up before radio and television became household fixtures and nuclear warfare a persistent threat.

By the time he is five, the child who is tense, overanxious, excessively rebel-lious, or unusually withdrawn is already noticeable. The problems of such a child should be taken seriously, not pushed aside with the vague hope that he will outgrow them. The child should receive thoughtful attention and, if it appears necessary, special outside help.

Enjoying independence

A child of kindergarten age is quite independent and enjoys doing things for himself—if he has not previously been pushed too hard or had too many de-mands made on him. He can usually wash himself, although his mother or father will have to help in neglected or hard-to-reach spots. He is able to take care of his own toilet needs, although sometimes he will need a reminder, for he finds it hard to leave his play. He feeds himself easily and with a minimum of mess. He still likes to eat many things with his fingers, but he is becoming in-creasingly skillful with fork and spoon and may even try to use a knife. He also has definite likes and dislikes in food. Most five-year-olds prefer foods that are not mixed together. They do not enjoy creamed vegetables as much as raw vege-tables, or puddings as much as fruit or jello for dessert.

Youngsters of this age can dress themselves, although they still get things twisted sometimes. They cannot always tie their shoelaces or manage tight buttons or small fastenings. They may still need help getting into a difficult snowsuit, especially when they are tired or out of sorts. Parents can help by trying to provide clothing with self-help features—ample armholes, large buttons or snaps in places the child can reach, rubbers that are loose enough to put on easily, and cardigan rather than pull-over sweaters. If these provisions are made, dressing can be a source of fun and pride to a child.

When one takes care of a child from babyhood, it is sometimes hard to keep pace with his growing ability. Many a mother does not even know until she visits kindergarten that her youngster can put on his own snowsuit. Mothers need great self-control to refrain from quickly doing for a child something he is doing slowly and ineptly by himself. Yet such help robs him of satisfaction in successful accomplishment, satisfaction all children need for building self-reliance and the courage to meet difficult situations. The five-year-old wants to test out and rely on his own powers, and he should be encouraged, though never pressured, to do so.

The five-year-old also shows his independence by liking to be trusted with

errands or by performing simple tasks in kindergarten and at home. He will go proudly to a nearby store and bring home a loaf of bread, change and all. He will usually carry out directions faithfully and be elated by his success.

The five-year-old is home-centered in spite of his growing independence. When he was four he sometimes ventured out of bounds to explore the neighborhood, but at five he likes to stay near home base. His mother is the center of his life—he likes to be at home and near her. Some five-year-olds show anxiety if they think their mother won't be at home when they get back from kindergarten. They enjoy their father, brothers, sisters, and friends, they enjoy their teacher and kindergarten, but their mother is most important. They constantly seek her support and approval.

An age of conforming

Five often seems an age of conforming. Perhaps this is why it is a good year to enter kindergarten. Most five-year-olds want to learn. They are much better able to settle into the routine of the group than they were at four. Five seems to be almost a resting point between the out-of-boundness of many four-year-olds and the extremes of six-year-olds. The five-year-old wants to do what is expected of him. He often asks whether he is doing something the right way, or he turns to his mother or father or teacher with "May I go?" "May I do this?" He wants to fit into his environment and seldom rebels against it.

This is the age when a child begins to take some responsibility for his own actions and to know the difference between right and wrong. It is often said to be the age at which his conscience is developing. Until now he has been dependent on his mother or father or some other adult to tell him what is acceptable behavior; now he is beginning to understand for himself, although he often turns to an adult for guidance and reassurance. He still thinks of good and bad in terms of specific situations—it was bad to do this or good to do that. Because the child is interested in conforming at this age, he can often be taught to adjust to the needs of the group and to respect reasonable authority. The child who goes to kindergarten during this year of equilibrium has a better chance of learning to adjust to the schoolroom situation with a minimum of strain than does the six-year-old who goes to school for the first time without a kindergarten experience.

study of a child

Brain Injury

Even slight damage may affect development

When a child does not respond and react as do most youngsters of his age, the reason is not always readily established. If he appears normal mentally and strong and healthy physically, with no serious sensory defect or crippling condition, his parents are not likely to consider that the cause of the puzzling behavior may be organic impairment, the result of brain damage. Often it is not until kindergarten age that behavior deviations become apparent and really disturbing. The school is likely to notice them first; parents generally become aware of them only when the school helps focus their attention on the child's total growth and reaction pattern.

It was not until Danny Ward was five and in kindergarten that doubts arose about his development. Miss Rosen, his teacher, at first thought of him as a friendly, pleasant, though exceedingly restless little boy. She soon recognized that he was less skillful on playground apparatus and with block construction than most of her other children, and that he was less fluent in relating his experiences. But in the first few months of school she was not particularly concerned about Danny; she was aware that some youngsters need more time and practice in learning skills than do others.

As time went by, however, Miss Rosen came to realize that Danny's pleasant smile was vague, that his restlessness seemed uncontrollable, and that his motor and verbal skills did not improve despite her patient help and repeated demonstrations. Furthermore Danny's speech was hard to understand, and although she encouraged him to enunciate correctly, he was either incapable of reproducing sounds correctly or reverted to incorrect ones as soon as her careful coaching ended.

Now and then Danny attempted simple songs and rhymes which the other children had learned readily, but for the most part he didn't pay attention long enough to learn the melody or words. Even when he did have some small success, he sometimes forgot the song or verse the next time it was repeated.

Danny's play with clay and finger paints was very immature, but it was far more successful than his efforts to draw or color pictures. Long after other children's drawings were recognizable as tree, flower, man, rabbit—whatever the subject—Danny's could not be identified. Generally Danny was affably willing to try to follow his teacher's directions, but his efforts brought him little or no success. This did not appear to bother him. He seemed unaware that he had copied a letter incorrectly or produced an unrecognizable picture. He would often ask Miss Rosen, "Shall I write my name now?" To her encouraging assent he would make an unintelligible mark on his paper and hand it to her with a satisfied smile. He seemed to want to please his teacher, but was unable to do as she directed.

Danny knew the meanings of many words, but his concepts were often faulty or bizarre, resulting in vague or far-fetched responses. He could see, but he saw inaccurately—shapes and letters appeared incomplete or distorted. Matching pictures was an apparently impossible task for him.

In the most ordinary daily activities, Danny had trouble getting along. He was inept and untidy at lunch, while the other kindergartners were capable and reasonably neat. He needed a great deal of help with his coat and his boots, though the other children managed theirs easily. When his mother or teacher encouraged him to try again, he frequently yawned as he answered, "I'm too tired."

118

But he was seldom actually relaxed, even during story time. Picture books didn't interest him for long. During games he often wandered away from the group. Many times during every school day he distracted other children from group activities by his constant squirming, his incessant getting up and down, or his monotonous repetition of a phrase or a question.

After several months of consistent, patient effort to help the child, Miss Rosen felt that everything she had done was fruitless. Speaking to Dr. Carol Gray, the school psychologist, she wondered if Danny were not a candidate for a class for retarded children.

"How could he possibly go to first grade?" she asked, both discouraged and concerned. "Should he stay with me another year? And if he did, would it do any good, do you think? He certainly hasn't made much progress this year, not at all like most of my children."

"Suppose we see how he does on some tests," Dr. Gray suggested. "From your description, giving him a psychological examination won't be easy, but the results should help us in planning for him."

Somewhat to his teacher's surprise, Danny's test results were not those of a mentally subnormal child. "Still," said Dr. Gray, "I certainly agree that Danny could never get along in first grade next term. He has definite limitations and he is a difficult youngster to handle in a group. I'd like very much to talk with his mother. I'd like to know how he is at home and how his parents manage him. And I'd like to know something about him as an infant and as a very small child, before he came to kindergarten. He may just be extremely slow in developing. And there may be unwise management at home without the family realizing it. I'd like to know his pediatrician's opinion and whether he's had an eye examination and a hearing test, although I didn't note any obvious physical problem that might be contributing to the situation. Call Mrs. Ward, Miss Rosen, and set up an appointment on one of my days here next week."

Mrs. Ward arrived at the designated time for a conference. She was cheerful and interested, with no sign that she expected any difficulty about Danny's going into first grade in the fall term. She was puzzled and alarmed when Dr. Gray suggested a second year in kindergarten.

"But he'll be six even before this term is over," she protested. "Don't children start first grade at six? His brother wasn't six until November of the year he started school."

"I see Robert is in sixth grade now," Dr. Gray observed, looking at the record she had at hand. "How would you compare the two children when you think of their baby years, Mrs. Ward? For example, did they walk and talk at about the same age?"

"Danny was twenty months before he walked," Mrs. Ward replied. "But really, that doesn't have any bearing on going into first grade, does it? And I thought we weren't supposed to compare children," she added defensively, ignoring the comparison that she herself had already voiced.

"How about talking?" continued Dr. Gray, for the moment overlooking both question and comment. "When did Danny start to talk?"

Mrs. Ward thought for a moment. "Well," she said slowly, "there were a few

words at——oh, about the time he started to walk, I think. But——well——
I guess he was past three when he really began to talk. I know that even now he
doesn't always express himself clearly. He's always in such a hurry to tell something or ask for something. You know how children are." She smiled a little
uncertainly.

"And your older boy?" Dr. Gray asked. "When did Robert walk and talk?"

"Earlier. Earlier for both," Mrs. Ward said frankly. "We always thought he
was very bright. But we'd always read that no two children are alike. So it didn't
worry us when the baby seemed different. We just let Danny go ahead at his
own rate. Isn't that what psychologists advise?"

Dr. Gray nodded. "But can you recall whether Robert was at all like Danny in
other ways—playing with blocks, looking at books, drawing pictures? Did he
listen to stories? Recite Mother Goose songs and rhymes? Could he count?
Name colors? Undress and dress himself?

"Because here in kindergarten," Dr. Gray added gently, "Danny has not been
doing what the other children do, or what Robert did when he first came here.
We don't compare one child with another child and look for each to develop at
the same rate and in exactly the same way. You're perfectly right about that. But
we do consider as evidence of normal development what thousands of children
of the same age are like and can do. And we are concerned when there are
marked differences in a particular child. We want to help Danny. I've already
used some tests with him and they show that he isn't yet able to do what is expected of children who will be ready for first grade in the fall. It would be much
better for him to wait awhile before going into the regular grades. That would
give him a chance to learn some things he hasn't yet mastered."

"Are you suggesting," Mrs. Ward asked hesitantly, "that you think Danny is
——backward? Is there anything really wrong?" She and Dr. Gray talked for
some time and considered a detailed history of Danny's growth. Mrs. Ward
acknowledged that Robert's growth had been vastly different. Although Dr.
Gray was sure from the results of the psychological tests that Danny was not
subnormal mentally, she felt equally sure that certain special training was necessary if he were to progress and learn as other children do in school.

"Right now he's not responding like a child who is almost six," Dr. Gray
emphasized. "He is learning very slowly, and he needs a great deal of individual
attention. There are things you can do at home for him which I believe will help
considerably. We'll talk over those steps and work with you all we can."

Understandably, Mrs. Ward was greatly distressed. She grasped eagerly at the
suggestion that she and Mr. Ward discuss the situation in detail with their pediatrician. But first they had an oculist experienced in examining young children
check Danny's vision. After a difficult examination period, the oculist stated
that he had found no problem with Danny's eyes. He suggested that the child
was mentally retarded, but later agreed, when the results of the psychological
tests and school discussion were reported to him, that he certainly could have
been mistaken.

When the Wards consulted Dr. Donnelly, their pediatrician, he agreed that
Danny and his brother had shown different developmental pictures. He reported
that no endocrine deficiency was involved in Danny's case and that, as far as he

could determine with the restless and uncooperative Danny, there was no hearing loss.

"He's always been a hyperactive child," said Dr. Donnelly. "He can't help the extreme restlessness that his teacher noticed; his nervous system is geared that way. I'd say that the cause is probably some relatively slight brain injury that occurred either before he was born or during birth. It's very difficult to tell exactly."

Because they understood only vaguely the suspected basis for Danny's behavior, the Wards listened eagerly as the physician explained some of the known facts about brain injury. Unfortunate as the condition was, they were encouraged to hear that Danny could improve.

"You see," said Dr. Donnelly, "the effects of damage to the brain are not necessarily apparent in the early months of a child's life. Even when a toddler shows certain behavior reactions, we keep looking for change, hoping he'll outgrow them. When a youngster is strong and well, particularly, we're optimistic. And Danny has been healthy right from the beginning. Sometimes brain damage results from disease—meningitis, for example; sometimes from a serious accident, with a severe concussion or skull fracture. We know neither of these possibilities is true with Danny. That's why I say the injury occurred either before or during birth.

"It's the kind of condition that may be present in so mild a form or to so slight a degree that in many ways the child seems entirely normal. Yet in other respects his behavior may be puzzling and actually evidence abnormal development. Fortunately, though, damaging results may be only transitory, not permanent.

"Brain damage shows up in various ways. Sometimes the child may be unable to learn. Or he may be very distractible, or irritable, or disinterested in his surroundings, almost withdrawn. It's impossible to say what behavior will appear. Often there's faulty perception. He may not see a diamond as a diamond, for example. He may not visualize the corners at all. Or a printed letter may look very different to such a child than it does to other children his age. So he'll have trouble learning to read and to write, to recognize numbers, and so on.

"Conceptual disorders are common among brain-damaged children. By that I mean that the thinking processes are unlike those of normal children. For instance, when brain tissue has been damaged, a child does not seem able to group or classify objects logically. Given a number of familiar objects, such a child once said that of three things, a gong and a ball and a bell, the ball and bell went together because 'in the bell there's a little ball,' meaning the tip of the clapper. This is a far-fetched relationship. Most normal children would give the more logical grouping of gong and bell, because each makes a sound or gives a signal.

"Motor behavior is generally clumsy and awkward in these children. They have difficulty in making precise movements with both large and small muscles. And they can't coordinate their eyes and their hands. For example, when they're asked to make a mark on a certain part of a picture, the mark is off to one side, or above or below, but not *on*—not because they don't understand the instruction, but because the necessary messages to and from the brain aren't functioning normally.

"The condition is very puzzling, you see, because it exists in varying degrees and in varying ways. Speaking generally, we know that brain injury shows itself in motor impairment or in impaired mental and emotional processes—sometimes in both ways. It's not surprising that a mild condition of this kind frequently goes unnoticed, and a child is often punished for not paying attention, for being restless, for talking incessantly, or for not learning normally when actually he can't help himself.

"But fortunately he can be helped. And the earlier the condition is recognized, the more effective the steps taken to help. Your school psychologist seems to be on the right track. Seeing your boy over a period of several months has given the school a chance to observe how he acts, how he learns, how he is impeded in learning. Try Dr. Gray's suggestions. But be patient. Danny can make progress, I'm pretty sure, but remember it will be slow progress."

The school's counsel and the physician's concurring opinion were not easy for the Wards to accept, but they could not deny the facts as Dr. Gray presented them, and they recognized in Dr. Donnelly's explanation of brain damage some of the difficulties that they now saw were true of Danny. Although they had been aware of the wide difference between their two boys, their acceptance of one being very bright and the other much less capable had made them less critically observant of Danny than they might otherwise have been.

Robert had delighted them with his quick perceptions, good memory, and eager questioning, and they had enjoyed teaching him the many accomplishments possible for small children. They were charmed with his pleasure in coloring, his early interest in numbers, his finger dexterity. And their play with him encouraged further learning. Unthinkingly, they had simply considered Danny "such a baby," not recognizing that he was failing to absorb the knowledge and the skills that the routines of a child's day generally provide. His parents overlooked his awkwardness and did for him what he should have been practicing doing for himself.

"There didn't seem to be time," said Mrs. Ward. "Everything took him so long, and he'd get impatient and whine. I guess I just took the easiest way and did things for him myself." So Danny's parents dressed him, fed him, built towers for him, and colored pictures for him. They gave him no actual opportunity to learn the arm and hand and finger manipulations necessary to dress and feed himself, to build with blocks, and to color with crayons. When Danny showed little pleasure in nursery rhymes and songs, the family stopped trying to amuse him with them. When his restlessness made him seem totally disinterested in picture books, they stopped making any attempt to point out and name objects, or to have him identify and point to them.

"I suppose we kept waiting for him to be old enough to enjoy counting and coloring and reciting. The six year difference in age made it hard to remember just when Robert did all the things we supposed one day Danny would manage, too. He'd get cross when we tried to push him. So we just stopped and let him alone. He didn't seem unhappy. And he wasn't really naughty, just so fidgety and restless and so very awkward."

The Wards now accepted Danny's need for consistent, patient help in acquiring, at least to some extent, the skills he hadn't yet mastered. They were determined to do everything possible to remedy and improve Danny's ways. Danny's teacher and the school psychologist helped the Wards outline a definite plan to provide the kind of help he needed. For many months, Danny and his mother worked together several times each day to help Danny help himself. At first, he was rarely interested for longer than ten or twelve minutes, but gradually he was able to concentrate for somewhat longer periods.

Before long Danny had learned to put on his sweater and coat, to undress with just a little help, and to participate increasingly in the dressing process. He was also successful in other efforts: he learned the names of many objects he had scarcely noticed before, he described pictures briefly, he recited a few nursery jingles. His building with blocks improved so that he delighted in making towers "so high." Six-year-old Danny was beginning to master the many little accomplishments most children acquire at three and four.

When the Wards reproached themselves for having neglected their son for so long, they were relieved to hear Dr. Gray say that it was questionable if many of his recent achievements could have been learned much earlier.

"Some, yes," she said. "But any child must be ready to learn before he can be taught. See what he can do now, compared with just a few months ago. His second year in kindergarten will without question be more profitable for him than his first, and more rewarding for his teacher and for you, too. Let's look forward to the following year, when there is every hope that Danny will be ready to start first grade and make progress there. In the meantime, keep on working with him—ten, fifteen minutes at a time. He tires quickly and he is very distractible. But whenever he makes a step forward, show him how pleased you are. Praise and encouragement help everyone."

When there is reason for concern in a child's responses and reactions, establishing the basis for his behavior is of primary importance. Only when an accurate diagnosis, an understanding of the child's potential, and a realistic acceptance of his limitations have been reached can a wise program be initiated to help him overcome his difficulties. Remedial measures used in such a program may be medical, psychological, or educational—a combination of them is the usual picture. Unwitting neglect of any aspect of help is as much to be avoided as are unreasonable expectations. Each child should be encouraged to aspire to goals that he has a chance of accomplishing successfully. Working toward goals beyond his possible achievement can result only in disappointment, distress, and continuing difficulties.

The Preschool Years

FOR THOUGHT AND DISCUSSION

1. How can television be harmful to the healthy growth of the runabout?

2. Ask a five-year-old boy what his favorite television programs are and briefly analyze the programs according to their positive or detrimental value to the child you interviewed.

3. Write a brief description of how you think morally and scientifically complex questions should be answered for children.

4. Write a short dialogue showing how you would answer the following questions a four-year-old might ask: "What do kids in school do?" "What are the pedals on the floor of the car for?" "Where does the sun go?" "How does the refrigerator work?"

5. Would you consider sending your own child to a nursery school? Why?

6. How does a child's language ability affect his ability to cope with frustrations and anxieties?

7. How do a child's attitudes toward his own creative products differ when he is a runabout and when he is five?

8. Assume you could observe two children, one four years old and the other five-and-a-half, both appearing to be the same age. What age-group characteristics would you look for to identify the older child?

9. Observe a group of five-year-olds at classroom play and note evidences of their social development in their attitudes toward each other.

10. What are the basic conditions governing reading readiness? Are there dangers in overlooking these conditions and attempting to teach a child to read before he is ready? If so, what are they?

11. Why is it especially difficult for the parents of the runabout to achieve the "light touch" mentioned in Part Two?

12. Mrs. Stern, in the case story entitled "Another Baby in the Family," wanted to help her son avoid experiences she herself had had as a child. What were those experiences, and what caused them?

13. Recall the mothers in the three case stories in this section. Which of the three do you feel had the most positive attitude toward her child before consulting her physician?

14. Observe three children, one two-and-a-half, one four, and one five-and-a-half, and note the differences in their use of language. Is there a greater difference in pronunciation and fluency between the four-year-old and the five-and-a-half-year-old, or between the four-year-old and the two-and-a-half-year-old?

FOR FURTHER READING

ASHTON-WARNER, SYLVIA. *Teacher*. New York: Simon and Schuster, Inc., 1963. A significant, exhilarating book that records how one teacher met the needs of her primary children.

BARUCH, DOROTHY. *One Little Boy*. New York: Julian Messner, Inc., 1952. Describes one child and also examines interpersonal relationships and their impact on all children.

CHRISTIANSON, HELEN; ROGERS, MARY M.; and LUDLUM, BLANCHE A. *The Nursery School*. Boston: Houghton Mifflin Company, 1961. An appealing and informative discussion of the nursery-school child and the parent's role in the nursery school.

DEUTSCH, MARTIN. "The Disadvantaged Child and the Learning Process," pp. 163-179 in PASSOW, A. HARRY. *Education in Depressed Areas*. New York: Teachers College Press, 1963. Discusses the educational needs of children in depressed areas, emphasizing preschool education.

FRAIBERG, SELMA. *The Magic Years*. New York: Charles Scribner's Sons, 1959. Provides valuable insight into the typical problems that emerge at each developmental stage during the first five years.

GARDNER, D. BRUCE. *Development in Early Childhood: The Preschool Years*. New York: Harper & Row, Publishers, 1964. Useful for people working with children under six.

HAIMOWITZ, MORRIS L., and HAIMOWITZ, NATALIE READER. *Human Development: Selected Readings*. New York: Thomas Y. Crowell, 1960. A collection of outstanding articles on infancy, childhood, and adolescence.

HARTLEY, RUTH; FRANK, LAWRENCE; and GOLDENSON, ROBERT M. *Understanding Children's Play*. 8th ed. New York: Columbia University Press, 1952. Deals with the relationship between play and child development.

HYMES, JAMES L. *The Child Under Six*. Englewood Cliffs, N. J.: Prentice-Hall, Inc., 1963. A valuable book for both parents and teachers.

ILLINGWORTH, RONALD, M.D. *The Normal Child*. 3rd ed. Boston: Little, Brown and Company, 1964. An English pediatrician's guide to bringing up the normal child.

JOSSELYN, IRENE M., M.D. *The Happy Child*. New York: Random House, Inc., 1955. A psychoanalytic guide to emotional and social growth, stressing the importance of early childhood and the meaning of family relationships.

LANGFORD, LOUISE. *Guidance of the Young Child*. New York: John Wiley & Sons, 1960. Discusses the development of the preschool child and the ways adults can help him. Includes a discussion of the handicapped child in the nursery school.

MURPHY, LOIS B. *Personality in Young Children*. New York: Basic Books, Inc., Publishers, 1956. Vol. I describes methods for the study of personality. Vol. II is a study of Colin, a normal child.

MURPHY, LOIS B., and others. *The Widening World of Childhood*. New York: Basic Books, Inc., Publishers, 1962. Report of a pilot study at the Menninger Foundation of the ways in which normal preschool children cope with the new demands and difficulties they face in everyday life.

READ, KATHERINE. *The Nursery School: A Human Relations Laboratory*. 3rd ed. Philadelphia: W. B. Saunders Co., 1960. An outstanding text in nursery-school education. Contains criteria for evaluating nursery schools.

REEVES, KATHERINE. *Children . . . Their Ways and Wants*. Darien, Conn.: Educational Publishing, 1959. Describes children's emotional needs from nursery school through the school years by discussing what growing up seems to mean to the child.

RIESSMAN, FRANK. *The Culturally Deprived Child*. New York: Harper & Row, Publishers, 1962. A challenging discussion of the need for new approaches to underprivileged children.

WANN, KENNETH D.; DORN, MIRIAM SELCHEN; and LIDDLE, ELIZABETH ANN. *Fostering Intellectual Development in Young Children*. New York: Teachers College Press, 1962. A study of young children's understanding of the world, with emphasis on how much more they can understand.

The Primary and Middle Years

In our culture six is the age we have selected for the child to begin his formal schooling. He is now ready, and indeed eager, to join the world of school children. For the next six years he will be part of a special world which few adults can ever really enter. The elementary school child lives at home, attends school, and usually does those things that adults expect him to do—but in his private life, and among his friends, he stays apart from the adult world. He will be fascinated by it and try to understand it; he may even be eager to enter it someday. But his own feelings, the understandings he has with his friends, the games they play, and the secret words they share are those passed on from child to child and shared with only the most perceptive adults. The child runs home eagerly to tell his mother all about nursery school or kindergarten, but once he enters first grade he seldom shares his world in all its vivid living with an adult.

School years have their ups and downs. For some children they are almost entirely satisfying and rewarding, and for some they are generally disappointing and discouraging. For the great majority of children, however, there are both good times and bad. Most children start school eagerly. They want to learn. They want to read. They want to enjoy school. Yet somewhere along the way we lose too many of these eager youngsters. By the sixth grade and sometimes even earlier, there are those who do not learn willingly—outwardly, at least, they have lost their curiosity and come "like snails unwillingly to school." It is our task as teachers and parents to reduce this number of unwilling or discouraged learners as much as we possibly can, so that all our children can take advantage of the years of education that are offered to them.

It is often right at the beginning that we allow youngsters to falter, when they are just starting to master the tools they will need for further learning—basic skills in reading, writing, spelling, and arithmetic. We give lip service to individual differences in children's ability to master schoolwork, but this is of little value unless we apply what we know about the child to the work that we ask him to accomplish. It is essential, if we are to educate all our children, that our expectations for them fit their abilities, so that each one may be encouraged to go on learning—so that none becomes discouraged by his inability to meet unrealistic goals.

It is also the adults' task to help each child develop responsible attitudes, not by scolding him because he is irresponsible, but by giving him opportunities to act in a responsible manner and by encouraging and recognizing his responsible behavior. It is during the elementary-school years that a child either learns the meaning of responsibility or develops the attitude of "getting by." Sometimes we limit our concept of responsibility to the carrying out of certain specific tasks at home or at school. We forget that responsibility also means getting up and going to school, accomplishing assignments, going home after school, acting fairly with other people. This kind of behavior needs recognition, too. Children learn to be responsible when responsibility has meaning for them.

During the years from six to twelve many parents overload their children with activities that involve additional responsibilities—for getting to lessons, for practicing, for accomplishing. It is no wonder that sometimes a child of this age cries out, "You never let me do what I want!" or, "I never have time for myself!" Between school and homework and extracurricular activities and organized club groups, many a child literally has no time for himself. Perhaps we have overdone the emphasis on opportunities and achievement to the detriment of individuality, creativity, imagination, initiative, and even the ability to entertain oneself. This question requires serious thought on the part of parents and teachers. How much assigned responsibility can the child carry during these important years without having to sacrifice something else important to his best development— some freedom to follow his own interests, some time to do what he wants?

Activity is the keynote to the elementary years. Children usually remain eager learners if they are allowed to take part in the process of learning, but too often we make them seat-sitters. Our culture demands that at six, a highly active age, children shall be required to attend school for six hours a day and often to sit still for relatively long periods. Teachers and parents are not always sufficiently aware of the relationship between growth needs and behavior difficulties when they reprimand restless children or expect them to stay too long in their seats in the classroom. The inability of many elementary-school children to sit still for more than a short time is a by-product of the rapid growth of their large muscles, their high energy drive, the fatigue that follows the too concentrated use of the small muscles, sometimes the strain of using the eyes before they are fully ready for close work, and the difficulty of controlling and inhibiting movement.

Differing energy drives among children make conforming to classroom demands more difficult for some children than others. A child who has a placid temperament or a low energy drive, or one who is well coordinated may have less problems in school than a child with high activity needs. Our problem as adults is to recognize how much learning of different kinds we can expect of children in six short years. We must help each child to find his place in the schoolroom and to attain his maximum growth without experiencing too much strain and tension. If each child has a feeling of accomplishment during his elementary-school years, he is more likely to continue being eager to learn and willing to put out the effort that will be required to continue his schooling.

chapter 8

A Period of Transition

Being six

Being six years old has a special significance for almost every child. He has looked forward eagerly to the time when he could proudly say, "Now I am six and I can go to school all day."

Six is one of the turning points of the child's life, because here he steps beyond the family circle into the larger world of the school and the community. Until now his relationships have usually been limited to his family, the few children on his block, and perhaps playmates in nursery school or kindergarten. In each of these situations his parents, especially his mother, have been closely involved, and the child has spent over half his day at home. But now that he is six, the child must find his own place and make his own friends under new conditions. At home the child is loved and accepted because he is a member of the family group; but when he starts first grade and is away from home all day, he learns— as he began to learn in kindergarten and even earlier—that among his peers he must *earn* acceptance. Just being Billy Smith is not enough; he must succeed because of his individual worth and because of the contribution he can make to the group.

The kindergarten year was one of transition between the home and the school, between the life of a child protected by the home and that of a first-grader encountering the often rigorous demands and competition of school life. Many factors combine to determine the child's adjustment to this new environment, but probably the two most important are *his pattern of individual growth* and *his background of home experience.*

Pattern of individual growth

Progress in physical development varies among different children, but by six a child has usually lost most of his baby contours. Although his growth at this age is less rapid than during earlier periods, his legs are lengthening and he is gaining in both height and weight. The child's body type is evident at six; the broad, solidly built boy or girl can be expected to weigh more in proportion to height than the slim, rangy youngster, and yet neither is underweight or overweight. While the child's body is gradually changing shape, so, too, is his face. His jaw is lengthening as permanent teeth replace baby teeth and as new molars come in.

The six-year-old's internal organs and framework are growing and changing, even though this development is not easily observed. His heart is still in a period of rapid growth, but his brain has almost achieved its full weight. During this year, the child's eyes are still not mature in either size or shape, and their relatively shallow depth probably accounts for a continuing tendency toward far-sightedness. This defect is usually corrected naturally between the ages of eight and ten, when the child's eyes attain adult size and shape. Although eye and hand preferences are well established, a six-year-old still has difficulty in coordinating eye and hand movements. His muscular development is also uneven, the large muscles being more advanced in general than the small ones. Precise movements continue to involve a considerable effort and strain for the child.

A six-year-old is particularly susceptible to contagious diseases. With his tremendous energy, he makes a difficult patient, especially during convalescence, and to keep him quiet his mother must be resourceful and prepared to help him shift his activities quickly from coloring books to toy trucks (or dolls) to clay modeling to cutouts.

Patterns of physical, mental, emotional, and social growth have many variations, fast and slow, steady and irregular. For example, a child of above-average mentality whose overall development is slow may be mentally ready for school at six, but emotionally and socially he may be more like a four-year-old, as yet unprepared for school. Similarly, a big, robust boy may be far ahead of his classmates physically, but socially and mentally immature. Too often we judge such a child by his size alone and pigeonhole him accordingly. We are apt to say, "A big boy like Jack shouldn't act like such a baby."

Variations in growth patterns make it necessary to know not only what children of a certain age are like in general but what each child is like in particular. Behavior problems at home and at school often develop because the adult in control, either parent or teacher, does not recognize a child's level of maturity. Many youngsters are regarded as incapable of adapting to first grade or as "difficult" children when, in reality, they are frustrated because they haven't yet reached the level of maturity attained by the majority of the class, or are bored because they have long since passed it. In a class for six-year-olds some children are still babyish, immature emotionally, and unable to adjust socially, whereas others are secure, self-reliant, and able to hold their own in their group.

Background of home experience

A first-grader's home experience is the second crucial factor in his school adjustment. If his parents have shown him affection and acceptance so that he comes to new experiences with the security of his home to help him, then he will usually be able to cope with school. If, on the other hand, he has been under strain during his early years—if his family has moved often and has failed to give him compensating love and security, if they have had to live in cramped and inadequate quarters with money worries taking precedence over the child's need for attention and affection, if his parents have been over-demanding, or if they

have had serious marital problems—the child is likely to come to school tense and fearful. The boy or girl who has been too rigidly trained or made to feel unwanted will also find it hard to adjust to the classroom, as will the child who has been overprotected and babied by his parents.

Obviously, then, six-year-olds cannot all be treated alike. *Each child is different, bringing to school a special native endowment, a special rate and pattern of development, and a special home background.*

Although there is no typical six-year-old, certain characteristics seem to be predominant in this age group. One of these is the need for physical activity. At this age children rush about in their play, jump up from the table at mealtimes, and wriggle in their seats at school. Their whole bodies seem to be involved in everything they do. When they read, they move their lips, shuffle their feet, and twist their fingers in their hair. When they write, they screw up their faces, bite their lips, and pull themselves back and forth in their chairs. They may try hard to sit still, but they are unable to do so for long, because they have trouble controlling their movements voluntarily. It is clearly unwise to put a strain on these youngsters by expecting them to sit still for more than a short time. Unusual restlessness at home and at school is often a sign that the child has too little opportunity for physical activity.

Six-year-olds carry over this pattern of activity even in their thinking. They learn better by participating actively than by sitting and listening. They count more easily if they have objects to move. They absorb ideas better when discussions and explanations are accompanied by, and grow out of, chances to handle all sorts of materials, to experiment with tools and art equipment, to look after details of housekeeping, and to care for a pet or a class garden.

Six-year-olds enjoy using their hands. Although they like to try to make things, they are usually still clumsy and cannot be expected to produce perfect results. Since the small muscles of the arms and hands are not completely developed, it is still hard for many children to write or to do handwork that involves much skill or control. Even apart from their lack of skill, they usually cannot

maintain their interest long enough to carry an activity through to a conclusion completely satisfactory by adult standards. Most children of six can, however, learn to paste and cut; to use paint, crayon, and clay; and to handle simple tools with a fair degree of skill. Their work will be crude, but their creative efforts should not be discouraged by placing too much emphasis on perfection.

Children vary considerably in physical maturity, and standards should not be so high that those developing slowly are discouraged or pushed to the point of tension. We cannot force muscular development and coordination; we can only cooperate with the degree of maturity found at any level.

Playgrounds—training schools of childhood

Activities that require use of the large muscles should continue to be stressed throughout this year. Six-year-olds should still have plenty of opportunity for climbing and hauling, for running and jumping, and for free, active play. They like to use wagons and scooters and to build with large blocks and boxes and boards. They are not yet well coordinated in their physical skills. They are learning to bat a ball or to jump rope, but they have far to go before they master these skills. Yet even if their movements are still rough and jerky, six-year-olds enjoy learning new skills. Adults should encourage and give opportunities for this learning but should not try to push children toward accomplishments beyond their ability. A well-developed child may perform easily on the trapeze, but other children, not yet ready for such stunts, can only stand and watch with envious interest. Someday they, too, will try.

The playground has been called the training school of childhood. It shows not only the kind of activity children of six need and enjoy but also the behavior patterns they are developing. They climb, jump, and run; they also shout and fight for their rights. They appear to have forgotten how to take turns, a social technique they had apparently mastered in nursery school or kindergarten. Now each child wants to be first and will push, fight, and quarrel for the apparatus. Each wants to be the leader; each wants to win and finds it hard to lose. Children of this age need to be taught again how to take turns and how to get along together. Some of their rough-and-tumble play and aggressiveness is necessary, however, for it is part of learning to hold one's own and of experimenting with independence. Competition is often keen, and many children boast and compare possessions, heights, and even families in trying to assert themselves and achieve status in the group.

Six-year-olds need adult supervision, though with a minimum of interference, to show them they don't have to be rough and rude in asserting themselves to meet the challenges offered by their playmates. Shy or slowly developing children, who might be overwhelmed by the usual playground activities, may need special help for a year or two until they are able to hold their own in the active group.

Increasing independence and imagination

Children of six are trying to leave babyhood and to free themselves of the behavior of little children. They do not want to be treated as they were during

their preschool years. We would be concerned if this growth drive did not appear —children must drop baby ways and exchange their dependence on their parents for the increasing independence and vigor of childhood.

Group activities gain popularity in the first grade, although few children evidence group loyalty or responsibility. At six a child often enters a game enthusiastically only to leave if he does not get the part he wants, or if he loses, or if something else attracts his attention. Such typical behavior shows that this is still a transition period between the individualistic play of the preschool child and the team play of the middle-grade boy or girl. Some immature children will remain at the level of individualistic play throughout the year, and for them group participation will be hard. These children should be encouraged to take part in group activities, but not compelled to do so.

In spontaneous play, girls and boys usually show different interests. Girls dress up and play house; boys play cowboys and Indians or spacemen. Occasionally girls join the boys in chasing and fighting games, and sometimes boys mix with girls in playing house or store, taking the parts of storekeeper, father, or delivery man. Best friends, however, are almost always of the same sex, and play in small groups is preferred. Although friendships are still shifting, they tend to last longer among the more mature children.

Dramatics have a prominent part in the spontaneous play of six-year-olds, as in that of five-year-olds. This delight in simple, informal acting develops out of the

interest or activity of the moment. Dramatic play is a source of learning as well as pleasure and therefore can be a valuable classroom tool. Dramatic play situations should be kept simple, however, since rehearsed or elaborately planned affairs are apt to destroy this rich, creative means of teaching and learning. A child of six quickly becomes self-conscious in a directed situation.

Love of dramatization carries over from play to conversation. A six-year-old tells a story with gestures, often moving his whole body expressively as he talks. He likes to add his own touches, and it is a mistake to scold him for telling something that is not completely true. Actually he is expressing his imagination as he weaves his story. The child only gradually begins to realize the difference between reality and fancy. An adult can help him differentiate between the two by asking understandingly, "Was it really that way, Jimmy?"

Six-year-olds love to laugh and enjoy a joke. Affection, warmth, friendliness, and a sense of humor can all help adults live happily with children who are six.

His learning and his limitations

Eagerness to learn is one of the most endearing traits of six-year-olds. Theirs is the age of *why,* and of trying to find clues and answers to their own questions. In this way children orient themselves to a world much bigger than the family or the block. They need to have adults encourage and respond to their efforts to express themselves. How their efforts are acknowledged, their questions answered, and their curiosity stimulated will determine their subsequent attitudes toward learning.

Children at this age learn by concrete situations and direct participation. A child's own environment challenges him first; he asks questions and seeks answers to what he has seen and heard. This may include much that he has been exposed to through television and books concerning other lands and perhaps scientific activities such as space travel. To most six-year-olds, the distant past, even if vividly presented by television, still remains vague and only slightly understood. Time, like distance, is not a clear concept for them; they are interested in the present, in what is happening *now*. Six-year-olds cannot plan much for the future, nor should they be expected to accept responsibilities that involve perception of time. "We will do this after recess" is more meaningful to a roomful of first-graders than "in half an hour." Perhaps because time still has so little meaning, many first-graders are likely to dawdle, and, if made to hurry, become irritated or upset.

Responsibility and routine

Six-year-olds like responsibility. Because they want to identify with adults and do what they think is grown-up, they imitate the mannerisms and actions of their mother, father, or a beloved teacher. They like to help set the table, wash the dishes, or make a simple dessert. At school they want to feed the goldfish, erase the board, and pass the papers. Even cleaning up is a coveted task if a word of praise makes the workers feel they have accomplished something.

Although a child's behavior at home may disturb his parents, he may appear quite grown-up when he is out. This ability deserves praise but should not be taken to mean "He can act that way all the time if he wants to." The effort of being grown-up all the time is too much for active, restless six-year-olds and should not be expected.

Six-year-olds have a hard time making decisions, and they should not be expected to make too many. Routines eliminate the need for some choices and give six-year-olds a feeling of security. Children of this age are reassured to know that meals come at certain times and that one activity follows another in regular order in the schoolroom. But this does not mean that programs for first grade should be rigid. On the contrary, freedom and adaptability within the program are needed, even while broad limits and sequences are clearly marked.

A turning point

Primarily, six is an age of transition. The child is not a more integrated, better-adjusted five-year-old. He is a different child, actually less stable, less robust, less decisive, and often less cooperative. He is changing physically, mentally, emotionally, and socially. He is trying to identify with older children and even with adults. He wants to be grown up, but at the same time he feels very small and dependent on the affection of the adults about him. Rigid discipline or a home or school atmosphere that is lacking in affection holds him back. He wilts under criticism and disapproval and becomes discouraged easily. When he is nine he will be able to take criticism in his stride, but now he needs encouragement, praise, and understanding. His explosiveness and violent changeability are normal and must be expected. Because his coordination is not perfected, the six-year-old still needs help—help that may seem out of proportion to his size. Parents, for instance, should be on hand at dressing time or when a new toy won't work, and teachers may need to help when coat sleeves and snowpants are hard to get on.

Emphasis on academic achievement can destroy a first-grader's confidence. Grades or marks should not be mentioned, but each child should be helped to read and write and do numbers when he is ready—and not all first-graders will be ready at the same time. Any effort to force a child to learn or to show independence before he is ready only defeats itself, rendering learning more difficult than it should be. On the other hand, if a child who is ready to progress is not permitted and encouraged to do the work he is capable of doing because other children are not ready, he may become bored and restless and find school lacking in challenge. Such a child may turn to his own thoughts, interests, and home activities for stimulation and show little interest in what he is asked to do at school, or he may sit back and develop the habit of not living up to his potential. If adults can catch the point of readiness, the child will pass more smoothly and efficiently from early childhood into the more complex and demanding school-age period.

This is a time for learning, not for polished achievement. We adults are often impatient, expecting too much of six-year-olds. We should judge children's success by their steady growth, by the progress they make over a period of months, rather than by a particular achievement at a particular time. If we expect more of six-year-olds than they are ready to give, we may set up tensions that will hinder their learning and affect their whole relationship to the school situation. A flexible program to meet the needs of all the children in the first grade cannot be overemphasized if each child is to have the best possible start in school.

Compliant Johnny

Good behavior may conceal disturbing emotions

Ignoring known results of research, many adults consider a child's behavior undesirable and suggestive of poor adjustment only when it disturbs or annoys them or interferes with their own comfort. It is true that frequent disobedience or quarrelsomeness, temper outbursts or defiance may well evidence poor adjustment and indicate a need for professional help, especially when the child's parents are at a loss to understand and correct such reactions. But it is equally true—and not as often recognized—that a pattern of yielding, compliant behavior and (possibly fearful) submissiveness also may evidence poor adjustment and suggest the need for help. A "good" boy or girl really may be too "good" and not a happy, relaxed child.

Johnny Gifford was six and had almost completed the first grade. He liked school and in the first months hadn't had any trouble with his lessons. But as the year wore on he gradually experienced increasing difficulty with classwork. He never seemed ready to begin when the other children were starting on a project. He was still assembling a well-sharpened pencil, a clean eraser, and fresh paper when they were well along with the task. And he seemed to make very slow progress once he did get started. Time and time again, dissatisfied with the results of his efforts, he would erase the words or numbers he had written, sometimes even recopying an entire page. The end of a period found him far from finished with work that most of his classmates had already completed.

Miss Eaton was a very young teacher on her first assignment. She thought of Johnny chiefly as one among her thirty-five children who never made her day difficult. She considered him "good as gold" and never worried about him. She was aware that lately Johnny's schoolwork had fallen below his earlier accomplishment, but she assumed this was a passing phase. At any rate, his work was fairly acceptable and she had no doubt that he would be able to go on to the next grade.

But when Johnny's report card indicated that he was slow and seldom finished his work, his mother was displeased. She appeared at the school the next morning and announced firmly to Miss Eaton, "He's never given any trouble before, and we're not going to have anything start now. I know he can learn as well as the others, and if it's necessary, you can punish him to make him do better. Whatever he's doing wrong must be nipped quickly. He must get a better report card next month. Probably he should have special tutoring."

Mrs. Gifford spoke quickly and decisively. Her chief reaction was indignation that her son was not bringing credit to his family. He had disturbed the routine of doing exactly as she expected; she found this difficult to tolerate. She had always considered Johnny's docile obedience a reflection of the "good job" she was doing in bringing him up. Quiet, self-effacing Johnny had followed all the regulations imposed at home, and Mrs. Gifford was determined that he would meet her standards of schoolwork as well. So a plan of tutoring was arranged. Miss Eaton questioned the need for it, but Mrs. Gifford was convinced it was necessary, though greatly upset that such special attention should be required.

Johnny accepted the new arrangement submissively, although it meant giving up a good deal of his playtime. Actually, he did not seem to want much contact with other children after school. He had few friends. He was seldom invited to another child's house, and he rarely asked if he might have a boy over to play. He wanted to do better in school. He had been worried because, as hard as he tried, he never seemed to accomplish what was expected of him.

After a few sessions, however, the tutor felt that Johnny's knowledge of basic skills was really adequate. He read well and his number work was good. It was the amount of time he took that interfered with his being successful in the classroom. She soon noted that his slow progress with a lesson was generally due to his dissatisfaction with his own work, his recopying material that he had already carefully reworked, and his erasing what another child would have considered acceptable. He was unsure of himself in every situation, afraid to go ahead, seeking constant reassurance that he was doing as he was supposed to do, anxious lest he had misunderstood instructions.

The tutor, realizing that working alone with Johnny showed her what a teacher in a busy classroom might fail to notice, arranged to see Miss Eaton.

Young Miss Eaton felt challenged by Johnny's problem, partly because she thought she might have been somewhat at fault, partly because she sensed that the mother's attitude was somehow involved in the situation. She discussed the matter with the school principal, Mr. Jamison, and arranged an appointment for Mrs. Gifford to talk to him. At about this time, however, Johnny developed a severe cold, and because he stayed home during an entire week, Miss Eaton went to his home with some of his schoolbooks. Her report of the visit suggested to Mr. Jamison a possible basis for Johnny's troubles and his tense, anxious manner.

"Johnny was lying on the living room sofa," Miss Eaton related, "and his mother said that since I was there with him she would go out to do some errands that Johnny usually did. She said it almost as if he had caught cold just to inconvenience her.

"When she had left, Johnny told me worriedly that his illness was making his mother do a great many extra things. It seems that usually he cares for his own room every morning. He makes the bed and dusts before he leaves for school. And he always sets the table, helps with the dishes, polishes ash trays and plant holders and that sort of thing. Another of his jobs is to keep the bookshelves in perfect order, dusting the books and ornaments and seeing that they are properly arranged. Every minute seems scheduled for him. Of course Mrs. Gifford is a wonderful housekeeper," Miss Eaton continued. "I telephoned only a little while before I went over to the house, so nothing special could possibly have been done. The place was spotless, everything exactly in order and looking as if it had just been polished or pressed or scoured."

While Miss Eaton was chatting with Johnny, who had been delighted to see her, she picked up a book, glanced through it, and replaced it. A little later she examined a lovely pottery bird, admiring the exquisite workmanship. Johnny became disturbed and restless, and when Miss Eaton questioned him, he blurted unhappily, "The book should be on the next shelf, not where you put it. And the bird you were looking at—it should face the window and you made it face the other way. My mother doesn't like it if things aren't right. She says there's a place for everything and everything should be in its place. She scolds if I don't fix things right after I dust."

Johnny was apologetic for his implied criticism of Miss Eaton, but he apparently could not risk displeasing his mother. Miss Eaton cheerfully replaced the articles as he directed, and Johnny relaxed. She asked him then if his father, too, was particular about everything, if he was strict. The reply was unexpected.

"Daddy tries hard," Johnny answered seriously. "But he's different. Mother says it's the way he was brought up. She says she's going to bring me up right. I heard her tell Daddy so one night," he added confidentially. "That was once when he wasn't being neat, and Mother told him I was just like him, and he was a bad example. But Daddy's nice. He's fun, and I like him."

Before Mrs. Gifford returned from her errands, Mr. Gifford came home. He entered cheerfully, tossing his coat on the end of the sofa, placing his hat on the table, letting his newspaper slide to the floor. "Hello, Johnny," he said, giving the boy a pat on the head. "Isn't it nice of your teacher to come to see you! Where's Mother?"

They chatted easily for a few moments and soon Johnny said, "Mother's taking a long time. I guess I'm making a lot of extra work for her." He looked anxiously at his father.

Mr. Gifford's expression became serious. "Have you been good?" he asked. More questions followed: Had Johnny taken his medicine? Had he eaten all his lunch? Had he been any trouble to his mother? "It's good that you have your schoolbooks now," he continued, with a faint smile for Miss Eaton, "so you can catch up with all the work you're missing. Mother's worried about that, you know. She wants you to be promoted."

Johnny sat up excitedly. "I have to be promoted!" he said shrilly. "I have to be! Mother said nobody in her family had ever *not* been promoted!"

Miss Eaton soothed him. "I'll help you, Johnny. You'll be back at school soon. And I'll leave these lessons for you to do while you're home."

When Mr. Gifford went to the door with her a few moments later, Miss Eaton asked him, out of Johnny's hearing, if a great deal wasn't expected of the boy. She told Mr. Gifford about the earlier conversation.

"My wife's a wonderful woman," he said, a little uncomfortably. "I know she's set in her ways, but really, she means everything for the best. She feels our son should be taught early to do everything just as she tells him. She wants John to be different from his untidy father," he said with a self-conscious smile. "And she's right about his schoolwork, too. Of course she's right."

Mr. Jamison felt that Miss Eaton's visit had been very enlightening. It suggested a home situation which was difficult for the boy and which was perhaps tied in with his school failure. After talking with Mrs. Gifford, he was sure his surmise was correct. He tried to show her how Johnny was caught between the opposing standards of his parents. For children want to please their parents; that is how they win the good will and approval so important to them. Thus when the home has two standards because the parents have opposing viewpoints, the child in that home becomes confused. In trying to please both parents, Johnny was having a hard time of it. Punishment was not the answer, as his mother seemed to think.

"Maybe you're right," said Mrs. Gifford finally, though grudgingly. "But Johnny will have to do as I say. I can't change at my age. I've learned to put up with his father's careless ways, but I won't have my child spoiled."

It was not easy to persuade Mrs. Gifford that her overexacting ways not only had created too many demands on Johnny, but had confused him because of the friction they caused with her husband. Mr. Jamison urged Mrs. Gifford to try to maintain a balance between her standards and her husband's. He pointed out that at least outward accord between mother and father was essential to help establish a feeling of self-confidence and security in the child. Without these, his schoolwork was only one aspect of his life which might be affected. His total adjustment was likely to suffer.

Parents are not always as rigidly demanding as Mrs. Gifford, yet their standards, whatever they may be, affect their children. In Johnny's case, his mother was a stronger willed, more dominating personality than his father. Johnny was zealous in meeting her demands and tried hard to live up to her expectations by being meticulously clean and orderly. Johnny's father was gentler and more affectionate, an easy-going individual. His ways were vastly different from his wife's. In seeking to meet his mother's requirements, Johnny often felt as if he were somehow criticizing his father. That made him feel guilty. Then when he occasionally left a toy on the floor or neglected to hang up his coat immediately on entering the house, he felt disloyal to his mother. That made him feel guilty, too. It was a problem he could neither understand nor resolve.

The dilemma worried the youngster considerably. And he did not leave the worry at home, where it originated. Often in school something would remind him of one or the other parent. He would begin to wonder a little resentfully whether he had done everything he was supposed to do before leaving the house. And he would speculate about whether his father really was a bad example, as he had heard his mother say so many times. Then he would feel guilty to have had critical thoughts about his parents.

Johnny's docile behavior at home had been the outgrowth both of his guilt over these criticisms and his fear of arousing his mother's wrath. He had learned that if he did as he was told and said little, life moved more smoothly. But he could not control his feelings as he did his actions. Often he felt angry or rebellious even as he was carrying out instructions; frequently he disliked his mother intensely while he was doing exactly as she directed. He wondered about his father, who clearly did not live up to his mother's expectations. But he admired him greatly and wished he could be like his father.

It was a very disturbing state of affairs for Johnny. At school he had been obedient because he feared that his teacher as well as his mother would criticize him. His own demands on himself for perfect papers created a large part of his difficulty with classwork. And these demands reflected his mother's requirements, which were beyond the child's achievement and worried him constantly.

Johnny's outward docility was a symptom. It needed to be recognized and understood. The healthy, happy child is often casual and careless, but generally he is eager, responsive, and active. Tractable and submissive moments can be observed in all children, of course, but when they aren't mixed with enterprising, alert, investigative moments—when the child never chafes or protests or murmurs—the situation is suspect. Handling the compliant child is easier than managing the rebellious one, at least for the time being. But the compliant child's very passivity, his resigned acceptance of the demands on him, is unhealthy. His withdrawn, meek, acquiescent behavior may cover angry and resentful thoughts, or puzzled and anxious ones.

A wholesome environment at home helps to forestall such reactions. Parental accord, at least in the presence of the child, is important. Arguments and recriminations between parents confuse children and interfere with their healthy emotional growth. When a child is not merely well behaved but *too* well behaved—too obedient and compliant—there is trouble somewhere. The sooner his behavior can be understood and corrected, the better the prospect for that child to reach inner contentment. This comes largely from the feeling of having his parents' approval and of being able to accept himself.

chapter 9

Slowly and Steadily Ahead

A new phase of development

The seven-year-old is much like the six-year-old in his physical growth, but in his feelings and in his attitudes toward life he is more mature. He has now entered another phase of his development, so his experience in the second grade is on a different level from that of the first grade. Teachers and parents should be aware of his new growth needs so they can anticipate and understand them.

The child's physical growth continues steadily and slowly; there is nothing spectacular about it. His annual expected growth is two to three inches in height, three to six pounds in weight. His legs continue to lengthen rapidly. Although his large muscles are still better developed than his small ones, the child is gradually becoming more skillful in using his small muscles and in coordinating his hand with his eye. Consequently, his writing is improving, although he still grasps his pencil tightly and shows considerable tension when forming letters. His eyes are not fully ready for close work, and he may often rub his eyes. This may indicate that the eyes are under some strain, and it certainly suggests the need for caution in emphasizing schoolwork that requires constant use of the eyes.

This is the period when the child is losing his baby teeth. He will have an increasing number of gaps as the months go by. Most children have already acquired their six-year-molars and are now getting their central incisors. Children usually do not experience great difficulty in cutting these teeth, although sore gums may cause an occasional child to be irritable.

The seven-year-old no longer takes an afternoon rest even on Saturday or Sunday, but he sleeps approximately eleven hours at night, usually starting for bed between seven and eight o'clock. He tires easily and often shows fatigue during the afternoon session of school; he should have a rest through a change of activity in the afternoon and should be encouraged to balance active play with quiet pastimes.

Physical activity and language development

A healthy seven-year-old is full of vitality and energy. Although he is not so continually active as the six-year-old and is more likely to balance his activity with periods of relatively quiet play, he still likes to do tricks—turning somersaults, hanging by his knees from a trapeze, or climbing to the top of a jungle gym, a tree, or a garage roof if one is available. He has usually put aside his tricycle by this time in favor of roller skates, a two-wheeler, a jump rope, a scooter, or a coaster wagon. On the whole, though, even though the seven-year-old attempts more kinds of activities, he is more cautious and less likely to take chances than when he was six.

Like the six-year-old, the seven-year-old often seems restless. He learns better if he is encouraged to be active while he learns. He still counts more easily and effectively if he has objects to move. He understands better if he can work ideas out in a sandbox or take some part in other projects. He wants to use his hands to explore, to make things, and to learn. He enjoys painting, clay modeling, and carpentry and is learning to handle tools with increasing skill. With many children, abstract thinking is barely beginning.

Language develops rapidly from six to seven. The seven-year-old carries on vivid conversations. He likes to talk, although his conversation usually centers around himself and the things he has done or around his family and their possessions. He tends to dress up his story and usually tells it eagerly, often with accompanying gestures. He still enjoys dramatic play, both in school and in spontaneous play with other children.

The child can now use language effectively in expressing disapproval. Instead of fighting, the seven-year-old sometimes hurls words at his antagonist and walks off the scene. He expresses his feelings toward his parents and their requests in no uncertain terms if he thinks they are unfair or if he does not want to comply.

Books, television, and movies

The seven-year-old still enjoys songs, rhythms, and stories. He knows the tunes of familiar songs and comments if other children do not sing correctly. His interest in stories has increased, as has his attention span; he can now listen or read for a longer period of time and can carry over the thread of a story from day to day. Now that he can read some books himself, he may delight in reading alone, although he still enjoys hearing stories read by his teacher or his parents. He is now well enough grounded in reality to enjoy fairy tales and myths and to recognize and accept the difference between an imaginary and a true story. Poems are still favorites, and the child will call for the ones he likes; he may even know many by heart. His interest in factual stories about real things is increasing; he wants to know how machines operate, what electricity is, and all about rockets and space ships. He often brings to school a fund of knowledge he has obtained from watching television, from reading many of the fascinating but simple science books for children, or from talking with his father or other adults. Many of the questions an alert seven-year-old asks require accurate, informative answers. Occasionally a teacher will find a seven-year-old who knows almost more than she does about his favorite science interest.

Animal stories continue to be popular with the seven-year-old, but now he enjoys stories about real animals rather than fanciful, talking creatures. He likes stories about other children and perhaps is beginning to be absorbed in the various series of books about boys and girls. This is the time to encourage his going to the library and choosing the book he wants.

Comics absorb more of the child's interest. While he may have enjoyed looking at comics for several years, he can now begin to read them, exchange them with his friends, and borrow them back again. Each child has his favorite or favorites, which he may read and reread.

The child's interest in stories carries over to television. Many seven-year-olds come dashing in from play toward the end of the afternoon eager to hear the next installment of a favorite program, and some watch television three to four hours a day. Many children watch without being concerned by the violence or problems they see portrayed; others are upset and may even have nightmares following an overstimulating television program. It is sometimes necessary for parents, or for a teacher through discussion at school, to help choose the more desirable programs. If a child is high-strung, his mother or father may have to limit his choice by saying "You may listen to any of these programs," instead of leaving the decision entirely up to the child. If television is used wisely and not allowed to interfere with outdoor play and other more creative activities, it can add an enriching dimension to a child's life.

Movies may begin to become part of the seven-year-old's life, but they are too stimulating for many youngsters of this age. If the child attends movies, they should be carefully selected and the child should arrive after the previews of other pictures. Few movies are planned for children, and many introduce a child to adult situations and experiences he is unable to understand. They can cause confusion in his mind as he tries to gain increased understanding of grown-ups and their world.

Standing up for his rights

The seven-year-old is learning to stand up for his own rights on the playground and will sometimes stand up for the rights of another child, especially where property is concerned. Most seven-year-old boys will fight for their rights if necessary, or else will walk off indignantly and refuse to play. A certain amount of aggressiveness is necessary at this age, for the child must adjust to the rougher ways of the playground. In another year, gangs will be forming and the youngster, especially the boy, will find it even more necessary to hold his own with the crowd. The adult's problem is to help children stand up for their rights without becoming ill-mannered, unkind, crude, or rough. This is not an easy task and it distresses some children. Shy, withdrawn youngsters may need considerable help during this year and, in some instances, protection from situations that are still too difficult for them.

Children of this age like to be first, to get the best grade or to paint the best picture. They like to win the race or have the biggest piece of cake. They each want their turn and demand it if they don't get it.

Dependence and independence

The seven-year-old is sensitive to what other children think about him and to whether or not he is liked. At the same time, he is also reaching for the approbation of adults and is becoming increasingly sensitive to their approval or disapproval. These two desires often conflict, because the patterns, values, and standards of the adults' group and of the child's group frequently differ.

Because the child is trying to imitate adult behavior and to relate to the adult world, it is more important than ever that his relationship with the adults about him be warm, friendly, and encouraging. The primary teacher has an especially important role to play in the development of the child under her guidance, for the youngster will seek a close relationship with her and will want to please her. If she is rigid or repressive, the child will be less likely to develop into an independent personality and less able to think for himself. The seven-year-old often finds it hard to take criticism from an adult and sometimes cries or blames the adult. On the other hand, he accepts leadership and guidance devotedly. By encouraging him and at the same time allowing him some independence, a teacher who is kind, understanding, and responsive will help the child to develop a great deal during this year.

It is important to recognize the seven-year-old's drive toward independence—a drive often overlooked because of his outward dependence on his teacher and parents for directions and reassurance. The seven-year-old wants to grow up, to leave behind the manners and dress and behavior of the little child, and to assume the standards of his peers or of children a year or two older; yet he does not quite trust himself and often seems anxious for fear he will do things incorrectly. If there is too much adult control, he will rebel against it, yet he continually turns to adults to make sure that he is right. If he is not reassured, he may temporarily give up trying until a little redirection or encouragement gets him started again. His teacher and parents need to be supportive in their attitude and yet at the same time encourage him to be independent and spontaneous.

A good year at school and at home

Seven is a good year for schoolwork because the child is anxious to do well and to learn how things are done. It has been called "the eraser age" because the seven-year-old erases as much as he writes, trying constantly to make his work more nearly perfect.

Differences in ability to do schoolwork are becoming evident by this time. The child who is having difficulty will need support and encouragement if he is not to grow discouraged when he sees others going ahead more rapidly. The attitude of both teacher and class toward the slow learner will be important. Seven-year-olds are not too young to learn to accept and respect differences in ability.

At home as at school, seven is generally a good year. The seven-year-old has learned to do many things for himself—even though he often dawdles and dreams while he is doing them. He still needs a patient reminder from his mother that he will be late for school, or that dinner is almost ready and he should wash his hands. But he is beginning to see for himself the need to wash his hands and even to help around the house. He likes to have a job at home, just as

he likes to help at school. Again, he may not always carry out his task efficiently, but he is learning to do his share. He can take care of most of his physical needs. He can bathe and dress himself, tie his shoelaces, and brush his teeth.

Although the seven-year-old is beginning to understand what time is and how to tell time, he still lives primarily in the immediate present and cannot plan realistically for future goals. He may worry about being late for school, but he cannot yet take full responsibility for getting there on time. He still dawdles and moves as slowly as if time meant nothing, although sometimes he will hurry if he is told that he must leave for school—his dash into his clothes may be a sudden contrast to his dreamy dawdling.

The seven-year-old is ready for a small allowance. He understands what money is for, and that food and clothes and other things that he wants must be paid for. He usually knows the names of the more frequently used coins and their relationship to one another—that a nickel and five pennies are the same and that a dime is worth two nickels. With a weekly allowance seven-year-olds begin to learn about spending and saving.

Reaching out for new experiences

One of the most striking contrasts between six and seven is that whereas a six-year-old is content with whatever happens to be going on—being taken to the park or riding his bike—a seven-year-old reaches out for new experiences, trying to relate himself to his enlarged world. He is often dreamy and absorbed, seeming to take things into himself rather than going out toward them. He likes other people and wants to be with them; he is gradually becoming more sensitive in his feelings toward them and more aware of their feelings toward him.

148

The seven-year-old reaches out for new experiences in various ways. He explores actively when his parents take him to the zoo or to some other place that he likes to investigate. But now that he has learned to read, he can explore the world by himself through reading books.

His ethical sense is beginning to develop. He is able to take some responsibility for his own actions. He is concerned about right and wrong, often criticizing his playmates if they do things he does not think are right and perhaps tattling to his teacher or his parents. Sometimes tattling is an attempt to win adult approval, but frequently it is an outlet for the child's anxiety and concern, an attempt to reassure himself that whereas the other children are wrong, his own behavior is right. He may also ask, "Is it all right to do this?" "May we go there?" He is still seeking patterns of behavior and wants to be sure that his are the right ones. He still does not completely understand truthfulness or honesty. He may pick up little things that he likes—a pencil, a piece of chalk, an eraser—and slip them into his pocket. He is more truthful than he was at six, but he is still learning.

Seven is a responsive age and it is easy to impose on the child's eagerness to please. Because he turns to adults for guidance, he can easily become too dependent on them, too inclined to give in to authority at the expense of his own feelings and drives. He is often overanxious for fear that he will not be able to achieve the standards set for him by his parents or teacher. Since he is becoming more critical of himself and is sensitive to failure or being made fun of, this is no time for sarcasm, ridicule, or even too much teasing. It is up to adults to steer a middle course that gives the seven-year-old the support, encouragement, and guidance he needs, while at the same time encouraging him to become independent and self-reliant.

No Place Like Home?

Sometimes a foster home is best

There is an old couplet that tells us, "East, west, Home's best." And certainly it is true that in general home *is* much the best place for a child to grow up. Most parents love their children and want to provide adequately for their happy, healthful development. Few situations suggest taking a child away from his home. He is usually better off living with at least one parent, if this is possible and if arrangements can be made for his care when the parent must be away or at work. But it is wise to consider every situation individually. Sometimes unusual circumstances make foster-home placement far more wholesome than a child's own home. Sometimes it is better for him to leave his family, despite the traditional counsel that "Home's best."

Huntley Williams lived in a large, comfortable apartment in a pleasant neighborhood. There was a playground nearby, and a school was conveniently located. His family was in good circumstances and able to provide him with more than the ordinary necessities. But by the time he was seven, Huntley had a long history of troublesome behavior—a type of behavior more frequently found when a child lives under conditions of deprivation with little supervision, few comforts, and no recreational facilities. He was defiant and impudent at home. He had twice run away. He disobeyed constantly, told lies, appropriated whatever he fancied, and showed no remorse when scolded or punished. The family was understandably disturbed, but their disturbance showed in anger and harsh treatment rather than in an effort to understand the untenable situation.

It was the child's aunt who finally approached the school for help. She said that since he was three, Huntley had been a problem. He would throw his food on the floor, refusing to eat. Without apparent reason, he would throw things out of the window—fruit from a dining-table bowl, the telephone pad, a number of guest towels. He was destructive with his toys, careless of his clothes, and adamant about refusing to accept any routine responsibility. He forgot errands, neglected piano practice, and ignored meal hours.

The aunt considered that the climax of his misdemeanors was his taking a ten-dollar bill from her purse. Huntley denied knowledge of the money until confronted with clear evidence that he had changed it for smaller bills and spent them for ice cream and cokes and dime store toys for the neighborhood youngsters. When it was useless to deny any longer having taken the money, the boy shrugged and refused to talk about it further.

All this was utterly baffling to Huntley's family. It was only too apparent that their method of constant scolding and frequent whipping, of depriving the child of an allowance and television had been wholly ineffectual. They felt puzzled when the school said that Huntley was not considered a problem—that his class-work was well done and that he had not been part of any disciplinary action.

True, he often argued with other children and was inclined to be noisy and talkative in class, but he had not been thought very different from most boys his age.

The family decided to consult a child-guidance center. It has been recognized that often a child who is considered "bad" in one situation will show acceptable behavior in another. This apparent paradox can be understood only when all the circumstances are known. We need to study thoroughly both the child himself and all the conditions of his daily living—not only current conditions but those that have prevailed throughout his life. For the behavior of a child at any time may be the result of what has occurred many months or years before.

The guidance-center staff found Huntley's physical condition excellent. His mental ability was superior. But when they considered his social relationships, they found that Huntley's schoolmates disliked him and that he had no real friends. It became evident that Huntley had taken the ten dollars to buy things for other children which would, in effect, buy their friendship. The social worker then tried to understand why such a step seemed necessary to Huntley, why he had not been able to make friends without bribing. That brought into the picture the boy's family situation and the emotional interrelationships in the home.

The surface circumstances included a comfortable home, excellent medical care, and piano lessons with a fine teacher. But they lacked even one acceptant, understanding, sympathetic adult through whom Huntley might have gained emotional security. Beneath the surface of his everyday living smoldered bitterness and resentment and unhappiness.

Huntley's parents had been divorced after his mother deserted the family to live with another man. The boy was then two years old. His father had never wanted a child and had always resented him as an added burden. When his wife chafed under the restrictions imposed by an infant, he was even more bitter. Yet when his wife left he saw no recourse but to make some plan to care for Huntley. He arranged to live with his mother, an aged and eccentric widow, and his older sister, also widowed, who was a high-school teacher.

Huntley was undoubtedly confused by the many changes that occurred during those days. He clung to his nurse, the most familiar and the most attentive of all the people around him. When she left—unable to get along with the demanding grandmother—Huntley could not be consoled and cried for days.

Elderly Mrs. Williams had never been anything but coolly interested in Huntley. She had disliked her daughter-in-law and had rarely seen her; she was indignant that her only grandchild should have his mother's maiden name. She had finally agreed to sharing a home with her son only after considerable inner struggle, because, she said, she "knew her duty." Small wonder that the baby cried for his nurse and feared his grandmother, who rarely smiled at him, rarely expressed either affection or approval. Her "duty" did not include loving the boy. She was a rigid disciplinarian and was in complete charge. Huntley's father was increasingly absent from home and, when there, never questioned the grandmother's demands or decisions. If she complained about the child, the child was spanked. When this had no effect, he was deprived of privileges or locked in his room.

151

Huntley's aunt remonstrated with her brother once or twice when she noted marks on the boy's body after his father had struck him with a cane or a leather belt. But she had little to do with the child and was often away weekends and evenings as well as during the day.

When she spoke to the social worker at the child-guidance center, she mentioned that on several occasions, after he had been punished, Huntley had failed to come home until very late at night. "His father punished him severely," she said, "but it didn't do any good. The next day he came home even later!" It evidently never occurred to her that there was little at home to attract the boy.

When an appointment was arranged with the psychologist at the guidance center, it was hard to convince Huntley that he was there not to be punished but to be helped. His sullen manner changed only slowly to responsive friendliness. He *did* want to be liked. He spoke about wanting the children on the playground and down the block to be his friends, and he told how his grandmother had always interfered. She said he "showed his poor blood" by seeking the company of the neighborhood boys; she ignored his protests that errands and tasks were always required when he wanted to go out to play; and she never permitted him to bring a child to the house.

Huntley had real need of other children, need of being accepted by them. But they called him "chicken" and "stuck up" when he didn't join them at play. He was rejected at home, and to be rejected by the children, too, was more than he could bear. To treat them had seemed a way to entice them to be friendly. This was the background for his taking money from his aunt's purse.

It was impossible to convince the family that Huntley was not a confirmed delinquent, an incorrigible thief, and a liar. They would not grant that the vastly different behavior he showed at school and at home involved them seriously. The grandmother refused to concede that she had played any part in the unhappy developments. The father admitted frankly that he stayed away from home so much because "The devil himself couldn't live peaceably with the old lady," and said that he didn't entirely blame the boy for his misbehavior. Nevertheless, Mr. Williams was too distraught by his own emotional problems to be really concerned about his son. The aunt bluntly summed up the situation: "I don't suppose we could expect Huntley to grow up normally in our abnormal household."

Fortunately, it was possible to arrange for Huntley to go to camp for the summer and for him to live in more favorable surroundings in the fall. The social worker from the guidance center found an understanding and sympathetic family with two children of their own who were interested in caring for the child. As is usual in such cases, Huntley's foster family would be paid for their part in supervising the boy and for providing him with room and board. In return they would be giving Huntley a chance, finally, for more normal development. Mr. Williams also accepted the idea of continuing the boy's treatment with a child psychologist as necessary in helping him to achieve an adequate adjustment.

For Huntley, his own home clearly had not been best. One can only speculate about what might have been accomplished if the father had accepted his own need for psychiatric help, if the grandmother had been less rigid and resistant, or if the aunt had been a warmer and better-adjusted personality. Before reaching his eighth birthday, Huntley had been antisocial, yet sought sociability. He had sensed rejection, and sought acceptance.

Because Huntley was young, it was not too difficult to help him, and after a period of time many of his scars healed. But for many months he needed professional help in learning to rechannel his emotional responses. He continued to do well in school, and he did better outside of school than he had ever done before. Because there was no longer any need to rebel against authority, he could accept deserved discipline and respect reasonable controls. He no longer felt the need to lie, nor did he have to appropriate what did not belong to him in order to buy friendship. He lived as an accepted member of a well-adjusted family. He felt loved and wanted. He had time to play and friends who accepted him and liked him. Given an opportunity to develop in wholesome surroundings, away from his own family, all went well. The home situation had been the problem, not the child.

Unusual as Huntley's circumstances may have been, less drastic conditions can lead to similar reactions. When a child feels unloved and unfairly treated, his unhappiness and confusion often result in unacceptable behavior. The conditions of his home life must be investigated—and, if need be, corrected—if he is to become a healthy and successful individual.

chapter 10

An Eager Year

A dividing line

The third year in primary school is the dividing line between early childhood and the more mature middle years. The eight-year-old is not a little child, nor is he yet quite so settled and responsible as he will be at nine. He resents being treated as a small child and being talked down to by adults, but he still depends on their praise and encouragement and still needs to be reminded of his responsibilities. Because he looks so much more grown-up than he did at seven, adults often grow impatient when his actions are less mature than his appearance.

The eight-year-old is very much aware of the adult world and is trying to find his place in it. He wants to be more grown-up. At home his manners may be lacking, but when he goes out to dinner or to a party that he considers grown-up or exciting, he may surprise his parents with his courtesy and good behavior. He is not so dependent on his teacher for emotional support as he was at seven, but he seems even more dependent on his mother. During this year he makes many demands on her. He continually wants her to play games with him, do things with him and for him, listen to his talk, and always be at hand when he wants her. Perhaps this is part of being neither a little child nor quite ready to grow up. While he dislikes being dominated or overdirected, the eight-year-old still needs his mother's support and wants to feel close to her.

Eight is an eager year. The child seems ready to tackle anything and he often shows more enthusiasm than wisdom in what he tries. For this reason, he usually has more accidents than in other years. The eight-year-old wants new experiences; he wants to try things out, to see how they work, to find out how they are made. Often he may attempt more than he can do, and so the results disappoint him or he is not able to complete his project. But if his eagerness is wisely directed, this can be a profitable year in the child's development. Adult guidance that cooperates with the child's enthusiasm and channels his curiosity and vital interests can be invaluable to him. On the other hand, the adult who dominates, overdirects, and overcriticizes can cause tension and anxiety in children of this

age. Parents and teachers who are working with eight-year-olds need to be aware of these children's sensitivity; the children want to be guided and helped in achieving their goals, yet they are unable to accept much criticism. They cry easily if corrected too harshly and resent being "bossed."

Physical growth and physical problems

Physically the eight-year-old continues to develop steadily but slowly. His arms are lengthening, and his hands are growing larger. His eyes are beginning to accommodate more readily to both near and far distances, so that he is better able to handle reading and other schoolwork that requires close focusing of the eyes. Eye-hand coordination is also definitely improved. Near-sightedness often develops during this year, however, and the child's eyes should be checked regularly and glasses prescribed when necessary.

At eight a child's permanent teeth are continuing to appear, usually the incisors first and then the lower bicuspids. By this time the novelty of brushing teeth has worn off and many children grow careless. They need to be reminded to take proper care of their teeth and should be taken to the dentist for regular check-ups.

Since the large muscles are still developing, children need continued opportunity for movement and active, outdoor play. They continue to run, shout, climb, and punch one another. The small muscles are much better developed than they

were at seven and children are able to use them more effectively and with better coordination. They write much more evenly and can do craft work with tools that require some skill in manipulation. The girls enjoy simple sewing and weaving and often spend hours with paper dolls and other cutouts, cutting carefully and efficiently.

During this year some children, particularly tall, thin youngsters, develop poor posture. This may be an indication of fatigue, of emotional tension, or of poor nutrition. It is possible, however, to interest children in learning to sit and stand correctly—not by nagging and scolding but by building their interest in the development of their bodies and teaching them why good posture is desirable.

Social activities and organization

Baseball, soccer, and other organized games delight the eight-year-old. He tries to learn the rules and may become quite bossy in insisting that they be followed. Sometimes his group will invent variations of the rules or make up new rules. On rainy days or in the evenings he is enthusiastic about table games—Monopoly, Parcheesi, rummy, hearts, and many other old and new favorites. Erector sets, chemistry outfits, model airplanes, trains, and boats keep the boys busy. The girls play countless involved games with their dolls.

The eight-year-old wants a best friend, although he will quarrel and argue with him often. Boys often fight with each other, while girls call names and have

battles of words, but children of this age can usually work out problems between themselves without adult interference. They are beginning to develop a sense of loyalty to each other. Many of their friendships will shift during the year, but some youngsters will remain best friends and carry their friendship over into another year.

Just as they want a best friend, so children of this age also seem to enjoy having an enemy. Sometimes two children single out other children as enemies; sometimes a group of children singles out one child or another group. If hostile feelings get out of bounds, adult intervention and adroit redirection may be necessary.

Until this year, boys and girls have played together some of the time, even though they have chosen their best friends from members of their own sex. Now we see a marked difference. Boys and girls are pulling definitely apart in their interests and their activities. Sometimes they even gang up against each other and call names or tease. They are entering the period when their interests will focus on friends of their own sex, the period of gangs and clubs. At this age the gang or club may not be well formed, and its purpose and membership may change frequently. But the children's desire to be a member of the gang is emerging and will grow more intense during the next few years. Boys and girls are beginning to consider it important to be like their friends and to belong to the group. Parents and teachers sometimes find this stress on belonging difficult, for it becomes increasingly evident that the child may follow the pattern of his group rather than adult directions when the two do not coincide, particularly if he is unhappy in his relationships with adults.

There are, however, strengths to be gained from belonging to the group. The child needs the security it gives, the opportunity to identify with others of his own age and sex, the opportunity to make and carry through plans and rules of his own. He learns the value of cooperation better in his own group than in any other way. The eight-year-old cannot take much criticism from adults, but he is capable of considerable self-evaluation at his own level and is able to take and give criticism within his own group. The wise parent or teacher will not try to hinder the establishment of gangs and clubs but will utilize their potentialities for helping the child learn to relate to others and work cooperatively with them.

The adult-supervised group cannot take the place of the children's own group, but it can be of additional value during this year. The eight-year-old responds positively to group activities of many kinds. His teacher finds him a willing member of the classroom group and can thus plan and think more frequently in terms of the group as a whole than was possible in the first two years of primary school. Class projects, club activities after school, organized games, and recreational projects fit the child's needs and interests. He participates enthusiastically in competitive games such as spelling bees, arithmetic games, or simple desk games. A well-planned program of both indoor and outdoor games provides not only fun but valuable learning for the eight-year-old. Through games he can enjoy wholesome competition and can learn to be both a good winner and a good loser.

A program of after-school play activities is particularly valuable during this transition year, although eight-year-olds are not always mature enough to carry through these planned activities by themselves. They may start an organized game of baseball or soccer on the corner lot, but they get confused and usually end up in squabbles and disputes. They can work through some of their quarrels by themselves, but they are usually relieved if a friendly adult helps get them out of the muddle. When they are older, self-direction in such organized activities will be increasingly valuable to them.

Eight-year-olds resent being grouped with six- or even seven-year-olds—"those babies," as they call them—in school or recreational activities. Physically they may be nearly like the younger children, but their interests have moved far beyond the interest of most six- and seven-year-olds. Consequently, they often rebel against group activities in which they are asked to play with younger children.

Dramatic play, movies, and television

Children's earlier interest in "acting" grows even stronger during this year, and their play is frequently dramatic. The boys may copy a favorite television program; the girls still dress up, play house, or plan plays to put on for their families or friends. In addition to dramatization in their informal play, eight-year-olds are also ready to take part in simple dramatics in the classroom; they thoroughly enjoy putting on a play. These dramatizations should still be simple and within the abilities of the children, participation being more important than a finished performance.

158

Movies, comics, and television have become a definite part of the eight-year-old's life. Many eight-year-olds go to the movies once a week. They are addicts of western and Indian pictures, stories of war, of space, and of adventure. But they do not want to be too scared and often close their eyes or cover their ears during a frightening scene. The girls like musicals, and both the boys and the girls enjoy animal stories and some comedies. Neither the boys nor the girls usually care for love stories—all but the most romantic of these children wish "all that stuff" was left out.

Most youngsters of this age watch television in the late afternoon or early evening, and some spend as much time in front of television as they do in school. They follow their favorite serials enthusiastically and also enjoy some of the comedy and game programs. But after frightening or overstimulating television programs, some eight-year-olds have nightmares and sleep fitfully. Parents need to consider their children's individual reactions in permitting or denying this activity. But if they do permit their children to watch television, they should carefully supervise the programs that the children are allowed to see instead of simply allowing them to watch any program they happen to turn on.

Reading interests and problems

Eight-year-olds read and reread comics, then exchange them with their friends and pore voraciously over the new crop. Children who have trouble reading will probably prefer comics to books, but most eight-year-olds enjoy books if their interest and delight in them has been encouraged. Parents and teachers should be particularly aware of the attraction comics hold for children of this age and should help the children to develop a wider interest in reading by introducing them to books full of adventure and humor. Fairy tales and stories about historical figures, animals, children, western adventure, and space travel appeal to the eight-year-old. Many children still enjoy reading aloud; others prefer reading to themselves.

This is the age when differences in reading ability begin to pose a real problem. The child who is still having difficulty learning to read finds it continually more difficult to keep up with his schoolwork and with the other children, because reading skill is now necessary for successful accomplishment in almost all areas of the curriculum. He often feels discouraged and defeated. He may develop a permanent dislike of school, even resulting in some cases in truancy. His concept of himself and his ability may be so severely damaged that he develops permanent feelings of inferiority, unless his parents and teachers are aware of his difficulties and help him to overcome both the reading problem and the emotional problem connected with it. Merely holding him back a grade will not meet his problem, nor will forcing or scolding him, because various developmental and emotional factors are usually involved in a reading difficulty. A special reading or guidance teacher may be able to help identify these factors so that the child can deal with them and subsequently go on to improve his reading. The child who is having trouble reading needs not only specialized attention in reading, but also a great deal of support from his parents and teachers. Certainly he needs opportunities for success in other areas to keep him from feeling discouraged and ashamed of his failure in learning to read.

Collections of all kinds intrigue the child who is eight. His pockets will be full of odds and ends, but his interest is also beginning to focus on more carefully planned collections. These may vary from bottle tops or playing cards to stones, bugs, or stamps. His interest is not always prolonged, however, and his collections may change frequently. Parents can help by encouraging the collector, by providing a place for him to keep his collections, and by not throwing away treasured objects because they seem useless by adult standards. Similarly, teachers can help by encouraging youngsters to bring their collections to school and tell the class about them. A child who is having difficulty in reading can often become an excellent collector and receive a much-needed feeling of achievement as he shares his collection with the class.

Money is beginning to play a significant part in the life of the eight-year-old. He understands the purpose of money and the simpler aspects of its use. He has some conception of saving for items that this week's allowance won't buy. If his allowance is not big enough for his needs, he will seek opportunities to earn small sums of money. He plans ahead, counting the weeks it will take him to save enough to buy a pair of roller skates or a model airplane. Often he is quite unrealistic and starts saving for unobtainable items. Often, too, he spends his money unwisely. But even if he makes mistakes, he needs the experience of having his own money and spending it in his own way. A small allowance is desirable for the eight-year-old. Discussions at home and at school about how money can be used and saved will be interesting and helpful to him. The ideas presented in these discussions should be within the realm of reality for the eight-year-old—saving for a baseball bat is reasonable and comprehensible, whereas saving for college is beyond both his means and his understanding.

The eight-year-old is developing a better understanding about time. He can tell time and can relate it to the events of the day. He can wear a sturdy watch and be relied on to use it. He knows at what time meals are served, when school begins, and when he must be in bed. Yet he is not always ready to take complete responsibility for going to bed, getting up, or arriving at school on time and must still be reminded by his parents if his routines are to function at all smoothly. He has the habit of putting things off. "In a minute" appears frequently in his vocabulary.

At eight the child also understands about days and months and years, and he is trying to relate himself to a past and a future. He is showing an interest in things that happened "long ago," although he is often extremely confused about just when past events occurred. He may think that his grandmother lived in the time of the Pilgrims, that she used a spinning wheel and was afraid of Indians. But at least he realizes that there *was* a past in which people lived and did things. His world now extends beyond the present; he realizes that people live and die, that there have been people before him and will be people after him. This is an adult concept and shows that he is growing up.

An expanding environment

The child's thinking is reaching beyond his immediate environment. He knows now that children live in other parts of the country and of the world,

As the eight-year-old learns the value and some of the uses of money and generally becomes more responsible, he enjoys being trusted to run simple errands such as shopping at the neighborhood grocery or drugstore.

some living much as he does but some differently, and he wants to hear stories about them. He may pore over maps of the states and pictures of other places. He is beginning to notice racial, national, or regional differences among his own classmates; sometimes, through the influence of the adults in his environment, he may have begun to develop feelings and prejudices concerning these differences. Because he is noticing people, this is an excellent year to encourage a friendly interest in boys and girls of other countries, other races, and other backgrounds—pointing out the differences but stressing the many similarities.

Not only is the eight-year-old beginning to develop understanding, sympathy, and acceptance of other people and of their needs and rights; he is beginning to understand himself better. He sees himself in relation to other people. He realizes now that some children do things better than he does, that others are not so capable, and that different people excel in different activities. He usually accepts himself and is not too concerned about his weak points unless the adults about him have put too much pressure on him, made too many unfavorable comparisons, or disturbed him with their concern over his achievement or ability. He shows a capacity for self-evaluation and will even sometimes laugh at himself for something he has done. He often makes excuses for himself, but almost as often resolves to do better. He frequently sets high standards for himself and tries to live up to them, as well as to the standards set by the adults around him. Some children develop considerable anxiety about their ability to succeed in school-work or in games and sports. Some are already afraid they may not be liked by

other children. This anxiety is apparent often among children who are successful as well as among those who are having some difficulty.

The eight-year-old is full of energy. He may not be so easy to guide as the seven-year-old. He may be more argumentative and have more spirit, but he is also alert to the world around him and interested in people. He may not practice his skills as carefully as he did at seven, but he is eager to find out about things and is a stimulating companion. He may be careless about his clothes, unwilling to help at home, noisy and bossy; but he is also lovable and friendly. The third year in school can be a good one for parents, teachers, and children, for most eight-year-olds will respond well to sensitive, intelligent adult leadership and guidance.

study of a child

Adele Had No Friends

*Social difficulties sometimes stem
from unrecognized conditions*

There is increasing acceptance of the concept that all behavior has some cause. But sometimes it is not understood—or at least not remembered—that no single cause can explain so complex a result as a child's behavior. Factors intermingle and their impact may be almost baffling when one tries to understand a child. If parents find themselves unable to understand and cope with their child's problems, they are wise to seek the aid of experts. Both medical and psychological aid may be desirable, even essential, to correct an existing condition.

This was true in the case of Adele Moffat. Just before her eighth birthday, her mother began to feel concerned that the child had no friends. To the suggestion that a birthday party be planned, Adele had said dejectedly, "Who would I ask? Nobody'd come. Nobody likes me."

Mrs. Moffat realized abruptly that Adele had only occasionally been invited to a party or even to another child's house to play after school. She thought uncomfortably of the many mornings she had watched Adele start for school alone, while other groups of youngsters went on their way, walking together. "I actually haven't thought much about it before," she said to herself, "but I wonder why she isn't getting along better with other children."

Mrs. Moffat had to acknowledge to herself that her child was often a bit surly. Frequently she was inclined to go to her room rather than stay sociably with the rest of the family. Perhaps she should be coaxed to be with them more. She recalled how seldom Adele spoke at the dinner table. Usually Adele's brother Richard, who was more than a year younger, monopolized the conversation. Even if Adele were asked a question directly, Richard would answer before she had a chance to reply. Mrs. Moffat resolved to curb Richard's talkativeness.

When guests came to the Moffat home, Adele rarely wanted to stay downstairs. She would sometimes say she had homework to do, sometimes just disappear without saying anything. Later her parents would find her alone in her room, reading and munching candy bars. They had been accustomed to smile tolerantly. "We've been almost proud she's been thought a bookworm," Mrs. Moffat said to herself, half accusingly.

That evening she and her husband discussed Adele and decided perhaps she needed more stimulation and more attention. "Let's see if we can get her into some kind of class outside of school," suggested Mr. Moffat. "Music, maybe? Or dancing?"

"Not dancing," replied Mrs. Moffat decidedly. "I don't think that would do. She's——well——sort of heavy for that. I'll see about music lessons."

Adele was not particularly interested, but made no objection to being enrolled in a beginner's class at a music school. The other students were about her age, and her parents hoped that she might become friendly with one or two of them. But, as the weeks passed, she made only slow progress with her music and none at all in making friends. In the meantime, her schoolwork seemed to suffer, perhaps from lack of application to homework—perhaps, her parents thought, from too heavy a schedule. She did seem tired often. After a particularly poor school report, Mrs. Moffat, wondering how matters might be improved, made an appointment to talk to Adele's teacher.

Miss Tice, the third-grade teacher, was inclined to think the Moffats were asking too much of Adele. "She isn't as quick to grasp things as some of the children are," she noted. "She really requires more time for her schoolwork.

163

Music lessons probably put her under considerable pressure. And you say she hasn't done very well with her music either."

Mrs. Moffat agreed. "Sometimes I get discouraged," she said. "I think Adele does, too. She isn't especially interested in anything, though she does like to read —at least she has a book in her hands a good deal of the time, along with some popcorn or candy. She doesn't seem to have many friends, either. How does she get along with the other girls in her class? Do they like her?" Mrs. Moffat almost hesitated to ask.

Miss Tice was thoughtful for a moment. "I don't recall any special incidents with the other girls," she said slowly. "Adele is usually rather quiet. She doesn't volunteer much in class, but she seems to follow along with whatever we're doing. She never gives any trouble. On the playground," she continued, "I don't think she ever takes a very active part in games. She's more likely to be off by herself, watching, or maybe just standing at the door, waiting for the bell to ring to go back to her room. She's not very energetic, or very social. She seems to try in class, although as you know from her report, her work isn't very good. She hasn't been absent much. I suppose she's all right physically?"

Mrs. Moffat seemed a little startled at the question. "Why, I think so," she answered. "She seems all right. She certainly is big and husky. The only thing I can think of is that she's always tired mornings when I call her. I know she gets to bed early enough. She's never been nearly as lively and active as her brother. We've often mentioned that. But we didn't think it was anything to be concerned about. After all, children aren't all alike. She's very like my husband's sister, as a matter of fact—big and slow and deliberate. But her aunt is always good-natured and easy-going and friendly; I'm sure there's nothing wrong with *her*. I just wish Adele were as cheerful."

"Well," said Miss Tice, "I'll see if I can manage to get her more interested in games at recess. Perhaps she needs more encouragement. I *have* noticed she's never picked first when the children are choosing sides. I think probably it's just because she's heavy and doesn't run fast. She gets winded quickly. They do tease her a bit about that. I've heard them call her "Fatso" and "Jumbo" and names like that, but I don't think they mean to be unkind."

When the school visit was reported to Adele's father, he, too, thought of his sister. "I can't believe a little extra weight can be really serious," he said. "Lots of people carry too many pounds without having problems develop. At least," he added, a hint of doubt creeping into his voice, "you don't hear of problems about overweight unless it's *extreme* overweight. Why, Del can't be *much* too heavy, do you think?"

"It might have something to do with her being more tired than a child ought to be," considered Mrs. Moffat. "And if she's getting self-conscious about it and being teased at school, I suppose that makes things pretty unpleasant for her. Even so, I can't see any relationship between her weight and the sort of schoolwork she's doing, or not being popular or never being interested in doing anything. Well, I suppose it might be a good idea to see what Dr. Mann has to say about it."

The pediatrician had known Adele well when she was a small child, but since her general health had not presented any difficulty beyond an occasional cold, he had not seen her for a long time. He listened thoughtfully to Mrs. Moffat before seeing Adele.

"You're concerned about several things, aren't you?" he said. "But you seem skeptical that Adele's weight has anything to do with your worries. Yet often we do find a connection between conditions that don't seem to have any bearing on each other. Suppose we look her over and see what a thorough physical check will tell us."

Mrs. Moffat's skepticism changed when, later, Dr. Mann discussed with her the findings of the examination and the laboratory tests. He had investigated in detail the total picture of Adele's body functioning and considered it in relation to the story her mother had told. Mrs. Moffat, impatient with herself for what she now realized was too casual an acceptance of her daughter's difficulties, was relieved that Dr. Mann's verdict was no more serious than it was. He was sure the problem could be solved once it was given proper attention. He urged that it not be ignored any longer, suggesting that both an inherited tendency and uncorrected habits contributed to Adele's excess weight.

"It's primarily a matter of metabolism," he explained. "There are glands of internal secretion that regulate the body in many ways. When one such gland isn't functioning efficiently, it can both influence the functioning of another and directly affect the way the whole organism responds.

"The thyroid gland produces a substance called *thyroxin* which the body needs. When not enough thyroxin is manufactured, the individual shows it in several ways. These may hardly be noticeable when the lack of thyroxin is only slight, but they are very marked when there is a really serious deficiency of it. In very mild cases the condition is not likely to be thought of as a factor interfering with health and happiness. But it *does* interfere—with work output, with the inclination to be social, with activity in many areas. It can be a very hampering condition. A mild hypothyroidism—that's the name for a mild underfunctioning of the thyroid gland—seems to be at least part of the cause of Adele's difficulties. There simply hasn't been enough thyroxin poured into her blood stream to meet the ordinary demands of daily living. And so to you she has seemed tired, without the vigor and pep we expect in truly healthy children. In examining her I noted that her skin was dry, and her hair, too. Not markedly so, but suggestive of something needing investigation. And all her movements, even her speech, are unusually slow, don't you think? She's not interested in active play and doesn't even have enough energy to be social.

"The overweight problem is not always a matter of underfunction of the thyroid, by any means. But it can be related. When anyone is disinclined to be active, to move energetically, he doesn't get enough exercise. That encourages a gain in weight. And when food intake is greater than the energy used, the pounds do mount up. This is especially true when there's an overindulgence in sweets. It's certainly been true with Adele. Fortunately, thyroxin can be easily supplied, and I'll give you a prescription. It's important to see that Adele takes the pills regularly."

"For how long?" inquired Mrs. Moffat, already relieved that there was something definite and simple that could be done to help Adele.

"Possibly always," was the answer. "We'll see. It's a simple enough way to supply what isn't being produced in as large an amount as the body needs. I'll want to check her at regular intervals for a time, to be sure the dosage is correct for her. Sometimes we can decrease it after a while; sometimes we find more must be given. We'll repeat some of the laboratory tests now and then to be sure we're on the right track.

"And, of course, attention must be given to her diet, too. Not too many sweets. It's difficult to restrict a child entirely, but here's a list of things to be avoided and a suggested diet. Encourage Adele to be more active, to participate more in outdoor sports. Don't hurry things too much, though. First let's give the medication a chance. When she's feeling less lackadaisical, she'll want to play more. I've seen a listless child surprise his parents when he started to play baseball every day. Skating and tennis and bicycling and hiking—all the things that children normally love—will have much more appeal for Adele when she feels more normal." He paused for a moment.

"I think, though," he went on seriously, "that there's more than your little girl's physical condition to be considered. She doesn't strike me as a happy, cheerful youngster at all. You say she doesn't make friends, and her teacher told you that the other children tease her and leave her out of their games. I think you should pay attention to the emotional factors in this picture.

"Health isn't only physical fitness, you know. Mental health is very important. Why don't you see if her school has a psychologist on its staff? Or consult one outside of school if you can. A child psychologist should be a great help here.

"Problems of this sort often seem to form a lengthy chain. The physical problem brings about a situation that affects emotional reactions and even intellectual functioning. We find social relationships somehow tied in with it, too. Bring her in to see me again in three weeks, and, in the meantime, look into the psychological aspects of Adele's problem."

The school psychologist had not known Adele previously. There had been no major emotional upset at school to suggest referral to her. Adele had handled her lessons fairly adequately, although when her record was checked carefully it was apparent that she had a much greater potential for achievement than her accomplishment suggested. Her overweight had also been thought a relatively minor problem. But the combined results of these elements had made for a situation that was on the way to becoming a serious one.

Adele had become increasingly uncomfortable about her appearance, and the self-consciousness that resulted interfered with easy social relationships. Her apparent unfriendliness was largely a defense; rather than be hurt by teasing or unkind remarks, she avoided other children. Her apparent slowness in understanding and responding to situations had little to do with innate capacity; it was actually a slow mustering of thoughts and responses. She had as much to say as her younger brother did, but before she could put her thoughts into words, he would have replied. Her hesitancy in expressing ideas was not because she lacked ideas; it was partly because her reactions were slowed by unrecognized physical handicaps, and partly because she felt unable to compete with her brother and with other children. She was both chagrined and disheartened, especially when it seemed that her mother and father enjoyed Richard's companionship more than they did hers and when, alone in her room, she heard her brother laughing and talking downstairs with his friends. On the playground, too, she was slow-paced and sluggish. Her indifferent skill at games was emphasized by her shortness of breath after only slight exertion. The extra pounds she carried were both an actual and a figurative burden.

Adele was aware of her mediocre success academically and socially. She did not know why she was so often out of sorts and cross. She only knew she felt uncertain of herself and unpopular—and that somehow a malted milk, or a chocolate bar, or a handful of cookies helped her feel more comfortable.

After medical and psychological aid had been continued for some time, there were marked changes in Adele. Her improved physical condition was reflected in increased participation on the playground. Her greater understanding of her feelings and behavior resulted in a more cheerful attitude and encouraged her to be more social. And, sensing a change in her parents' response to her, she felt a new contentment with herself and with her family.

Mr. and Mrs. Moffat made a conscious effort to show the deep affection and love that they had for Adele. They drew her out gently and listened to her patiently, responsive now to her need for their attention. They were careful not to continue giving disproportionate notice to the lively Richard. They no longer smiled tolerantly when Adele started to leave them chatting sociably with visiting relatives and friends. Instead, they included her as much as possible in the conversation and felt when she did go to her room that she went because it was time for homework or for bed. They knew now that formerly she had disappeared not because she was so conscientious about her lessons, but because she was so sensitive and ill-at-ease.

Adele's weight loss was matched by her loss of discontent and uneasiness. As her appearance improved, she became more self-assured. Her interest in school grew, and her grades gradually improved. She was no longer apathetic or so frequently irritable. After a time the changes in Adele were met with a change in the way other children reacted to her. When she was invited to go to a Saturday movie with two of her classmates, all concerned counted it real progress.

No single factor should ever be considered the cause of poor adjustment. When a child's entire life situation is reviewed, many elements are disclosed as causative factors. Each element must be understood, and the interaction and interrelation of the various elements must be discerned. Only then can measures be planned to improve the total picture. Implementing such measures can transform a disconsolate, inept child into one who can function adequately and contentedly. Few accomplishments are more gratifying than having played a part in effecting such a change.

chapter II

In Balance

The individual nine-year-old

The nine-year-old is fairly responsible and dependable. He understands explanations; he is interested in trying to do things well; and he is beginning to have a strong sense of right and wrong. His abilities are clearly apparent, and his real interests are beginning to develop. Individual differences are distinct. The nine-year-old is an individual with a definite personality of his own.

At nine the wide variations in development that will become increasingly noticeable at ten, eleven, and twelve may be beginning. In their interests, nine-year-olds are closer to ten- or eleven-year-olds than to seven- or eight-year-olds, whom they think of and sometimes refer to as "just children." This is especially true among girls, a few of whom may be nearing preadolescence.

Physically, most nine-year-olds are much the same as they were a year ago, but a little longer legged, better developed, and closer to physical maturity. During this year girls who mature early may reach the growth plateau that precedes the pubertal growth spurt.

The whole body is continuing to grow steadily and is nearer its adult functioning. The lungs and the digestive and circulatory systems are still growing but are almost mature in function. The heart is not yet fully developed, and some children may strain it during this year if allowed to compete physically to any great extent with older children. The eyes are much better developed—although they will not reach adult size until ten, they are able to accommodate to close work with less strain. Children often get their first and second bicuspids at nine, and their teeth often need straightening. If this seems indicated, parents should consult a dentist promptly, since treatment is sometimes started during this year.

Nine-year-olds are becoming increasingly skillful with their hands, and their eye-hand coordination is greatly improved. Individual differences in coordination are increasingly apparent. Both boys and girls enjoy crafts and shop work, and some can carry out many kinds of careful, well-planned craft work. Others, however, still have trouble with handwork that requires any great degree of skill.

Nine-year-olds demonstrate an increasing ability to organize themselves and to work cooperatively in carrying out a specific project, especially if it is one they have thought of themselves. These boys, for example, are collecting supplies to stock their basement club room.

The nine-year-old's attention span has greatly increased. Boys may spend a morning or an afternoon with their erector sets, chemistry outfits, tools, or stamps. Girls may sew, weave, or even attempt to knit. Even though these children are capable of sustained attention, adults should not plan activities of long duration for them, because interest and self-motivation are important determiners of attention span. Forced or required attention for too long a time is wearing to children and usually results in tension and restlessness.

The nine-year-old has original ideas and interests and is capable of carrying them out. He often makes his plans and goes ahead without any adult direction or encouragement. He carries on a project over quite a period of time, thinking through and planning each step with almost adult care. At the same time, as soon as a project ceases to interest him he may drop it without finishing it or giving it a further thought.

Nine-year-olds still need and enjoy active, rough-and-tumble play. But sex differences are showing up increasingly. The boys shout and tear around. They like to wrestle and punch each other—in fact, punching is often a mark of extreme affection reserved for best friends. The girls also enjoy active group games but are usually less noisy and energetic than the boys. They turn to quieter activities or to roller skating, ice skating, jump rope, and jacks. Both groups are talking more. They may rush onto the playground shouting but soon congregate in groups and begin to talk. Sometimes they just sit around talking at random; at other times they make plans or discuss the activities of their club or gang. Their plans are often too elaborate to be carried out, but the talk is good and the youngsters enjoy it and grow with it.

Increasing interest in skills

At nine the child often is a bit of a perfectionist. He is becoming critical of his own performance. He wants to do things the right way and so may work hard to perfect a skill or to recopy, on his own initiative, a piece of work that looks messy to him. He is no longer satisfied just to paint a picture; he wants a semblance of reality in what he paints. He asks for help now and is interested in techniques and skills, not only in his schoolwork but also in his play. He wants to be an accomplished ball player, to pitch and catch like an expert or at least like the older boys he admires. He wants to improve his swimming; he is no longer content just to splash around. Girls want to know how to cook and sew as well as how to take part in games and sports. Children need to develop skills that other children appreciate and admire, so this is a good year for parents to take time with both boys and girls encouraging them and helping them to learn new skills.

Parents and teachers can overdo the teaching of techniques and skills at this age, however. For even though the child wants to know how to do things, his ability and his capacity for sustained interest may not equal his initial enthusiasm. Adults must be aware of the child's present ability and future capability in order to set standards and goals that will encourage the child in his desire to

learn instead of discouraging him. It is extremely important that any teaching of skills be done in a spirit of enjoyment. The adult who is overinsistent, who drives too hard or demands a perfect performance, can destroy a child's initial desire to acquire the skill and his pleasure in using it, whether it be playing the piano or pitching a ball.

Competitive games

Nine-year-olds enjoy competitive games—team games, relay races, and jack tournaments, for example. But the competition easily gets out of bounds. Winning becomes very important to the children and they can turn cruelly on the boy or girl who fails to make a point or "loses" for their side. A child who is skillful in games can take these jibes in stride, knowing he can do better next time and receive applause instead of blame. But a child who always misses or is clumsy can be deeply hurt. Such a youngster may pull away from the very physical activity that he needs and become a spectator rather than try to play. Nine-year-olds need help in learning sportsmanship. They should be encouraged to play their games for the fun of playing and to keep their competition within reasonable limits. Choosing up teams without occasional adult advice or supervision, for example, can result in excessive competitive pressures. Some children are seriously hurt by team captains who willingly choose only children who play well and then grudgingly accept the others. It is no wonder that some children shrink at the embarrassment of always being the last chosen or the one left out.

Reading interests and abilities

Wide developmental variations in both reading interest and reading ability are apparent by fourth grade. Many nine-year-olds are great readers, whereas others are hardly interested in books. A reading span of four to five years is not unusual in the fourth grade. Some children can read as well as adults and are enjoying their first experience with the classics; others are still at first- or second-grade level. The choice of reading materials for children of this age must be wide indeed if some children are not to be bored and others discouraged by the level of reading to which they are held. The school or class library must contain books at various levels of reading difficulty and yet equal in their level of interest.

The nine-year-old is beginning to put aside fairy tales and much of the fantasy and imaginative play of his earlier years. He is relating not only to his immediate environment but to his community, his country, and even other countries. His interest goes beyond that of the third-grader. The alert fourth-grader likes to study maps and play travel games. He enjoys writing letters to children in other countries, either as a member of a group or as an individual. He may ask discerning questions about other peoples and about world conditions.

At nine the youngster is beginning to understand his own country and to develop loyalty and pride toward it. He wants to know about the different parts of his country and the different kinds of work that people do in it, though he is actually not so interested in the work as in the trappings: the cranes on a construction project, an astronaut's space suit, or the Army's planes and tanks. He enjoys trips to a dock, a factory, or a farm and asks innumerable and often surprisingly intelligent questions about the things he sees. He is beginning to be interested in heroes and great men. He wants to know about Washington and Lincoln, and sometimes voluntarily chooses biographies when he goes to the library. His interest in science is also increasing, and he often tries experiments on his own or reads widely among science books available at his vocabulary level.

This is a stimulating year for parents and teachers, even though the child's growing independence and individuality may sometimes make it a difficult one. The nine-year-old is beginning to think for himself, to develop his own ideas and point of view, to realize that sometimes there is more than one valid opinion and that perhaps his mother, his father, or even his teacher does not have all the answers. He may be quite outspoken and critical of the adults he knows, despite his genuine fondness for them.

The nine-year-old responds best to the adult who treats him as an individual and approaches him in an adult way. He enters eagerly into making plans, whether for a project or party in the schoolroom or a trip with the family, and his ideas and suggestions are often worth considering. He is more cooperative and responsive when he is included in making the plans than when he is told "This is what we are going to do."

A child of nine is also willing and able to take responsibility. He likes to be trusted with handling the family baggage on a trip, going to market, repairing something for his mother, getting the props together for a school play, or being responsible for a research project. He is often shy when asked to take part in a play or program if parents or other adults are present, and he is apt to be embarrassed if he is praised in public. He does, however, like recognition for what he has done and responds well to deserved praise. He also tends to be very fair and will usually refuse to accept credit for something he has not done. He will even give the credit publicly to his friend or to the person he feels deserves it.

The nine-year-old will accept criticism or punishment if he thinks it is justified, but will be most indignant and outspoken if he feels that an adult or another child is being unfair. He frequently argues with other children over fairness in games, taking sides and upholding one faction or the other. This is a good sign, for it shows that he is really beginning to understand right and wrong and is trying to develop standards of acceptable behavior. He is also beginning to understand more about truth and honesty and about property rights and personal rights. He is developing sympathy for and loyalty to others.

Nine is a good year for helping youngsters develop standards that build character. This is best accomplished by using specific situations and experiences rather than by sermonizing. For example, if a boy borrows a baseball from his friend and then loses it, he learns responsibility by paying for it from his allowance or from money he's earned doing jobs for his mother.

At nine a child is more frequently able to make up his mind and come to decisions than he was during the earlier years. He should be given as many opportunities as possible to exercise a measure of independence and make decisions for himself. He will make mistakes, but he is ready to learn from his occasional failure of judgment, as long as the learning takes place in situations where failure will not have too serious consequences. The fourth-grader is able to be on his own quite a bit. An overnight visit to a friend's house, a trip by himself on the bus downtown, the purchase of school supplies, or even a well-planned train trip to his grandparents' is not beyond many nine-year-olds.

The nine-year-old is not only responsible—he is also beginning to be reasonable. One can talk things over with him and present a point of view. He will listen to the reasons presented by an adult, but he will also want the courtesy of being allowed to present his own reasoning. If he is not too emotionally involved in a situation, he is frequently capable of modifying his plan or changing his mind if another course is suggested to him. He can accept the need to put something off, to reschedule the picnic for next week if the weather is poor today.

He can also understand a reasonable explanation in regard to the family budget. He may be disappointed that he cannot have a new bike now, but he can understand that the family cannot afford it and accept a promise that he will receive it on his birthday in the spring. He is even able to see the necessity of contributing some of his birthday money toward the bike or of earning his share. He is best guided by a simple, clear-cut reason for a decision that must be made. He is reasonable in accepting punishment if it is fair and may even see the need for being reminded that his conduct was undesirable. If he must be punished, the most effective punishment is that which has a reasonable tie-in with the situation for which he is being punished.

Influence of the group

Clubs and gangs are stronger among nine-year-olds than they were among eight-year-olds. Although the membership and purpose are still of short duration and likely to change frequently, some firm and loyal friendships may develop during this year. The child is increasingly influenced by his group. He wants to be like the others, to talk like them, to look like them. If a boy's friends wear their shirttails out and use objectionable expressions freely, parents may temporarily lose the battle for neatness and correct speech. They may have to be satisfied with a compromise to dress up on Sundays and refrain from using tough

language at home. Unlike the boys, girls of this age are usually becoming more interested in clothes. The basis of their attitude is the same as with boys—the desire to be like the others—but with girls this usually leads to a growing interest in well-brushed hair and a more attractive appearance. Some girls even talk with great superiority about "those awful boys, aren't they messy?" Not all girls, of course, are neat at this age. Some are tomboys, just as careless and indifferent to their appearance as the boys.

Just as children copy each other in clothes and interests and mannerisms, so they may also follow loyally the whole behavior pattern of their friends. Usually this pattern is not undesirable—it can, in fact, provide the child with many valuable experiences—but there is always a possibility that any group of children, primarily boys, may get into trouble or even minor vandalism, especially if they haven't enough opportunities for recreation after school. Parents and teachers should be alert to this possibility so that they can redirect the activities of youngsters who seem headed for trouble. Success in redirecting a trouble-prone youngster is usually possible only if an effort is made to redirect the entire group. Working with an individual child or removing him from the group seldom brings satisfactory results, for the pull of the group is so strong that a child who is forbidden to be with his friends tends to feel defiant or rebellious and will usually find ways of rejoining them despite parental objections.

The left-out child

Having friends and belonging to a group mean a great deal to nine-year-olds. Consequently, parents and teachers need to be particularly alert to notice and help the child who is being left out by his classmates. Nine-year-olds are general-

ly conformists. Often they leave out the child who is in any way different from themselves, whether he is unusually bright or a bit slow, whether he speaks with an accent or dresses differently than they do, whether he has a special talent or is handicapped in some way. In the earlier grades children are not so keenly aware of differences as they are at nine. Nine-year-olds need help in learning to accept others. Sometimes they must be checked if they become too thoughtless and unkind.

The teacher may be able to help the left-out child win acceptance by placing him in a favorable position in relation to his classmates, so that they begin to like and appreciate him. She may, for example, seat him next to a friendly child or draw him skillfully into a group project in which he can make a valuable contribution. Parents may help, too, by inviting other children to the home. There are times, however, when it seems impossible to obtain acceptance for a certain child —sometimes even an especially attractive or talented one. Such a child will need special help, understanding, and support in learning how to adjust to the group and to a difficult situation. Careful thought should be given to the problem of finding ways to compensate the child who is on the fringe of the group and providing him with other outlets of self-expression.

Half mature and half a child

The fourth grade is an important year in the child's development, for it marks his entrance into the upper years of elementary school. More will be expected of

176

him in the way of being personally responsible both for his behavior and for his schoolwork.

Because the nine-year-old seems mature and capable in many ways, adults sometimes overestimate his maturity and expect too much of him, becoming impatient when he seems childish in some of his reactions. They should remember that, despite his seeming maturity, he is still not far from being a young child. He may have a greater understanding of truthfulness, but under pressure may not remain truthful. He may be independent in many of his decisions, but turn to his mother or teacher for help in some little thing she feels he should be able to handle for himself. Because the nine-year-old is half mature and half a child, it is best to let him lead in the direction of independence, to encourage him when he wants to go ahead, but to willingly help him without ridiculing or criticizing him when he occasionally reverts to more dependent, childish ways.

study of a child

Runaway Mark

*Delinquency threatens
in the absence of emotional security*

It is generally acknowledged that security is an important childhood need. But too often it is assumed that when a child's parents provide him a home and clothes, and see to it that he is well fed and reasonably clean, they have furnished that necessary security. Physical security, however, does not necessarily bring with it emotional security. And it is emotional security which children must have if they are to develop strong and healthy personalities.

Feelings of insecurity may influence a child's unacceptable behavior in ways not directly related to the child's basic problem. Sometimes he rejects social relationships, fearful of further rejection. Sometimes he dreams away his time at school, and his lessons suffer. Quarrelsomeness, fighting, and insistence on his own way are other possible accompaniments of insecurity. Nightmares, digestive disturbances, puzzling fears—the patterns that may develop are almost infinite.

In the case of Mark, insecurity was symbolized by running away. At nine he was a year behind in school, not because he was incapable of doing adequate schoolwork, but because he had been unable to withstand the impact of a home made stormy and puzzling by difficult family relationships. He had become

177

confused by the circumstances of his life and needed help before he could face his situation rather than flee from it. His parents, too, needed help, both for their own sake and for the sake of their children. In order to create a less disturbing situation for Mark—one that he could learn to handle—they needed help in working out their marital problems.

During his earliest years Mark had been pampered and indulged by his parents, and he had become accustomed to having things his own way. Discipline was rare and haphazard. His parents usually gave in to him if Mark nagged or pleaded. They seldom insisted on anything that he found distasteful. But the arrival of a baby sister when Mark was not quite six brought a number of changes. His mother was busier than he had ever remembered her being before, and his father seemed preoccupied. Both parents were less patient with Mark than they had been and they were less apt to humor him. They also began to punish him and to criticize him more frequently than they had ever done before.

When Mark entered first grade, his parents said openly that they were glad he was old enough for school. Since he had not gone to kindergarten, this was the first time he had had to meet a situation without his mother. He did not like sitting quietly, taking his turn, or concentrating on what his teacher planned instead of doing something of his own choosing. School was an ordeal for him.

Mark's seeming inability to adjust to first grade led the school authorities, after a time, to advise keeping the youngster home for another semester. They indicated to his parents that they favored delaying school entrance because Mark had not yet reached his sixth birthday and seemed to be very immature. Mark's parents felt there was justification for the school's counsel and agreed to the postponement, although they were somewhat irked by it. So again Mark managed, in a sense, to get his own way. He stayed with his mother. He avoided distasteful activities.

But staying with his mother was no longer the same for Mark. It was not only the new baby; it was a different feeling in the home. Another woman had attracted his father's interest, and his parents were constantly arguing and exchanging recriminations. Once or twice a quarrel more violent than most really frightened the boy. When one day his mother took the baby and left home, Mark was completely bewildered. The part-time maid was replaced by a housekeeper who stayed all the time. She did not like children particularly and was unreasonably demanding of Mark when his father was not at home. Mark could not understand why his mother was away for so long. His confusion was increased when one day the housekeeper failed to appear and his father brought another woman home to live with them. "She's our very dear friend," explained his father.

A few weeks of unpleasant scenes followed: scolding, neglect, impatience, denial were daily worries for the child. He decided to find his mother and ran away. When the police brought him back his father, really distressed and remorseful, was for a time more attentive and gentle. But Mark was unhappy and soon made another attempt to run away. This time when the police brought him home, his father whipped him and notified Mark's mother of what was happening, thinking she would send for the boy. Instead, she came home. The parents now decided that perhaps the damaged emotions of all could be salvaged. The other woman left, and a reconciliation was effected.

About this time the new school term started, and Mark was again enrolled at school. His attendance was intermittent due to a succession of minor illnesses and also to lax supervision on his mother's part. He had indifferent success with his lessons, and he was not promoted at the end of the term. So the following September Mark started first grade all over again. This time things were more peaceful at home and he learned to adapt somewhat better to being one of a group in the classroom. He mastered his lessons without special difficulty and at the end of the year was promoted to second grade.

But Mark's path was still not smooth. He was inclined to tease smaller children and to fight with boys his own size. He did not get along with his teacher, who criticized his poor work and frequently scolded him for fighting. Unfortunately, she did not try to find the reasons for either his poor work or his quarrelsomeness. One day, after the teacher had criticized his reading, Mark failed to return for the afternoon session. Another time, when he had been reprimanded for being noisy and inattentive, he became sullen and did not come to school at all the following day. But although he had missed a number of days at school that year and had done only mediocre work, he was again promoted. School, however, became more and more distasteful.

At nine Mark started third grade. His absences increased, and he became adept at leading his mother to think he had been at school and his teacher to believe his parents had kept him at home. Actually he was wandering about, spending a great deal of time at the nearby railroad yards, where he learned to evade the questioning of any workmen who happened to wonder why he was there. He was joining in the escapades of older boys and learning from them both a vocabulary and attitudes which were unwholesome and undesirable.

When the school's attendance department finally brought it to the attention of Mark's parents that the boy had regularly been playing truant, his father whipped him and told him he had to go to school. Mark did attend school the next day, but that night he didn't come home until very late. His mother scolded him severely and Mark, seemingly contrite, promised to "be good."

But he had started a pattern which did not change for the better. He had often stayed away from school; now he often stayed away from home, too. His parents were angry and bitter at all the sleepless nights spent and all the time lost from work in looking for the boy. They saw no reason for Mark to behave as he did, and his father felt the only solution was to "try to beat it out of him." Mark felt increasingly unloved and unwanted. He liked home less and less.

By this time Mark, ignoring the school's repeated warnings, was absent from school more often than he was present, and he slept away from home as much as he did in his own bed. His parents couldn't manage him. The attendance officer who had time and again picked Mark up at the railroad yards or sleeping in a protected doorway was genuinely concerned about this nine-year-old—so defiant, so glum and sullen in voice and manner, so insistent on staying away from both school and home. He referred the case to a social agency, and an experienced, skilled worker was assigned to investigate the situation.

For the first time since he had been a very small boy, Mark now felt that an adult was sincerely interested in him. He had many conferences with the social worker and, as his initial wariness gave way to friendliness, he responded well. He was gradually helped to verbalize his antagonism for his little sister, his resentment over his mother's having deserted him, his fear of his father's beatings, and his dislike for his teacher. The social worker helped him to understand that there are some situations in life which cannot be changed, from which one cannot run away, and that one must adjust to them. His sister was there to stay, *but his mother still loved him.* His parents were not always amicable, *but their quarreling between themselves didn't mean that they weren't interested in him.* His father had whipped him, *but he had been worried about him* and hadn't known how else to handle Mark's disobedience. His teacher was really interested in helping him learn, *and her criticisms had been to correct him,* not to humiliate him, as he had felt.

The social worker spoke with Mark's parents and with his teacher, interpreting for them the boy's frustrations and insecurity and giving them suggestions for handling him more wisely. She recognized that there was less open quarreling between Mark's parents, but because she sensed that their marital situation was still filled with hurt feelings and dissatisfaction, she strongly advised marital counseling.

She also arranged for Mark to attend a Boys' Club several afternoons each week and to go to camp for two weeks in the summer. A remedial teacher helped Mark to reach the achievement level of his class and to feel increasingly successful in his schoolwork. And the parents were also persuaded of the importance of spending more time with the boy, of helping him to feel an important member of the family group, of taking occasional Sundays for excursions or trips or other recreation together, so that Mark could sense his place in their affections and accept sharing them with his sister.

Change in Mark was slow but steady. Unacceptable behavior was less and less in evidence. Reassured, Mark no longer felt the need to run away from his problems. He could now go to school without resenting his little sister's staying home with his mother and without dreading that he would return to find his mother gone. He could now come home after school feeling accepted by the family and no longer fearful of being beaten or sarcastically criticized by his father. Once he felt secure in his parents' affection, he was able to accept the routines of school and home and to respond to the ordinary requirements of life.

There are times when every child experiences some degree of fearfulness and worry. Every child is likely to react to certain circumstances with resentment and jealousy. But in homes where a good parent-child relationship provides emotional security, the sense of being loved and wanted helps the child recover from the tensions that are inevitably aroused in the course of his growing up. Without this bulwark, the child feels uncertain and unhappy.

Insecurity and unhappiness are often the groundwork for delinquency, but an understanding of them can help channel predelinquent behavior constructively and acceptably. An alert and interested teacher can often see to it that appropriate professional help is enlisted to solve difficulties before they become overwhelming. Delinquency need not develop.

The Slow-Learning Child

Appropriate goals depend on potential

Not all children are bright children. Not all are even of average intelligence. But if the limitations of a child's intellectual endowment are recognized, a great deal can be done to help that child live as a social member of a group and experience the satisfactions important to every youngster. These satisfactions—generally considered basic needs—include successful achievement, approval by family and teachers, and acceptance by other children.

When Edith's family moved, she was nine years old. She had gone to school in a small town for three years. Now she had to adjust to a large new school in a different city. She knew none of the children and she was understandably somewhat shy and hesitant. The school building was strange, the routines were different, the whole situation was unfamiliar. But Miss Tyson, the fourth-grade teacher, hoped that as Edith became accustomed to things she would adjust to her new school and be able to meet the grade requirements. For Edith was friendly in a quiet way, seemed responsive to Miss Tyson's efforts, and was trying hard to do well.

The routine review at the opening of the school year was not too difficult for Edith, since Miss Tyson started from almost beginning fundamentals. Edith was attentive and did her work systematically, and the results were passable. But as the difficulty of the assignments increased, Edith's attention wandered frequently and her obvious efforts to succeed in her schoolwork were no longer effective. Although her interest didn't lag and she continued to be cooperative, her work fell below the standard of the grade.

Because no record had been sent from the school Edith had previously attended and because her mother hadn't noted that Edith had ever had any difficulty with schoolwork, Miss Tyson was at first uncertain whether the child simply felt strange and confused in a new environment, or whether she lacked the capacity to respond more adequately to the academic program. Over a period of time Miss Tyson observed Edith carefully, alert to the patterns of behavior that she was showing both in the classroom and on the playground, and gradually she reached the opinion that a limited scholastic potential was at the root of Edith's problems. This conviction was soon substantiated by the results of psychological tests, which showed that Edith's mental age was about two years below her chronological age. Her intelligence quotient was in the low eighties. According to the psychological diagnosis, Edith had "dull normal intelligence"; she was "a slow learner."

Outwardly, Edith did not seem very different from the other children in her class. She was physically sturdy, as tall as the average nine-year-old, as attractive as any child in the room. Although she was more passive than most of the children, she was pleasant and friendly. But even though Edith was cooperative and worked industriously, she had little to show for her efforts. As the academic work in her class became more complex, she often failed to comprehend instructions. Like many slow learners, she had little capacity for self-criticism and tended to be satisfied with almost any results. Finishing a lesson always pleased her; whether she had done it correctly or incorrectly did not seem to worry her.

Edith's thought processes were slow and inept, and her memory was uncertain. Even when she listened attentively, she needed repeated explanations to grasp a new concept and a great deal of practice to remember and apply it. Her arithmetic papers generally included many incorrect answers. Her spelling was better, but only passable. In reading, she sought help with new words, then often failed to recognize the same words when they appeared again in another context on another page.

Edith's muscular coordination was no better than her thinking. There was markedly poor development of the small muscles of her hands and fingers, making her inept with pencil and crayon. Her coloring always went over the lines, and when she wrote, she held her pencil in a tight, cramped position that resulted in crowded, uneven, sometimes barely legible writing. In rhythms she was frequently out of time with the music. She could not follow a rapid tempo or a change in the beat.

The same lack of muscular skill was apparent on the playground. Edith ran awkwardly, and her reactions were slow. She could not throw a ball accurately, and when she tried to catch one she often fumbled or dropped it. She was uncertain and clumsy on playground apparatus and made many mistakes when playing a game with specific rules.

Often Miss Tyson observed Edith on the edge of a group, watching the others. Her posture seemed babyish: feet apart, abdomen thrust forward prominently, a hand held up loosely away from her body. Most of the time she was rather apathetic, remaining wholly apart from the gay, noisy play of her classmates. When she did occasionally play with other children, she was friendly but passive, never protesting the loss of a turn to a more aggressive child. With adults, Edith seemed a little shy and hesitant, but always polite and sweet.

Despite her inefficient thought processes and movements, Edith rated high in "effort." Despite her discouragingly poor results, she persisted with surprising determination. While reading, she moved her lips as she tried to fathom the words, following line after line methodically with her fingers. While working arithmetic problems, she counted almost aloud, doing sums with her fingers.

Edith's family was aware of her slowness and had been patient and understanding in the face of her limitations. Their continuing affection and attention had resulted in the wholesome attitudes Edith exhibited. She felt that people liked her, and so her behavior made her likable. But now more than patience and understanding were needed. Special help in schoolwork was essential. Miss Tyson realized that with the best will in the world Edith would probably always fall short in many of the skills that other children acquired with comparative ease; but with special help the child could be expected to do much better than she had ever done in the past.

182

Recognizing that Edith had never acquired an adequate foundation in reading and numbers, Miss Tyson felt she needed a fresh start. In that way she could achieve a firmer mastery of the fundamentals and, at the same time, could experience encouraging success by working with material simpler than the regular class assignments. Because it was impossible for Miss Tyson to find time in her regular day to give Edith this necessary special help, she urged the girl's parents to arrange for private tutoring. She offered to meet with the tutor to suggest what she felt was particularly necessary for Edith and, if the parents wished, to check with the tutor later regarding the child's progress.

Going back to materials of second-grade difficulty, the tutor prepared a "book" with Edith which had story sequences, matching exercises, and vocabulary and classification sections interesting to a nine-year-old but simple enough for a child with very limited reading skill. She encouraged Edith to tell a story, which they would then organize to put in their book. Edith looked through magazines for illustrations to cut out and paste on appropriate pages. Each story was utilized further as a basis for writing and spelling.

When manuscript writing was introduced, Edith was helped materially by the similarity of the symbols she found repeated in both her reading and her writing activities. At first she copied stories written down for her; then, as she progressed, she was able to write simple stories herself. She gained facility in recognizing words and phrases and in reproducing them. She learned to spell as she learned to read and write. A typewriter with large letters was provided at home, and slowly Edith developed the ability to find and strike the right keys. She found enormous enjoyment in thus producing straight lines and legible characters.

Edith was stimulated as she had never been before by the results of her efforts. She grew less dependent and was delighted when Miss Tyson commented before the class on her progress. With the difficulty of lessons scaled to her possible successful accomplishment, Edith was experiencing a totally new satisfaction. She could read, and read without help. She could write, and her writing could be read. What was more, she was learning to type, a skill which most of the other children did not have. Edith found pleasure in having accomplished something that the others admired, a pleasure she had never before experienced.

The simplest concepts of primary science books were incorporated in Edith's work as time went on. And together she and her tutor arranged a number book, illustrating Edith's own experiences. For the first time in her entire school experience, Edith was really enjoying her lessons. She recognized that she was accomplishing something, that she was learning. Miss Tyson was generous in her praise of the little girl and gave her much encouragement when she produced increasingly better papers in class.

Edith, of course, also participated in regular classwork. She listened more carefully to discussions, understanding more than she had formerly, enjoying the experience as never before. She even began to offer an occasional spontaneous comment. By the end of the school year Edith showed gains in more than academic skills and knowledge. She was becoming more self-reliant, more willing to stand up for her rights on the playground, and more aware of herself as a person in relationship to other persons. She continued to be friendly, but gained a quiet self-assertion.

Edith's parents realized that they could not expect her to learn as effectively as other children of her age or to participate in classroom activities on a par with them. But Edith was able, through the help of Miss Tyson's interest, to learn within the limits of her abilities and to participate in the class to the extent that she was capable. She retained her admirable qualities of attention, interest, and effort. And as she grew in social skills she lost her former helpless, forlorn dependence.

Only a discerning teacher can provide this kind of awareness of an individual child's special needs. And only an understanding family can implement the teacher's suggestions. When in addition, an interested, skillful tutor can be engaged and there is cooperation between teacher, tutor, and parents, progress can be most encouraging. Special aid may be needed for many months or even years, but there can be every hope that such efforts will bring further all-round growth for the slow learner and increased satisfaction for those concerned in helping him. Regardless of the amount of specific subject matter mastered by such a youngster during a school year, it is deeply gratifying for a teacher to see developing—in return for the extra time, thought, and planning necessarily involved—a much more effective and far happier child.

chapter 12

Rounding Out Childhood

Looking forward to adulthood

The ten-year-old is rounding out his childhood years and is alert to what it means to grow up. He often seems to be looking forward curiously and eagerly to adulthood. He is not yet caught up in the rapid physical, emotional, and social changes of puberty. He is usually only on the edge of being personally involved in them; he isn't yet as preoccupied with himself and his own age group as he will be when he reaches puberty. Consequently, he is detached enough to look at the adult world calmly, appraisingly, and often critically. He is not yet there, but he knows that he will be someday soon.

Ten is a profitable year for teaching and learning. The child's interest in people, in his community, and in world affairs is keener than most adults realize. The ten-year-old is interested in social problems in an elementary way and likes to discuss them. He is becoming aware of differences among people, of social justice and injustice. He wants to know why there are criminals and hungry people. His ideas about democracy are forming. His attitudes and prejudices are shaping up in wholesome or unwholesome ways. He is forming feelings about authority and about cooperating with it. He is gaining concepts of law and order. His ideas are broadening, and he is picking up a whole new fund of information from newspapers, magazines, and television. If adults will take his growing concerns and interests seriously and meet him at his level of thinking, a youngster can grow astonishingly in his social concepts. This is the year when social studies should probably become the core of the curriculum, for it is the year when the fresh awareness of these boys and girls can be channeled into a constructive approach to the meaning of real citizenship in our democracy.

During this year parents and teachers must try to help the child identify with the adult world in such a way that he is neither overinhibited by it nor resentful and rebellious toward it. Some children are too anxious to conform to the standards grown-ups set; thus they tend to lose their spontaneity and bury their individuality. It is the adult's task to help the youngster develop responsible attitudes —not by scolding him when he is irresponsible, as he surely will be at times—but

by giving him opportunities to act in a responsible manner and then encouraging and praising him for these actions. The ten-year-old is so anxious to accomplish and to receive adult approval that he may often undertake more than he can manage.

Responsibilities and frustrations

At ten the child is a bit steadier, a bit more grown-up than he was at nine. His talents and skills are becoming more definite. By this time, we can usually spot the youngster with special abilities or outstanding interests. Such a child will now need encouragement and special opportunity to develop his talent if he is to fulfill his early promise. But *every* ten-year-old—whether outstanding, average, or slower than average—needs encouragement and opportunity to follow a special bent or interest. He likes to do things well and wants to learn new skills, but he does not take himself quite so seriously as he did when he was younger. Now he can look at his work more critically, without going to pieces if it doesn't come up to his standards. He can even say, "I guess I goofed." He is ready to plan his day and accept more responsibility for getting things done on time. He makes a good committee member and likes to be given an opportunity to plan and carry through a project either with a group or on his own.

Despite a growing ability to take things in stride, some children are overly conscientious at ten and become worriers. They worry if they cannot get their homework done, or if they are not sure just what they should do. Because of adult emphasis on grades and academic success, fear of failure is becoming a real concern even to children who do well in school. If parents and teachers are aware of this fear of failure, they will try to be even more careful to assure each child enough successes to offset his inevitable feelings of failure—and to see that these feelings of failure are merely occasional rather than constant. In this respect, it is important to set achievement goals in school realistically and on an individual basis. Continual failure in the classroom gives a youngster a poor estimate of himself, which often discourages him or causes him to develop a rebellious "don't care" attitude toward those who put impossible demands on him.

The ten-year-old is increasingly able to take care of himself. He feels more secure in taking long trips away from home. He can go to the library and enjoy browsing on his own and even take responsibility for getting his books back on time or paying a small fine out of his own allowance. He can enjoy a museum on his own or go to the Saturday movie with his friends. Boys want to go to the playground or park to play ball. They also enjoy camping with their cub pack, even if it means being away from home for a week or even longer.

The ten-year-old is beginning to take more responsibility for his pets, although he still needs an occasional reminder. He is able to handle some household chores without too much fussing, although he does best when working along with an adult whom he likes. He may want to be paid for some jobs now, because his wants are increasing and he likes the feeling of earning his own money. This is a trait to be encouraged. There are many simple, extra jobs about the house or the neighbors' houses that a ten-year-old can do.

Pressures for achievement must be kept within realistic limits of what a child *can* achieve. Too often at this age, a child begins to doubt himself seriously and to develop inferiority feelings which may become permanent. Or his interest in learning may be discouraged by assignments too difficult or too easy for him, assignments given to all children regardless of their ability to complete them. Many children, especially boys, begin to dislike school because they feel inadequate to accomplish the kinds of tasks the school requires. If sufficiently frustrated, they may play truant from school, take part in acts of vandalism, or establish predelinquent patterns of behavior. We don't yet have adequate information about the nonverbal boy, but we do know that many more boys than girls have difficulty in mastering schoolwork as it is usually taught. There are, for example, four boys to every girl in remedial reading classes. This problem requires thoughtful consideration if we want to avoid turning active, restless boys away from school toward more exciting activities.

Friends and family

The ten-year-old is physically active. He likes to rush around and be busy, so much so that he may easily overload himself with activities. This is the club-joining age when both boys and girls proudly wear their uniforms and enjoy the ritual and activities of their meetings. They become loyal members of their particular organization, willing to carry their share of responsibility and to keep promises made to the group, but they easily drift away if the program is not interesting.

The organized club does not take the place of the groups or clubs that children form spontaneously. These continue to hold appeal, although they tend to shift and change as interests change. Boys are likely to run together in a more permanent group or gang than girls and are less selective in their membership than girls. They will usually take in any boy who can hold his own, make some kind of contribution, and keep up with their activities. Girls are more apt to gather in groups of two and three. Being someone's best friend is an important experience, although feelings are frequently hurt as best friends shift and change. This is the time of note passing, especially among girls, and of sharing giggling, whispered confidences.

The ten-year-old has grown in self-control. He may still get angry and occasionally lose his temper, but he does not flare up or cry as easily as he did when he was younger. Girls cry with frustration or hurt feelings more often than boys, who rarely give in to tears now unless they have been badly hurt or have had an overdose of frustration. Ten-year-olds hurl words back and forth and call each other names. They frequently have their feelings hurt during such explosions, but they rarely harbor grudges and are usually quick to patch up their quarrels.

At home the ten-year-old is usually good-natured. He likes his family and is often proud of both his parents. He wants them to visit school and still talks things over with them. There is little indication of the rebellious need to break away and express his independence that may become apparent in a year or two. Youngsters still enjoy going on picnics or trips and playing games with their family. Boys enjoy taking a special trip to the ball park or going fishing with their father, while girls enjoy shopping with their mother.

188

At ten most youngsters are careless about taking care of themselves, their clothes, and their rooms. Their beds may look rumpled instead of neatly made, although some girls are beginning to want attractive rooms. Many ten-year-olds drop their clothes on the floor, yet they may be very particular about what they wear. Boys dislike dressing up or wearing a shirt or a color that the other boys might call sissy. Girls are beginning to exhibit definite tastes in clothing and are increasingly influenced by their friends', rather than their parents', tastes.

Hobbies and interests

This is still an age of collections. Ten-year-olds start many collections spontaneously and sometimes drop them just as quickly. On the other hand, the collecting of stamps, car and airplane models, rocks and crystals, or nature specimens may now shape into a permanent and valuable interest, even leading ultimately toward a career choice. Children should be encouraged in such hobbies and given adequate space and time to pursue them.

Most girls of this age are physically, mentally, and socially more mature than most boys. The sexes are beginning to separate more definitely in their interests and activities. Boys increasingly like rough-and-tumble games. They play baseball, football, and other team sports. They like to ride their bikes. Girls enjoy their bikes, too, and will roller skate and jump rope, following innumerable, complicated jump-rope patterns and games. But they also enjoy quiet pastimes—making things and playing jacks or cards. They are concerned with personal relationships. Some still play with their dolls or paper dolls, or dress up and play-

189

act situations about marriage, families, babies, and, increasingly, teen-agers. Others are putting these games aside as too "babyish."

Although the two sexes mix in school activities and planned parties, in spontaneous activities boys stay with boys and girls with girls. Sometimes a boy and a girl of similar interests enjoy playing together when no other children are around, but in the company of other boys and girls they often pretend they don't like each other. There is often considerable real and feigned antagonism between boy groups and girl groups, with the boys teasing and the girls provoking the teasing to some extent, then squealing and running away. The girls may complain to grown-ups that the boys are interfering with their activities—a very real complaint at times.

Ten is the age, too, when hero worship is beginning. The early interest in biography has continued, but now these youngsters are personally identifying with their heroes—not only with heroes in books, in movies, or on television, but also with living people whom they admire. They are already daydreaming about the great things they will do and about situations in which they and their hero (or heroine) are involved.

The ten-year-old is developing a growing capacity for abstract thinking. He is becoming increasingly concerned about what is wrong and what is right. He is sensitive to unfairness, cheating, and lying, and he may turn on a friend or even an adult in righteous indignation if he detects or suspects this kind of behavior. He is beginning to ask searching questions and to be increasingly concerned about God and life and death. He asks many questions and wants thoughtful answers—occasionally he rejects an answer given by his mother, father, or teacher. He is now aware that people have many varying opinions, and that different adults, even among those he admires, have different standards of right and wrong.

At ten a child is often bewildered by the many diverse standards he sees being followed in the adult world. As he begins seriously to question and wonder about right and wrong, he needs help and guidance, especially during this year when he is still strongly influenced by adults. Adults responsible for his guidance must let him know what their values are and why they believe in them. This is a formative year. In the next few years the child must struggle, as he grows up, to choose his own values and begin to live by them. He will be likely to choose wisely if he has had sound guidance and a desirable pattern to follow during his childhood.

A plateau year

For most children, ten might be called a plateau year. It is a point of resting and of bringing together all that they have achieved and learned during the childhood years—of getting ready for the changes that will soon take place as they enter puberty. But things will not go so smoothly for all ten-year-olds; some, particularly among the girls, will already be approaching the restlessness of preadolescence. Most ten-year-olds, however, seem well adjusted, absorbed in their own affairs, and vigorous in carrying them out. They seem to be coordinating and applying what they have learned during early childhood and, at the same time, to be reaching ahead toward their teen years and interests. Ten seems a fairly steady, well-knit interim before the preadolescent and adolescent years begin. It is a good year in which to build for the future.

study of group interaction

There's Always a Reason

Recording of an actual class discussion

A child's attitudes and behavior are enormously influenced by his school relationships—not only contacts with his teachers but also interaction with other children. Often discussion among a group of youngsters, under sympathetic and understanding adult guidance, can bring desirable changes in the actions and feelings of the children involved. Particularly in the area of health and personal development, schools are placing increasing emphasis on the values inherent in skillful group guidance in the classroom.

An actual example of group interaction and group learning can be illuminating. Following is a partial transcript of a recording made of a group of ten- and eleven-year-olds in a classroom. They started by reading a story:

Teacher: What's the name of the story, Patsy?
Patsy: "You Show How You Feel."
Teacher: Do you think you show how you feel?
Patsy: I don't know. I've never thought about it.
Teacher: Well, let's see if Tom showed how he felt.

> "Look, Tom!" Ellen said one day. "I'm getting better and better at drawing people. Here's a picture I made of you."
>
> "Hm-m," said Tom. "It's not bad. But you didn't get the back right, Ellen. It's all bent over."
>
> "But that's the way you *looked!*" exclaimed Ellen. "I watched you coming home from the park, and you looked just like that."
>
> "Well," said Tom, "I *felt* like that, but I didn't know I looked that way. I got over to the park late, and the others had all the players they needed for the ball team. I was mad because they didn't wait for me. So I just came on home."
>
> Tom made an interesting discovery when he looked at the picture Ellen had made of him. He learned that his feelings showed in the way he walked, in his *posture.*

If you look around you, you will see that this is true. You can often tell by the way people walk, stand, or sit whether or not they are tired or sad or uncomfortable. How does a person walk when he is discouraged? Who can show us?

Nancy: Well, he walks all slumped over, and he looks sad and unhappy. Like this.
Teacher: Did you ever see anyone walk like that?
Several children: Yes. . . . I did.
Teacher: Did you ever walk like that yourselves?
Several children: Yes. . . . Sometimes. . . . Sure.
Teacher: How does a person walk when he is happy?
Carol: He skips along. He doesn't even walk.
Teacher: Could you show us how you'd go if you were just as happy as could be, Carol? . . . That's it. Now look at the picture below. Can you find the one who seems to be angry?
George: Well, I think this one, because his fists are clenched and he has a mad look on his face.
Teacher: Which one looks unhappy?
Paul: The one that's all slumped over. His hands are up to his face, and his face is down to his desk, and in his face he looks all sad.
Teacher: Why do you think he might be unhappy?

192

Jack: Well, maybe his pet's killed or maybe lost.

Teacher: What's that on his desk, do you think?

Tom: It might be his arithmetic paper, and he might have got a bad grade. I think he couldn't get his problems.

Teacher: Which child seems very happy?

Marjorie: The one that's skipping, and her face looks as if she's happy.

Teacher: What do you suppose has made her happy?

Patsy: Well, it might have made her happy that she got an *A* in spelling or an *A* in something else that she got a *B* in last year.

Teacher: That's one thing. What else might it be?

Jean: Well, she could have got something done. Gotten it right.

Teacher: What else might have made her happy?

Janice: Being chosen for the play.

Teacher: That's very possible. Now let's think for a moment. We've talked about posture, and you know what it means, don't you?

Group: Yes.

Teacher: Sometimes our posture shows how we feel. But what are some of *the things that make us feel that way?* What are some of the things that we have to have to be happy? Can you name a few things that you just *have* to have if you're going to be happy? I'll write them on the board. Nancy?

Nancy: A mama and a papa to love you.

Teacher: Yes. What else?

Fred: Friends.

Teacher: We need to feel people care about us. What else do we have to have to be happy?

Jean: Clothes.

Teacher: That's interesting. Why do you feel you have to have clothes? What is there about your clothes that makes you happy? Jackie?

Jackie: Well, I think we should be happy that we have clothes and that we're not like the people overseas who don't have them. Like Patsy—she brought a letter from a girl she writes to who has only two dresses, one for school and one for Sunday. Patsy wondered if she could send her some clothes and things.

Teacher: We're both happy and thankful, aren't we? You were going to say something about clothes, Rose?

Rose: We can be happy for clothes because in the winter we won't have to go around cold or anything, and we're lucky because we have snowsuits and jackets and hats and scarves and gloves. And the same in the summer——you don't want to go out and get all sunburned, so you have some light, thin dresses so you won't get sunburned or get too hot.

Teacher: Clothes make us comfortable, yes. Then there's something else about clothes. Why do we change the kinds of clothes we wear, get different kinds of clothes? Fred?

Fred: Well, because then——if you had the same kind all the time, you'd get sick of them and you wouldn't have anything to wear——and, well——

Teacher: But suppose you had things to wear. Suppose your mother made you come to school wearing short pants and a bow tie. (*Laughter*) . . . How would you feel?

Fred: I don't like short pants.

Teacher: Why don't you?

Fred: None of the kids wear short pants!

Teacher: If everybody else were wearing short pants, you'd probably like them and hate the long. Why is that? Anybody have any ideas? John?

John: We like to be like other people. We like to dress like them and do the same things they do.

Priscilla: Isn't that the reason women wear funny hats sometimes? Sometimes these ladies, these ladies go downtown, and they wear big hats, and I think they look so funny.

Nancy: But that's the style. That's the thing. We wear the clothes we do because we like to be like other people, don't we?

Teacher: We don't feel just right if we're different, do we? Well, what are some of the other things that we need to be happy? Someone said a moment ago that he thought this little girl in the picture was happy because she got good grades, a good report card. So what's one of the other things that you might say we need to be happy?

Barry: Good grades in school.

Teacher: They help, don't they? Now see if you can tell why these children I'm going to read about did the things they did. See if you can tell me what need they had that wasn't being taken care of. You remember the kinds of needs we mentioned. Who can tell us about them? What do we need in order to feel happy?

Susan: Somebody to like us, like a mother and daddy.

Sarah: Do things good, get things right.

Teacher: And was there something else we need to be happy? Does anyone remember?

Fred: It was about clothes——

Teacher: Yes. It was about being pretty much like other people, in the clothes you have and what you are allowed to do and the way you live and so on. Now listen to this little story and see if you can tell what need wasn't being taken care of.

> Jerry went slouching out of the room, the very picture of unhappiness. In his hand he carried a crumpled arithmetic paper—ten problems on it and all ten wrong!

What need wasn't being taken care of with him?

Priscilla: Well, it was success 'cause he didn't know how to do those ten problems.

Teacher: That's the idea. Here's another story:

> Henry was in the fifth grade, but he couldn't do any of the fifth-grade work very well. There was one thing Henry could do though. He could cause a disturbance, and he often did. He threw erasers when the teacher wasn't looking, pulled the hair of the girl who sat in front of him, and sometimes put his feet in the aisle to trip those who passed by.

Did you ever see anybody act like that?

Sharon: A boy sat right next to me who was always trying to do that, and he was always talking to Mike. But I'm glad, for one thing, he stayed back. I mean,

194

I'm not really glad, really, just sort of happy 'cause he was always——well, bothering and everything.

Teacher: Well, why do you think he did the things he did? Did you ever stop to wonder?

Sharon: He wasn't brought up right. He didn't act right. And he swore. He swore right in the schoolroom, and he did all kinds of naughty things. He threw spitballs, and he got up all the time from his seat, and he leaned over me to talk to Mike and——

Teacher: Could he do the work?

Sharon: No.

Teacher: Well, then he was needing——what?

Sharon: Success?

Teacher: Yes. And what about those other things, about how he was brought up?

Nancy: He needed a family that would help him get along. The thing he really needed was a family that would help him.

Teacher: You think maybe they just didn't spend enough time with him?

Sharon: I guess they just didn't care.

Teacher: Well, what about this one now, this girl?

> Annabelle began coming right home from school and spending her time reading books. "Annabelle," her mother would say, "why aren't you out playing? You used to spend all your time with Helen and Mary, and now you never seem to be with them."
>
> "They're silly——and mean, too," Annabelle answered. "I don't want to have anything to do with them or any of the other girls, either. It's more fun to stay home and read."
>
> It wasn't until weeks later that Annabelle's mother learned what had happened. Helen and Mary and a few other girls had formed a club, and they hadn't invited Annabelle to join.

What do you think was the matter with Annabelle? What did she need? What happened that made her act that way? Joan?

Joan: Success?

Carol: No, I think it was something else. She needs friends to play with.

Teacher: What had happened? What had her friends done that made her unhappy?

Joan: They left her out of the club.

Nancy: Last year when we were in fourth grade, Dorothy and——I forgot who else it was, but Dorothy and her, they had a club. And they always went up on the fire escape and just went up there and played. I was in it for a while, and then I went out 'cause they were just too snobby. They're older, and they think they're smarter, and I didn't like that much. There were a few girls in it that I liked 'cause they were nice, but of course some girls acted snobby too 'cause they were older than we were.

Priscilla: Well, once I was over at a girl's house, and she had a swimming pool, and she had another girl there, and she and this other girl wouldn't let me go in the swimming pool. I felt so bad 'cause they wouldn't let me go in and that made me feel mad. And then one day she came over to my house, begging for me to play.

Teacher: Has anyone else ever felt left out?

George: Well, I was playing with Johnny, and this Gordon came over, and they shut the door and locked it and left me in there.

Teacher: How did you feel?

George: Just left out.

Teacher: Together we've seen that we show unhappiness in different ways. We may show it in our appearance, as Jerry did the way he slouched. Sometimes when we aren't happy ourselves, we may tease and annoy others—like Henry, remember? Or we may draw away from people and just go home, like Tom in the story we just read. Tell me this, what might cause a boy to become a show-off? Do you know somebody who is showing off all the time?

Group: Yes.

Teacher: Why do you think a boy might do that?

Tom: Well, there's a boy in my neighborhood. He thinks he owns the street. He comes over to our house, and he runs through our garden and my dad doesn't like him to come over. And the neighbors——he goes over there and climbs all over their garage and on top of it. And Mrs. Justin tells him to get down, and he doesn't. He keeps right on.

Teacher: Why, do you think? Did you ever stop to wonder why he does things like that?

Paul: I think because his mother doesn't care if he does stuff like that. She doesn't even know.

Teacher: You think that's it. Does anyone else have any other ideas?

Carol: I think it's sort of his own fault. I know him, and I think it's just his own fault.

Teacher: Does he have good friends? Do you know him, too, Judy? What do you think it is?

Judy: I don't think his mother knows it.

Teacher: Well, why do you think he annoys other people? Does he need something, like Henry? Does he make good grades in school?

Judy: No. My sister's in his room, and she says he doesn't get good grades.

Teacher: So perhaps because he needs to feel successful and also needs to feel his parents care about him and about how he acts, he's just not very happy. What were you going to say, Joan?

Joan: He doesn't have many friends. The only friend he's got is his brother.

Teacher: You had something to say, Nancy?

Nancy: Well, I think when he was little, they let him get away with murder. Why does he have to cut up on other people's property when he could go on his own property?

Carol: Prob'ly he's mad and wants to make somebody else mad, too.

Fred: They don't have any space. They've got just a little house, and there isn't a yard. . . .

Teacher: And maybe he would like to have a place to play like most of the children, you mean? I think that's very possible. He doesn't feel happy in being different. Is that it?

Fred: Yes. Yes, that's it.

196

Teacher: Suppose now we talk about some other things, because there are so many different things people do. What do you suppose would make a girl steal some money from her mother's purse to buy cokes for another girl?

Patsy: Well, maybe she liked this girl, and her mother was always nagging her and telling her not to do this and that.

Judy: Maybe the girl did her a favor, maybe lent her a dime for popcorn or a candy bar or something, and she didn't want to tell her mother, and so she stole something to pay this girl back because she didn't have any money to pay her back out of her very own money.

Teacher: Perhaps something like that. You were going to say something, Betty?

Betty: Once my girl friend bought me something, and I had to pay her back. I didn't have any money to pay her back with. All I had was some money in my piggybank, and my mother had put it away in a dresser drawer, and it was locked, and I couldn't get it open. And so I got a dime out of my mother's purse, and she didn't know it, and I gave it back to her, but she found out I did it anyway.

Teacher: And what happened?

Betty: She straightened it all out. She didn't whip me or anything. She told me to tell her everything I did, even if it was bad. 'Cause then she could explain it to me, and I could see I shouldn't take what wasn't mine or do anything else bad.

Teacher: That helped you, didn't it? Now, we've talked about things we need to make us happy. We need to feel loved. We need to succeed in the things we are expected to do. And we need to feel that we belong and are like other people. And we've discussed different ways we behave when we don't have the things we need—love and success and feeling like the others. Now can we put all this in a few words that we can remember when people do things that bother us? Patsy?

Patsy: We could ask ourselves, "Why did he do that?"

Teacher: And we could say to ourselves, "Remember, there's always a reason." Maybe we could say, "He might be like that because he didn't get good grades." Or we might think, "Well, maybe he's so mean because he thinks people are mean to him" or "Maybe he'd be different if he had friends." And then perhaps we can do even more than just think those things. Perhaps we can plan how to make him feel he's liked or help him some other way. And of course we can remember about our own feelings, and try to understand ourselves better, too.

Children with worries and troubles may be reassured by reading specially selected stories and talking over their meaning. By identifying with characters whose problems are like their own, often they are helped to express their own negative and difficult feelings. When a child feels free to say, "I remember once when I——" or "I felt just like that when——" he is provided with a kind of safety valve, which can release many unacceptable responses. Annoying or "bad" behavior of children of all ages is often their fumbling to rid themselves of upset feelings. With increased understanding of themselves they can tolerate their own feelings better and learn to redirect their actions. And with help toward understanding others their social relationships can be greatly improved. Group guidance offers a helpful means of averting many problem situations as well as considerably easing others.

chapter 13

Growing Toward Adolescence

Different levels of physical maturity

Every class from the fifth grade through junior high school will contain some children who are on the threshold of puberty, or beyond it, and some who remain young boys and girls in their physical development, their thoughts, and their interests. Because of their different levels of physical maturity, children in these grades are difficult to plan for at home, in recreation groups, or in our present school grouping. Parents, teachers, and community recreation leaders need considerable skill and understanding to plan a program that benefits and interests those who are still youngsters and those of the same age who have already begun to mature physically and socially.

Youngsters who are *not* approaching puberty will remain much as they were in physical appearance and development. But those who *are* beginning the cycle of puberty will show changes in their growth patterns and often in their attitudes and behavior. These boys and girls are generally called *preadolescent*.

The increased production of the pituitary hormones and the increased release of sex hormones first cause noticeable bodily changes about two years before puberty. A plateau, during which the child gains in neither height nor weight, usually occurs before these changes become evident. This is followed by a rapid spurt in growth when a child may grow four or five inches within a year. Some girls will reach as much as ninety percent of their adult height during this period. A boy's growth tends to be of longer duration.

About half of all children put on excess fat at this time. Naturally many children and their parents become alarmed, for fear this rapid growth is abnormal. But if the child has not been overweight during his earlier school years, he will probably not retain the excess fat of the prepubertal period, unless his weight growth is complicated by emotional problems that lead to overeating.

At the same time that the child is gaining in height and weight, his arms are growing longer and his hands bigger. Girls' hips are broadening, and their breasts are developing. Boys' shoulders are broadening as their skeletal frame begins to enlarge and their muscles develop. Their pigmented pubic hair is be-

ginning to appear, indicating that in about three and a half months the first ejaculation will probably occur. In girls, menstruation is likely to occur about eight months after the appearance of pubic hair.

Since all the parts of the body do not develop at the same speed, the child may become self-conscious because of seemingly too large hips or hands or feet. Much preadolescent awkwardness—the dropping and tripping over things that adults often find so trying—is due to this uneven physical growth. Girls frequently feel embarrassed about their sudden growth in height or weight or about the development of their breasts. They may hunch over in order to seem smaller or to hide their growing breasts. However, more girls seem to be embarrassed about their height or weight than about breast development, which some girls proudly consider a sign of growing up. This may be due to the fact that many girls find themselves both taller and heavier than the boys during this period.

Most girls begin to show signs of maturing around eleven and menstruate at about thirteen. Most boys mature physically between fourteen and fifteen. The range is great, however; girls may menstruate between ten and sixteen and boys may mature between twelve and sixteen, with a few starting earlier, a few later. This variation among children points up one of the big problems of the preadolescent period. Even in the sixth grade, some girls will already be menstruating and others will be nearing their first menstrual period. It is much less usual for boys in the sixth grade to enter puberty, and comparatively rare for boys to be sexually mature by this time.

Explaining variations in maturity

If parents and teachers are aware that pubertal changes may take place, particularly among girls, as early as the tenth or eleventh year, they can avoid many problems and better understand and help the early maturing youngsters. The neighbors may say that parents are letting their child grow up too fast, but the parents and teachers will know that the child cannot help it. His early maturity must be recognized. A child who is beginning to experience the problems of early adolescence cannot be treated in the same way as others of his age who are not yet preadolescent.

Explaining the different times of maturing to children can spare them unnecessary bewilderment, fears, and feelings of inferiority at being different. Children should know what to anticipate in physical changes and in new emotional reactions and problems during the coming years. They especially need to realize that girls usually mature earlier and are for a few years often bigger and better developed physically than boys. Children need opportunities to talk through the problems and anxieties that may arise when they find themselves either far in

The interests of preadolescent girls are as varied as their levels of development. For example, some girls in this age group are still tomboys, interested in building model ships and planes; others are becoming interested in boys, in dressing up, and in going to parties; while still others are primarily interested in the new intellectual challenges of the upper elementary grades and junior high school.

advance of their friends or far behind them during these years of maturing. Group discussions in school can often provide opportunities to talk about these problems, especially when the children who are physically more mature can be grouped together. This separation can often be achieved by forming groups on the basis of common interests. The teacher's function within such groups should be to stimulate the discussion, listen to the children's reasons and opinions, and then present his own point of view.

Living with the preadolescent

The preadolescent's seeming laziness may be founded in very real fatigue. He is growing so rapidly that he is often tired and just doesn't want to do anything. Children who are not nearing puberty are usually so alert and energetic that the early maturing child, easily fatigued because of his growth spurt, may stand out in sharp contrast or may even seem difficult and uncooperative.

The preadolescent is sometimes more difficult to live with than other children of his age who are not so near puberty. His moods change quickly. He may be eager to start a project in the morning, but by afternoon be depressed and unin-terested in it. Girls may cry frequently over seemingly insignificant events or remarks. The preadolescent becomes overcritical of his parents and his teachers, although at the same time he may also hero-worship or develop a crush on an adult to whom he is particularly attracted. He wants to grow up, but he seems afraid to leave the security of childhood behind him. He may seem responsible and capable today, exceedingly childish tomorrow. He often expects and wants help from his teachers or his parents—yet he resents being told what to do.

The preadolescent is constantly contradicting, arguing, and taking issue with anything his mother, father, brothers, sisters, teachers, or even his friends say. He especially attacks his mother and disagrees with her constantly. He hates house-hold chores and may be uncooperative when asked to help, yet he is likely to be polite and helpful to people outside of the family. He resents being teased, but he loves jokes and often tries them out on his friends or on grown-ups. He responds best to teachers or to parents who crack jokes with him and laugh at his humor.

Preadolescence has been called a period of disorganization. A preadolescent will rebel at going to bed, at keeping clean, and at wearing the kind of clothes his mother thinks suitable. Boys are often untidy, uncooperative, and sometimes use language which distresses adults. Some girls follow this pattern, too, but most girls are interested in dressing attractively and being cute. They often reject the girl who is sloppy, rough, or tomboyish.

Preventing delinquent behavior

Preadolescents are often overanxious and competitive, both in their play and in their schoolwork. If they are under too much pressure to excel in grades, sports, or some other activity, they may resort to cheating. It becomes increasingly im-portant for teachers to recognize individual differences in ability to master schoolwork, so that the demands of the curriculum can be suited to the capacity of each child. The child who fails or is made to feel inadequate because the work assigned is beyond his ability may seek compensation in group activities that border on delinquency. Groups of boys, and sometimes girls, may steal from the dime store and accuse a child of being chicken if he does not go along. They may issue dares to each other that can have serious consequences, or they may share in the excitement of vandalism.

A child who gets involved in even minor delinquent behavior needs parental guidance to understand the seriousness of what he has done. His parents should help him to take responsibility for his action and to make amends, when that is possible. It is a mistake to allow potentially dangerous or destructive activities to slide by as merely "mischievous" or a "passing phase." This is the age of the alibi. Consequently, it is important that parents check their child's behavior and, if they find undesirable activities, try to discover the reasons behind them. If necessary, both parents and child should receive professional counsel to help prevent more serious behavior in the future. Sometimes delinquent behavior develops because a gang of boys has outgrown childish games and, with no new activities to take their place, hasn't enough to do. In this case, a better recreation program should be planned to meet the normal restlessness of this age group. Or, if there is an adequate program, these children need to be drawn into it.

It is wise to allow preadolescents to let off steam a bit, to express their thoughts and their feelings. A listening adult needs to be understanding and to have a sense of humor to meet the ups and downs of this period, since scolding, nagging, or taking offense at signs of disrespect will only make matters worse. Parents must still be ready to exercise their veto, however, if the preadolescent gets out of bounds. He needs to know that adults are still in control and that he is expected to behave in a responsible way. But it is better for the adult to respect these children's maturity and to trust that they can and will make adequately sound decisions than to treat them as difficult children or to show lack of confidence in them. When correction is necessary, it should be given in a friendly, matter-of-fact way with a firmness that will make it stick.

Social activities

The gang or group is very important to a child of this age, whether he is nearing puberty or not. As one of the gang, he has the feeling he needs of belonging and being like the others. But for youngsters who are nearing puberty, the character of the group is changing and will change even more. Such a child loses much of his earlier interest in the secret code, the secret word, and all the mystery he used to enjoy. He becomes more interested in sports and in things the gang can do together. Boys keep this gang interest longer than do girls.

Friendships are important to the preadolescent. The more boys like one another, the more frequently they seem to get into fights. But they are developing loyalty and the capacity to stand up for each other. Girls tend to have on-again-off-again relationships. They get angry at each other over little things and then make up again. They have long talks on the telephone, calling one another incessantly. Trouble and misunderstanding are likely to develop among youngsters of differing maturity levels. The more mature children tend to group together with interests of their own.

Preadolescence is a trying time for both parents and teachers, because the opinions of the peer group are becoming increasingly important. Acceptance by the peer group often means more to children of this age than their relationships with adults. They are beginning to use "but all the other kids do it." In the classroom, group contagion spreads quickly, and a teacher may find her whole class

up in arms against her. Parents, too, have a difficult time if their standards for their own child's behavior are different from the standards imposed by other parents. Youngsters are often quite unreasonable if they feel they are being asked to do something that will make them seem in any way different from their friends.

In our culture, early dating sometimes begins before children really want it or are ready for it. Formerly, it was believed that boys' and girls' interest in each other began as a result of emotional feelings paralleling puberty and that this interest grew in intensity during the adolescent years. But today, fifth- and sixth-graders are often interested in the opposite sex; some are even dating before junior high school. They have been given a cultural pattern through television, movies, books, and comics that emphasize boy-gets-girl stories. Many adults have also accepted this pattern and push their youngsters into early dating.

This premature growing up is usually undesirable. If dating and pairing off are encouraged during preadolescence, youngsters may desire a faster pace of social life as they go through junior high. Early dating also creates uneasiness among youngsters who are growing up at a slower pace, causing them to feel inadequate when, in fact, their interests and activities are the ones appropriate for the end of the elementary-school years. The majority of fifth- and sixth-graders, especially boys, are not ready for dating and pairing off or really interested in it. But they are often made to feel that this is expected. They must prove to themselves and others that they can be popular and have a girl friend or boy

friend. Most children, if left to their own interests, would prefer to enter boy-girl relationships more slowly. A precocious social life, if permitted to flourish in the fifth and sixth grades, results in a vanishing childhood, depriving children of time in which to prepare themselves for their adolescent years.

This is the time for parents to meet together and set up standards for their children's social life. They should emphasize group activities and parties appropriate for elementary-school children rather than for young adolescents. While parents, teachers, or community agencies may provide some kinds of opportunities for early maturing children to learn more adult social skills, these children's interest in dancing and pairing off should not be allowed completely to dominate the social activities of the elementary school. Preadolescents enjoy swimming, hiking, roller or ice skating, games, picnics, and hobby groups in which both boys and girls can take part. Membership in organized groups such as Boy Scouts, Girl Scouts, Camp Fire Girls, and 4-H should be encouraged.

Fifth- and sixth-graders are active, growing children who need many wholesome outlets for their energy and their expanding interests. They should not, however, be overloaded with after-school activities of adult choosing. Too many lessons after school, no matter how worthwhile, can overburden a child and leave him little time for free choice in developing his own interests.

Interest in team games is high among preadolescents, but skill is important and the child who hasn't enough skill to hold his own will often withdraw from the game and become a spectator. Boys usually continue to like baseball, football, soccer, rowing, swimming, bicycle riding, and construction activities such as making model airplanes. Girls like sewing, cooking, gardening, swimming, hiking, skating, and dancing. Both groups enjoy pets and are now able to care for them. They enjoy movies, radio, television, and comics, although by this time their interest in comics is sometimes on the wane.

Differences in reading ability and reading interests are very apparent. Some children greatly enjoy reading; others show little interest in it. The children who read seem to want facts as well as imaginative stories. Some like nature stories and books about science, travel, and mechanics; many enjoy series of books about boys and girls. Others are reading and enjoying the classics, although some do not yet like romantic stories. The girls usually become interested in such stories sooner than the boys.

Many preadolescents are also showing a stronger interest in music. They are anxious to own a transistor radio of their own and want to turn it on when they study. They are also becoming interested in records and may begin to collect them—popular singers, rock and roll, jazz, and occasionally musical comedies seem to be the favorites.

Those things that have given stability to the younger child will give stability also to the preadolescent—warm affection from parents and teachers, an understanding of his particular pattern of growth, recognition of his individual personality needs, a vital school program, encouragement of his skills and his hobbies, being given a sense of belonging and of being accepted, and an opportunity to be as independent as his maturity will permit. Proper support and encouragement will help a youngster pass through the years of preadolescence and adolescence without too much difficulty.

study of a child

Paul and Paul's Father

A parent's plans sometimes need rethinking

When it is possible to obtain a detailed picture of how a child has lived and grown and developed, clues are generally uncovered that help in interpreting any disturbing behavior that the child may exhibit. But sometimes, even after a thorough study of his life, a child's behavior remains puzzling. The clues to its origin are not always in the child himself but may lie instead in a parent's unconscious expression of his own troubles and the resultant tensions in his relationship with his child. Such a concept is not easy to understand, and such a situation is surely not easy to handle. When a school child is involved, he is fortunate if his teacher senses a problem that is beyond her province and secures expert help in identifying and solving it. Paul's story is a case in point.

At twelve Paul Werner was repeating fifth grade. He had spent much of the previous school year lost in daydreams. He hadn't acquired the necessary facts and skills for more advanced classwork, nor had he reached the quality of social adjustment that made relationships with other boys successful. He had seemed immature in so many ways, including physical strength and growth, that he had been retained in the same grade at the end of the term. His teacher hoped that the following year might find him more responsive socially and better able to handle his schoolwork.

But Paul's new teacher, Miss Spahn, found his behavior the same in his second year in the fifth-grade. She wondered if something could be done to bring him the satisfaction of real experiences in place of his continuing dependence on the vicarious delights of daydreaming. She felt that until this was done he would make no further progress either academically or socially. And she worried because he seemed so hopelessly acceptant of his lack of success both in classwork and in making friends.

Paul, according to the intelligence and achievement tests in his record, was not among the very bright children in the class, yet he had adequate ability to do schoolwork creditably. He seemed healthy, though he was small for twelve. Neither his vision nor his hearing was faulty, so apparently sensory impairment did not contribute to the fact that his school achievement was far below his possible level of accomplishment. Miss Spahn was puzzled by the situation and wondered if Paul's life at home might offer a clue to his behavior.

When she made an opportunity to talk with Paul one afternoon after school, he revealed enough of his home life to disturb her. Judging from the incidents that the boy related, she felt that he must have a harsh, demanding father and an ineffectual mother. Paul spoke somewhat haltingly, but it seemed as if he welcomed an opportunity to talk things over with a sympathetic listener. "He looks frightened," thought Miss Spahn, "and so unsure of himself and apologetic for everything." Anxiety was apparent in the child and perhaps fear even greater than he was expressing. Although she couldn't isolate any particular incident as significant, Miss Spahn felt that the boy's story should be investigated. She decided to seek expert advice in the matter.

Miss Spahn, though well aware that her information was incomplete, could give a number of facts to the consulting psychologist who served the school. Paul lived with his parents and a twenty-year-old brother, Charles, in a small, comfortable house on the outskirts of town. They were near enough for Mr. Werner to go to work in town and for Charles to attend the local college, but far enough away to permit a vegetable garden, some chickens, and a wide lawn surrounded by a trim hedge. Mr. Werner was very proud of his home. He wanted everything shipshape all the time. The grass was always smooth and green, and the vegetable garden was without a single weed; even the chickens seemed well cared for. The porch was inviting, with its chairs and swing seeming to stand waiting for the family to have the leisure to enjoy them.

It was Paul who cared for the garden, so that it always looked freshly weeded when his father came home in the evening. It was Paul who fed and watered the chickens and who kept their quarters almost as immaculate as his mother kept the house. Paul swept the porch daily. He also raked the leaves and cut the grass. Sometimes he counted the number of things he did every day and compared his responsibilities with those Charles assumed. Charles trimmed the hedge when it needed it and painted the porch furniture each spring. But nothing else was expected of him. When Paul pointed out that he was doing most of the work, Mr. Werner rebuked him, reminding him that Charles had more important things to do. Charles was the one who would someday make them all proud; Charles was the student. Someday Charles was going to be a minister with his own church and have widespread recognition as a learned and important person. Charles needed all the time he could get to study.

"And you, Paul. How did you do in school today? Bring your reader and let me hear you," was the inevitable end of such a conversation with his father.

That was why Paul stopped talking about the work he had to do. His father was never pleased with his reading and would make him go over the material again and again. The words soon became meaningless as he stumbled through them in a monotone, outwardly compliant but inwardly despairing and rebellious. The reading sessions usually ended with Mr. Werner in a temper and Paul in tears. The boy became convinced that he was slow and stupid, as his father said. He wondered why he should even bother to try since his father was never pleased anyway.

"You *must* learn!" Mr. Werner would rail at him. "To use your hands only is not enough. You must study. Be like Charles. If you don't study, you will never amount to anything. What do you want to do, work with your hands all your life?"

Once Paul had ventured, "Papa, you work with your hands, don't you?" That, he found, was not to be mentioned again. His father's temper lasted longer that day than ever before. In between his own sobs and his father's roaring, Paul gathered something about being one's own boss, not depending on the whim of an employer, and earning enough money to buy shoes for sons who wore them out too fast and new dresses for a wife who, because she was only a woman, thought clothes important.

Paul was frightened and upset. It was easier to try to work just as his father demanded than to raise questions about doing more than his share. It was better just to listen quietly when his father was "in a state" than to try to say anything in his own defense. He soon developed the trick of letting his thoughts wander away from the tempest. He took *himself* away, even though physically he stood dejectedly before his father. He would tell himself a lurid story of being so big and strong that he could whip anybody, strike out at anyone who failed to follow his orders exactly. Or he would fancy a world in which only boys and women were present, never young men or older men. Everyone in his dream world was cheerful, easygoing, and casual. No one cared particularly if dust showed on a table top or if weeds grew in the garden. No one was interested in anything connected with studying and learning from books. Life was good in his dream world.

When daydreaming is practiced often enough, it becomes a pattern of response whenever it seems desirable to avoid something difficult or uncomfortable. Thus Paul gradually became more and more accustomed to using this habit of removing himself from his father's scolding and upbraiding and soon learned to avoid any embarrassing or uninteresting experience in the same way. He found that he could remove himself just as effectively from other children's teasing, from the teacher's reprimands when he did an exercise incorrectly, or from her explanation of a new task which he did not understand and felt was far beyond his ability anyway.

"If you'd only pay attention," Miss Spahn would say. "You can't learn if you don't listen." Paul would turn his eyes toward her. But he would not be listening even when he seemed to be. He would be lost in his daydream, where he could feel successful as he never could in his actual experiences.

Although Miss Spahn's picture of Paul's home life was incomplete, it did suggest the desirability of trying to enlist the parents' cooperation in helping Paul to more adequate adjustment. When the parents were invited to come to school to talk with the teacher and the school psychologist about Paul's progress, Mr. Werner came alone. He greeted them bluntly with, "You want to tell me my Paul is not smart enough for school?" It seemed he wanted to say it first, before anyone else could. He looked relieved, almost pathetically so, when he was informed that Paul was certainly smart enough for school. The reason for concern, the psychologist explained, was that the boy was not progressing as well as he could. The school thought that if his parents and his teacher worked together they might help him to do better.

Mr. Werner immediately became excited. "He must be punished," he said firmly. With rising anger he told Miss Spahn that not a week went by that he didn't have Paul read to him or that he didn't criticize the way Paul was doing his schoolwork. "That I should have such a son!" he ended. "If he doesn't study medicine as I planned for him, he will have a hard life like me. His brother Charles will do better. He's smart. He will be a minister. I want Paul to be a doctor and I know there must be a way. What can I do?"

The psychologist assured Paul's father that what he must *not* do was punish his boy for not learning. After Miss Spahn left the psychologist and Mr. Werner to confer alone, they talked for a long time about the general feeling of disappointment Mr. Werner had with regard to Paul. The psychologist recognized sympathetically his great concern lest the boy turn out to be a failure in life. And she tried to point out gently that reasonable, attainable goals are far wiser than arbitrary aims which take no account of ability. She stressed that Paul was still too immature to make the kind of definite and specific plans for his future that Mr. Werner had been nourishing. Mr. Werner seemed appreciative of the school's proferred help.

It is not always easy to convince a parent that his tactics are not helping but are actually harming his child. In the Werners' case it required a series of interviews between Mr. Werner and the psychologist. After his first anger had died down, however, Mr. Werner cooperated completely. In time he came to understand how his own feeling of insecurity had made him plan almost fiercely to help his children to a happier life. Although actually his income was ample to care for his family comfortably, he felt keenly that only the professions were worthy means of earning a good living. He was somewhat ashamed of his own status as a skilled workman.

As he told his story, Mr. Werner emphasized his own father's disappointment in him when, as a youth, he had not done well in academic studies. He listened to and accepted the psychologist's suggested explanation that he had probably been feeling guilty all his life for having been a failure in his father's eyes. His efforts to draw his sons into the professional fields (their grandfather had been a chemical engineer) were his unconscious atonement for his own feeling of not having met his father's expectations. His extreme demand for exactness, his orderliness, and his overemphasis on cleanliness were all further evidence of his own inner personality problems. His quick anger when Paul did not meet his demands was the result of feeling that, in essence, he was again disappointing his own father, for Mr. Werner was convinced that only by the success of his sons could he compensate for his own early rejection of a career that would have necessitated rigorous academic studies.

Mr. Werner's several hours with the psychologist were well spent. It became clear in the course of the conferences that Paul's daydreaming could not be brushed aside as simply a persisting naughty trick, but had to be considered as a habit pattern acquired for a purpose. Paul was understandably upset by his father's repeated expressions of dissatisfaction and displeasure. And since no one likes to feel unsuccessful or enjoys scolding and criticism, it was not strange that he sought to evade such discomforts by building up soothing fantasies wherein he felt capable and accepted and secure.

"You do expect a great deal of Paul," said the psychologist, "both in school-work and in jobs around home, and evidently you are frequently annoyed with him. Perhaps you're demanding too much."

The psychologist helped Mr. Werner to see that many of the demands he had been making on Paul were really inconsequential and that his attitude toward the boy had been belligerent. By his very insistence that Paul was slow and incapable, Mr. Werner had contributed to making his son feel inept and stupid. Instead of encouraging him, he had consistently discouraged him.

Mr. Werner gradually became able to reëvaluate the entire situation. He began to show genuine, warm interest in his son and placed less stress on scholastic perfection. He granted that a happy life, spent in congenial work, was possible for people other than students. He conceded that his older son's studiousness and eagerness for a career that required years of academic preparation were no reasons to insist on similar inclinations in his younger boy. Paul's talents might not lie in the same direction as Charles', but Paul could be helped to be as successful *as a person,* which was, after all, even more important. To anticipate for him a career that appealed to his father, but that was probably inappropriate for Paul's particular interests and abilities, was unrealistic.

The search for reasons to explain Paul's daydreaming and his difficulties with schoolwork led far from the child himself. But in helping Paul's father to understand and improve his *own* attitudes and behavior patterns, the school psychologist also gave indirect help to Paul. As a more relaxed atmosphere was created in the Werner home, Paul became a happier child and eventually, therefore, a more successful and better-adjusted student. As Paul Werner's story illustrates, there are some areas of investigation and counseling which clearly lie beyond the training and skill of the classroom teacher. They are not within her province. Nevertheless, the children she teaches are influenced by so many apparently unrelated factors that she must be alert, as Miss Spahn was, to situations calling for the help of someone trained and experienced in dealing with serious personality adjustment problems.

study of a child

The Story of Elizabeth Holmes

Early maturity may be confusing

That children change as they grow is recognized by everyone. But sometimes changes in behavior are so marked that they become disturbing to adults charged with the care of children. This is particularly true when the adults don't recognize the underlying cause of an undesirable change. Once they are aware of the reasons behind a child's reactions, they can make plans to help him reach more acceptable ways of behaving. Until those reasons are uncovered, there may be weeks of concern and discontent for all involved.

That was the case with Elizabeth Holmes, who, as a bright nine-year-old, had ranked high in her fourth-grade class. Elizabeth was a big girl and the picture of sturdy physical health. As a fourth-grader she got along well with her classmates and enjoyed a secure home situation. She had understanding, college-trained parents.

But Elizabeth in fifth grade presented a vastly different picture. She had celebrated her tenth birthday early in the summer. Shortly after she returned to school in September, she showed few of the desirable attitudes and behavior patterns so apparent during the previous school year. Both her mother and her teacher, Miss Lewis, were gravely disturbed.

Elizabeth seemed painfully self-conscious. She kept a compact in her desk and examined her face frequently during class periods. She bemoaned her many freckles and pimples, and tried to powder or rouge over them. She no longer enjoyed being with children her own age. Instead she turned to a little clique of girls in seventh and eighth grade and sought to establish herself as one of them. Since they were considerably older than Elizabeth, their interests had changed from activities typical of ten-year-olds to whispers and giggles about a handsome movie star, a good-looking boy, what to wear, how to fix their hair. Some of them accepted Elizabeth as a sort of pet and, though they often laughed at her, the group did not discourage her "hanging around" with them.

During class one day, Miss Lewis corrected Elizabeth's poor posture. The child burst into tears. Another time when Elizabeth stumbled against a table and upset a vase of flowers, Miss Lewis suggested that she might be more careful. Elizabeth blushed furiously. She was so disturbed by the reprimand that she was unable to participate in class discussion during the following period. Soon after this, the other girls in her room began to tease her because of her obvious infatuation with Miss Lewis. Elizabeth gazed soulfully at the teacher, kept offering to do unnecessary errands for her, brought her one gift after another, and seemed unable to keep from caressing her teacher's sleeve or shoulder whenever an opportunity presented itself. Elizabeth became interested in romantic movies. She collected pictures of actors and was embarrassed when her classmates laughed and ridiculed her ecstatic comments. She wept dramatically on one occasion when Miss Lewis commented disapprovingly on her new enthusiasms.

Her mother observed changes at home, too. Elizabeth demanded clothes that were inappropriate for a ten-year-old and privileges that were unsuitable. She developed ways of behaving that she had never shown before—evasions and even deceptions, a haughtiness which was sometimes ludicrous, and a sensitiveness that made every day increasingly difficult for the entire family. Her parents were bewildered—worried and yet annoyed, concerned and yet impatient, too.

"She's just a little girl," they said. "What are these notions she is developing? Why is she so hard to manage all of a sudden? It must be the big girls at school she has been tagging after. They're a bad influence on her." Mr. and Mrs. Holmes forbade Elizabeth to go around with the eighth-graders. But this only made matters worse. Elizabeth became increasingly rebellious, flew into a temper when she was crossed, neglected the chores that she had always attended to before. She was restless and sullen and often rude.

Elizabeth alternately tried standing on her dignity with her parents and cajoling them into permitting her to stay up for an evening party or go to a movie with Carl, an eighth-grade boy. "Oh, Mother, why can't I even go to a movie? His parents have promised to take us and pick us up and we'll be home by ten thirty! Please let me go, Mother!" When Mrs. Holmes was firm in her refusal, Elizabeth withdrew. "Very well, Mother. If you insist. But you just don't understand! Things have changed since you were my age." And Elizabeth went crossly to her room and closed the door with a bang.

"It was funny, in a way," Mrs. Holmes said, relating the incident later to Mr. Holmes. "She tries so hard to be grown-up. She really felt unhappy, though, and I was sorry for her. But such notions, at her age!"

Elizabeth's schoolwork began to reflect the entire disturbed situation. Instead of being well up in her classes, Elizabeth handed in assignments late. She was so inattentive in class that she was unable to follow the group activities, and she seemed unable to concentrate on new material. When Miss Lewis spoke to her about her increasingly poor achievement, Elizabeth breathlessly implored, "I'll try, really I will, Miss Lewis. *Please* don't think I don't want to please you. I can't stand it if you talk to me like that!" And she cried almost hysterically.

Finally Miss Lewis and Elizabeth's parents talked over the matter together. Why these different and unfavorable reactions in fifth grade, after so successful a school experience throughout the earlier grades? Why the changed emotional responses at home, the demand for greater freedom and for social relationships which were so patently inappropriate for a ten-year-old? Fortunately, Miss Lewis had been sufficiently interested in Elizabeth to discuss her difficulties with the school nurse and the physical education teacher. They supplied the clues that eventually helped the Holmeses to understand Elizabeth.

Often when a parent or teacher sees a child day after day, he fails to notice physical changes that are taking place. Then something happens to bring them into focus—last year's coat is much too small, food demands change radically, complaints of lassitude or undue restlessness are so obvious they cannot be ignored, or a "peaches-and-cream" complexion becomes rough and pimpled. Such things had actually been true of Elizabeth, but because they emerged gradually, they had not been noted as specific changes.

On the first cold day Elizabeth put on her last year's winter coat and found that it was absurdly small across the shoulders and chest. It was also too short in the sleeves and in length. Formerly an active, eager little girl, always occupied with engrossing interests, Elizabeth had rarely seemed to be fatigued. Now she appeared to tire easily and was often lost in a daydream as she listlessly attended to her few chores about the house. Her always healthy appetite had grown so much that the child never seemed satisfied at mealtime. Candy and cookies and the richest kind of sundaes became routine after lunch and again after school. Before bedtime Elizabeth was sure to be heard at the refrigerator or the cookie jar. In her room there were often papers from chocolate bars and bags with only a few pieces of candy remaining. She spent her entire allowance on sweets.

The increase in Elizabeth's weight, the records showed, had been tremendous. She had grown more than twice as fast as ten-year-olds generally do. She had gained nearly twenty pounds during the past year. And during the first two months of the fifth grade, she had grown still another inch and gained four more pounds. No wonder last year's coat did not fit this year. No wonder her once smooth face was marred now with patchy places and pimples.

The changes in height and weight were accompanied by other physical changes. Elizabeth's hips had widened, and her breasts had developed. Together with these evidences of an early puberty, she showed the muscular incoordination and clumsiness which often trouble the preadolescent before he learns to handle his rapidly developing skeletal and muscular structures. The frequent moodiness, the occasional spitefulness, the restlessness, and the sensitiveness which had become characteristic of Elizabeth were all part of the change brought about by her approaching maturity.

Elizabeth did not understand why she should look so different from her classmates. It worried her and made her self-conscious. If she stood half stooped over, perhaps those embarrassing breasts would be less conspicuous. If she used make-up, maybe she could conceal the facial blemishes. If she sought the companionship of older girls—girls already well along in their pubertal development and so more like herself in appearance—she need no longer feel so different, so out of sorts with herself and with her whole world.

When the reasons behind all of Elizabeth's annoying reactions became clear, neither Mrs. Holmes nor Miss Lewis felt so helpless. They recognized that Eliza-

214

beth needed aid in understanding and accepting herself in her new role. "How could I be so blind!" lamented her mother. "But I somehow never thought a ten-year-old was about to menstruate. How wrong I've been."

It was clearly appropriate for Elizabeth to learn more about how girls grow and develop. Her mother explained menstruation to her. Much of Elizabeth's confidence in her mother returned as the two talked together about physical development and functions. Her rebelliousness was gradually replaced by a greater acceptance of the reasons why her parents had to refuse some of her perfectly natural desires. As she was helped to develop new interests, her preoccupation with boys and movie stars and clothes was no longer so all-absorbing. Dancing had once fascinated her, and it was not difficult to reawaken that interest and to arrange for dancing lessons. She was also enrolled in a children's dramatic group.

With Elizabeth's energies absorbed by these new and more acceptable activities, the adults' worries decreased. Elizabeth became less depressed and confused. Her schoolwork reflected her greater inner relaxation. She concentrated more successfully on her lessons and was therefore more successful in completing them. She was clearly growing in her ability to live with her new maturity. Because she now realized that her differences from her classmates were temporary, she acquired a new perspective concerning herself. She no longer felt it necessary to be always on the defensive against them. Instead, with the help of her mother and teacher, Elizabeth was enabled to substitute for her half-ashamed awareness of her early maturity a kind of pride that she "had gotten ahead of the other girls." Maturity became more than a matter of physical growth and functioning. There was increased maturity in social relationships and in emotional stability as well. Both at home and at school, Elizabeth was again functioning contentedly and acceptably.

The Primary and Middle Years

FOR THOUGHT AND DISCUSSION

1. Why is a normal child's sixth year often called the "turning point" in his growth? Are the conditions governing his acceptance as a member in a society different from when he was four or five? Give reasons for your answer.

2. Observe a group of kindergarten children at play and note in their activities how closely they tend to identify with their own sex and how much they interact with the opposite sex. Do the same with a third-grade class and a sixth-grade class. How does the proportion of identification and interaction change over these three periods?

3. Discuss briefly the differences between spontaneous and adult-directed group activities of children between six and nine. Give an example of an activity where adult direction seems to be profitable and one where adult direction could easily be detrimental.

4. Does dramatization play a significant part in the child's development? If so, what is its significance?

5. Observe a group of second-graders in classroom and playground activities. Note the types of dramatic activities that occur and the frequency with which they occur.

6. Select five library books for children in the second grade and five for children in the fifth grade. Compare the types of characters and events used, the use of language, and the degree of reality.

7. Consult this week's television listings and make out a schedule of the most valuable programs for a six-year-old and for a nine-year-old. For each program you select, name the one being shown at the same time that you feel would be least valuable (or most detrimental) to each child. Give brief explanations for your choices.

8. In "Paul and Paul's Father," who seems to be primarily responsible for Paul's problem? Recall the children in the other case stories in this section and in the first three sections. Do the origins of these children's problems and the methods of solving them form any recognizable pattern?

9. How important is the character and attitude of the classroom teacher to a child's healthy growth during his primary and middle years? Recall your own elementary teachers and decide which of their characteristics you would imitate and which you would avoid imitating if you were an elementary teacher.

10. Observe a sixth-grade class and note the range of physical development in the children. Has the range increased or decreased since the third or fourth grade?

11. Which of the following statements do you feel would mean more to a six-year-old: "You may watch television three hours from now" or "You may watch television after supper"? Explain your choice.

12. Put yourself in the position of planning a trip to a state fair for next month with a child of seven and a child of ten. How do you think each child would react to the knowledge that he was going?

13.   Observe first-, second-, and third-grade classes and note how the three teachers vary their use of language in order to further the language development of the children in their grade levels.

FOR FURTHER READING

ALLPORT, GORDON W. *The Nature of Prejudice*. Garden City, N.Y.: Doubleday and Company, Inc., 1958. A thoughtful, penetrating study on the development of prejudice.

BERNHARDT, KARL S. *Discipline and Child Guidance*. New York: McGraw-Hill Book Company, 1964. A practical book on discipline in each age period. Written by the director of the Institute of Child Study at the University of Toronto.

BUHLER, CHARLOTTE; SMITTER, FAITH; and RICHARDSON, SYBIL, *Childhood Problems and the Teacher*. New York: Holt, Rinehart & Winston, 1952. Gives insight into the kind of problems a teacher may meet in the classroom, with suggestions as to the kind of help these children need.

CLARK, KENNETH B. *Prejudice and Your Child*. Boston: Beacon Press, 1963. An objective discussion of prejudice, with suggestions for how schools, community agencies, and parents can deal with children's prejudices.

CUTTS, NORMA E., and MOSELY, NICHOLAS. *Teaching the Disorderly Pupil in Elementary and Secondary Schools*. New York: David McKay Co., Inc., 1957. Offers a great many practical suggestions for helping the disorderly pupil in his adjustment to the classroom group.

DAVIS, ALLISON. *Psychology of the Child in the Middle Class*. Pittsburgh: University of Pittsburgh Press, 1960. Discusses the emotional development of the middle-class child in relation to failure, achievement, and a sense of personal identity.

D'EVELYN, KATHERINE E. *Meeting Children's Emotional Needs*. Englewood Cliffs, N.J.: Prentice-Hall, Inc., 1957. Discusses some of the basic emotional needs of children and offers practical suggestions about teaching procedures to help meet these needs.

ERIKSON, ERIK H. *Childhood and Society*. New York: W. W. Norton & Company, Inc., 1963. A psychoanalytic approach to childhood. Contains stimulating material for those who have some background in the field.

FRENCH, JOSEPH L., ed. *Educating the Gifted*. New York: Holt, Rinehart & Winston, Inc., 1959. A survey of studies about and programs for gifted children.

GESELL, ARNOLD, and ILG, FRANCES L. *The Child From Five to Ten*. New York: Harper & Row, Publishers, 1946. A companion volume to *Infant and Child in the Culture of Today*. Contains a great deal of practical information about the personality growth of five- to ten-year-olds.

GETZELS, JACOB W., and JACKSON, PHILIP W. *Creativity and Intelligence*. New York: John Wiley & Sons, Inc., 1962. Describes new methods for measuring creativity and discusses specific issues which should be taken into account when dealing with potentially gifted students. Includes case studies.

GILES, H. HARRY. *The Integrated Classroom*. New York: Basic Books, Inc., Publishers, 1959. Summarizes research on intergroup relationships and provides helpful material for the teacher, including a resource list of books, pamphlets, and films for children.

GILLHAM, HELEN L. *Helping Children Accept Themselves and Others*. New York: Teachers College Press, 1959. Discusses how to help children whose self-image has been destroyed because they are handicapped or members of a minority group.

GORDON, IRA J. *Children's Views of Themselves*. Washington, D.C.: Association for Childhood Education International, 1959. Gives insight into the feelings of children in the classroom. Pamphlet.

GORDON, IRA J., ed. *Human Development: Readings in Research*. Chicago: Scott, Foresman and Company, 1965. A collection of sixty-one articles concerning research and theory on human development from birth through adolescence.

HAIMOWITZ, MORRIS L., and HAIMOWITZ, NATALIE READER, eds. *Human Development: Selected Readings*. New York: Thomas Y. Crowell Company, 1960. An unusually interesting collection of readings, including some on the elementary-school years.

HARRIS, IRVING D., M.D., *Normal Children and Mothers: Their Emotional Opportunties and Obstacles*. New York: Free Press of Glencoe, Inc., 1959. Examines some popular assumptions about parents and children by means of a study of the family backgrounds of 54 eight- to eleven-year-old, normal, well-adjusted girls. Also reports on a follow-up study four years later.

HARTLEY, RUTH; FRANK, LAWRENCE; and GOLDENSON, ROBERT M. *Understanding Children's Play*. 8th ed. New York: Columbia University Press, 1962. Deals with the relationship between play and child development.

HAWKES, GLEN R., and PEASE, DAMARIS. *Development From Five to Twelve*. New York: Harper & Row, Publishers, 1962. Emphasizes the child in school and with his peers.

JENKINS, GLADYS GARDNER. *Helping Children Reach Their Potential: A Teacher's Resource Book*. Chicago: Scott, Foresman & Company, 1961. Discusses some of the attitudes and approaches toward children that will help make it possible for the children to fulfill their potential. Based on discussions with teachers.

LOOMIS, MARY JANE. *Preadolescence: Three Major Concerns*. New York: Appleton-Century-Crofts, 1959. A useful addition to the small amount of literature available about the preadolescent.

McCANDLESS, BOYD ROWDEN. *Children and Adolescents*. New York: Holt, Rinehart & Winston, 1961. Cites research on the behavior and development of young people.

MILLER, DANIEL R., and SWANSON, GUY E. *Inner Conflict and Defense*. New York: Holt, Rinehart & Winston, 1960. Report of a study of child-rearing practices and social factors that predispose children to handle inner conflict in one way rather than another. Has practical implications concerning the desirability of various methods of handling children's behavior. Especially helpful in understanding preadolescents' defense mechanisms and ways of expressing themselves.

MORSE, WILLIAM C., and WINGO, G. MAX, eds. *Readings in Educational Psychology*. Rev. ed. Chicago: Scott, Foresman & Company, 1962. A stimulating collection of articles. Contains original reports of research and applications of research findings to the practical problems of teaching.

RITHOLZ, SOPHIE. *Children's Behavior*. New York: Twayne Publishers, Inc., 1959. A continuation of the Wickham study of 1928. The present study includes parents' and children's attitudes as well as teachers' and mental hygienists' attitudes toward the relative seriousness of children's behavior problems.

ROGERS, DOROTHY. *Mental Hygiene in Elementary Education*. Boston: Houghton Mifflin Company, 1957. Stresses the importance of the elementary-school years as preparation for future competence and mental health.

RUSSELL, D. H. *Children's Thinking*. New York: Blaisdell Publishing Co., 1956. Based on more than 1000 research studies of how children think, conducted both in this country and in other countries.

SARASON, SEYMOUR, and others. *Anxiety in Elementary School Children*. New York: John Wiley & Sons, Inc., 1960. The first report on a long-term research project. Presented in readable form with practical implications for parents and teachers.

SEIDMAN, J., ed. *The Child: A Book of Readings*. New York: Holt, Rinehart & Winston, Inc., 1958. A collection of articles and reports of research.

SHACTER, HELEN S. *Understanding Ourselves*. Bloomington, Ill.: McKnight & McKnight Publishing Co., 1945. A readily understandable presentation of methods of meeting or avoiding difficulties in everyday experiences. Illustrated with anecdotal sketches of actual children.

SPOERL, DOROTHY, ed. *Tensions Our Children Live With*. Boston: Beacon Press, 1959. An excellent collection of short stories to stimulate discussion about social relationships among children from the third to the sixth grade.

STENDLER, CELIA BURNS, ed. *Readings in Child Behavior and Development*. New York: Harcourt, Brace & World, Inc., 1964. An excellent and up-to-date collection of readings based on an interdisciplinary point of view.

STEVENS, ISCOE. *Personality Development in Children*. Austin: University of Texas Press, 1960. Points up the many factors entering into the development of personality as children grow.

STONE, L. JOSEPH, and CHURCH, JOSEPH, *Childhood and Adolescence*. New York: Random House, Inc., 1957. An outstanding book in the field of child development. Contains an excellent chapter on the meaning of maturity.

STRANG, RUTH. *Helping Your Gifted Child*. New York: E. P. Dutton & Co., Inc., 1960. A practical approach to meeting the needs of gifted children at each level of their development.

WARNER, RUBY H. *The Child and His Elementary School World*. Englewood Cliffs, N.J.: Prentice-Hall, Inc., 1957. Points up the new experiences that the child faces as he starts to school.

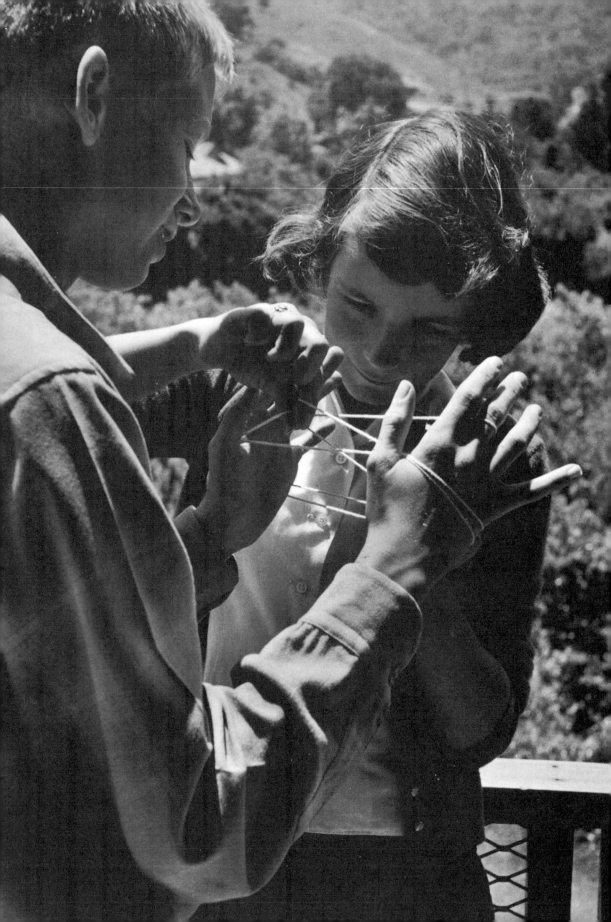

part five

Adolescence

During adolescence the young person must reweave the patterns of his life so that out of the disorganization of preadolescence may come the maturity he will need as an adult. This change does not come about all at once. The adolescent must still go through a good many years during which he will often be immature and dependent. Yet parallel with this continuing immaturity will be evidence of increasing independence and often a surprising maturity of thought and judgment. During these years perhaps more than at any other time, parents and teachers must try to keep a balance in meeting the adolescent's needs both to become more independent and, at the same time, to continue relying in some degree on adults.

Because boys and girls mature at varying ages, we cannot say that adolescence begins or ends with any certain year. Some children mature rapidly and are ready for adulthood and its responsibilities when others of the same age are still immature, still working through the adjustments of adolescence. Youngsters differ, too, in the ease with which they make these adjustments. How they will adjust is determined by their attitudes, abilities, and personalities; and these factors, in turn, will have been affected by their past relationships and experiences. Many adolescents will have grown steadily toward an emotional maturity basic to good adjustment; others will have had experiences that have delayed rather than furthered their development.

Our interest in the adolescent years and our recognition of the very real strains and adjustments involved have made us highlight this period, setting it apart from the rest of the growth process. As a result, the difficulties boys and girls may have at this time are often so overdramatized and overemphasized that many parents and teachers and even some adolescents themselves have come almost to dread these transitional years. Yet they are valuable years, vital in the total developmental picture. Adolescence is indeed a period of heightened growth activity, but it must be regarded as part of the normal sequence of growth, continuous with what has gone before and with what will follow, not as an isolated headline. Rather than dreading these years, we should consider carefully the role that we, as adults, can play in guiding young people through the period of adolescence, so that they will be able to step with some confidence into their places in the adult world.

The current trend toward playing up and setting apart the adolescent years is unfortunate for another reason. It provides adolescents a cultural pattern—actually a blueprint for behavior—that is not always a desirable one. Through books, magazines, movies, television programs, the creation of a teen-age market, and even classroom discussions, we often push boys and girls into thinking that it is natural for them to want to look alike, think alike, and be alike. We imply that they are expected to be rebellious and to break away from the influence of their parents and other adults. We state that the standards of their peers are more important to them than the standards of an adult world. But even though rebelliousness and the desire to conform are commonly observed conditions of adolescent development, they are not always as essential as the popular image of "normal" teen-age behavior would indicate. All adolescents do not feel the need to conform or to rebel to the same degree, and many of them find that their popular image makes it unnecessarily difficult for them to be themselves and to mature in their own way.

The adolescent does, of course, face several major adjustments, and his parents and teachers should be aware of these. The first, and perhaps the most basic, is the problem of finding a personally satisfying answer to the question, "Who am I?" In order to further his search for his own identity, the adolescent must become less dependent on his parents, then gradually identify with and assume a more adult role. He must be able to attain a certain degree of self-control and emotional maturity. He must be able to make decisions, to use good judgment, and to meet new situations without constantly turning to a teacher or parent for support and guidance.

Another adjustment adolescents must make is to the complicated physical, emotional, and social changes involved in recognizing and accepting their roles as men and women. Associated with this adjustment is the adolescent's desire to learn about members of the other sex and to establish normal, happy, healthy relationships with them.

Boys and girls must also begin thinking about a vocational interest during their adolescent years, so that they can plan toward establishing themselves as self-supporting, self-respecting adults. They must find their strengths and weaknesses, their interests and aptitudes, as they come to the time when they must fit into a realistic situation, translating the daydreams of their childhood into actual possibilities for their adult life.

These are difficult, complicated adjustments. Young people need the wise support and understanding of their parents and their teachers as they try to work through the problems they must inevitably face at some time between the years of twelve and twenty.

chapter 14

Not Quite Grown Up

Changing moods

The changing moods of the preadolescent period generally continue through early adolescence, sometimes with increasing intensity. The teen-ager may be happy and self-confident one day, despondent and self-doubting the next. His likes and dislikes are often strong. He is rarely tolerant of other people. He may be generous at one time, but revert to childish selfishness within the same hour. He wants to be with his friends, but at home he may bury himself in his room, demanding utmost privacy, or he may withdraw within himself, barely responding to his family. His moods are influenced by heightened physical changes, by self-consciousness that comes from his increased awareness of himself, and by cultural pressures which demand that he be acceptable to his peers. The struggle to belong, to be accepted, puts an added strain on the young adolescent as he becomes physically mature.

The adolescent's changing moods are difficult for teachers and parents to accept, even though they may have some understanding of the cause. The adolescent is often easier to guide and live with in school than within the family; he may respond better to the group situation and to the guidance of his teachers because he feels his parents are too close to him and too identified with his childhood. They are the ones from whom he must break away in order to become an adult. Although he may love them, frequently enjoy being with them, and often turn to them for support, he also rebels against them and pushes aside their attempts to help him as he struggles to grow up. He wants their interest, yet he often rejects both their affection and their help. This seems to be particularly true at about the fifteenth year, which might be considered the point at which the younger adolescent begins to grow up and feel that he is really becoming a young adult. Living day in and day out with a young adolescent while he is trying to break some of his home ties and establish his independence is not easy. Parents need encouragement during this period, but too often they receive only condemnation.

Marked physical changes

Most boys and girls enter adolescence during their junior-high years, although a few, particularly boys, will not do so until they are in high school. The special problem of the junior high school is that it includes students in such different stages of development. In no other growth period is this variation in physical development quite so marked. In a single classroom we find some youngsters still in the spindle-legged stage of late childhood and others with the developing figures of young men and women. By the eighth grade, approximately two thirds of the girls have matured and may be called adolescents, whereas two thirds of the boys are still preadolescents. By the ninth grade, almost all of the girls and a majority of the boys will have matured physically.

Although growth proceeds more slowly after the growth spurt of the preadolescent and early adolescent periods, definite and striking changes continue to be apparent. The adolescent's appearance changes from that of a child into that of a young man or woman. Adolescent girls gradually lose their boyish appearance as the distribution of fat becomes more feminine. Their hips grow wider and rounder, and their breasts become larger and better formed. Boys also change in appearance as their muscles develop and their shoulders and chests broaden. Their voices deepen gradually, but in early adolescence they are often embarrassed as their voices fluctuate between a childhood soprano and a developing bass or baritone. In fact, growth in general is uneven through the early years of adolescence, and the teen-ager may feel awkward and embarrassed because of it.

Many young adolescents feel generally uneasy and dissatisfied with their bodies or their appearance, although they are no longer so concerned with whether or not they will mature normally. Differences in body size, proportion, height, or weight now worry the teen-ager in a new way—he fears that this is the way he may always be. "I don't want to be a big woman like my mother." "I don't want to be a short guy." "My mother is awfully fat, and I'm getting heavy, too. I'm afraid I'll be fat by the time I'm twenty." Until this time the short boy could always hope he would grow tall, and the tall girl could think, "The others will catch up with me." But now that they are almost grown-up, these teen-agers become aware that their height, bone structure, and general proportions are the ones they will always have, although they can, of course, gain or lose weight. Sometimes teen-agers are very unhappy about their appearance and need help in accepting it. Again the cultural pattern, with its emphasis on small, slender girls and tall, manly boys, is not helpful. Body build is an inherited trait and many young people fall far short of the unrealistic ideal that is so persistently held before them.

Acne or other facial blemishes, scars, birthmarks, or even freckles can distress an adolescent and render him painfully self-conscious. Body odors embarrass him. His need to wear glasses or even the kind of hair he has may disturb him, especially at the beginning of adolescence. These things may seem superficial to adults, but they are serious to the youngster. Because of the dramatic changes that have taken place in his body, his attention is naturally focused on it. He will need greater maturity before he can value himself primarily on what he is and what he can do rather than on how he looks. He now assumes, "I am what I look like." Adults should take these feelings seriously, not criticizing the adolescent or laughing at him, but giving constructive help and friendly reassurance. Adolescents need help in growing toward the realization that the kind of person they are is determined by much more than personal good looks.

Self-centeredness, belonging, and conforming

In the early years of adolescence, a boy or girl is usually self-centered. He is so deeply concerned with answering the question "Who am I?" that his thoughts are focused almost entirely on himself. He uses his friends as a mirror for himself. He constantly asks them questions about himself: "How do I look?" "Do you think Jim likes me?" "Did I do all right?" "Let's have a truth session." When his friends start talking about some other subject, he listens to them just so long, then he must bring the conversation around to himself again. He is self-conscious as well as self-centered. He uses his friends to support him. As he grows more mature and more sure of himself, he will become increasingly able to turn from this self-questioning and to develop a real interest in other human beings, going out to them in genuine love and affection.

Belonging to a group reassures the adolescent. He seems to crave its security and its power to bolster his waivering self-confidence. He is most conservative and he will often try to submerge himself further in his group by conforming to the group pattern—appearing and behaving as the group dictates. Adult stand-

ards of behavior do not matter nearly as much as the standards of the group. Often a boy or girl who does not really want to do everything his group is doing does not dare to be himself but tries instead to be what the others think he should be. He may do unwise and silly things in his efforts to be popular or at least accepted by the others. Group contagion is strong. At junior-high parties many youngsters get so excited and wound up that they behave in ways they would never think of as individuals. At school a normally friendly girl or boy may be unfriendly to those outside his group if group pressure demands it. He may feel unhappy about this and a bit ashamed, but he goes along. As one girl said, "I have to pretend to be that way or I won't have any friends." Many young adolescents are so concerned about what others think of them that they can pay little attention to anything else, with the result that their schoolwork and their own real interests may temporarily suffer. They face an arduous, complicated task in living up to the demands of the group. They are often strained, unhappy, and worried during these years for fear they will not be able to hold their own with others.

Often in their desire to make the grade socially, teen-agers pass up friendships or acceptance in groups which could give them real companionship but which seem to lack prestige. Instead, they hang on at the fringe of a supposedly better group, feeling left out and unhappy. A great deal of adolescent tension and irritability stems from the worry over belonging. This anxiety has been heightened by a cultural pattern that puts a high premium on belonging to the right group, an emphasis felt not only by adolescents but by adults, who often consider

conformity a virtue and in some instances a necessity for holding a job or attaining a promotion. Conformity is probably not an innate adolescent need but one that has been fostered as a community pattern. As the need for individual ability is reëmphasized, we can hope to see a lessening of the pressures on the adolescent to be so completely like the others.

Teen-age standards and behavior

By and large, junior-high-school students are drawn toward boys who are good in sports, adequately attractive, and popular. They admire girls who are pretty by the particular standard of the group, talk easily, and enter into all the chatter and plans of the group.

The great loyalty boys often develop for members of their group or their team is less frequent among girls. Girls are more concerned with cliques, and can be quite cruel in excluding others and letting them know they are excluded. Girls greet their special friends with squeals and shrieks in the halls, save seats for them at the lunch table, and call them on the phone as soon as they get home. They love to gossip—even about each other. Many girls seem less secure and less motivated toward purposeful activity than boys.

The junior-high boy or girl does not understand the person who does not conform to his own, usually narrow, standards and is often openly intolerant of him. He either wholly accepts or wholly rejects most classmates—there is very little middle ground. If not guided and helped to develop an understanding of other people, he can, in his insecurity, be quite unkind and thoughtless toward a person who does not fit in. He may reject a member of a minority group or of a different religious belief, a youngster whose appearance or clothes are different, one who is especially successful academically or one who is a slow learner, one who has special talent or strong interests of his own, or one who refuses to go with the group. Sometimes it is a student who is too popular. Even adolescents who are attractive and eager to be friendly are sometimes rejected because, for one reason or another, they do not fit in with the particular group pattern. Adults need to be aware of the heartaches suffered by those who are not accepted by their peers, in order to give them the support and guidance they need.

Differences in social maturity

It is natural, normal, and desirable for boys and girls to begin to be interested in one another during junior high school. The point at which the interest develops will be an individual matter, based on the youngster's maturity, self-confidence, interests, and sometimes his childhood experiences with friends of the opposite sex. If a boy or girl feels inadequate or is too young when he first tries to date, he may withdraw and be unwilling to try again until he is more sure of himself. Boys and girls who are not ready for dating in junior high school should not be pushed into it. They will date when they are ready.

Many boys are almost dragged into social life in junior high school by the girls. This is unfortunate but understandable. Since many of the girls mature earlier than the boys, they become interested in boys before most of the boys are genuinely interested in reciprocating. Girls often take the initiative toward boys their own age and often are met with a complete lack of response. They telephone boys—much to the boys' irritation—invite them to parties, and try to attract their attention in whatever way possible. Parents and teachers need to be aware of this problem. They need to interpret the situation to the girl who has matured, and see to it that she has plenty of opportunities to work and play with boys in group activities. If a girl matures very early and is far ahead of her group, it may be wise to provide her with carefully chosen opportunites to get to know boys who are slightly older than she is.

Many of the problems we meet in junior high school girls—overdone hairdos, too much lipstick, too much chasing after boys—are the result of this difference in development between boys and girls. They reflect the normal interest in dating of the girl who has matured before the boys she knows are ready to respond, and the feelings of frustration and failure she experiences because "the boys don't like me." Many young girls begin to think they are social failures because boys are not interested in them.

Even though many boys catch up with the girls in social maturity by the end of junior high, some boys and girls continue to be ill at ease with each other. Boys may hold aloof for fear of being turned down, of being clumsy, or of somehow embarrassing themselves. Many boys will date only popular girls, feeling too insecure to date the girl on the fringe of the group, however attractive she may seem. In the same way, many girls turn down a date with the "wrong" boy. Consequently, popular boys or girls may have many opportunities to date, while others just as attractive have none. Often adolescents want to go steady as social security, as insurance against being left out. They change partners frequently and seldom feel any deep attachment for their steady.

By the time boys and girls are in the ninth grade, they usually want opportunities to be with the opposite sex. They need places where they can gather and get to know each other in informal surroundings. This is a different and more valuable experience than pairing off or going steady—experiences that should belong to the older adolescent as a prelude to selecting a mate. Parents should open their homes so that their teen-age sons and daughters feel free to bring friends there. Schools, churches, and community agencies can provide opportunities for young teen-agers to participate in hikes, swimming parties, picnics, dances, dramatics, operettas, folk dancing, and hobby groups. Young people who are actively doing things together can get to know one another during early adolescence without relying exclusively on dating.

Parents must continue to take considerable responsibility for guiding the activities of the younger adolescent, who is not always ready to judge wisely or to make sound decisions. They must sometimes use their veto quite firmly even in spite of their child's anguished protests. There are times, indeed, when adolescents want and need to rely on their parents' judgment and decisions. Sometimes this makes them strike out at their parents, resenting their own immaturity at the same time that they are seeking and accepting the security their parents offer. The adolescent does not like the idea of controls, yet at times he wants and must have the security controls can provide. "My mother won't let me go there" or "My father makes me get home at midnight" is sometimes a convenient shel-

ter for the adolescent, even though the same teen-ager may storm at his mother and father for being old-fashioned and too strict when the restrictions aren't so convenient.

Academic problems and opportunities

Because of the many emotional demands on a youngster during his junior high school years, schoolwork sometimes takes second place. A boy or girl who has done well in elementary school may begin to grow careless about homework and about handling in assignments. Yet many boys and girls respond positively to the wider academic program of the junior high school. They become genuinely interested in a subject and may even find a major interest leading toward an eventual career. They enjoy changing teachers, working in the laboratory and shop, and being assigned more difficult lessons. They often become attached to a particular teacher, developing crushes which they discuss avidly. Teacher influence is at a high point and can be most valuable in guiding the student and developing his values and interests at this crucial period in his development.

Individual differences in ability to do schoolwork become increasingly apparent in junior high school. The child who still cannot read well finds himself in very real difficulties. Now, even more than in preceding years, different programs of study suited to children's differing abilities and goals are essential. Each program must be offered as one of value, so that a youngster does not feel that he has failed because he is following one channel of study rather than another. In schools in which the major emphasis is an academic, college-oriented curriculum, many youngsters fail and begin to consider dropping out of school. Such failure

particularly is serious, during junior-high years, when boys and girls are trying to find out what kind of a person they are. They need help in finding their strengths as well as their weaknesses if they are to become useful citizens, competently using their own abilities.

study of an adolescent

Agnes and Her Parents

Misunderstanding motives causes difficulties

Children who "run the family" are not unusual. They accomplish this in various ways. Sometimes they use a persistent cough or a sharp abdominal pain that disappears when the parents give in to a demand. Sometimes they apply scathing criticism that compares their parents unfavorably to other parents, until the mother and father feel they can recover their child's good will only by meeting an unreasonable request. Or they may get their way by refusing to study or by misbehaving at school, especially if the parents set great store by high grades and participation in school activities. Yet none of these ways of behaving is likely to be really satisfying to a boy or girl, and all are certain to be disturbing to the family.

The Fowler family was faced with a situation that bewildered and disturbed them all. The parents had been lenient and protective; they were now distressed that their teen-age daughter was difficult to please and seemingly impossible to control. Fourteen-year-old Agnes was confused and unhappy. She baffled the adults who knew her, both at home and at school. Her schoolmates wondered about her and although they sometimes envied her doing as she pleased, they did not like her. Endowed with a pretty face and provided with pretty clothes, Agnes could have been attractive and popular. Instead, she drew attention chiefly because she was sullen, scoffing, and rude. She had failed to establish friendly or even agreeable relationships with either grown-ups or her schoolmates. She was defiant when corrected or reproved and she flaunted her disregard of school regulations. Her school record was poor, and she showed little desire to do anything to improve it.

To a teacher who had once tried to reach a responsive chord, talking sympathetically and warmly in an effort to break through her aloof manner, Agnes had given the insolent rejoinder, "Why should you care? I'll get along without you, thank you!"

"I don't understand that girl," the teacher said later at a faculty conference. "She *can* be sweet. Yesterday I saw her being very gracious to a visitor who stopped her to ask for information. And not long ago she was lovely to a frightened youngster who came to meet his big brother and got lost in the halls. But she's never been very sweet to me!"

"I think she's unhappy," said another teacher, "but I can't imagine why. Her parents certainly seem interested in her. Why don't they do something? She really needs help."

"Perhaps they don't know what to do," ventured another faculty member. "Perhaps *they* need help, too."

And they did. Mr. and Mrs. Fowler were greatly concerned about Agnes' attitude and behavior. She ignored all responsibilities at home—never making her bed or helping with the dishes or even being reasonably careful with her belongings. Yet she found continual fault with her mother's housekeeping. She expressed dissatisfaction with the way the family lived, the car they drove, the clothes they provided her, and the size of her allowance. She seemed unaware of anyone's comfort but her own, turning up the television when others preferred quiet, insisting on listening to a program that only she found interesting.

The Fowlers were worried, too, about some of Agnes' habits which they felt threatened her health. She indignantly rejected the idea of a regular bedtime, saying she would go to bed when she felt tired. Mornings, she usually had to be called several times before finally getting up. Then she would either scurry off to school without breakfast or sit down for an unnecessarily prolonged meal. As it got later and later, her mother would hover about, half pleased at the appetite Agnes showed, half irritated that she would again be late to school.

When her parents suggested a movie or a drive, Agnes either refused to accompany them—while also refusing to stay home alone—or found some fault with the plan they proposed. When, on a rare occasion, they said in exasperation, "We're going—you can do as you please," Agnes would retire to her room until it became evident that they would actually leave. Then she would emerge with tear-stained face, holding her head or her side and bewailing a terrible pain and a family without feeling. Finally her parents would give up whatever they had planned and express great concern about her pain. Yet on several such occasions when they consulted a physician, he found nothing wrong.

Mr. Fowler finally realized that other tactics were necessary. "She's not sick," he declared flatly. "We've been told that again and again. I hate to think so, but maybe the school counselor was right after all when he said we ought to see a psychologist about Agnes."

The counselor's concern for Agnes' poor scholastic and social record as well as her obviously poor emotional adjustment had prompted him to suggest to the Fowlers that psychologic help would be desirable. He had told them that the local mental hygiene society could give them names of professional individuals qualified to provide such help. This suggestion had, at the time, brought indignant refusal.

"What will people say?" had been Mrs. Fowler's concern. "My daughter's not crazy!" was Mr. Fowler's angry retort. And they had refused to discuss it further. With no clear notion of what psychologic help involved, Mr. and Mrs. Fowler dreaded it and assured each other that Agnes would out-grow her problem. They tried to forget the warning that an emotional problem is more likely to be grown into than to be out-grown.

Only desperation now drove the Fowlers to follow the school's suggestion.

They felt almost despairingly, that their daughter was afflicted in some strange way for which there might be no help. Thus, they were relieved to learn from the psychologist whom they consulted that Agnes was not behaving in a totally unheard-of manner.

"Growing up is very disturbing to many young people," Dr. Barton said. "Many of them cannot face becoming self-reliant and independent. That may be part of Agnes' trouble. Often we find that the trouble we see in children as they approach adolescence began years back, in their early childhood. Then we must search carefully for the basis of their problems, so that we can give them the help they've needed for a long time. What was Agnes like as a little girl?"

Mrs. Fowler reviewed the early years of Agnes' life, expressing again her dismay that "a good, happy child should get so difficult" and emphasizing the devoted care Agnes had always been given. "I had to work, but she always had the finest care," said Mrs. Fowler. "I wanted her to have everything I had missed when I was a girl—good times, pretty clothes, and a lovely home. I wasn't happy without them, but she isn't happy with them. I can't understand it."

The Fowlers reluctantly agreed to Dr. Barton's suggestion that she see Agnes alone. Mr. Fowler worried, however, that "the child will be upset, all alone here," and Mrs. Fowler protested that she was "so close" to her daughter that her presence would not be undesirable.

Dr. Barton eased their apprehension, and explained that it would be best if Mrs. Fowler came with Agnes to introduce her, and then left. "Let me handle it from there," she said, making a mental note of Mr. Fowler's uneasy concern. And she wondered about the "closeness" Mrs. Fowler had stressed. Was the mother correct in thinking that the situation was difficult now, yet so happy earlier? It was obvious that many answers had to be found, and she cautioned the Fowlers against thinkng that one or two meetings with Agnes would produce these answers.

"And after this first time," advised Dr. Barton, "let her handle her appointments herself. She and I can arrange between us when she'll come in. And don't question her when she gets home. Take time to listen to whatever she may say, but let her tell you spontaneously, not in answer to questions. Leave it up to her. Our visits will be more helpful that way."

It was only after considerable time that Agnes was sure Dr. Barton really accepted her and was genuinely interested in her. As she gradually became less resistant and more able to express her feelings freely, Dr. Barton was able to help Agnes understand the influences of her developing years, tying together situations remembered from early childhood with her teen-age reactions to those situations. It became evident that Agnes had never felt really loved and wanted at home. She had at first been completely in the charge of a housekeeper. She saw her mother mornings to say good-bye before Mrs. Fowler left for the business she and her husband had established. "Be a good girl," Mrs. Fowler would warn. Or, "Be careful! You'll muss my hair!" when the little girl put up her arms for a hug. And in the evenings Agnes recalled her mother's being tired, irritable, impatient of noise, and objecting even to Agnes' eager shout as she heard the key in the front door.

When Agnes was old enough for kindergarten, the housekeeper was dismissed. The childish interpretation which Agnes recalled was that the housekeeper hadn't liked her enough to stay. Agnes was not happy in kindergarten. Nor was she happy at home, although she now had more time and supervision from her mother than before.

"I seem to remember feeling Mother didn't want to be bothered with me," she almost shamefacedly told Dr. Barton one day. "I guess I wasn't a very nice little girl, or my mother would have been more interested."

Early in her school life Agnes had had a severe attack of scarlet fever. A long convalescence followed, which apparently brought an about-face from Mrs. Fowler. Dr. Barton wondered if Mrs. Fowler had suddenly recognized that she had been giving her child only indifferent attention. When Agnes became sick, did she feel guilty for her neglect? Or had she come to sense from the child's reactions that the extra income she brought in by working could not provide everything a child needed to be happy?

Whatever the reason for Mrs. Fowler's changed attitude, Agnes remembered that during her illness her mother became watchful and solicitous, gratifying every whim she expressed. Apparently Mrs. Fowler then gave up her business interests, staying at home most of the time.

Agnes' reaction to her new situation was not unmixed. Pleased though she was, she was also puzzled and a little uncomfortable about interfering with her mother's work, which for so many years had been given prime importance. Wondering how long it would be before her mother returned to the office, and evidently anxious to make the most of the new state of affairs, she became very demanding. She seemed to feel it necessary to keep testing the love which she now heard proclaimed frequently. Her demands became more and more unreasonable, but they were rarely refused.

As time went on, recurring periods of financial stress arose in the Fowler home. Yet the parents continued pampering the child and lavishing unnecessary luxuries on her. Agnes accepted them somewhat uneasily, aware of sacrifices her mother and father were making yet unwilling to give up this tangible evidence of their affection. She felt confused, guilty, and actually deeply unsure of their love for her.

Agnes' attitude toward her mother and father was projected on others. She became convinced that no one really had much use for her. She was anxious and hurt at feeling unwanted, yet her manner was distant and aloof. Rather than risk being rebuffed by others she rebuffed them first. In this way she was unconsciously trying to avoid having her feelings hurt.

Dr. Barton was finally able to show Agnes that she was able to be kind to a stranger because there was no risk of injuring an established relationship. But being pleasant to an acquaintance involved, in Agnes' confused thinking, the chance that her warmth would not be met with equal warmth. Feeling ill at ease with people and fearful of being hurt by them, Agnes had continually built up ideas that they disliked her.

"Your way has been a sort of shield," said Dr. Barton gently. "I don't think you want to be unfriendly, but you're afraid to be anything else because you're afraid someone might not be friendly to you. You used to think your mother was unfriendly when she went to the office. Then later you felt upset when she ignored the office for you. Really, she went to work and left you to earn money to get you nice things. She thought she was being the best mother in the world.

234

But you were too little to understand that. And later she gave up working because she really did love you very much and realized you needed her at home. But you didn't understand that, either. You couldn't, because you were so mixed up in your feelings about her."

It took many discussions such as this to help Agnes understand her feelings. But she came slowly to the conclusion that her unhappiness was not based on real facts, after all. People did not dislike her. She just expected them to. Seeing herself, her parents, her teachers, and her schoolmates in new perspective gave her a different understanding of how people feel toward each other. Gradually she tried more friendliness, more overt responsiveness to others. Slowly her defensive behavior was replaced by a warmer, easier manner.

Mr. and Mrs. Fowler needed to understand Agnes' problem more fully, too. While at first they had said uneasily to each other that Dr. Barton's interpretations were "exaggerated" and even "fantastic," they could not deny the changes in Agnes over a period of time. They saw that her complaints of aches and her sullen antagonism stopped; her provocative disregard of other people's wishes decreased; her responsiveness to others increased. Finally accepting Dr. Barton's explanations of causes and effects, Mr. and Mrs. Fowler began to learn how to readjust their own ways of feeling and behaving toward Agnes. As time passed, family tensions lessened and Agnes, particularly, was more relaxed both at home and at school. As a result, she was able to concentrate more successfully on her schoolwork. She found, almost to her surprise, that more efficient studying gave her higher grades and more peace of mind.

Crisscrossing motives and frustrations, wishes and anxieties, often tangle the lives of parents and children. The threads can be unraveled if the family learns to understand where the tangle started. First, of course, they must accept the idea that help is desirable and that cooperation is necessary. The attitudes of all concerned generally need rechanneling before relationships move smoothly. But if attitudes can be changed, inner relief and satisfaction can usually be expected to replace confusion and discontent after a time. Then outer evidences of inner satisfaction will be increasingly apparent in improved relationships with others and in greater success in daily tasks.

Behavior of disturbed young people can usually be redirected if, without too long a delay, their excessive willfulness, swaggering, contrariness, and seeming unreasonableness are correctly interpreted. These reactions may be evidence not of defiance or rejection of authority but of a need for help.

chapter 15

Almost Adult

Approaching physical maturity

The older adolescent of high-school age is leaving adolescence and moving closer to the adult world. Physical changes are almost complete. Many high-school students have the body of an adult. Few girls increase in height after their sixteenth year, although some boys continue to grow until they are almost twenty. Many high-school boys are fine athletes and girls of the same age are becoming graceful and poised. Their body proportions are stabilizing, and the extreme awkwardness of early adolescence is passing. They no longer have as many physical adjustments to make.

As growth slows down and the symmetry of the body develops, girls come to accept their prettiness, often rather matter-of-factly, and begin to use their attractive appearance as a tool for social success. Girls whose height or weight or general appearance is not in the current style of good looks may continue to be anxious about their appearance, but many older girls are beginning to learn that personality can be more important than mere physical attractiveness. Older boys become proud of their manly appearance and are often more vain than the girls. Some boys, however, continue to worry about their size or build or complexion.

Sometime during high school a boy begins to show the first sign of a beard and will probably need to start shaving once or twice a week. This is an important time for a boy. He is proud of his beard and should not be teased about it. His father may mark the occasion by presenting him with a good razor as recognition of an important event that is bringing them closer together. Unfortunately, many adults don't realize the significance for a boy of the first signs of a beard and treat its appearance with amusement and often ridicule.

Continuing conflict with parents

Adolescence, like other periods of normal growth, involves progress as the needs, problems, and interests of the adolescent grow and change. Those of

236

sixteen-, seventeen-, and eighteen-year-olds, who are almost adults, are quite different from those of young adolescents. High-school students chafe much more than younger adolescents under adult pressures and restrictions that deny them the right to grow up. Older teen-agers feel grown-up, and in many ways are, but the culture still treats them as though they were children. This pressure results in much of the moodiness and continued rebelliousness of the later adolescent years.

In his attempt to achieve adult status, the adolescent sometimes expresses his criticisms of his parents quite frankly and freely. This, like so many other aspects of adolescence, may be hard on his mother and father. He no longer sees them through the eyes of childhood, but now compares them with other parents and other adults. Just as the parent often sees only the problem side of his adolescent son or daughter, so the adolescent may temporarily see only what he feels to be shortcomings of his parents or his home. Perhaps his need to establish his own identity makes it necessary for him to find fault with his home, so that he will feel less guilty about breaking away. During the final years of high school, many boys and girls experience considerable conflict over their very real attachment to their parents and their equally great need to become emotionally independent of them. They may feel anxiety and tension as they rebel against their parents or criticize them.

Too often parents and their older adolescent children come into unnecessary conflict because they lack understanding of each other's point of view. Parents are not always fully aware of their son's or daughter's need to assert his growing sense of independence. If they can allow their child to express his point of view and even his criticisms, within reasonable limits, without being too upset by his outbursts or taking them too personally, the child will usually be able to work his way through to a more adult relationship with them. But if his parents cannot take some measure of his adolescent rebellion without growing angry, punitive, or rejecting, the conflict may increase and lead to a decisive break between parents and child. Parents must guard against losing patience with their older adolescent. It is wiser for them to listen as he tries to work through his confusion and to provide him support, guidance, and steady control when necessary.

Belonging and breaking away

A high-school boy or girl will usually turn to others of his own age for support in his attempts to find himself. In his uneasiness about breaking away from dependence on his parents and childhood patterns of behavior, he seems to feel reassured if he is surrounded by others similar to himself in competence and experience. Those of his own age do not threaten his ability to decide for himself, as adults so frequently do.

Older adolescents show a developing maturity as they offer sympathy to one another and try to help their friends along. They give each other advice, often better accepted than any adult's. Either in pairs or in groups they talk long,

Adolescents are not primarily concerned with winning the approval of their parents or other adults. Their main social goal is to be popular with other adolescents, a goal which takes up a large amount of their time and energy every day.

earnestly, heatedly, and often intelligently about their ideas and interests. They are all absorbed in the same problems of growing up and struggling to be free of adult domination. They are concerned over the same social successes or failures and the same dating problems. They can talk together about their future, their worries about school, and their likes or dislikes of teachers.

During their high-school years many adolescents will have gained enough self-confidence to begin to shake off some of the influence of their group. They will then be able to risk being individuals, making judgments and holding opinions of their own. They will be able to begin following their own interests and choosing people whom they enjoy for friends, rather than being limited to members of their group. The insecure adolescent who never takes this step toward greater independence from his group but continues to need its support may remain permanently in the stage of early adolescence and never become fully capable of thinking or acting for himself.

Some young people, in their efforts to belong, develop feelings of inferiority that make them behave in ways that cause adults to shake their heads. Some develop a man-of-the-world or woman-of-the-world attitude with which they try to impress their friends. In a loud voice, they boast and boss and criticize others, especially the leader of the group. They are sure they could run things better themselves. Or they become smart alecks who try to attract attention by being

Cars are important to teen-agers. Without a car, they have to be chauffeured to school, to sports events, and, most embarrassingly, on dates. For some teen-agers, a car assumes too much importance as a symbol of material and social success.

different, by doing or saying startling things, by clowning or laughing at their own jokes. Some teen-agers are afraid to express their own opinions at all and generally just parrot someone they admire. Others don't seem able to fit into the group pattern, or don't want to. They withdraw too deeply into their books or hobbies or lose themselves in daydreams.

Channels of social development

Two channels of social development are involved in the adolescent's need to find himself in his group. One is his continuing relationship with those of his own sex, and the other is his newly developing relationship with those of the opposite sex. Although we usually think of adolescence as the years of developing relationships between the sexes, we must not overlook the fact that friends of the same sex are still very important. Boys in particular continue to feel great loyalty to their group. Often a boy of this age transfers his allegiance from the gang to the basketball team, the football team, or the baseball team. But where teams or other organized groups do not exist, gangs often continue to fill a boy's need for close companionship with a group of his own sex. Without purposeful activity, these gangs may develop serious delinquent tendencies during the senior-high-school years.

Even though teen-agers are increasingly drawn toward members of the opposite sex, their closest and most intimate friendships continue to be with members of the same sex, even during the later years of adolescence. A girl tends to choose a personal friend as a confidant within her larger group of girl friends. Although

she continues to be part of a group of girls throughout high school, she no longer finds the group all-absorbing. She will readily turn down an activity with the girls for a date, and the other girls will accept her action as a matter of course. For boys of this age, on the other hand, the group still usually comes first. Boys may have close personal friends, but the gang or the team often remains more important to them. A group of boys, furthermore, will continue to consider a member disloyal if he misses a club or team activity to take his girl out. A boy may even stand his date up if some plan of his group demands it. Despite the great loyalty among friends, youngsters of this age may criticize each other a good deal and even have serious disagreements and quarrels.

The high-school student is concerned about going steady, which may now mean much more than "I have someone to go to the next party with," as it did to the younger adolescent. High-school students sometimes think seriously about marriage—and an increasing number of them do marry, if not during their last years of school, then just as soon as school is over.

The parental role

Many parents worry about their adolescent son or daughter and tend to become overrestrictive, thus making it more difficult for the young person to become responsible and independent. One reason for their fear is the realization that the mistakes of adolescence, unlike most mistakes of childhood, may affect their child's entire adult life. The couple who marry before they have finished school, the boy who fritters away his time in high school and is then unable to enter college or get the job he wants, the girl who bears an illegitimate child, the youngster who chooses the wrong group of friends and gets drawn into activities that border on delinquency—all of these naturally cause parents grave concern.

The parental role with sixteen-, seventeen-, and eighteen-year-olds will become one of counselor. These teen-agers look, act, and feel grown-up, yet their judgment is not always so mature as their appearance would suggest, or as they think it is. They are seldom easy to guide and they may make serious mistakes, despite the best efforts of parents, teachers, or counselors. If mistakes are made, the role of the adult is to help the young person face his errors and work his way through them toward greater emotional maturity. As one seventeen-year-old said, "It's not the trouble you get into, but the way you're helped to come through it that's so important."

What many adults do not see is that underneath manifestations of adolescent rebellion is the teen-ager's need to make decisions and to take more responsibility for himself. This should be permitted and encouraged whenever the possible consequences of a mistake in judgment are not too serious. But with the greater freedom accorded him, the older teen-ager must also be expected to shoulder more personal responsibility for his decisions and his actions. It is important that he become fully aware of this change in his status, and that he fully realize that he will be held responsible in his own home as well as in the adult world. But because the older adolescent looks so mature, adults frequently find it hard to remain patient and to accept his mistakes. They forget that he is not yet an adult. His sprawling awkwardness, his morose and defiant moods, and his daydreaming often leave his parents and teachers bewildered and baffled.

Pressures and responsibilities

Although adolescents often seem noisy, rude, inconsiderate, and difficult, they also have another side. Many are in earnest about developing their abilities and hobbies. They may also have an intelligent interest in world affairs. Often they are anxious about their futures, wondering and planning and daydreaming about what they are going to do with their lives. They have realistic choices and decisions to make between an immediate job or further training in a trade school or college. They are faced with questions of earning money and becoming self-supporting. Even in high school, most boys are up against the problem of having enough money for dates or for running a car. In fact, this has become one of the major distractions that may keep a boy from concentrating on his academic work. Most boys are also concerned about their future. Will jobs be available? Will they have to spend time in military service? Will there be war? Can they plan a future? Those who have decided to go to college are faced with the pressures of getting into college when the competition for places is becoming increasingly keen. Others who are less talented or less interested academically face the problem of continually falling behind or failing in their work. If they try to solve this problem by dropping out of school, they run into the even more serious problem of trying to make their way in an adult world that has no real place for them.

Often adolescents who seem to lose interest in their schoolwork and do poorly because it has no meaning for them show surprising alertness and ability when they take courses relating to their own interests. They often respond, for example, to vocational courses or courses in which they can have an opportunity to talk about things that are happening among young people or about social or political problems. Even students so disinterested in school that they have truanted regularly may respond to a half-day-school and half-day-work project in which their studies are related to their job. They may settle down and accept responsibility as they have never done before.

Adolescents who seem disinterested in school usually respond, too, to opportunities for assuming responsibility that has meaning for them. They will work hard if they are allowed to plan some of their own activities, help develop their own programs, make their own decisions, and carry them out. They will often do a capable job in school councils and committees, in club activities, and even in community affairs if they are made to feel that they are needed and wanted. Adolescents need a motive and a purpose in their work. If these are present, they frequently do a better job than many adults would believe possible.

Adolescents sometimes get into trouble because adults have not met them halfway in giving them opportunities to be mature. Studies have shown that most adolescents would prefer a real job after school, on Saturdays, or during the summer to demanding extracurricular activities. But though high-school students want to work, even summer jobs are not readily available to them. We must do what we can to encourage the growing young person at each point where he is willing and able to take responsibility. The adolescent, like the little child, should not be pushed too rapidly, but if responsibility is not offered to him as he shows readiness for it, he may remain immature and continue to play the part of a child, irresponsible and self-centered.

In learning to be responsible, the adolescent will react better to guidance than to domination. He will need many opportunities to talk things over, for he is often confused. Comments from members of his family, his teacher, or his activity sponsors often help him to gain perspective and to sort out his thoughts. He needs adults in the background to guide and encourage him without condemning his failures, to give him the feeling that they trust him to act on his own but are still ready to give help when he needs it. He likes to discuss ideas with older people who will listen to what he is trying to say and help him think things through. He will seek out those adults who take him seriously.

The adolescent's desire to be treated as an adult may serve as a cue for wise parents and teachers—although it is a cue that is frequently hard for them to follow, for today the high-school youngster may act like an adult and tomorrow return to childish, irresponsible behavior. Growth in the adolescent, as in the child, does not proceed equally at all times and in all areas. The adolescent is

often still emotionally immature—"a full-grown body entrusted to an inexperienced mind." All this helps make adolescence a difficult period for both young people and adults. It is a challenge to adults not only to help the adolescent but to *permit* him to achieve maturity and become part of the adult world.

living with an adolescent

Family Troubles

Parents, too, must accept reality—
and maturity

Some parents, concerned about undesirable personality characteristics in their children, hopefully expect that as the children mature they will grow out of these ways. Other parents, pleased with the development their youngsters are showing, complacently assume that the fine attitudes and behavior will continue. Both hopes may go awry: children may grow further into rather than out of unacceptable ways, and the acceptable responses of childhood may not continue if circumstances change so that they are turned in another direction.

When Lynn Rogers was a baby, her mother called her "my big girl" and took pride in her rapid gains in height and weight. During Lynn's first school days, her mother felt deep satisfaction in seeing her child stand first in line—the tallest, best coordinated, and sturdiest in the group. Mrs. Rogers' maternal satisfaction was reflected in her attitude toward the child. Sensing this approval, Lynn developed healthy feelings of adequacy and competence which were definite assets to her. She played well with other children but was not dependent on them. She fell in cheerfully with her mother's proposals for activity but also had her own ideas and desires.

Mrs. Rogers took credit for this happy situation. She had taken motherhood seriously and tried to keep abreast of current recommendations on child-rearing. She liked hearing herself referred to as "a wonderful mother" and delighted in feeling that she was free of parent-child problems.

But one day, after her daughter had entered high school, Mrs. Rogers overheard a remark that made her vaguely ill at ease. "That big girl *hers?*" the question floated to her over the heads of the audience watching a school play. "Why, she must be sixteen! I didn't think . . ." The speaker's head was turned away, and the rest of the comment was inaudible.

Mrs. Rogers eyed Lynn with a new kind of awareness. Lynn was fourteen, not sixteen. She did give the impression of being older than she actually was because she was well developed physically and she had enviable poise for her age.

"If people think she's sixteen now," mused Mrs. Rogers, "what will they think in another year? And that will make *me* seem . . . Goodness, how old will they think *I* am?"

Without realizing it, Mrs. Rogers changed subtly in her behavior toward Lynn. One evening she said to her husband, "Our date's off for tonight. The Kanes can't come—no sitter."

"Why don't we go over there?" suggested Mr. Rogers. But Mrs. Rogers objected to leaving Lynn alone.

"It's just down the block," urged Mr. Rogers.

"I don't mind, Mother," Lynn said. "I have lots of homework. There's plenty to do. You go ahead."

But, to Lynn's surprise, Mrs. Rogers could not be persuaded. It did not occur to Lynn that her mother preferred to think of her as too young to stay alone.

Some time afterwards, the Rogers arranged for a Saturday luncheon in town with some friends who were stopping briefly between trains. Mrs. Rogers left everything prepared for Lynn's lunch and gave her minute instructions.

"We'll be back by three, and I've left the telephone number of the restaurant in case you need us."

"Oh, Mother, for goodness' sake," Lynn protested. "Why should I need you? I can get my lunch, and I have homework and a new library book. I'll be all right."

But at the luncheon Mrs. Rogers seemed distracted. She hurriedly ate her meal and finally said, "We're terribly sorry we can't wait until your train leaves. But Lynn's all alone."

"Lynn's fifteen now, isn't she?" the friend commented.

"Not for another two months," stressed Mrs. Rogers. "I don't like the idea of our little girl home alone."

"Our Jeannie is about Lynn's age, and she baby-sits," was the casual reply.

Several months later Lynn was invited to a dance for which she was to have a new dress. When her mother found a shopping trip impossible, Lynn said eagerly, "Let me go alone. I know what I want and you let me choose most of my own dresses anyway!" Somewhat reluctantly her mother agreed, naming the salesperson to see and the price limit.

That evening Lynn proudly showed her purchase. "Isn't it *darling*?" she exclaimed.

Mrs. Rogers eyed the dress critically. "The color's not right for you, dear," she said, then added decidedly, "and the style is much too sophisticated. And Lynn, you have too much lipstick on. Wipe it off, dear."

"Daddy," appealed Lynn, "don't you think it's mean of Mother to say that? It's a beautiful dress and just the kind the other girls are getting."

"Their mothers will have to decide about them," Mrs. Rogers said quickly, before her husband could reply. "We'll find something more appropriate in time for the party. This isn't at all right for a little girl."

"I'm not a little girl!" snorted Lynn. "I'm in high school. And it's not a party, it's a dance. Oh, Mother. . . . Daddy. . . ."

"Don't whine, Lynn," interposed her father. "You know your mother knows more about these things than I do."

Lynn went upstairs dejectedly. In her room she pirouetted before the mirror. "What's the matter with Mother?" she muttered. "I don't see what's got into her. She objects to everything lately. It's a beautiful dress, and it would be perfect for the dance." But Lynn took off the dress and reluctantly replaced it in its box. On few occasions had she felt angry or rebellious when doing as her mother directed. But now anger overwhelmed her. She was puzzled at her own feelings and disconsolate at her mother's attitude.

Downstairs Mrs. Rogers was answering her husband's somewhat amused question. "No, indeed, it's *not* all right," she said, more sharply than usual. "The child looks like a——a senior in that dress. Why, she's just started high school. She has lots of time to dress like that."

"She's a sophomore," said Mr. Rogers mildly, "and this dance seems pretty important to her."

"Of course it is," Mrs. Rogers agreed promptly. "And I want her to look just right. She just hasn't the judgment to select clothes yet. After all, she's only fourteen. I never should have let her shop alone."

"Her birthday's not far off," Mr. Rogers reminded her. "You know, Lynn's going to be a young lady soon, and we might as well realize it. She's practically fifteen."

But some months later Mr. Rogers was no more ready than his wife to accept Lynn's being a "young lady." Late one afternoon Mr. Rogers answered the bell and found a tall boy at the door.

"I'm Chuck Johnson," he said. "Is Lynn ready? She said she'd go for a ride with me. It's my last day before I go back to school." He nodded toward a car at the curb.

Before calling Lynn, Mr. Rogers spoke to his wife. "Chuck Johnson's home from school. Says Lynn's going for a ride with him. What does she mean, going out for a ride with a boy who's so much older than she is? I won't have it!"

Mrs. Rogers was moved by two feelings simultaneously: how nice that Lynn was attractive and sought after, and how discomfiting that her girl was so mature that she was going out with a senior, almost a college student. "It dates me," she thought ruefully.

The smooth, pleasant days that the Rogers had been accustomed to now became increasingly disrupted. Lynn was argumentative. She sulked and accused her parents of not understanding her. "You treat me like a baby," she objected more than once. A sullen, forced politeness replaced her natural courtesy. Over the months a succession of incidents brought tears and objections from Lynn and distress and irritation to her parents.

One evening when Lynn was out, Mr. Rogers looked at his watch, peered out of the window, even opened the door to look down the street. "It's late," he said to his wife. "Think we should call and find out when she left the party? She ought to be home by now." After worrying a while longer, they telephoned Lynn's hostess and became even more worried when she told them that the party had been over for an hour.

"She'll probably be coming along soon," the hostess said comfortingly—and a little amusedly, too, Mrs. Rogers felt. "They've probably stopped for another coke, to talk over the evening."

Somewhat disconcerted at the tone, Mrs. Rogers became increasingly provoked and upset. When she finally heard Lynn's laugh at the front steps, she promptly took her to task for being so late.

"You've spoiled the whole evening!" Lynn cried.

"You know when you're supposed to be home," Mrs. Rogers answered. Then, attempting to soothe her daughter, she added, "When you're older it will be different."

Lynn stormed impatiently, "I'm as old as the rest of the kids at the party. They didn't have to be home this early. You're trying to keep me a *child!*"

Disagreements between Lynn and her parents increased. Why did she have to account for every minute? Why couldn't she choose her own clothes? What was the matter with her make-up—all the girls used that much. And she liked her hair that way—couldn't she even pick her own hair style! Why shouldn't she go out with Chuck even if he was eighteen? She'd be eighteen, too, in a couple of years. And so it went. The whole family was tense and unhappy.

An unusually tempestuous outbreak came some time later when Mrs. Rogers asked Lynn if she had replied to an invitation received a few days before. Lynn could not accept but had not yet said so.

"You'd better call right away. Thank Alice and tell her how sorry you are," directed Mrs. Rogers. "And be sure to ask about her mother—she's been ill. Tell her you hope you can get together soon. You don't want her to misunderstand. Remember, you had to refuse her last invitation, so say . . ."

"Oh, Mother!" Lynn interrupted crossly. "Can't I even *talk* without having you outline every last little thing I should say?"

Mrs. Rogers was annoyed and hurt and worried. Was this her child talking? She wondered if Lynn was showing the same kind of behavior at school—if she was rude, or always insisted on her own way, or was defiant.

Mrs. Rogers arranged to talk things over with Miss Young, the school counselor, hoping for help in handling Lynn's new reactions. "My little girl is worrying me," she began, and recited the story of the past months.

"I wonder, Mrs. Rogers," suggested Miss Young when she had heard the story, "if the chief difficulty isn't that your little girl is a *big* girl, and you haven't realized it. You're making it very hard for her to continue the fine, independent behavior you've always encouraged. She's able to take over more and more responsibility now, but you don't seem able to let her."

In quick protest Mrs. Rogers said, "But she's so very young!"

"Not really," Miss Young replied. "She's fifteen now, you reminded me. She's making a completely natural and normal struggle for a kind of emancipation. You'll find the atmosphere around home will be much more agreeable for all three of you if you can loosen your hold a bit."

"I'm not sure I know what you mean," began Mrs. Rogers. But almost as soon as the words were out she added, "Oh, I guess I do, really. But you're rushing things so. Isn't she still a child? Does she really have the judgment to make decisions for herself? How can I be sure?"

"It takes a lot of faith when they're this age," Miss Young admitted. "But here at school we've had no report of Lynn's rebelling or being discontented with regulations. Basically I think Lynn's doing all right, considering all the demands that maturing makes on a youngster. Most of all, right now, she needs the emotional security that can come from her friends. She has to feel that she's one of them, and she has to feel liked by them. Otherwise she's going to be uncertain and miserable."

"Lynn's very well liked," Mrs. Rogers said defensively. "She has lots of friends."

"But she'll still be uncertain and miserable if she feels that you and her father disapprove of everything she and they want to do. She deeply needs to feel that you both have confidence in her—all the more since her own confidence in herself is a little shaky right now. She's reaching toward adulthood, and she'll probably make some blunders. But she needs to be free to make mistakes in order to learn not to."

Mrs. Rogers sighed. "What shall we do?" she asked helplessly.

"Accept the passing of the years," was Miss Young's frank response. "Accept the changes they bring. Let me talk to Lynn about some of these things. You know, teen-agers can generally talk more freely to someone outside the family. They don't want to hurt or anger their parents—their parents' disapproval is a threat to them; it frightens them. So they keep some things back from you, and often deny their thoughts even to themselves.

"But honestly, Mrs. Rogers, I don't believe Lynn's problems are as great as you imagine. After I've seen Lynn, come back and let's talk more specifically. I might have some suggestions for changes at home. I've talked only in general terms today because each family situation is different, but there will be some suggestions specifically right for your family."

Many parents find it difficult to accept their children's inevitable growing up. Some are loath to relinquish the pleasures of lovably dependent youngsters. Some sense for the first time, in seeing their children's new maturity, that they themselves are no longer young. They find that being the parents of a young adult calls for a new picture of themselves. And they dread the adjustment this involves.

Normal living is dynamic. Nothing about it remains the same very long. Parents often need help in adjusting to life's continued advance, just as young people often require help in adjusting to its continued and changing demands. A first essential at any age is to accept reality. Accepting the changes it brings then becomes less difficult.

study of an adolescent

Should Alec Go to College?

Wise planning takes study and cooperation
between home and school

It is relatively simple to point to a youngster who is rebellious, one who is unsocial, or one who is failing in school as probably having an underlying emotional problem which requires attention. Not so apparent is the student who is disturbed by uncertainty about his future even while he manages to carry on fairly successfully with each day's activities in and out of school.

School was well under way in the fall of his senior year when Alec Schwarz sought out the school counselor and hesitantly revealed his troubled state of mind. Always a good student, he expected to meet high-school graduation requirements in February, a term ahead of his class, since he had gone to summer school one year and had carried an extra subject during several previous semesters. But Alec had been expecting to remain in school during the spring term in order to complete college entrance requirements in certain subjects. He had been surprised when his father had begun to argue against that plan.

"Dad wants me to go into business with him," Alec said to Mr. Daniels. "He says he's been keeping the shop just for me. And in another few years, if I start in pretty soon, he can take things easy. I know he's worked hard. And he's a great guy as far as I'm concerned. But I just don't like the shop. I don't want to go into that business. It makes me feel terrible to say so," he added unhappily.

"What do you want to do?" was the counselor's natural question.

"I don't exactly know. That's one of the troubles. My dad says if I had a clear idea of what I wanted to prepare for in college, he might see the point of my going. But since I don't definitely know, he thinks it would be four years of just marking time, taking courses, and then not having a thing to earn a living with."

"You're a good student," said Mr. Daniels. "You've said you like science best of your subjects. There are a great many possibilities for earning a living as a scientist," he added with a smile, "and you might do a little more definite thinking about them. For example, geology, chemistry, physics, biology, agronomy, are all possibilities within the scientific field. And of course there are many fields other than the scientific which might prove interesting if you knew more about them. If you like, we can use some vocational tests, which often throw a great deal of light on problems like yours."

"Can I take them right now?" urged Alec eagerly. "Maybe I can tell Dad the results tonight and get it all settled."

"No, because it takes considerable time to give, and score, and evaluate the tests. And tests don't work magic, you know," Mr. Daniels cautioned. "They can be very helpful, but they are only one part of sensible planning. We can't expect all the answers from them—or, in fact, any answers at all in a minute."

The following day Alec's father, informed of his son's conversation with Mr. Daniels, telephoned the counselor. "Alec has a fine opportunity to walk into an established and successful business," he said. "It will assure his future, so college really doesn't seem necessary." Mr. Daniels suggested that Mr. Schwarz come to school to talk matters over, since it was too important a matter to settle hurriedly over the telephone.

"I'm leaving on a business trip tomorrow," replied Mr. Schwarz. "That's why I'm phoning you. I'll be gone for almost three weeks, but I'll call you when I get back. In the meantime, talk that boy of mine out of wasting time at college," he suggested genially. "I never went to college, and I'm doing pretty well for my family."

250

The three weeks gave the school an opportunity to administer a battery of tests to Alec. "We already know your potential for college work from the scholastic aptitude test you took last spring," said Mr. Daniels. "We'll go on from there."

"I never was sure what the results of that meant," said Alec. "How could that sort of thing tell you about what I'll do in college—if I get there!" He was politely skeptical.

"That scholastic aptitude test," explained Mr. Daniels, "is given in high schools throughout the United States. The results give us a measure of your potential as a college student, in comparison with that of students from schools all over the country. Thousands of records have been gathered, so we know how well a student should do on this type of test if he is to have much chance of doing well in college. Of course, a good score doesn't say you *will* do well. Test results just indicate the possibilities. What happens depends on you. It's important to know if college training is a wise plan. And it's also important to know what to emphasize in college, what courses are appropriate for a particular student, what he's interested in. So tomorrow we'll check your interests."

The next day, explaining the interest inventories to Alec, Mr. Daniels said, "No right or wrong answers to these. And no exact time limits. This approach isn't to tell us what you know or what you can do, but *what you prefer doing* from among several possibilities."

"That ought to do it," Alec said later, confidently giving Mr. Daniels the completed inventories. "Now you have all the answers about me."

"Think so?" asked Mr. Daniels mildly, holding up another folder. "This one," he said, "does have right and wrong answers. We'll see what you make of it tomorrow." It was a test of mechanical aptitude and it was followed by a test of mechanical comprehension.

"It's not just what you know," explained Mr. Daniels. "We want to find out the sort of thing you might have a special aptitude for—the sort of study you are likely to learn most easily and quickly and enjoy most. It's possible to investigate several aptitudes—science, art, accounting, perhaps salesmanship, and others, too. Then, later, we'll think about the results in terms of your personality, because we sometimes find that what seems a good idea for a particular student in terms of his ability to learn isn't appropriate in terms of the kind of person he is. Some people are good at work that requires great attention to detail. Others aren't. Some people feel happier if they do about the same sort of thing day after day. Others prefer varied activity. A laboratory research worker doesn't generally have the same interest in people and skill in personal relationships as a practicing physician, for example. Yet they both must have an interest in scientific matters, and they both need a certain level of general intelligence. A salesman and a teacher both should like to work with people, but not every teacher would make a good salesman, nor would all salesmen be able to do a good job in a classroom. Personality characteristics are an important phase of this kind of investigation."

In spite of his impatience and his early skepticism, Alec began to see the value of the many different approaches.

"They're all interesting," he observed, when Mr. Daniels finally decided enough information was at hand to form a basis for intelligent planning. "And I can see there are different ways of helping find out about a person. But suppose," he said thoughtfully, "suppose someone seems cut out for a job his folks can't swing—like being a doctor, with so many years of studying, and then interning, and then a residency. He doesn't earn much all that time, does he? So for a long time when he can't make a living, he needs help from his family. What about that?"

"Good point," said Mr. Daniels. "Counseling has to be practical and realistic to be worthwhile. Sometimes for economic reasons what seems an excellent plan simply can't be worked out. The family has to be consulted, of course. But money isn't the only thing to think about. Health and age and sometimes a particular handicap, like poor eyesight or a crippled condition, might rule out a first choice entirely. But fortunately, particular combinations of ability and interests and aptitudes and personality characteristics are usually appropriate to several different kinds of work. For instance, a student might find he liked mathematics and science and disliked English composition and literature courses. He might think this meant he was cut out to be a great success as an engineer. But those special likes and dislikes could apply in some ways just as well to chemists and mathematicians and physicists and architects.

"It's wise to know what to rule out as well as what to rule in. So we shouldn't skip anything that might be helpful to know. That's why our investigations have to be so broad. That's why we need to study your interests and personality characteristics as well as your general and scholastic ability and your special aptitudes. Then all those facts about you have to be balanced with whatever limitations there may be, like your health or funds or family obligations."

"I suppose it was sort of silly to think everything could be found out in an hour or so," acknowledged Alec. "I didn't know there were so many different kinds of tests."

When the various test results were analyzed, it became apparent that Alec could certainly profit from further schooling; indeed, it would be a waste of talent if he didn't go on with his studies. His general intelligence and scholastic ability were superior. Success in college and graduate study was almost certain, provided he applied himself to the work involved and did not allow distractions to interfere too much. His interests were widespread; there was no single area in which a significantly high indication appeared, but several were significant in some degree. That is often the case when the individual being studied is in his early teens and has had limited experiences. He doesn't really know about enough possible activities to pinpoint a specific area of interest. Frequently he is only vaguely aware even of his own father's business life.

Mr. Daniels finally discussed the whole situation with Alec's father. "Let's consider your son as a person," suggested Mr. Daniels. "What you want in the long run is for him to be happy and contented in life. Happiness, of course, is complex and it doesn't always routinely follow financial success, as we all realize. Alec is a healthy boy with a good mind. He likes to study, and he has been successful in his studies in every field. He gets along well with people, too. You've had few worries about him. But Alec wants something now that you question seriously. He wants to go to college—and that takes time and money.

And because he isn't entirely certain just what he wants to do when he finishes a college course, it seems to you very impractical."

"Yes," interrupted Mr. Schwarz. "You're right. He doesn't know. He's just a boy. Let him start in the business—he's got the brains, and he knows how to get along with people—and I guarantee I can make him a success in business. He doesn't need college. I didn't go to college."

"I agree college isn't necessarily the best plan for everyone. But I think it is for Alec," replied Mr. Daniels. "And let's not lose sight of the fact that a college education provides a great deal more than a way of earning a living. It helps many people to a better way of life, so that they lead especially productive and happy lives. And more and more often, as you know, top jobs are open only to college graduates. Alec should have an educational background at least as complete as the people he might employ in years to come.

"Of course, we all know some college graduates who don't seem either especially successful or especially happy, but that doesn't prove college training is of no value. If a capable boy can have the advantage of college, it would be too bad to deprive him of it. Particularly when, like Alec, he is eager to go.

"You've told me you made a success starting from scratch," added Mr. Daniels. "But remember that you did what *you* wanted to do."

"Yes, and now I want Alec to be a success, too," said Mr. Schwarz, missing the point in his eagerness to convince Mr. Daniels.

"We're agreed on that," answered the counselor. "But he must make his own success. At least he should be allowed to try. It's true he doesn't yet know exactly what he wants to do as his life work. You say he can be told. That's where we don't agree, because I feel an intelligent boy—and Alec is very intelligent—should have a chance to find out for himself.

"Bright as he is, though, Alec is still young. He has very little idea of what working and earning really mean; he's had almost no work experience. So when he says now that he doesn't like the idea of going into the business you've built up, I believe that's partly because he feels he's being forced. Kindly and 'for his own good' as you say. Still, if he went into your shop now, he would feel it was *your* decision, not his. That could have unfortunate results. Even now he's restless and disturbed at the prospect, yet he hates to disappoint you, and he's pretty miserable about it all.

"Feeling upset isn't a help to success in whatever you do. Even if Alec is allowed to follow his own inclinations, he'll certainly be unhappy if he thinks you feel he's being foolish or disobedient. Or if he follows your plan under pressure from you, he might start out being resentful at not having chosen his work independently. Feelings influence quality of work and often interfere with progress at work, in school, or on a job. That's particularly true of teen-agers who are pulled in two directions at the same time, wanting to please their parents but needing to sense a certain independence.

"Why not give Alec a chance to mature a little more? Let him go on and graduate here in June with his high-school class. Then even one year at college would benefit him. After all, the more a person knows, the better advantage he can take of any opportunity. Decide after a year whether his continuing in college seems wise."

"I'll think it over," Mr. Schwarz finally agreed. "If I'd had such a business opportunity when I was sixteen, I'd have grabbed it. But as you say, we're all different. Well, if I let him start college next fall, maybe in a year he'll come to his senses. Or maybe," and Mr. Schwarz smiled broadly with a hint of less rigid conviction, "maybe I'll come to mine!"

Sometimes a boy or girl feels guilty about his feelings when they are not in accord with his parents' plans. He may be reluctant to express his feelings—being confused at feeling rebellious yet not knowing how to get help in working out his problem. The boy or girl is fortunate whose school can provide the needed help, but generally that help requires cooperation from the home. The school can often be the mediating agency between children and parents, partly because discussion between teachers and parents is less emotionally tinged than that between children and parents. It can be more rational and logical for that reason.

Parents need to be willing to listen, to recognize the possibility that their ideas may be less wise and desirable than they had thought. Being careful to avoid undue pressure, they can continue to guide their children in terms of the children's potentialities and individualities. By respecting the individuality of each child—recognizing abilities and aptitudes, interest patterns and personal characteristics—home and school together can help young people toward happy and successful living.

Adolescence

FOR THOUGHT AND DISCUSSION

1.   Is our cultural pattern an important cause of many adolescent anxieties? If so, describe a few of the aspects of our cultural pattern that could cause such anxieties.

2.   Describe the kinds of groups that adolescent boys and girls form. How do the attitudes and loyalties within groups formed by girls differ from those within groups formed by boys? Can you give reasons for such differences?

3.   Observe the boys in an eighth-grade class and note the range in their sizes and in the pitch of their voices. Does the range of growth seem to be greater among the boys than among the girls?

4.   Observe a group of adolescent boys in physical education group activities and comment on the following questions:
a.   Who is the group's leader?
b.   In what ways does he function as a leader?
c.   Describe the boy you have chosen as the leader and try to explain what gives him his status.
d.   How do the members of the group respond to him?
e.   Do the members of the group imitate him in any way? If so, how?
f.   Are there any boys who do not seem to be a part of the group? If so, are there any apparent reasons?

5.   What are some of the services and activities that the public schools provide to help deal with adolescents' problems?

6.   Compare the early life of Agnes, in "Agnes and Her Parents," with the forms of childhood growth generally recommended in earlier sections of *These Are Your Children*. Does her early childhood differ in any way from the forms of childhood growth recommended? If so, how has it affected her? Why did her problem seem to become more severe as she entered adolescence?

7.   Compare the origins of Agnes' problems with the origins of Lynn's problems in the case story, "Family Troubles." Is there an important difference? Discuss this.

8.   What are the general conflicting attitudes between parents and children that cause problems of growing up throughout adolescence?

FOR FURTHER READING

BANDURA, ALBERT, and WALTER, RICHARD H. *Adolescent Aggression*. New York: The Ronald Press Company, 1957. A research study which identifies the child-training factors and the family relationships that lead to the development of antisocial, aggressive behavior in adolescent boys.

BLAINE, GRAHAM B., JR., M.D. *Patience and Fortitude: The Parent's Guide to Adolescence*. Boston: Little, Brown and Company, 1962. Discusses the problems of young people in their relations with and attitudes toward family, high school, college, society, and sex. Also discusses some solutions to these problems. Based on Dr. Blaine's experience on the counseling staff of Harvard. Valuable for teachers as well as parents.

BLOS, PETER. *On Adolescence*. New York: Free Press of Glencoe, Inc., 1962. A psychoanalytic interpretation of the adolescent period.

CAVAN, RUTH SHONIE, ed. *Readings in Juvenile Delinquency*. Philadelphia: J. B. Lippincott Co., 1964. A competent, current selection of readings.

COHEN, ALBERT K. *Delinquent Boys: The Culture of the Gang*. New York: Free Press of Glencoe, Inc., 1955. Discusses the frustrations of the working-class child as he finds himself ill-equipped to meet the pressure of middle-class standards.

COLEMAN, JAMES S. *The Adolescent Society*. New York: Free Press of Glencoe, Inc., 1961. A study of ten high-school social systems, exploring the impact of the teen-ager's social life on education.

CONANT, JAMES B. *Slums and Suburbs*. New York: McGraw-Hill Book Company, 1961. Also a Signet book, 1964. A report on the differences between opportunities for children in slum schools and in white, suburban schools.

ERIKSON, ERIK H. *Identity and the Life Cycle*. New York: International University Press, 1959. Selected papers on the adolescent's search for identity.

FRIEDENBERG, EDGAR Z. *The Vanishing Adolescent*. New York: Dell Publishing Co., Inc., 1962. A challenging, original approach to the problems of adolescence.

GALLAGHER, J. ROSWELL, M.D., and HARRIS, HERBERT I., M.D. *Emotional Problems of Adolescents*. New York: Oxford University Press, Inc., 1958. Explores the basis of emotional difficulties and ways in which the adolescent can be helped toward sound emotional development.

GRINDER, ROBERT E., ed. *Studies in Adolescence*. New York: The Macmillan Company, 1963. Well-selected, current readings.

HECHINGER, GRACE, and HECHINGER, FRED M. *Teen-Age Tyranny*. New York: Fawcett World Library (Crest), 1964. A thoughtful discussion of the teen-age culture and its effect on teen-agers, their parents, and the culture of the entire country.

HORROCKS, JOHN E. *The Psychology of Adolescent Behavior and Development*. Boston: Houghton Mifflin Company, 1962. Well supported with research and references.

JOHNSON, ERIC W. *How to Live Through Junior High School*. Philadelphia: J. B. Lippincott Co., 1959. Based on answers to questionnaires sent to several hundred seventh through eleventh graders. Includes practical suggestions.

LICHTER, SOLOMON O., and others. *The Drop-Outs*. New York: Free Press of Glencoe, Inc., 1962. A study of intellectually capable students who drop out of high school.

MARTIN, JOHN M., and FITZPATRICK, JOSEPH P. *Delinquent Behavior: A Redefinition of the Problem*. New York: Random House, Inc., 1964. A valuable study of the theories of delinquency.

McCANDLESS, BOYD ROYDEN. *Children and Adolescents*. New York: Holt, Rinehart & Winston, Inc., 1961. Brings together many references to research on the behavior and development of children and adolescents.

PECK, ROBERT F. and others. *The Psychology of Character Development*. New York: John Wiley & Sons, Inc., 1960. Results of a sixteen-year study on the motivation patterns in children's moral behavior.

PENTY, RUTH C. *Reading Ability and High School Drop-Outs*. New York: Teachers College Press, 1956. A study of dropouts, with recommendations for a more adequate program in developing reading skills. Also reviews some of the research in the field.

REMMERS, H. H., and RADLER, D. H. *The American Teenager*. Indianapolis: The Bobbs-Merrill Co., Inc., 1957. Results of a Purdue University poll of 15,000 teenagers.

SCHREIBER, DANIEL, ed. *The School Dropout*. Washington, D.C.: National Education Assn., 1964. A report of the symposium, *Project: School Dropouts*. Contains considerable information and some challenging articles.

SEIDMAN, J. ed. *The Adolescent: A Book of Readings*. Rev. ed. New York: Holt, Rinehart & Winston, 1960. A competent selection of 72 articles on adolescence.

STONE, J. JOSEPH, and CHURCH, JOSEPH. *Childhood and Adolescence*. New York: Random House, Inc., 1957. Contains an outstanding chapter on the meaning of maturity.

STRANG, RUTH. *The Adolescent Views Himself*. New York: McGraw Hill Book Company, 1957. Gives the adolescent's own point of view.

TUTTLE, HAROLD SAXE. *So Discipline Baffles You?* New York: Exposition Press, 1963. A series of case studies concerning junior and senior high school discipline problems, with methods used in handling them.

WILSON, EUGENE, and BUCHER, CHARLES. *College Ahead! A Guide for High School Students and Their Parents*. Rev. ed. New York: Harcourt, Brace & World, Inc., 1961. A realistic book with emphasis on considering the student's interests and needs before deciding whether he should attend college or which college he should attend.

Home, School, Community Work Together

Although parents have the first responsibility for providing an environment suitable for the healthy development of their children, we cannot leave this to the parents alone. Many fathers and mothers carry their responsibility well. Others, however, are inadequate, and their children must not be deprived of their right to grow and develop as fully as possible. It is the responsibility of the community to see that no child shall be denied an opportunity for healthy growth.

Children are a part of their community. They cannot be isolated from the life around them. It is all the adults of the community, not only individual parents, who set the standards that influence children's developing concepts concerning education, religion, ethical values, and citizenship. Children will learn the prejudices of the adults in their community, will copy the example that is generally set before them—even when parents would wish it otherwise. If there are slums, inadequate schools, low salaries for teachers, lack of support for law enforcement, or indifference to religion and moral order—it is *all* the children who suffer, not just those whose lives are intimately touched by the specific problems.

Therefore it is the task of the citizens in a community to see that no child goes hungry or lacks adequate shelter or clothing; that areas are set aside for wholesome, health-producing play activities; that there is a seat for every child in a school where attention will be given to his individual capacities; and that treatment centers are available not only for those who are physically ill or handicapped but also for those who have emotional problems that are too big to be solved by the family group. It is also the responsibility of the citizens in a community to see that no child is discriminated against because he is different from some of the other children—that the atmosphere in the community is such that there is compassion and concern for all children.

chapter 16

Education for Family Living

Ready for the years ahead

The test of our wisdom and skill in guiding our children toward maturity will be measured by the values and attitudes that they carry with them as they build their own families. Our guidance will have been successful if we have helped them to understand themselves better—their own drives, feelings, and needs— and to accept comfortably the roles that they will play in the family of tomorrow. If we have helped our children to enter their adult years with these insights and with the possibility of building successful relationships with others and with their families, we also will have done our part in helping the next generation start a step ahead in their emotional adjustments.

Living in a happy home with parents who have achieved a successful marital adjustment is the best preparation children can have for developing desirable attitudes and values concerning marriage and family life. Unfortunately, not all children have this background, and so the teacher and the school, the church and the community have a responsibility to see that all boys and girls are helped to understand what it means to become a man or a woman capable of successfully guiding a family of his own. This is not an easy task. To do it successfully, we must help children develop respect for the human body, for the creating of life, and for life itself.

These are attitudes which children absorb as they grow. Adults cannot teach them just by sitting down and talking to a child, giving him a book to read, or even providing a course in school, helpful as these methods may be. Children acquire their "sex education" from babyhood onward through the many ways in which the adults around them show their feelings, attitudes, and acceptance or nonacceptance of their sexual role and relationships. Children begin their preparation for marriage as they learn how to love and be loved by other people.

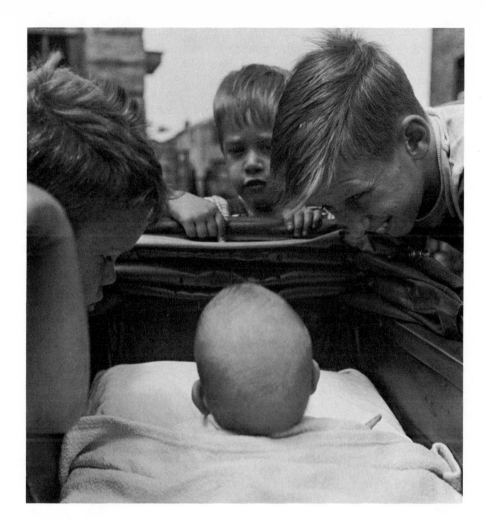

Learning to love

We used to think that sexual feelings developed suddenly at puberty, but we now realize that their beginnings are present in infancy and are part of the child's normal growth pattern. We cannot distinguish between those elements that tie a child in close affection to his parents and his friends and those that later cause him to love and to marry. They are part of the same life force. An adolescent does not suddenly or mysteriously gain the capacity to understand and deal successfully with sex. The attitudes, insights, and behavior patterns that are involved have been developing steadily throughout his life. They will influence him as he tries to understand his increasing sexual drives and interests. The ways in which he learns to love and be loved are as much a part of education for marriage as are the physiological facts of reproduction.

A child's ability to eventually achieve a satisfactory marriage and family life begins with his early attachment to his mother as he suckles and cuddles in her arms. It grows through the early years as the little child begins to develop deeper feelings for both his father and mother. It continues through the stage of close friendship with youngsters of the same sex in grade school and on into attachment for members of the opposite sex during adolescence. It culminates in marriage and the beginning of a new family cycle. If we are really to help boys and girls, we must understand this gradual growth cycle in learning to love.

The school years are not a time of completion but rather of finding out, of learning, and of building attitudes and values. The child is trying to orient himself to the adult world and to his place in it. With manifestations of sex everywhere about him, it would be a dull child indeed who was not curious about the beginnings of life and about the differences and relationships between the sexes. The ways in which we attempt, both in the schoolroom and the home, to fill a youngster's need for certain kinds of experience at each level of development are important. We need to be aware of the normal curiosity which all children have about sex and of the questions and situations that are likely to arise in the normal process of their growing up. What counts is the way we answer their questions during each period of growth and the way we help them to understand themselves, to live successfully through each stage, and to progress normally into the next phase of development.

The roles of the sexes

Children need help in understanding their roles in a complex and changing society. This is particularly important today when the roles of the sexes, except

for the physiological role, are moving away from traditional patterns. The difference between the activities of the sexes is diminishing. In many cases children see their mothers and fathers doing similar work both at home and on the job. Their parents will probably even dress similarly at times. Yet strong cultural pressures remain for boys to behave as boys and girls as girls. Crying is taboo for even little boys, but permissible for girls. Boys are given greater freedom to be aggressive; they are encouraged to stand up for themselves, to wrestle and fight. They are not expected to play with dolls or to go in for housekeeping games, even at an early age. Yet at home boys may be expected to wash the dishes, make their beds, and dust the house. Often they see their fathers as well as their mothers doing these things. Girls, on the other hand, soon find out that fighting is not permissible and that they are expected to be more gentle and well behaved than boys; dolls and housekeeping games are encouraged, but playing football is frowned on.

In spite of the many changes in the traditional roles of men and women, identification with one's own sex remains essential for normal, healthy development. Such identification should become complete during adolescence, but it has been in process since early childhood. Even during the preschool years, children normally begin to identify with those of their own sex. The little girl takes her mother as her pattern of what a woman should be and copies her ways. The little boy watches his father and tries to walk and talk like he does and to imitate those qualities he thinks of as manly. During the grade-school years this attempt to find oneself as girl or boy continues. Girls grow close to each other as

best friends or members of a club, and boys identify closely with each other in sports or in their special gang. Through these experiences and by imitating older boys and girls whom they admire, they learn what behavior and attitudes society expects of each sex. With adolescence, girls usually identify again with their mother or with a mother substitute, a greatly admired teacher or some other woman. Boys identify with their father, an athletic coach, or some other father figure. There is also a heightened attempt at this time to imitate successful, admired members of one's own sex within the peer group.

Most adolescents are able to accept themselves fully as man or woman by the end of high school. But some need special help if they are to accept their role without undue conflict. The child who has had a conspicuously unhappy relationship with those in his life who exemplify the basic pattern of his own sex may reject that pattern and identify with the parent, or some other adult, of the opposite sex. A mother who intensely resents being a woman may make it difficult for her daughter to accept the feminine role. Or a father who wanted a son may bring his daughter up to value manly activity and scorn feminine values, so that the daughter may find it hard to make the transition to the feminine role as she grows older. Similarly a mother who, wanting a daughter, has brought her son up to be too gentle and effeminate, who disliked cutting his curls, and who taught him to be "her sweet little boy" and to stay away from the other boys because they were "too rough" may make it almost impossible for the child to assume the masculine role as he grows up. Although not many children have this particular problem, those who do will need understanding and sometimes the expert help of the school psychologist or the community guidance clinic in order to work through their problems and develop more normal, healthy attitudes.

Questions about reproduction

Children normally ask many questions about reproduction—not only about where babies come from but why their mother is different from their father, why girls can have babies and boys cannot. These questions vary with the age of the child. He will ask the same questions many times over as he grows and feels the need for more information. At whatever age he asks them, his parents should answer his questions simply, honestly, and—if at all possible—at the time they are asked, remembering that a child often learns more from the *way* something is said than from the actual words. A good general rule is to answer only the specific question a child asks. When he wants more information, he will ask for more—if he feels that his parents are willing to answer his questions. Too often in our eagerness to teach the child we give him far more information than he is seeking or can absorb. Too much information given too soon only bewilders and confuses. Until the child is six or seven, providing simple information in answer to his questions is usually the wisest course to follow.

Children at the primary level need information on the physical differences between the sexes. This often needs clarifying for children all through the early primary grades. Children of primary-school age will also ask questions about where babies come from and how they are born. The coming of a new baby in their own family or in the family of relatives or neighbors can be used as a rich

One of the ways that parents can help their children build healthy attitudes toward reproduction is by preparing them carefully and lovingly for the birth of a new baby in the family. Here a child is intrigued by listening for the baby's heartbeat.

experience in helping children understand the mystery of birth. Pets, at home or in the classroom, can also provide a valuable learning experience, especially if baby animals are born.

Stories about family relationships, new babies, and typical family experiences are helpful to the child who is learning to establish his own relationships. Because many children today are growing up in homes that do not follow the traditional family pattern, care must be taken to reassure these youngsters by talking about the many different kinds of homes in which children grow up. There are homes in which there is only one parent or in which grandparents or other relatives are taking the place of father and mother. There are children who have been adopted, and others who are living with foster parents. There are many children from homes in which both parents are working. All these youngsters may be growing up in *good* homes and receiving loving care, and they should not be made to feel left out or different because their family is not like the typical family of mother, father, and children that is pictured in almost all readers and stories for young children. They should be helped to recognize that it is

the love within the family group and the responsible care the adults give the children that makes a family and a home.

At eight and more markedly at nine, children become increasingly interested in babies. Girls delight in them, hover over them, and want to take care of them. Even the boys often show a real interest and pride in their smaller brothers and sisters and may sometimes like to look after them. Along with feeling an affectionate interest in babies, children are also curious about their origin and are still often confused about the birth process. If they don't receive correct explanations of these things from the adults closest to them at this time, they may gather sketchy or erroneous ideas from other children. Much of children's sex play and sex curiosity comes from lack of information, from unsatisfied but normal curiosity, or from wrong information and attitudes given to them by their playmates.

Answering children's questions

The child who listens to the radio and to adults' conversation, watches television, reads papers and magazines, and observes what is going on about him will not only ask questions about the differences between the sexes and about where babies come from but may want to go into these things in greater detail. A helpful technique is to turn the child's questions back to him in a conversational way, asking him what he thinks about it. In this way we are often able to go beyond the surface question and find out just how much the child really knows

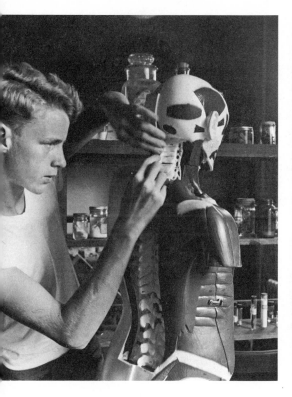
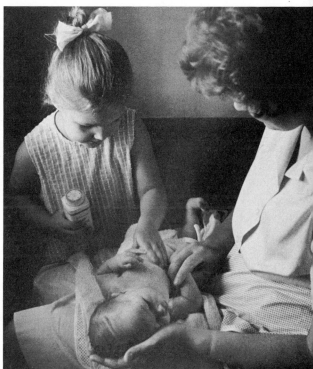

and whether he has obtained inaccurate information that is confusing him. We will then be able to correct mistaken notions and fill in the gaps in what he already knows.

Even after children have been given factual answers many times, they still may fail to understand fully and may return to get a clearer answer or more information as their concepts grow. If we are able to keep the channels of talk open, we will be able to meet their needs as they reach out again and again for more information. We must also be sensitive to what is underneath the question—there may be anxiety, guilt, or fear which we need to understand.

The years from ten to twelve are probably the best time in which to make sure that children have the physiological information they will need to understand the coming changes in their bodies. This is also the best time to make sure that all boys and girls have the basic knowledge of how life begins. Youngsters should have this information by the end of the sixth grade and preferably earlier. They can receive it much less emotionally during these years than they will be able to after they become adolescents. The information given to children of this age should be specific. They should understand the physiology and function of the reproductive organs of both sexes, menstruation, nocturnal emissions, the birth process, and the sexual roles of male and female. It is preferable to give this information as part of a general course of study that deals with all parts of the human body, so that children will learn to think of their sexual organs simply as part of their body and not something on which to focus special attention.

Understanding the child's present information and attitudes is of special importance during the preadolescent periods, when the mass media expose a child to confused concepts of the relationships between men and women and between teen-age boys and girls. On television and in movies he sees materialistic values, amoral standards, and even deviant sexual practices. He needs help in sorting out ideas and information that will help him to build healthy sexual concepts as distinguished from those that will confuse him or foster unwholesome or oversophisticated desires and patterns of behavior.

Preadolescents are more likely to seek information from their friends than they are to ask direct questions of either their parents or their teachers. But adults should take the responsibility for presenting correct, factual material to preadolescents—through discussions, films, and books—and for helping them develop wholesome attitudes toward their roles as boys and girls, and later as men and women.

Meeting problem situations

During the elementary-school years, children cannot be fully protected from inaccurate playground sex information, undesirable words, pictures on toilet walls, or possible exposure to sex play. Occasionally, there are more serious problems of experimentation among some of the children. Sometimes the presence of a sex offender in the neighborhood may make it necessary to warn children for their own protection.

The way we meet these situations influences the attitudes our youngsters develop. If we meet them with tension, overexcitement, disgust, anger, or an attempt to punish, shame, or frighten the children involved, we have failed in our responsibility. We should understand that curiosity about sex and sex play are most often only natural attempts on the part of youngsters to find out about themselves. It is best to respond not with anger and stern punishment but with the realization that children who are too concerned with sex need information to satisfy their curiosity and help in establishing wholesome attitudes to replace undesirable ones. Often, too, they need other outlets for their energy besides those that are being supplied in the regular routines of either home or school. Even acutely serious situations should be treated as problems to be worked through rather than as misdemeanors to be punished. The children involved need help, probably from a counselor, a psychologist, or a psychiatrist, if they are to be able to change their behavior. We are best able to help children, instead of further entrenching their wrong attitudes toward sex, when we approach these situations with calmness and insight.

In order for the adult to help a child with a problem, the relationship between the two must be warm, friendly, and accepting, not driving or condemning. We may not like what the child does. We may tell him that some actions are not socially acceptable. But we must make it clear to the child that we care what happens to him in spite of what he has done. In no situation is this more important than in meeting sexual problems that arise on the playground or in the school building. However serious the problem, punishment is the wrong answer. Adults must rather look for the cause and seek to help the child build healthy attitudes.

The physiological changes that herald puberty are those that change the child's body into that of an adult capable of reproduction. These are gradual changes, built upon the physical and psychological development that has been proceeding since birth. The adolescent begins to experience an intensity of certain drives and emotions that he has not known as a child, ones that he will need as an adult. But with his new physical maturity, even with the best of knowledge and attitudes, he may still lack the judgment that should accompany the power of reproduction. Adolescents must be helped to understand that maturity of judgment doesn't automatically accompany physical maturity. During the adolescent years

they should be guided toward developing sound judgment and a responsible attitude about sex, so that when they are ready for marriage they will be able to build stable family units and enter confidently into the responsibilities of family life.

By the time boys and girls are physically mature, most of them know something about the physical facts of reproduction. They need more opportunities, however, to talk through the emotional and social relationships between the sexes and the values and attitudes that are important if they are to use their sexual drives happily and well. It is still the task of adults to help young people think through the complex feelings, attitudes, and responsibilities that face them when they have reached physical maturity.

Teen-agers often ask questions dealing with feelings and emotions and with ways to get along with the opposite sex. But there are other questions that they do not ask so readily, questions about the physiological changes that are so obviously taking place and about their own roles as they develop into young men and women. At first, physical changes may seem strange and even distressing, especially if the young adolescent has not been prepared for them. The growth in weight, the development of the breasts and hips, the beginning of the menstrual flow are bewildering experiences to many growing girls and need careful anticipation and interpretation. Boys are often concerned by their changing voices, their need to shave, their developing genitals, or their nocturnal emissions. Adolescents need time to adjust to these changes, opportunities to ask questions about them, and help in understanding them.

The older adolescent has more serious questions to face, many of which he does not easily express. Should I go steady seriously? Shall I marry now or when I leave school? What about heavy petting? What about intercourse before marriage? What about birth control? If I am pregnant, what shall I do? What about abortions? What about homosexuality? Why doesn't anyone date me—is something the matter with me? What about venereal disease? If I remain a virgin will boys want to date me? Such questions are perturbing to adults who do not like to believe that high-school students are concerned about such problems.

Guiding adolescents

If parents and teachers are to be truly helpful in guiding adolescents, they must be aware not only of the heightened sexual drive, particularly among boys, but of the change in the cultural pressures that are being put on older teen-agers. The excitement of heavy petting and even of intercourse is becoming an accepted activity in many adolescent and adult circles today. In some adolescent groups participation in such experiences is played up and made to seem a highly desirable part of growing up. Boys and girls who do not want to become involved in this kind of activity are often made to feel that they are behind the times and are frequently left out of social groups that they consider clever and sophisticated and fun. These boys and girls must feel the steady support of parents and teachers and the approval of the larger community if they are to withstand the pressures of this growing pattern of sexual intimacies.

Many adults and young people take the position that where there is a real emotional attachment, sexual intimacies are part of the deepening feeling for one another and should be permitted. Unfortunately, those who encourage this point of view do not seem to be aware of the transient nature of the feelings adolescent boys and girls have for one another and the fact that one involvement frequently leads to another. There is genuine cause for concern in the increasing number of high-school marriages, often resulting in the disruption of education; in the high rate of divorce among those who have married under twenty; in the increasing number of illegitimate births, with all the resulting heartache; and in the growing incidence of venereal disease among young people.

Many parents and teachers recognize the importance of preparing children for the physiological and emotional changes of adolescence, yet they find it extremely difficult if not impossible to talk with youngsters about these things. In fact, many parents find the difficulty so great that they put it off from year to year until the child enters adolescence totally unprepared or with only the haphazard and often erroneous facts and attitudes he has picked up from his playmates, from newspapers, movies, television, comics, or from adults' scattered remarks and innuendos. In the same way, many teachers are embarrassed or perplexed when the students ask direct questions about sexual matters or when situations arise that involve questons or problems of a sexual nature.

Although sexual matters are being discussed today with increasingly greater freedom, many adults still find it difficult to talk about them with their children. This is a natural result of the training that many present-day adults received in their own childhood. One reason for their difficulty in explaining sex to their youngsters is that they have no pattern to follow in their own experiences. As children, many of them received very inadequate information, and the information they did receive concerned only the so-called facts of life. These were presented as something totally apart from the rest of living. To this lack of adequate preparation for life and family living have been added the parents' and teachers' varying personal experiences and adjustments, all of which color their attitudes. Many significant factors apply in this connection: the way their own parents lived together, their parents' opinions about the relative value of a boy or a girl in the family group, the amount of affection they received as children, their parents' attitudes when a baby was born or coming, the punishment they may have received for asking questions or for trying to find out about their bodies, their own adjustments or difficulties as they left the home circle and tried to make friends with other young men or women, their feelings of success or inadequacy. All these things help to determine whether adults can talk naturally and simply with children about the beginnings of life and the relationships of men and women, and whether they impart wholesome or distorted attitudes. Sometimes teachers and parents may need to seek help in understanding their own problems and attitudes before they can be sufficiently free, comfortable, and clear in their own thinking to help a growing child.

Additional resources—books and the school

Among the readings and reference sources listed at the end of Part Six in this book, teachers and parents will find books that may be helpful in answering specific questions that children ask throughout their years of growing up. The answers found in these books can be used as a guide, although each answer will need to be modified to fit the particular child or the particular question that has been asked. They must be phrased according to the individual's own way of saying things, so they will not sound cold and stilted but will show warmth and personal interest.

Books can be a valuable aid in giving adults the correct information to pass along to children and the confidence to discuss sexual matters frankly. But they are only a supplement. They cannot take the place of the day-to-day development of attitudes, the informal discussions, and the answering of questions as they arise in everyday life. If the parent is too tense or embarrassed to talk informally with his child, then he will probably be wiser to read a well-written book with a young child or to provide an older child with a book to read for himself. The reading list at the back of this section indicates which books are written for parents and which are suitable for children. Even if the parent gives his child a book to read, however, he should realize that he must still try to answer the questions that the reading may stimulate. The parent must always remember, too, that detailed factual information is not enough, that the child is seeking attitudes as well as facts.

Whether the school should provide education in family living through a formal plan of study is a question which cannot be answered categorically. It depends in great measure on the attitude and readiness of the community, on the teachers available, and on the religious background of the school. There is no question that the need for such education must be met in some adequate manner, because the readiness of our children to establish satisfactory marriage and family relationships is of such vast significance that those who are responsible for educating boys and girls cannot ignore it. It would be desirable for parents to educate their children in this field, but some parents cannot or will not do so. Thus the teacher often finds herself having to guide or counsel not only the child but in many cases the parents as well. Such guidance must be given wisely and with understanding of the feelings and inhibitions of those involved.

Rushing into this field with an enthusiasm which roughly pushes aside long-standing taboos or the sincere beliefs of the parents in the community is certainly unwise. If the school considers a formal course in family-life education the most effective answer to the real needs of the children in the school or the community, it is best, first of all, to study the parents' attitudes to find out how far they are willing to accept education of their children in this field. Before establishing such a program it is usually wise to meet with the parents, respecting their prior interest in this area and talking over the needs of the youngsters, the school's plan for meeting these needs, the factual material that will be covered, and the way it will be presented. Once the parents' cooperation and support have been obtained, the school can proceed on a sound footing, with parents and teachers working together for the benefit of the children. Such a preliminary procedure enriches the ensuing course of study for the students, whether it is given during one year or becomes a part of the total curriculum, because the parents are often able to add much by the type of support and approval that they give in the home. In addition, the materials presented in the group meetings frequently give added insight to many parents, lessen their anxieties, clarify their attitudes, and even give them factual information that they may not have had before.

Whatever the methods they use, if home and school can work together to develop in children respect for the human body, appreciation of the rights of others, mutual respect for each other, and an understanding of their own emotions and feelings, they will have given the children a firm basis for their own family life in the years ahead. Such education can contribute to lessening for these children many of the tensions and strains in personal relationships that surround so many adults today.

chapter 17

When Things Go Wrong

The problems of growing up

Growing up is especially difficult for some children. There are troubled young-sters in many homes and in all of our schools. Sometimes this is because of failure in the home, the school, or the community to provide adequately for the growth needs of these children. Many children face neglect or rejection by parents who are uninterested in them or too busy to pay them adequate attention. Others experience the insecurity of a home broken by desertion or divorce. Still others feel pressured and discouraged because of the unrealistic demands imposed on them by their parents or their school. In some cases, factors beyond parents' control touch the lives of children, producing anxiety or problems that are difficult for the children to meet—the tensions of the atomic age; racial or religious prejudice; poverty. Some children, too, have physical or mental handicaps which make it necessary for them to have special understanding and help if they are to meet life successfully, making the most of whatever capacities they may have.

A child has few inner resources and little practical experience to call on in meeting situations that are too difficult for him or pressures that are too great. Often he is not even conscious of the reasons for his hurt or distress. When a child finds himself frustrated by a situation he cannot meet, he can move in either of two directions: he can pull back and withdraw into his own personal world, or he can hit back. In the latter case the child's aggressive behavior is often met with punishment or counteraggression on the part of adults. This, of course, tends to complicate the problem further.

There are many manifestations of these two basic ways of meeting problems that seem too difficult for solution, and a child does not consciously choose one type of behavior over another. Various factors within himself and his environ-

ment determine which pattern of response he will follow. For example, Mark's insecurity drove him into meeting his problem by running away. Johnny, whose parents demanded a standard of perfection he could not meet, protected himself by being "good as gold" and never asserting himself. Agnes, who never felt really loved, rebuffed others because she expected that they would rebuff her: wanting friendship desperately, she nevertheless pushed it aside when it was offered for fear that she would be hurt again. Paul, with his feelings of never being able to match his brother's achievements, withdrew into daydreams.

At some point in their lives, all children find growing up difficult, even if they come from homes in which they find loving support. But if the satisfactions of growing up outweigh the problems it entails, most children are able to cope with their disturbed feelings and to meet most situations adequately—though not always without a struggle within themselves. Children who have the support of their parents and other adults—who are encouraged and guided as they grow up —usually show the greatest resilience. When problems become temporarily too great for these children, they can often be helped to meet them in a realistic and practical way by perceptive parents or teachers and sometimes even by other children.

The emotionally disturbed child

Some children's defeats have so outbalanced their successes that they will need professional help in order to work through the conflicts between their own deep needs and the demands of situations they have been unable to meet. Huntley and Mark were two such boys, both of whom might have become seriously delinquent if they had not received professional help in time.

In many communities such help can be obtained through the Mental Health or Child Guidance Clinic, through a physician specializing in psychiatry, or through a practicing psychologist. School systems that have a psychologist or counselor should be able to guide parents to appropriate sources of help. Parents can also write to their State Department of Mental Health for information about the resources available in or near their community. It is usually necessary to wait for an appointment, although many clinics have provisions for meeting real emergencies.

Emotionally troubled children can be found in all our schools—children whose problems, though deep, do not require hospitalization or placement in an institution. In some schools special classes have been planned in which children with severe emotional disturbances, who are too disruptive to a normal classroom, can be taught in a smaller group with a specially trained teacher. When this is possible, their personal needs can be met more fully. But most emotionally disturbed children, even if they are under treatment, will attend regular classes. Many will remain the problem of the classroom teacher.

Every child's problem is individual. To give effective help, even the expert needs to know a great deal about the particular child: his background, his parents, his past experiences, his temperament, his needs and wishes, and his inner resources for dealing with pressure and strain. It is possible, nevertheless, to group some of the problems together and to find common factors among them that are helpful as a guide in developing a program for the individual child.

The poorly socialized child

One type of emotional problem is typified by the rebellious child who dislikes everybody, usually because he feels that people dislike him and are mean to him. He is a poorly socialized child. His way of trying to meet his needs is the clumsy, inadequate one of fighting the world indiscriminately. He is hostile and defiant. He has no sense of fair play. When he dares to, he attacks or bullies other children. Yet he feels he is being picked on, and indeed he is not well accepted by other children or by any gang. He is usually a lone wolf. He is so difficult to manage and causes so much disturbance that he is sometimes called *the undomesticated child*. He achieves little at home or school and, as a result, develops a discouraging self-image. He thinks he is no good and may say so.

Typically, such a child lacked sufficient mothering in his early years. Often he had an immature or inadequate mother who considered her own needs and feelings rather than the developmental needs of her child. In a typical case the child is unwanted at birth. The trouble is intensified when the child's activity becomes annoying to the mother, and over a period of time continual conflict develops as the pattern between the two. Sometimes the father becomes involved in the battle of wills, but often he is a rather inadequate parent who fails to back the mother in her attempts to control the child and thus gives the child tacit permission to continue his rebellion.

We also find rebellious, poorly socialized children among youngsters who have been raised in institutions that provide no stable child-parent relationships and among youngsters who have had frequent foster-care placements. A child with such a background has lacked sufficient roots in any home. Adults have never seemed dependable to him, and he often gives little return for their kindness.

The rebellious, antisocial child may be helped to some degree by his classroom teacher or by someone else in the school system or community who can win his confidence. Great patience is needed, however, for the adult must not only try to win the child's trust but stand ready at the same time to disapprove his behavior when it becomes objectionable. The prognosis for such a child will improve if his parents can be helped to gain understanding before the antagonism between them and the child becomes irreversible. Sometimes, however, it is necessary to remove the child from his own home before treatment can be in any degree successful.

In dealing with the rebellious child, kindness and understanding must be backed by firm control. Sometimes a teacher will need the help of the principal or some male teacher in critical situations, as when a troublesome boy becomes so difficult that he has to be removed from the classroom. When an unsocialized child has been in trouble with the juvenile court, the school should be informed,

and the principal and the teachers should be aware of what kind of difficulty might be expected and how they should handle it if it does arise.

The child who dislikes adults

The child who dislikes adults may be well socialized as far as other children are concerned. As he gets older he may become a member of a semi-delinquent or delinquent gang. The youngsters who fall into this behavior pattern are almost always boys, rarely girls except when a girl is a hanger-on to a boys' gang. Where separate girl gangs do exist, they are usually more transient, more personal, and less likely to draw attention than are boy gangs.

The child who dislikes adults is part of a rebellious group and he is loyal to his group, following the pattern that the gang builds up in defiance of the adult world. He will steal from the dime store rather than be called chicken. With his gang he will participate in acts of vandalism, refuse to cooperate in the classroom, and generally tend to disturb and disrupt any situation he encounters. Emotional dissatisfactions contribute to a boy's desire for membership in such a gang. He is seeking the satisfactions that life has otherwise denied him by ganging up with other boys against adults.

In the classroom the influence of these boys may be a problem. Many of them are muscular, active, vigorous, and adventurous youngsters who, disliking school, find an outlet for their energy by cutting up in class or playing truant. Frequently they fail to develop adequate reading skills, and this in turn contrib-

utes to school maladjustment. Sometimes the school itself is at fault in neglecting to provide a program geared to the interests, needs, and capabilities of this group. Few schools, for example, capitalize sufficiently on the interest that many of these youngsters show in manual skills and shopwork. More can be done, too, by physical education departments in developing special programs for these boys. Obviously the school must set limits on the behavior of rebellious and trouble-prone youngsters, but it also has a responsibility to provide activities that will give them the experience of success and enable them to work off their energy.

Whatever teachers do in trying to meet the situation, they will have little chance of success unless they can reach the individual child through his group or separate him from it completely. The latter course is usually difficult to accomplish. A teacher or community leader who, on the other hand, can capture the interest of the *group*, particularly that of the boys' leader, is often able to help redirect their energy and need for activity into more desirable channels.

Children who are hostile to adults but have close friends among other children are rarely as emotionally disturbed as the child who is a lone wolf. But although they are more normal in personality, they can get into serious difficulties and cause serious disturbances in the classroom and in the community. It is from this group of boys who grow up with an increasing lack of interest in school that many of our drop-outs come.

The child who dislikes adult authority often has a father who lacks any real interest in him and has therefore neglected him. Often he has experienced inconsistent discipline, failure of direction, and insufficient warmth and affection from his father. An alcoholic father is not uncommon. Typically the mother has been adequately accepting of the youngster, at least in his early years, so that he has developed a capacity to like some people, but he directs this capacity toward other children rather than toward adults.

These children come most frequently from underprivileged areas, but they may be found in any neighborhood. Sometimes the parents of this kind of youngster can be awakened to see what is happening to their child. If they become aware that their child's activities with his group are bad for him and indicate a public failure on their part, they can sometimes be led to assume more responsibility for their child.

The over-anxious child

The over-anxious child who suffers from severe inner conflict is the youngster whom we often overlook in the classroom. Such a child is insecure, too inhibited, too dutiful, and too sensitive to criticism and failure. He is apprehensive and unsure of himself. As a rule he is overly concerned about examinations and grades. Such a child maintains contact with reality and tries to function effectively, but he is frightened, worried, and under strain. He is inclined to be timid, often more so with adults than with children. He sometimes literally worries himself sick, undergoing spells of vomiting, stomach aches, and headaches. The child's deep concerns, if not recognized, may lead to neurotic illness such as anxiety attacks.

Over-anxious children create no problem of classroom control. They usually work hard in school and live up to their intellectual ability, sometimes even achieving beyond the level that might be expected. They often need help, however, in finding their place in the classroom group. It is unwise to force an over-anxious child into classroom situations that appear to distress him. Speed tests and competitive situations are undesirable. The teacher should make an effort to encourage him and help him relax. Because the child will need a great deal of help in learning that he is liked for himself, the choice of a teacher for him is especially important. A warm, supporting teacher can help, but a rigid, scolding, or perfectionistic teacher can harm him and cause him to withdraw more deeply into himself.

Over-anxious children usually have parents who do not give much warmth and approval but hold very high standards for performance. These parents put so much value on achievement and grades that the child comes to feel that they won't accept him unless he is able to live up to their expectations. Such parents are often restrictive in what they permit the child to do, so that he becomes dependent rather than self-reliant.

Many of these parents are interested in their child but fail to understand him. It is sometimes possible to help them see that their child is too worried and anxious about his schoolwork, that they must give him more encouragement and praise. How much the child can be helped will depend largely on how the parents respond to their new insights. Sometimes both the child and the parents will need professional help.

The withdrawn child

The withdrawn child who pulls away from reality into a world of daydreams is a much more serious problem than the over-anxious child. He cannot be reached easily by his teacher or by anyone else. But even though it is difficult to establish personal contact with such a child, the teacher must make a special effort to do so, showing warmth and friendliness even if the child does not respond. A teacher sometimes takes this lack of response to mean a rebuff of her kindness, but often the child is actually unable to respond. The problem is sometimes complicated because the youngster does not relate well to the activities of the classroom. He may not keep his place in the book. He may, like Paul, go on daydreaming when directions are given. His schoolwork is rarely up to the level of his intelligence.

A friendly classroom atmosphere is likely to benefit a withdrawn child if he is not lost in the shuffle. Even with great effort on his teacher's part, however, he seldom relates easily to others. He may attract the disapproval of other children because he does not fit into the classroom program. He is often considered odd. He doesn't rebel or refuse to take part. Rather, he just is not there.

Constant encouragement will be necessary in trying to hold the attention of such a youngster in the classroom, to bring him closer to reality, and to help him find satisfaction outside his daydreams. Harshness and scolding will only work further harm. A teacher is usually able to help a little, but she must be prepared for the fact that she will have to make a large effort for a limited return.

A great deal still needs to be known about the withdrawn child. He is so hard to reach that it is difficult to understand the underlying causes of his problem. There are indications, however, that withdrawal from reality is more frequent

with children of parents who have exerted strict control over their child without accepting him as a person in his own right. Usually the parents have not rejected him but rather have been unwilling or perhaps unable to let him develop an individual personality. Frequently they have made all the plans, laid down all the rules, directed every movement. They may regard their child as a possession or extension of themselves, thus making it difficult for him to develop his own individuality. If professional counsel is sought, parents may be helped to modify their behavior toward the child. Both parents and child may need long-term professional help.

The apathetic child

Some children do poorly in school because they are discouraged with themselves and refuse to try. Rather than withdrawing into daydreams, they tend to be apathetic. These children are found most frequently in deprived areas, in city slums and poverty-stricken rural communities—wherever the blight of extreme poverty and neglect is found. They come from homes where there is little money, poor clothing, inadequate food. Many are in poor physical condition, lacking muscular tone, and often fatigued. Their parents, too, are often ill and, because of illness or general inadequacy, unable to give the encouragement and emotional support which children need. The children seem to have such a poor self-image that they no longer try—they just give up.

Culturally deprived children are a responsibility of the community that has permitted neglected areas to continue to exist. Before these children can become alert and motivated to do schoolwork, they need attention to their physical needs, correction of their physical defects, clothing to encourage greater self-respect, and then, gradually, experiences in identifying themselves as individuals. Their apathy toward school can only be changed as we help them develop self-respect and a self-image which enables them to believe that the effort of learning is worth while—because they *can* learn.

The over-active child

Over-active children constitute a difficult problem in many of our classrooms. These are restless, distractible children with short attention spans and poor concentration. They disturb the rest of the class and are often difficult to manage. They not only do not live up to their potential, but they frequently have trouble in learning to read and manage symbols. Sometimes they are wrongly considered to be of low I.Q. because they show up badly on group tests which do not adequately measure their potential. They have difficulty in conforming to classroom routine, in paying attention, and in sitting still.

Among these over-active children are those who have been called *unorganized children* because they have never developed an organized pattern of behavior. Such children usually have grown up in a haphazard fashion without adequate parental guidance. The expectation that they should conform to an acceptable pattern of behavior has not been made clear or has not been enforced. These children will need patient but firm direction as they are helped gradually to observe the behavioral limits that are essential in living and working with others.

With some other children, over-activity has an *organic* basis. These are children like Ronnie, and they are found in our classrooms more frequently than is generally realized. Obviously the diagnosis of brain damage is a medical one and cannot be made by observing behavior in the classroom. The classroom teacher *can,* however, recognize overactivity, distractibility, and a short attention span as possible signs of an organic problem. Indeed, she may be the first person to realize the seriousness of the problem, because she sees the child's behavior in relation to that of other children. If this behavior presents a serious management problem and the child seems unable to respond to attempts to help him control his overactivity, the teacher should discuss the situation with the principal and with the school psychologist, if one is on the staff. After further study it may be decided to contact the parents and suggest that the child be referred to a physician or a child-guidance clinic. Teachers are not qualified to suggest what the medical diagnosis might be, and it is advisable for them to stay out of this area. However, it is appropriate for them to ask for further medical or psychological study of a child when there is an unexplained problem in his behavior.

At present, the child with mild brain damage must often be taught in the regular classroom. Only in severe cases will he belong in a special class for severely handicapped children. Neither does he belong in a class for the mentally retarded, for his mental ability is usually normal and may even be superior. Sometimes, however, such a class is the only compromise available, because the child may have too much trouble in keeping up with normal children in school. He may be so easily distracted that he cannot function well in a group situation. And, as in the case of Ronnie, his capacity to perceive and to draw shapes may be grossly impaired—a limitation that affects his readiness for reading and writing. Sometimes he may have to be taught reading by a remedial or special teacher. His limitations may also mean that he will have to go more slowly than other children.

Scolding the brain-damaged child, telling him to pay attention and keep still, cannot be effective. His hyperactivity will crop out in one way or another. An organically damaged child needs a great deal of patience, tolerance, and steadiness, with as few distractions as possible. He should never be placed in the room of a nervous, tense, or insecure teacher, for this will inevitably generate too much friction.

The teachers' role

With both the brain-damaged child and the child who is overactive because he hasn't developed a structured pattern of behavior, the teacher should carefully watch for signs of restlessness building up. She may then send the youngster on an errand or find some other active job for him to do before he spills over in disturbing activity. Perhaps he can put books away on the library shelves, clean out the fish bowl, take care of the plants, or help the custodian rake the leaves or wash the blackboards. A wise teacher who sees tension mounting may sometimes even interrupt the class and have all the children do some exercises, or she may arrange the classroom schedule to provide more frequent breaks for physical activity and a change of pace, in order to keep one child's restlessness from being too upsetting to the entire group.

Having a hyperactive child in the classroom makes a difficult situation. The other children cannot understand the reason for the restlessness of the unorganized child, nor can they "see" the physical handicap of the organically damaged youngster. They are not likely to feel the same protective sympathy, therefore, that they do for an outwardly handicapped child, such as a youngster with a brace or one who is blind or deaf.

Because the child with an emotional problem must often be placed in the regular classroom, the teacher's attitudes are of major importance in determining not only whether the child will be helped but whether the teacher herself is able to carry on without too severe strain. A first step is for the teacher to understand the problem and the limits of what she can be expected to do for the child. This means that she should have continuing access either to the school psychologist or to some other professional person who understands the child's condition and can guide her as she works with the youngster in the classroom. Teamwork involving the family, their physician, a psychologist, and the teacher is essential if the child is to be helped.

The teacher will find it easier to tolerate the problems that the child brings into the classroom if she can emotionally accept him without feeling personally threatened by his behavior. She must try to avoid meeting the child on his own level. She should be on guard, for example, against feeling personal hostility toward the child who is a perennial troublemaker or the child who rebuffs her or does not respond to her attempts to help him. These are children in trouble, and their behavior is not always under their conscious control. It is important that the teacher do what she can for the emotionally troubled child—as she would for any child—but she must remember that failure to help him is not necessarily a personal failure.

Providing an atmosphere of emotional stability within the classroom is also important. Steadiness in classroom direction helps the withdrawing child to know what he can expect, and it shows the rebellious youngster that the teacher is in control and that she expects certain standards of behavior in the classroom. The confused teacher cannot successfully teach the confused child.

The physically handicapped child

Many children are handicapped physically rather than emotionally, although emotional disturbance may become part of the picture if the physically handicapped child does not have adequate support and guidance. The epileptic child, the child with cerebral palsy, the child who has been crippled, the child who is blind or deaf, the child who has diabetes or a heart condition—these are children who need special plans to help them meet the problems of their handicap. Although most of these children are able to use their minds as competently as boys and girls without physical handicaps, there will be situations that they cannot meet unless special provisions are made. Parents and teachers must help physically handicapped children to accept their particular disabilities realistically and to meet the frustrations that they will inevitably face because of them.

We can help children with physical handicaps to develop healthy personalities by accepting them as normal in other respects and by encouraging them to participate as much as possible in the activities of normal children. Encouraging them to be as independent as possible and to cultivate their own special interests

With help, physically handicapped children can learn to perform actions and understand concepts that their handicaps would otherwise deny them. The picture on this page shows a blind boy learning to kick a ball he cannot see. The pictures on the opposite page show deaf children learning to "feel" sounds they cannot hear. Note the concentration of the first boy, then the delight of the children as they feel the vibrations set up by sound waves.

284

and abilities helps them to develop a positive self-image and, as they grow up, to acquire an increasing degree of self-reliance.

The mentally handicapped child

Another large group of children who will need special help are the mentally retarded. Three per cent of our school children will test as mentally retarded, as approximately 120,000 mentally retarded children are born each year. Retarded children may be found in families of every level of intelligence. Fortunately, a retarded child is no longer considered a family disgrace. As scientific knowledge replaces superstition concerning the causes of mental deficiency, the stigma of mental retardation is rapidly diminishing. Research has already uncovered more than seventy causes for this condition. Heredity is now recognized as less important than was formerly assumed, while disease and injury of the brain are seen as more important. Even when heredity is definitely established as its cause, the mental defect is sometimes preventable with proper medical care. This is true, for example, in cases of phenylketonuria, or PKU—a metabolic disorder due to a hereditary enzyme deficiency. When this defect is recognized in infancy by a chemical test of blood or urine, mental deficiency can be prevented by feeding the child a special diet during the first years of life. This is only one of several hopeful breakthroughs in preventing mental retardation. The future is bright with hope for continuing progress in this field.

There are many degrees of mental retardation, and retarded children cannot be grouped together as if all their problems were similar. There are individual differences and needs among these boys and girls just as there are among children who do not have this handicap.

The *dependent retarded* are so severely handicapped that they must have

These mentally retarded children are participating in a special class where the work is geared to their capacity to learn. They are learning motor control and coordination through play activities and are developing their social skills through being with the other children in the class.

constant, kindly, nursing care throughout their lives. Only one of every thirty retarded children is in this group. None of these children will be able to attend school or even play with other boys and girls. They can never become capable of caring for themselves. Most of them will be cared for in institutions, although some will be cared for, at least in their early years, by parents or foster parents.

The *semi-dependent* or *trainable* children, as we call them when we think in terms of their educational needs, represent about four out of every thirty retarded boys and girls. These children will need constant supervision and care, but they are able to attend school in a special class, usually called the "trainable class." Many of these classes are presently organized and supported by parents, but there is an increasing tendency for public schools to assume responsibility for such classes.

Trainable children can learn acceptable social behavior, useful work, and care of their personal needs. Most of them will not be able to learn to read and write, although some can learn to read simple signs, write their names, or master simple counting. They enjoy uncomplicated games and rhythms, finger painting, clay modeling, and many nursery-school and kindergarten activities. A few are able to go somewhat beyond this level. If a sheltered workshop is available to trainable children when they become youths and adults, many can become contributing members of society. But they will always need someone who is responsible for their well-being, guidance, and protection.

The *marginally dependent* or *educable* children are estimated at twenty-five out of every thirty retarded children. These are the youngsters we find in the usual special-education classes in our schools. They can learn enough reading and arithmetic so that they can meet simple daily needs. Many of them will be able to function quite adequately in areas other than academic work, and some may show real talent in special areas such as art or singing or athletics. With a special educational program, most of them will be able to become self-supporting and to manage their own affairs quite adequately under circumstances that are not too complicated. But they will continue to need help and guidance in their vocational adjustment and in situations that require considerable judgment.

We are becoming increasingly aware that among children who test within the retarded range are many who have normal potentialities but are *culturally retarded*. They have grown up in disadvantaged areas in which they have missed the opportunities most children have to learn about the world and to build the concepts necessary to prepare them for success in schoolwork. Often their parents have been so culturally deprived themselves that they cannot provide for even the basic physical needs of their children. Some of these boys and girls have never seen themselves in a mirror or have never even realized that they have a name of their own or a personal identity. Some have had little opportunity to learn language, because in the crowded quarters where they have grown up parents seldom talk to their children and never read to them. Many of these culturally deprived youngsters can be helped to leave the group of the retarded if they are reached during their early years, if their physical needs are taken care of, and if they are provided with experiences that will help them develop intellectually.

More alike than different

Parents and teachers who are helping retarded boys and girls need to remember above all that these children are more *like* other children than *different* from them. They have the same needs for affection, achievement, and a feeling of personal worth. They need friends to play with, interests to follow, trips and experiences to open up the world to them. They need fun and laughter just as other children do. Retarded youngsters will also need special educational plans fitted to their mental ability rather than to their chronological age—activities and expectations appropriate to younger children of normal intelligence. They can never be expected to carry on the academic work that children their age experience in the regular classroom, to proceed at the same pace as more normal boys and girls, or to catch up with them. When mentally retarded children are accepted at their own level of performance, however, many of them can learn enough to become happy and productive citizens. Each has his own individuality and personality and his own needs. Each will progress and develop at his own rate. Each needs to be known and appreciated as an individual rather than pigeonholed as a "retarded child."

Parents naturally feel deep grief over a handicapped child, whether the handicap is physical or mental, but by their own realistic acceptance of the handicap they can help their child to accept it, too. The earlier they recognize the problem, the earlier they can begin appropriate treatment, guidance, and education, and the better the prognosis will be for the child's learning how to accept and live with his handicap. It is unfortunate if parents, in their grief, are unable or unwilling to recognize the problem for what it is or if they put off facing the child's handicap, hoping that he will outgrow it.

Parents will not be able to meet all the needs of a handicapped child by themselves. The community must help by providing both treatment and educational facilities that will make the care of these children possible. Small communities are not always able to afford all the necessary facilities, but these facilities can usually be supported by the larger units of county or state. The availability of such services should be called to the attention of all parents of handicapped children. If parents have not received such information and do not know how to secure it, they can write to their State Department of Health and their State Department of Education. These two departments will have information concerning all the possible help that handicapped children can receive within their state. There are also many national organizations to help the handicapped.

Parents of handicapped children also need opportunities to meet and talk with parents of other children who have similar problems. Through such contacts, parents are often able to support one another and share their solutions to some of the practical difficulties they must face in learning to live with their child's problem and the problems it makes for the whole family. The parents of retarded children, for instance, have helped one another immeasurably as they have come together across the country in units often sponsored by their national and state organizations. In these groups they have not only talked about their problems but have encouraged and sponsored research on the causes and treatment of mental retardation. They have worked for the organization of schools for trainable children, special classes in the public schools, recreational and religious activities suited to the needs of their children, and sheltered workshops and vocational opportunities for their grown sons and daughters.

One of the greatest needs of the handicapped individual is for personal acceptance and a recognition that he has a personality of his own. A young woman with cerebral palsy expressed it in this manner:*

Blessed are you who take time to listen to spastic speech;
For you help us to know that if we persevere we can be understood.

Blessed are you who walk with us in public places and ignore the stares
Of strangers; for in your companionship we find havens of relaxation.

Blessed are you who never bid us "hurry up"; and more blessed,
You who do not snatch our tasks from our hands to do them for us;
For often we need time rather than help.

Blessed are you who stand beside us as we enter new and untried ventures;
For our failures will be outweighted by the times when we surprise ourselves
And you.

*Courtesy of Vivian Moffitt, "Beatitudes for the Friends of the Cerebral Palsied." Reprinted from *Give Them a Chance to Talk* by Berneice R. Rutherford. (Minneapolis: Burgess Publishing Company, 1956).

288

Blessed are you who ask our help; for our greatest need is to be needed.

Blessed are you, when by all these things, you assure us that the thing
That makes us individuals is not in our peculiar muscles,
Not in our wounded nervous systems, but in the God-given self
Which no infirmity can confine.

Rejoice and be exceedingly glad, and know that you give us reassurances
That could never be spoken in words, for you deal with us as
Christ dealt with the slow and peculiar.

Now that families are becoming better able to accept their handicapped children without shame, many more parents are answering the special need of these children for love, affection, and a place in the family. This is the first and most important step in the emotional development of these children, as it is with all children. But there is still much to be done to obtain acceptance for the handicapped in the community, first as children and later as workers. This task begins in the schoolroom and in the neighborhood as adults, through their own attitude toward the handicapped, set an example for children. Sometimes children need direct teaching in the schoolroom, in youth groups, in the church school, and in recreational activities if, because of their difficulty in accepting differences, they taunt or turn away from those who are handicapped. Discovering that many handicapped people have something of value to contribute provides an added dimension in a child's development.

This girl has a speech defect. She is learning to form the sounds that she will use to speak correctly. Here, by blowing out the flame, she is trying to master the wh *sound.*

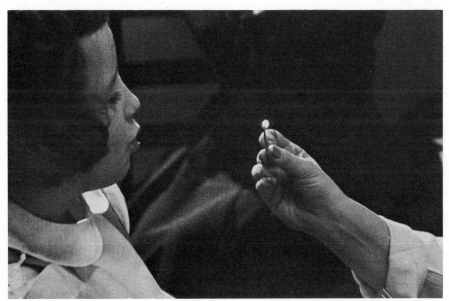

chapter 18

Living with Children at Home

The importance of the family

Even in the rapidly changing world of today the family is still the primary unit in our society. The outward forms of family life have changed, but children still start life as members of a family group, and each boy and girl reflects the influence of his family on his life. His mother and father, his grandparents, and even his great-grandparents leave their mark on him, not only through genetic influence on his physique, his basic temperament, his capacities, and his limitations but also through some of the attitudes, customs, and child-rearing practices that have been passed down from one generation to another. This family "lore" accumulates and is rarely discarded entirely, even though new cultural patterns may be added to it.

A child's *immediate* family influences him even more strongly, of course, through the ways they help him to grow up; through the feelings they have for him and those he develops for them; through the values, beliefs, and goals that they instill in him. Indeed, the family's influence is so great that if it is unhealthy it can handicap even a child whose heredity is sound and prevent him from developing his capacities. By the same token, a healthy family influence can build on sound heredity or even help compensate for some hereditary handicaps.

Those who work with problems of adjustment place a major emphasis on the effect of early emotional experiences in the home in determining how a child will feel toward other people and in determining his capacity to withstand the strains and frustrations he will necessarily meet as he grows up. During the last half century clinical studies have been accumulating evidence that every child needs the security of belonging, of being accepted, and of being loved. These studies have also shown that juvenile delinquents and seriously disturbed children seldom come from homes that provide a warm, affectionate, accepting atmosphere. Many of them come, rather, from unstable or broken homes in which they have been unwanted or neglected. It has also been found that in many cases children who have grown up in institutions where they had no personal relationship with

an adult have been retarded both in their mental growth and in their ability to relate warmly to other people. Research studies have also documented many cases of babies and young children who have suffered severe physical retardation when they have been deprived of sufficient mothering.

No satisfactory substitute for a home has yet been found for supplying the kind of care that children need. The family still remains the first group in which a child can feel that he belongs and have the experience of being cared for in a warm and personal way. A child whose family fails him experiences the deep void of being unwanted, a void which he may seek to fill all of his life as he turns from one group or person to another in trying to satisfy his need to belong.

Child-placement agencies are recognizing this need of children for a personal home and a personal parent-child relationship by trying to find foster homes for children whose homes have somehow failed them. When institutional placement seems the only available possibility, the placement-agency personnel look for institutions that try to give family-like experiences to the children in their care.

Such institutions try to divide the children into small groups with a mother-substitute and, when possible, a father-substitute for each group. Some social agencies are trying in still another way to meet children's need for a family by keeping impoverished families together, giving financial aid when necessary instead of taking children away from parents who cannot support them. It is now recognized that a home inadequate by many material standards may still be the best home for children if the parents are able to supply warmth and affection and interest in their children.

Providing and demonstrating affection

A great deal of misunderstanding has arisen over the stress placed on the parent-child relationship. Some parents take this to mean that they must lavish physical and verbal expressions of love on their children. Other parents think that they must give a child complete freedom to develop in his own way, never expressing their point of view, establishing their own needs, or frustrating the child for fear they will block his development. Still others place great importance on the providing of material things for their children. Some parents make their children the center of the family's life to such an extent that the children never learn that belonging is only real when one shares in meeting the needs of the entire group.

Children need parents who are warm, mature adults. Such parents welcome a baby at birth; accept his heredity and build on it; try to provide him with the best conditions for physical growth; and try to understand his particular pattern of growth. Through affection, encouragement, and consistent guidance and example they provide the child with the personal security that leads to self-confidence and mental health. Such parents may be found in almost every kind of home. Many children have grown to happy, competent maturity despite shortcomings in their physical surroundings, and many have grown into warped personalities in homes that supplied their physical needs in abundance. There are good homes and inadequate homes in every kind of neighborhood. Pleasant physical surroundings make growth easier, but it is the emotional relationships within the home that make the essential difference between a home in which growth proceeds freely and one in which it is hampered.

In a good home, parents want their children. They enjoy them. Even though family life engenders problems and worries and responsibilities, the parents feel that the rewards of having a family far outweigh any problems involved. In such a family, children receive affection, love, and the warmth of belonging. Affection is shown not only in the care given to the children but in the tone of voice, the arm around the shoulder, the fun together, the spontaneous laughter, the games, the stories at bedtime, and the willingness to listen and enter into each child's interests. Children are literal and so need the tangible proof of being loved that parents who enjoy their children can give.

As children grow up, the ways in which their parents show their affection and interest will naturally change. For example, small children love to roughhouse with their father or to be taken for a piggyback ride, while elementary-school children are more likely to prefer their parents' help in making an airplane or learning to sew a doll's dress. Teen-agers, while not always willing to confide in their parents, sometimes are anxious to have them listen to and help with their problems. But sometimes parents unwittingly lose the opportunity to express their affection for their children by establishing an unbreakable pattern of "doing things together" instead of allowing for spontaneous opportunities and impulses. The custom of a family evening around the fire, for instance, can be enjoyable if the pattern can be broken when one of the children wants to do something special or to go out with his friends. Plans should be flexible enough to be adapted to the family's growth and changing interests. Preschool children need and want the routine of always doing things in the same way, and even school-age children tend to cling to certain routines; but as children grow older it is the enjoyment of doing things together and being a part of the family group that is important, not the set time or plan. In fact, too rigid planning of family activities can even interfere with the enjoyment of them. An activity such as a picnic planned spontaneously when everyone is home will probably be more enjoyable than one that has been scheduled for every Friday evening.

Grandparents can add a sense of unity and continuity to family life. Children can learn from their grandparents, have fun with them, and, most important of all, love and be loved by them.

It is through the warm relationship that he establishes with his mother and father that a child learns how to love and get along with other people, including his own brothers and sisters. In every family with more than one child, there will be occasional tensions among the children—quarrels, disagreements, and jealousy—as each seeks to be first in the eyes of his parents. But parents can ease these tensions by gradually showing their children that they love and accept each one and that they will try to be fair with everybody. In such a family the underlying feeling of belonging to each other will be strong enough to balance the normal stresses of living and growing up together. When this feeling of belonging exists, the problems that do arise can be seen in perspective. Negative emotions, such as hostility and jealousy, will arise from time to time, but these will not constitute the family's basic emotional pattern.

A child needs to feel that he is completely accepted by his mother and father and that their love is not contingent on a particular kind of behavior. He needs to feel that he is loved not for his looks or his schoolwork or his good behavior but because he is himself. In a good home parents recognize each child's individuality and love each one as he is. They accept the child—the poorly coordinated child, the agile child, the child who learns easily in school, the child who learns best with his hands, the handsome child, the plain child, the handicapped or delicate child. If parents can accept their child as he is, they will then be able to help him grow within his own pattern. They will not try to turn him into the kind of child that they had perhaps pictured before he was born, nor will they try to make him like his brothers or sisters or the neighbors' children. They will help him to develop at his own speed and in his own way.

Parents' loving, consistent relationships with their children help the children meet the demands of growing up. This child, for example, has a cheerful matter-of-fact attitude toward toilet training, primarily because of her mother's steady encouragement and relaxed attitude.

A child grows best when his parents are consistent in their attitudes toward him and in what they expect him to do. A child should be able to count on the way his parents will usually react. The wise parent will not let his moods interfere with his basic feelings for his child or with the pattern of behavior he will expect his child to follow. He will realize that the child has many things to learn. The child is not born knowing what is right and wrong or what kind of behavior is considered acceptable in the part of the world where he lives. These are things that he will learn gradually as he grows up. The first pattern of behavior that he learns is the one that his parents teach him during his early years. What his mother and father say is right, the child accepts as right; what he is told is wrong, he believes is wrong. As he grows older, he will encounter other standards of behavior and will learn to make his own decisions about right and wrong, but if his parents' standards were inadequate or confused or inconsistent, he will have more trouble in knowing what he is expected to do and in learning to exercise sound judgment.

Whether the youngster will accept and follow the standards of his home as a little child and later as an adolescent will depend largely on the relationship that is built between him and his parents. If the child feels that he is loved and accepted and if he respects his parents' standards, he is likely to accept their guidance and learn the behavior they are trying to teach him. But if he is unhappy in his relationship with one or both of his parents, he may seem to accept the pattern through fear but not make it really part of himself, or he may rebel against his

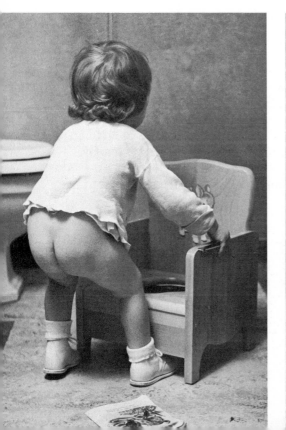

parents and refuse to do what they ask—whether it concerns toilet training or eating or coming home at a reasonable hour. The child who has warm feelings toward his parents is better able to resist being influenced by undesirable behavior which he may meet in his neighborhood, through his gang, or through questionable friends than is a child whose need for affection has not been met at home. A youngster who lacks affection will usually turn to anyone who will offer him the satisfaction and security of belonging, and he will be inclined to accept unquestioningly the standards and behavior of his new friends, even if the standards are ones he has been taught to consider unacceptable.

As parents teach their children desirable patterns of behavior, they will find it necessary to make rules and set limits. These will vary with the age of the children and with the particular family situation. Well-adjusted, happy children are found both in families where parents are strict and in families where parents are lenient. Whether the home is strict or relaxed, the essential again is *consistency*. Wise parents will not make a rule today that may be broken tomorrow because mother has a headache or father is busy in the yard and cannot bother to enforce it. If a small boy is forbidden to play in the street today, he should not be allowed to get away with it tomorrow. Inconsistency in rules is unfair to the youngster. It confuses him.

If a child is old enough, he should be allowed to help make the rules, because then he will better understand the reasons for them. Rules should be well considered and should be kept at a minimum, involving only the essentials of safety and consideration for other people. There need to be rules, for example, about crossing streets and about letting parents know where you are going; such rules are reasonable and children will usually conform to them. But rules should not be made for situations that may change so frequently that the rule cannot be enforced.

As a child grows, rules have to be changed to meet new needs and situations. The yard may be a reasonable limit for a two-year-old, but a four-year-old will become restless and rebellious if confined to the yard. He will want to ride his tricycle up and down the block and to play with other children a few houses away. The school-age child will find the limits of the block too small and will want to go to the playground or to visit a friend a few blocks away, while the adolescent will need the wider limits of the entire community and in some cases opportunities to go even farther away from home. Rules and limits should be made to fit the maturity of the child—the child should not be squeezed into the rules. Intelligent consistency and flexibility in setting limits give boys and girls a feeling of security. Children need to know what they may do and what is expected, and parents must expect of a child only that which he is mature enough to give.

Fitting punishment to the situation and to the child

In all homes there will be times when some form of punishment is needed. Such a method of teaching should be reserved for times when a youngster has deliberately done what he knows he should not do. In considering punishment, parents should understand both the situation and what can fairly be expected of the youngster at his particular stage of growing up. For example, they shouldn't

punish the toddler for breaking a pretty object, even though he has been told not to touch it; they shouldn't always expect the four-year-old to tell the truth or the school-age child to remember consistently without a reminder; and they shouldn't become too upset with the adolescent if he sometimes seems irresponsible. Punishment should never be used to try to curb actions that indicate a child may be under tension. Thumb-sucking, masturbating, nail-biting, stuttering, and failing in school are examples of behavior that cannot be helped by any form of punishment.

If punishment is to be at all useful, it must vary with the age of the child, with the thing he has done, and with the kind of child he is. One child can accept and understand the reasonableness of a punishment, but another who is more timid or sensitive may crumple under even a mild punishment. Punishment should be meaningful to the child so that it really involves him in a learning situation and helps him to remember the next time. The four-year-old who plays in the street might be restricted to the house or yard for a short time, and the nine-year-old who breaks a window because he played ball where he wasn't supposed to might make amends by mowing the neighbors' lawn or performing some other service to help pay for the damage he has done.

Although spanking is not usually a desirable punishment, a young child may be able to accept a mild spanking better than constant nagging. Each parent must decide for himself the kind of punishment that he feels comfortable in administering and that seems effective with his child. In every case the important thing is for the child to feel that, despite being punished, he still has his parents' love and affection. If he detects hostility or indifference in his parents' behavior toward him, even the mildest punishment may be too hard for him to take. In such a case punishment may increase the child's timidity or feed his rebellion. Punishment which is too severe creates fear and anxiety. Rather than teaching the child, it creates tensions that make teaching more difficult. To be of any value, punishment must be reasonable. It should never deprive the child of his self-respect or make him feel that he, as a person, is "bad." Punishment used too frequently often indicates that tensions are building between the parent and the child and that these tensions need thoughtful consideration.

Participating in family life

Children grow best in a home in which they participate. Taking part increases their feeling of belonging, of being valued, of being wanted and accepted. From the time they are little, children need to feel that they are part of the family— sharing in work, in play, in family celebrations, and later even in problems. Instead of mother and father making all the rules, plans, and decisions, the children should be drawn into planning a picnic or a vacation, discussing the purchase of a new car or a new chair, or talking over the question of allowances or how to stretch the budget.

Each family has its own way of doing things, but in the homes in which chil-

dren are the happiest and best adjusted, the children usually take an active part in the work of the household. Parents can teach or fail to teach invaluable habits and attitudes toward work by their own feelings about it. Children easily come to feel that they don't like to work if their mother complains about doing the dishes or if their father is conspicuously reluctant to leave his paper and clean up the yard. Whenever possible, parents and children should work together as a cooperative unit. Work in the home rarely goes smoothly when children are *told* to do jobs. It is better to talk over the work to be done and let the family decide together how it will be distributed. An opportunity for a child to change jobs as his interest lags will help to keep up his cooperation. It is not the specific job that is important but the fact that the child has a valued contribution to make.

Competition within the family is lessened when each member of the family has an opportunity to help with the planning and each uses his skills for the benefit of the family group. If one child likes to cook and does it well, the family may elect her to help make the desserts. Another who is learning about electricity in school and is clever at electrical repair work may get the job of seeing that the electrical appliances are in order. Some families hold a regular family council in which everyone, even the littlest child, takes part. Household work is discussed and assigned, problems are talked over, complaints are aired, and plans are made. Other families have less formal discussions—perhaps around the dinner table when everyone is present and some special point has come up. But whatever method is used, children grow best when they are real participants. In all families there will be decisions that must ultimately be made by the parents, but the children's ideas can be welcomed, considered, and talked over before a decision is reached. Children follow decisions more readily and with greater understanding when they have had a part in making them.

Many compromises have to be made and accepted in every family, but in a family in which everyone takes part in making decisions, the compromises are usually better understood and more fully accepted. Both parents and children have to compromise for the benefit of the family group. For example, parents have to be willing to put up with more mess and noise than they like, whereas children have to accept the fact that there are limits to the mess and noise which adults can tolerate.

As children grow old enough to understand, they are able to share in some of the serious family decisions, worries, and problems. Permitting children to know about family crises and to share in meeting them enables the children to come through the crises with the least possible strain. A conference behind closed doors or an anxious, abstracted look on a parent's face can worry and frighten a child more than a knowledge of the facts. "Daddy is having trouble with his job," or, "Mother is very sick with pneumonia, but Dr. Smith is coming and will do all he can to make her better. Will you help by giving Timmie his supper?"—such straightforward explanations give a child a sense of his own worth, of his responsibility in the family, that makes him better able to meet problems and troubles. Children who really share in the life of their family develop a family loyalty and a "we-feeling" which usually last throughout their lives and add to their emotional security. In addition, they receive invaluable practice in making decisions and in carrying responsibility. Sharing the fun, the responsibilities, and the problems of the family is essential if growth is to be at its best.

Some children never develop a clear idea of what their father does when he leaves the house to go to work. But this boy, by visiting his father's studio, seeing the paintings, and watching his father work, is developing such a concept—in addition to enjoying his father's company.

Helping children meet their problems

The wise parent remembers that growth does not always proceed smoothly. Even with the best of daily guidance, boys and girls will have problems and will sometimes get into trouble. Children need to feel that they can safely let their parents know what they feel and think. If their real feelings and hurts must go unexpressed, the repressed emotions may fester and come out in undesirable forms of behavior. Withdrawal, bullying, quarrelsomeness, headaches, and stomach aches are some of the many channels through which hurt or anger may find their way to the surface. Children need the release that comes from being able to say how they really feel and the security of being allowed to explode when they are under too much pressure. But parents cannot always accept the form of release that their youngster uses. They may often have to let the child know that they understand his feelings but don't approve of his way of expressing them because, in the process, he is hurting someone else or damaging someone else's property.

300

Sometimes a youngster becomes so disturbed that his parents are no longer able to give him the help he needs. It is not always easy for parents to realize that their child has reached this point and that they should seek the help of a guidance specialist. When a child fails to learn from his own experience or mistakes, or when he is unable to make adjustments, he needs professional guidance. This is also true when his mistakes become too serious, when he pulls away from life because of the pain his experiences give him, or when his relationships with his parents have become so tense that he doesn't respond to their efforts to help him. A child's problem is of a serious nature when any of the following behavior patterns become characteristic: withdrawal from others; preoccupation with health or with symptoms of illness; any other anxious preoccupation which interferes with schoolwork or effective living; delinquency; inability to accept his own sex or to be normally interested for his age in the other sex; chronic unhappiness or anxiety; troubled and obsessive thoughts; compulsive actions; irrational fears; or suspiciousness. Sometimes recognition of these symptoms may be gradual. At other times parents suddenly realize that a child's difficult behavior is becoming more frequent and marked—a customary pattern of behavior instead of an occasional one. It is important for parents to seek help for the child who shows any of these forms of behavior, for these are symptoms that indicate emotional tensions, tensions that cannot be relieved until they are fully understood.

Parents will not be able to fulfill all of their children's needs, and all children will have experiences that will make their parents unhappy. But if parents try to build a warm and stable home so that their children have an opportunity from babyhood on to develop good emotional balance, their boys and girls will usually be better prepared to withstand the problems of their environment, whatever they may be.

chapter 19

Teachers and Parents Work Together

Understanding the whole child

In understanding the individual child, his needs and his problems, the teacher and parent should meet and share their knowledge of the child whenever possible. The parent must help the teacher to see the youngster as he is in his family and neighborhood group; the teacher must bring to the parent her insight into the child's capacity to learn in the classroom and to live and work with others in the school environment. Teacher and parent must work in harmony—each one has the welfare of the child in mind, and each has a special contribution to make to the child's growth and development.

The parent is responsible for providing the emotional support and individual guidance his child will need as he is growing up. His concern for the child is and should be deep and personal. The bonds of affection must be strong if the child is to feel the security of belonging to his family group. This is essential if he is to become an emotionally healthy adult.

The teacher, too, feels deep concern for the individual child, but her responsibility is in two directions. Her primary responsibility is to teach. She must see that each child is equipped, insofar as possible, with the skills and knowledge that will enable him to meet his responsibilities as an adult in a complex world. In working toward this end, she must pay attention not only to *what* is to be learned but also to the individual boys and girls who are the learners. Only as she understands and recognizes that a child's emotional needs must be met if he is to learn effectively will she be able to fulfill her role as teacher.

When parents and teachers feel able to communicate with one another, realizing that each has the welfare of the child in mind, the child can be seen as a whole person, not segmented between school and home. His experiences can be brought together and seen in perspective so that parents and teacher, planning together, can help him to develop his capacities as fully as possible. Many potential problems never develop if, through the years, parents meet with teachers to discuss the needs and characteristics of their children. Through such meetings the parent can learn about the classroom program which has been planned or is being developed, and the teacher can gain valuable insights into the child's relationships with his parents and into his home conditions.

Parent-teacher conferences

The keynote of cooperative relationships with parents is not the teacher's professional training nor her understanding of learning processes or even of child psychology. Rather, it is her willingness to talk with the parents and to listen to them, in order to seek and understand more fully the reasons behind their child's behavior. If the child is having trouble at school, what do the parents think the problem is? Have they any idea how the problem arose? What action have the parents taken and what do they think the school should do? What can school and home do together? Thoughtful discussion between teacher and parents may seem to make little headway at times, but the conclusions they reach together are much more likely to lead to a successful plan for attacking the problem than are conclusions reached by the teacher alone.

The importance and benefit of teachers' giving parents a complete and detailed progress report on their children can hardly be overemphasized. A report, whether it is written or given at a parent-teacher conference, can give perspective both on the child's progress and on problem areas—perspective from which parents and teachers can then plan intelligently for the child. Such a report should be based, of course, on a child's own record rather than on comparisons with other children. (See "Guide for Parent-Teacher Conferences," page 332.)

Unfortunately, teachers can seldom get to know the parents of all their children. Often the parents whom they would most like to know will not come to school. Some are afraid of the teacher—a carry over, perhaps, from their own

School systems throughout the country are carrying on programs to help children who attend inner city schools both scholastically and socially. One such program, in which parents as well as teachers and school administrators are enthusiastically involved, is that of the Flint, Michigan public schools. Here, for example, fathers are building teaching aids that will be used in the inner city schools.

school days. Others are too busy or not sufficiently interested. Some are embarrassed to come to school because of inadequate clothing, work-roughened hands, or inarticulate language. Still others might like to come to school but do not realize that they would be welcomed by the teacher.

It should be made easy for parents to come to school—the door of the school should always be open. Parents should be informed, however, about when they can most conveniently confer with a teacher or principal. In some schools a parent may drop in at any time, but in others the teachers set aside special hours to see parents or to talk on the phone. Whatever the arrangements are, they should be clearly stated at the beginning of the year so that no parent need suffer embarrassment or be put off because he happens to come to school at an inconvenient time. Special arrangements should be provided if both parents work and neither can get to school at the times regularly scheduled for conferences.

The school in the community

It is easy to blame parents who never come to school for lack of interest in their children, but before doing so the school personnel should study their own policies. Has the school become part of the neighborhood? Parents in middle- and upper-class neighborhoods usually take it for granted that they may go to school. But in impoverished neighborhoods and in some neighborhoods with large numbers of foreign parents, the school must reach out toward the parents and encourage them to feel that this is *their* school.

Every teacher needs to become familiar with the disciplines, traditions, customs, taboos, and attitudes of the community in which she teaches, especially those of the homes of children in her class. A child who is well accepted in his own home or neighborhood may face a problem when confronted with a school situation where he meets, for the first time, a completely new set of social and ethical standards. Most teachers come from the middle class and are accustomed to middle-class standards of language, behavior, and values. But many children come to school from homes in which these standards do not exist. Children from lower-class homes often shock their teachers by using words that are offensive in a middle-class group. Yet these may be the only words they have learned, words that are commonly used within their families and their neighborhoods. If teachers take these children's efforts to express themselves in their own language as deliberate disrespect, communication between children and teacher will inevitably suffer.

Many communities also include national and racial groups that have customs different from those of the community as a whole. If these customs—many of which have a traditional value—are ignored or undermined at school, a child may lose his mooring to his family and even come to look down on his own parents. All parents are quick to sense whether their child's teacher respects their traditional ways or rejects them as being different from her own.

Although a teacher may want to help all children achieve the values and patterns of behavior she considers desirable and appropriate, she will be making a mistake if she fails to recognize the cultural pattern of the community, the reason and often the necessity for behavior considerably different from her own. She must choose carefully the behavior and attitudes that she will try to change and learn to recognize those that are better left undisturbed.

Understanding problems at home

Parents sometimes hesitate to talk with their child's teacher for fear that the teacher will be critical of them because their child has failed in some respect. Often teachers do blame parents when things go wrong with their children. This is easy to do and at times is justified. But as professionals, teachers should have some understanding of the causes behind parental behavior and should be able to accept parents of all kinds with patience and insight. By showing too obviously their disapproval of parents, they may lose the opportunity to gain an understanding of the home problem and may completely destroy any possibility of effective communication concerning the child's problem.

Many parents are on the defensive. Most of them want to love and understand their children; they would like to give their children the essentials for healthy emotional growth, but they are unable to do so because of conflicts, problems, or lack of emotional, intellectual, or financial resources. Even some parents who can accept their children's needs intellectually are unable to show the warmth and affection they feel. Perhaps they themselves as children were never really helped to learn how to show affection. Others, like Agnes' parents, have unresolved conflicts of their own which make them resent the burdens of parenthood and interfere with their enjoyment or understanding of their children. Some parents take out on their children tensions resulting from their own marital problems or from negative feelings that they still harbor toward their own parents and their own childhood. Sometimes they cannot seem to love a child or care for him adequately because he reminds them of undesirable or disappointing qualities in themselves or in a husband or wife or parent. There are parents, too, who need to exert authority over a child to make up for their own feelings of inadequacy and insecurity. Such parents may be unnecessarily harsh. Others would like to be kind to their children and to guide them well but fail because they interpret behavior exclusively in terms of "good" and "bad" or in relation to themselves— "Does it annoy me?" Such parents are usually unaware of their failure to interpret their child's behavior in relation to his developmental needs.

Unfortunately parents are sometimes so hampered by their own problems or inadequacies that they are unable to do what is best for their children. But as professional people, teachers should take an understanding attitude toward the parents' failures as well as the children's failures. In condemning a parent the teacher only widens the gap between home and school and makes fruitful cooperation virtually impossible. A teacher must be able to recognize the point at which she cannot reach a parent or hope to obtain the parental help that she feels a child needs. If a teacher anticipates that her inability to communicate with the parents is likely to have serious consequences for the child, she will want to talk with the principal, the school psychologist, or the counselor to see what plans can be made for the child. Sometimes, too, these individuals can suggest ways to steer parents toward the help that they need in working through their own problems.

A teacher cannot change an undesirable home environment. Yet by her knowledge of her students' home conditions, she can do much to give them the help and the support they need. Huntley, Johnny, and Mark suffered from emotional insecurity as a result of their parents' difficulties. In each case their feelings affected their schoolwork. A fairly stable home basis was eventually established for Mark and Johnny, but Huntley's original insecurity was aggravated by his abnormal family situation. The harsh and eccentric grandmother, the aloof aunt, the rejecting father made a happy adjustment impossible for the boy. A number of children, like Huntley, are subjected to the influence of many relatives in the home and to all the conflicts of in-laws who disagree with one another. Perhaps the household is divided by friction or divorce has created a problem, as it did for Huntley. Special problems are created, too, if one of the parents is physically handicapped—deaf, blind, or trying to direct the household from a wheel chair or invalid's bed. A father or mother may be bringing up the family alone. A mother may be working and thus have to be away from her children immediately before and after school. Sometimes an older child, particularly a girl, may be doing most of the housework and taking care of the younger children, or a boy may be holding down an after-school job to help the family finances. Such heavy responsibilities are likely to affect the preparation of schoolwork. Knowledge of a child's home life cannot help but make a difference in a teacher's attitude, her patience, and the techniques she will find useful when problems arise.

Home visits are not always possible, and in some school systems they are not considered advisable. In some schools, a social worker or a visiting teacher is assigned to gather information about the backgrounds of the children, particularly those who have problems and need help. A cumulative record of home visits, if it is properly kept, can be a useful source of information. Any information included in the cumulative record must be treated professionally, of course, and should never become a subject of gossip in the teachers' room.

Because children from the same family attend the same neighborhood school, a great deal of information can be compiled from their various records. Teachers who have known other children from the same families, and teachers who have taught a child in previous years can be valuable sources of information, as can the principal. The knowledge gained from these sources can then be added to the teacher's own assessment of the family situation.

Understanding problems at school

At times parents come to a conference at school feeling that the school rather than their child is at fault. When this happens, many teachers react indignantly. Although some parents blame teachers unreasonably for a child's failure, there are times when the teacher or the methods or policies of the school may indeed be at fault.

Although a child's growth is influenced first and most strongly by his home, even an adequately adjusted child may develop personality difficulties or fail in his schoolwork if the school environment is unsuitable. A child who has always done well in school may become anxious and discouraged if he has a harsh, uncompromising teacher or one who is inadequate and ill-prepared. A child who is constantly expected to accomplish work that is beyond him by a teacher who sets a single standard for all the children in her class may lose his cheerful disposition and become unhappy, withdrawn, or disturbed. A parent is justified in questioning whether the class atmosphere or a relationship with a particular teacher is the cause of a child's problem, if the child has shown a marked difference in his behavior and attitude toward school when he has moved into a new class. Such changed behavior may serve as a cue for the thoughtful teacher to question herself, to reëxamine her classroom methods and perhaps her feelings for a particular child.

Teachers are people, too. Each one brings to the classroom not only her knowledge and training but her personality as well. Just as the parents' personalities help to create a child's home environment, so the teacher's personality determines in great part the climate of the schoolroom. Sometimes a teacher finds herself unable to be patient and warm with her students, even though she desires to do so. She may be under strain and tension herself. She may have home problems and worries which crowd into her mind during the school day in spite of her attempts to forget them and to think only of her class. Or she may feel insecure because she lacks experience or adequate training. She may be afraid that her class will get out of hand, that she will not maintain proper discipline, or that the supervisor or principal will walk in at a critical moment. This may make her brusque and irritable, to the detriment of all her students and especially of those who are particularly sensitive or insecure.

Some teachers will be worried, strained, or anxious as a result of past experiences or present difficulties. Nevertheless, a teacher must be aware of how deeply her personality and her anxieties can affect the children in her class. If her problem or anxiety is not a passing thing but results in a pattern of behavior that prevents her from achieving a pleasant, calm atmosphere in her classroom, if her irritabilities affect her teaching, she should seek help and try to reach an adjustment that will make life more comfortable both for herself and for the youngsters in her class. Her own mental health must be good if she is to teach children effectively.

Homework and extracurricular activities

The everyday practices of school life can result in friction between home and school if parents and teachers do not discuss them and agree on them. The assignment of homework, for example, frequently becomes a cause of tension and misunderstanding. The teacher often feels herself caught in the middle between parents who want their child to have a lot of homework—who gauge his progress by the amount of work he brings home—and other parents who are concerned because their child has to work too late in the evening. Parents have a right to be concerned if homework interferes with needed outdoor recreation or sleep. Every child needs time to participate in the family group as well as in the school group, to do his share of work in the home, and to enjoy his hobby, his music, his books, and even some television.

Teachers must think through the relationship of homework to the total life of the child. Where a departmental system is used, teachers in the different departments need to check with one another to see whether the overall amount of homework required is realistic or whether each is making an assignment without regard to what the others are requiring. It is also important to differentiate assignments for children of different abilities. A fast learner may cover a long reading assignment in less time than it takes a slow child to read even a few pages.

Sometimes parents are justifiably irritated by assignments requiring the use of reference material that all homes do not have, especially if a library is not easily available. They are also likely to resent having their child encouraged to undertake a project involving expenses they cannot meet without financial strain, such as an elaborate project for a science fair.

If homework is to be assigned, particularly in the elementary grades, the school should help the parents to understand their expected role. Many teachers would be surprised if they could look into the homes of their students and watch the tension that frequently develops over getting homework done. Many parents dread the evening hours—which should be a pleasant family time—because of the nagging and pressures they feel obliged to use to make their children get their homework done. Many parents, too, try to help with homework but only succeed in confusing their children by using methods different from those that the school is using. Other tensions crop up in homes so crowded that boys and girls, particularly of high-school age, have trouble finding a quiet spot in which to work.

Homework that has a real purpose may have a place in the school program, but homework that is just busy work is unjustified. Both parents and children resent assignments that are given to be done at home but are never looked at, corrected, or returned by the teacher.

Extracurricular activities may also cause tensions between school and home. A play rehearsal scheduled too near supper time, costumes that take money and time to buy or make, committee work, band practice, or even punishment scheduled for after school with no thought of how the children will be able to get home—these may all prove potential points of irritation if parental cooperation has not been sought beforehand.

Parents also have a right to expect that school activities will be open to all boys and girls. Lack of money or suitable clothing should not form a barrier between students within the school. Activity fees, trips, or parties that are too expensive for some of the children in the school can upset and embarrass these children and their parents, especially if the children are forced to miss the event.

Explaining the school program to parents

Much of the misunderstanding that arises between parents and teachers revolves around the parents' feeling that their children are not learning enough.

One way of building cooperation between parents and teachers is to acquaint parents with the school's programs and curriculum. These parents are taking a one-month course in the new math that their children are studying.

Parents are proverbially fearful that their child will not learn to read and do his arithmetic. They need reassurance based on facts. Methods change, and parents need answers to their questions about why certain subjects are taught in certain grades and why others are held until later. They need to understand the reasons behind new methods of teaching. Many parents would appreciate more interpretation by the school of the aims and goals of the whole school program and, in particular, of their child's class. They want to know the policies of their school system. Parents can be informed in PTA meetings and, even more effectively, in small classroom meetings or in specially planned discussion groups. Written presentations sent out to each parent may also help, but they are not as effective as meetings in which parents and teachers talk over together the school's aims and methods.

Thoughtful parents are genuinely concerned about school policies and their effect on the education of their children. Teachers shouldn't be afraid of parents' honest questions or their honest criticisms. If school personnel show a willingness to talk over controversial matters and back their policies with factual statements, they will usually find that the questioning parent and the school can come to a better understanding of one another. This does not mean that groups of parents should be encouraged to run the schools—the actual educational direction must remain in the hands of the superintendent and the staff who have been professionally trained for this task, and teachers must be free to teach according to the methods that have been found to work best. But only as parents and teachers work together can each child's best educational growth be attained.

Building cooperation between school, home, and community

Parents can be drawn into the life of the school in many ways. Some schools do so by making the school a community center to which parents and children can come separately or together for many activities. A school building should be in constant use, symbolizing the place of learning in the community. Parents, children, and adults without children need to feel welcome, not only for lessons but for other community experiences. Some schools have hobby nights when whole families work together in the shops and the art room. Many schools are open in the evenings for adult education classes, thus drawing the parents into the building for educational interests of their own. Other schools open their doors for all kinds of meetings, for forums and community groups, for classes in citizenship. Some schools share their facilities with the recreation department for summer or after-school play. One city has opened a new school building which houses a county health clinic and a branch of the library. Parents who come to the school for many purposes usually have a much closer feeling for the teachers and the work of the school.

The relationship between the school and the parents may affect the work of the school as a whole as well as the way in which an individual child is helped to learn. When the school and the parents are not in sympathy and are not working together, the program of the school may be seriously damaged. Working for cooperation between school and home takes time, especially when classes are crowded and teachers are overburdened, but the effort can pay large dividends.

Children experience an infinitely better climate for learning when their parents feel that "This is our school and a fine one."

The Committee on Academic Education of the American Psychiatric Association feel that cooperation between home and school is of such significance that they circulated the following letter to their members:

*The School and Community**

Gone are those days when the child was sent to school for six hours and lived in the home as another world for the rest of the day. As educators, we create the school in the community in which we find ourselves. The outside forces affecting the community cannot be controlled or changed in a day, but the school can be molded, as a piece of soft clay in the hands of a skillful artist, to make it fit into its surrounding world and to make it take the form and shape that will attract and welcome the community.

There are three essentials for good school-community relationships:

1) Parents and teachers must know and trust each other. The school belongs to the people, not to the principal who is entrusted with its leadership. In the community-centered school, the parents come and go in the building with a sense of belonging, not intruding. The privilege of moving about the school unchallenged is wisely used by parents who recognize the aims of the educational program and do not abuse the freedom which is theirs. Mothers and fathers come in to walk through the halls and see the displays of pupils' work; to absorb the atmosphere of relaxation coupled with purposeful activity; to stop in a classroom and exchange a friendly greeting or to give Junior his raincoat for the unexpected shower. They come to the office to arrange for a private conference with the teacher; to make a complaint to the principal; or to consult the principal on a variety of personal needs.

This understanding of the place of the teacher and parent, where they are separate and where they merge, is reached through meeting and working together in Parent-teacher organizations, grade conferences, and individual conferences. This mutual trust is achieved through a thorough knowledge of and a belief in the philosophy of education being carried out in the school. This philosophy must be the common belief of parents and educators; it must be clearly stated and often repeated.

2) Teachers must know the community in which they work. To teach a child, the leader must know not only his abilities, desires, weaknesses and strengths, but also those of his forebears, for woven into the fibre of this small being are all the joys and sorrows of past generations, transmitted to him through the culture of the home.

The child brings to his teacher a mind and a body bearing the imprint of his family, his playground or street, his church and his social agencies. How, then, can the teacher meet him on common ground if she is not thoroughly versed in the mores of the community? The true teacher does more than help the child to

*By Courtesy of the American Psychiatric Association and Mrs. Margaret S. Douglas, Principal, P.S. 133, Manhattan, N. Y.

develop through the school hours of each day. She visits homes, attends community meetings, confers with representatives of community agencies, reads copiously and joins in some phases of the social and religious life of the people with whom she works.

3) There must be many opportunities for parents and other community residents to work in the school. The community-centered school, while urging its teachers to go outside and absorb something of the life of the people, also opens wide its doors and draws in the community. Parents take part in school activities, initiate community projects among the students, and feel a sense of responsibility for the care of the actual buildings and grounds. There will be many friends of the school, not parents, whose interest in the school will be cultivated and used for mutual benefit. Leaders from many walks of life will be invited in to inspire the children and make friends with them.

Outside organizations should be encouraged to use the school for entertainments, forums, athletics, and dances.

The school must belong to all of the children and all of the adults living within its borders.

All that has been said in these brief words is this; the school with its facilities and community with its broad background of experience have common needs that can be met when the two forces join.

Lack of mutual understanding and trust have been the only barriers to the unification of these two tremendous powers to be used for the good of our children.

part six

Home, School, Community Work Together

FOR THOUGHT AND DISCUSSION

1. Briefly describe the characteristics of the male and female sex roles, considering display of emotions, dress, attitudes, and pastimes.

2. Do you think the general pattern of the roles of the sexes is changing? If so, give specific examples of how any changes are manifested. Are there any definite causes for the changes you have listed?

3. Does the sexual impulse begin at puberty? If not, when does it begin? Explain.

4. How would you answer the following question asked by a five-year-old: "Where did I come from?" How would you answer a nine-year-old who asked, "How are boys different from girls?"

5. Can you think of two television shows and two movies in which you have seen specific cases of oversophisticated or deviant sexual behavior that you feel might cause an adolescent to develop harmful or unrealistic attitudes about sex? In each case, describe the type of behavior and explain why you think it could have a detrimental effect on the adolescent's normally healthy sexual attitude.

6. Is there any specific difference between an "emotionally disturbed" and a "mentally retarded" child?

7. What is the teacher's role concerning a possibly emotionally disturbed or mentally retarded child who is in her class?

8. Think back over all of the case stories in this book and attempt to fit those children whom you feel are emotionally disturbed into the categories mentioned in Chapter 17. In each case, point out similarities between the behavior of the particular child and the general pattern of behavior described for that category.

9. Can a usual cause be found for the problems of emotionally disturbed children? For each of the categories mentioned in Chapter 17, briefly list the *probable* causes of the problem. Compare the background of each child whom you listed as emotionally disturbed in Question 8 with the typical background in the category where you placed him. Are the case-story backgrounds similar to the backgrounds in the categories in Chapter 17?

FOR FURTHER READING

EDUCATION FOR FAMILY LIVING

CHILD STUDY ASSOCIATION OF AMERICA. *What to Tell Your Child About Sex.* Rev. ed. New York: Pocket Books, Inc., 1964. A dependable source of information for parents and teachers. Practical and helpful.

DE SCHWEINITZ, KARL. *Growing Up*. 3rd ed. New York: The Macmillan Company, 1953. A clear explanation of the process of being born and growing up—a guide for elementary sex instruction. Useful for both younger and older children and for parents.

FLANAGAN, GERALDINE L. *The First Nine Months of Life*. New York: Simon and Schuster, Inc., 1962. A complete, beautifully written and illustrated study of prenatal development and birth. For older children and adults.

GRUENBERG, BENJAMIN C., and GRUENBERG, SIDONIE M. *The Wonderful Story of You*. Garden City, N.Y.: Doubleday and Company, Inc., 1960. Discusses "How you were born, and how and why you developed as you did." For older children.

GRUENBERG, SIDONIE M. *The Wonderful Story of How You Were Born*. Garden City, N.Y.: Doubleday & Company, Inc., 1952. Excellent for elementary-school children.

LERRIGO, MARION O., and SOUTHARD, HELEN, in consultation with SENN, MILTON. The *Dutton Series on Sex Education*. New York: E. P. Dutton & Co., 1956. The series includes six booklets prepared for different age levels. Approved by a joint committee of the National Education Association and the American Medical Association.

LEVINE, MILTON I., and SELIGMANN, JEAN H. *A Baby Is Born*. Rev. ed. New York: Golden Press, Inc., 1962. An explanation of birth for children from six to ten.

LEVINE, MILTON I., and SELIGMANN, JEAN H. *The Wonder of Life*. New York: Golden Press, Inc., 1952. Factual sex information for the elementary-school child.

MUSEUM OF SCIENCE AND INDUSTRY (Chicago), and the UNIVERSITY OF ILLINOIS PROFESSIONAL COLLEGES (Chicago). *The Miracle of Growth*. New York: Pyramid Publications, Inc., 1956. Discusses human development from the time of conception. Relates biological facts in a way that reveals the miracle of life and growth.

STRAIN, FRANCES BRUCE. *Being Born*. New York: Appleton-Century-Crofts, 1954. Has become a classic in its field. For older children.

STRAIN, FRANCES BRUCE. *Love at the Threshold*. Rev. ed. New York: Appleton-Century-Crofts, 1962. Discusses dating, courtship, love, and marriage. For teen-agers.

WHEN THINGS GO WRONG

AYRAULT, EVELYN WEST. *You Can Raise Your Handicapped Child*. New York: G. P. Putnam's Sons, 1964. A practical, helpful book for both parents and teachers.

BOWER, ELI. *Early Identification of Emotionally Handicapped Children in School*. Springfield, Ill.: Charles C. Thomas, Publisher, 1960. Report of a study by the California State Department of Education. Includes a review of past research in the field.

GILHAM, HELEN L. *Helping Children Accept Themselves and Others*. New York: Teachers College Press, 1959. Discusses how to help children whose image of themselves has been destroyed because they are handicapped or members of a minority group.

GRAHAM, FRANCES K., and others. *Brain Injury in the Preschool Child: Some Developmental Considerations*. Washington, D.C.: American Psychological Association, 1963. Discusses procedures developed to measure vocabulary, conceptual ability, perceptual-motor ability, and personality characteristics of normal preschool-age children. Compares performance of normal preschool children with that of brain-injured preschool children and suggests systematic differences in the effects of injury depending on age at time of injury. Pamphlet.

JENKINS, RICHARD L., M.D. *Breaking Patterns of Defeat*. Philadelphia: J. B. Lippincott Co., 1954. Presents some of the more serious problems of childhood. Written for people working in fields that deal with human relationships.

JOHNSON, WENDELL, and others. *Speech-Handicapped School Children*. Rev. ed. New York: Harper & Row, Publishers, 1956. A thorough discussion of speech handicaps and the problems that children with such handicaps face in school.

JUNKER, KARIN STENSLAND. Translated from the Swedish by LANNESTOCK, GUSTAF. *The Child in the Glass Ball*. Nashville, Tenn.: Abingdon Press, 1964. The understanding story of a retarded child and the way his parents helped him.

KIRK, SAMUEL A., ed. *Educating Exceptional Children*. Boston: Houghton Mifflin Company, 1962. Thorough discussion of the educational needs of exceptional children.

LEWIS, HILDA. *Deprived Children*. London: Oxford University Press, 1954. A follow-up study of 500 problem children.

MARY THEODORE, SISTER. *The Challenge of the Retarded Child*. Milwaukee: The Bruce Publishing Co., 1959. Discusses the special needs of the retarded child and how they can be met. Written with insight into the problems of both the child and the parents.

MASLAND, RICHARD L.; SARASON, SEYMOUR B.; and GLADWIN, THOMAS. *Mental Subnormality*. New York: Basic Books, Inc., Publishers, 1958. Includes a thorough discussion of the effects of heredity and culture on mental development.

PERRY, NATALIE. *Teaching the Mentally Retarded*. New York: Columbia University Press, 1960. Offers practical suggestions for training the severely retarded child.

ROBINSON, HALBERT B., and ROBINSON, NANCY M. *The Mentally Retarded Child*. New York: McGraw-Hill Book Company, 1965. Includes the most recent knowledge on mental retardation and the application of such knowledge in planning for a retarded child at home and at school.

ROUCEK, JOSEPH S., ed. *The Difficult Child*. New York: Philosophical Library, Inc., 1964. A compilation of articles covering many aspects of the problem of the "difficult child." Offers remedial and therapeutic suggestions.

RUBIN, THEODORE I., M.D. *Jordi*. New York. The Macmillan Company, 1960. The story of a severely disturbed child as told by a psychiatrist.

SIEGEL, ERNEST. *Helping the Brain-Injured Child*. New York: New York Association for Brain-Injured Children, 1962. Aids in understanding and helping the brain-injured child.

SPENCER, MARIETTA B. *Blind Children in Family and Community*. Minneapolis: University of Minnesota Press, 1960. A book of photographs with text prepared by a medical social worker. Discusses ways in which the basic principles of child guidance apply to blind preschool children and suggests the kinds of help these children may need.

STRAUSS, ALFRED A., M.D., and LEHTINEN, LAURA E. *Psychopathology and Education of the Brain-Injured Child: Fundamentals and Treatment*. Vol. I. New York: Grune & Stratton, 1947. Offers clinical observations of brain-injured children and results of experimental psychological investigations, including studies of thinking and behavior disorders and of perceptual disturbances. Also describes general principles of and specific methods for teaching brain-injured children.

WRIGHT, BEATRICE A. *Physical Disability: A Psychological Approach*. New York: Harper & Row, Publishers, 1960. Outlines constructive ways in which handicapped people can be helped to cope with their environment and to develop their potentialities.

YOUNG, LEONTINE. *Wednesday's Children*. New York: McGraw-Hill Book Company, 1964. A discussion of child neglect and abuse. Written by the Executive Director of the Child Service Association.

LIVING WITH CHILDREN AT HOME

ACKERMAN, NATHAN W. *The Psychodynamics of Family Life*. New York: Basic Books, Inc. Publishers, 1958. A comprehensive study of the interrelationships of family life.

ARNSTEIN, HELENE S. *What to Tell Your Child*. Indianapolis: The Bobbs-Merrill Co., Inc., 1962. Offers help in answering children's questions about community dangers, divorce, mental illness, family moves, etc. Developed in cooperation with the Child Study Association.

BETTELHEIM, BRUNO. *Dialogues With Mothers*. New York: Free Press of Glencoe, Inc., 1962. Based on actual discussions with mothers. Useful for teachers as well as parents.

BOSSARD, JAMES H. S., and BOLL, ELEANOR S. *The Sociology of Child Development*. 3rd ed. New York: Harper & Row, Publishers, 1960. Based on sociological research relating to children and parents. Introduces interesting material on routines of family life.

BRIM, ORVILLE GILBERT. *Education for Child Rearing*. New York: Russell Sage Foundation, 1959. Analyzes the methods used in parent education and calls attention to areas in which research is needed.

GLIDEWELL, JOHN C., ed. *Parental Attitudes and Child Behavior*. Springfield, Ill.: Charles C. Thomas, Publisher, 1961. Proceedings of Conference on Community Mental Health Research, Washington University, St. Louis, 1960. Provides an interdisciplinary approach to maternal attitudes and child behavior as well as a review of some of the most significant research in this field.

316

GRUENBERG, SIDONIE M., ed. *The Encyclopedia of Child Care and Guidance.* Garden City, N.Y.: Doubleday & Company, Inc., 1963. A comprehensive reference book with excellent articles by outstanding professional people.

HARRIS, IRVING D., M.D. *Normal Children and Mothers: Their Emotional Opportunities and Obstacles.* New York: Free Press of Glencoe, Inc., 1959. A study of the family background of 54 eight- to eleven-year-old, normal, well-adjusted girls, with a follow-up study four years later. Examines some popular assumptions.

HEREFORD, CARL F. *Changing Parental Attitudes Through Group Discussion.* Austin: University of Texas Press, 1963. An interesting research study on the results of parent-education discussion groups.

LIEBMAN, SAMUEL, M.D., ed. *Emotional Forces in the Family.* Philadelphia: J. B. Lippincott Co., 1959. A symposium of outstanding contributors discuss the ways in which the American family is forming new traditions.

NYE, FRANCES, and HOFFMAN, LOIS. *Employed Mother in America.* Chicago: Rand McNally & Co., 1963. Reports on studies concerning the problems of maternal employment.

SEARS, ROBERT R.; MACOBY, ELEANOR E.; and LEVIN, HARRY. *Patterns of Child Rearing.* New York: Harper & Row, Publishers, 1957. A careful, intensive study of the child-rearing patterns of 379 families in the Boston area.

SMITH, I. EVELYN, ed. *Readings in Adoption.* New York: Philosophical Library, Inc., 1963. Articles on the various aspects of adoption. Useful for both parents and teachers.

TEACHERS AND PARENTS WORK TOGETHER

BAILARD, VIRGINIA, and STRANG, RUTH. *Parent-Teacher Conferences.* New York: McGraw-Hill Book Company, 1964. A manual to help teachers conduct conferences with parents. Includes many sample interviews.

D'EVELYN, KATHERINE E. *Individual Parent-Teacher Conferences.* Rev. ed. New York: Teachers College Press, 1963. Helpful reports of actual parent-teacher conferences.

HAVIGHURST, ROBERT J., and NEUGARTEN, BERNICE L. *Society and Education.* 2nd ed. Boston: Allyn and Bacon, Inc., 1962. Discusses school values, family values, and the influence of teachers' backgrounds on their relationships with children.

JERSILD, ARTHUR THOMAS. *In Search of Self.* New York: Teachers College Press, 1952. Comments on the role of the teacher and of the school in helping a child to better understand himself and to adjust to his environment.

JERSILD, ARTHUR THOMAS. *When Teachers Face Themselves.* New York: Teachers College Press, 1955. Helps teachers learn to know themselves and to develop healthy attitudes of self-acceptance.

LANGDON, GRACE, and STOUT, IRVING W. *Helping Parents Understand Their Child's School.* Englewood Cliffs, N. J.: Prentice-Hall, Inc., 1957. Contains clear, practical answers to what parents say they want to know about their children's schools.

PRESCOTT, DANIEL. *The Child in the Educative Process.* New York: McGraw-Hill Book Company, 1957. Excellent material on home and school working together and on the child in the classroom situation.

PRESTON, GEORGE H. *The Substance of Mental Health.* New York: Holt, Rinehart & Winston, Inc., 1946. An unusually clear presentation of what is involved in mental health.

REDL, FRITZ, and WATTENBERG, WILLIAM W. *Mental Hygiene in Teaching.* 2nd ed. New York: Harcourt, Brace & World, Inc., 1959. A practical, helpful approach to working with children in the classroom.

REEVES, CHARLES E. *Parents and the School.* Washington, D.C.: Public Affairs Press, 1963. Helpful in developing cooperation between parents and teachers.

RUBEN, MARGARETE, and others. *Parent Guidance in the Nursery School.* New York: International Universities Press, Inc., 1960. Suggests ways of sharing information about children in the nursery school with their parents. Foreword by Anna Freud.

STEWART, ROBERT S., and WORKMAN, ARTHUR D. *Children and Other People: Achieving Maturity Through Learning.* New York: Holt, Rinehart & Winston, 1956. Emphasizes the importance of understanding oneself in order to understand children. Provides insight into the classroom behavior of both teacher and student.

317

reference manual

Studying Children

This section presents additional material to be used in studying children. This material will highlight and reinforce important points already presented in *These Are Your Children* and will foster insights and skills not obtainable from reading alone. It will also provide a means of evaluating and checking statements given in the text.

Individual Study Guide

Understanding children

As the emphasis in today's schools turns more and more toward helping children achieve a wholesome adjustment, it becomes increasingly important that the teacher have a thorough understanding of the children in her charge. In order that each child be given counsel and guidance according to his particular needs, he must be understood *as an individual reacting in a social environment.* To be so understood, the complexity of factors inherent in the child himself and present in his background of situations and experiences— that is, the factors through which he has become *individual*—must be discerned and understood.

Each child differs from all other children in every trait. Physical development, mental ability, emotional maturity, social adjustment—all are unique for every child. So, too, are the influences that act upon him. In the interaction of his abilities and his limitations, the people he has known, and the situations he has experienced lies the explanation for the behavior, desirable and undesirable, that is characteristic of the child.

Conduct problems occur in normal children. Such problems may be easily detected when the overt behavior is unacceptable (as when a child has tantrums, steals, or truants), but they may not be so readily recognized when other people are not disturbed or affected (as when a child is excessively timid, shy, or fearful). In both kinds of responses—one shown in overt behavior, the other in inner personality trends—the child's conduct is problem conduct.

When a child's behavior presents some problem, when it is considered *unadjusted* behavior, effort should be directed toward making it more acceptable. The interested adult must realize that *often the overt behavior is only a symptom or manifestation of an underlying maladjustment.* To treat a symptom without understanding its cause is futile. Probably no more common error is made in dealing with problems of both adults and children than to stress the symptom and ignore the basic cause, which, if neglected, results inevitably in a continuance of undesirable behavior.

The causal elements of a behavior problem are not always readily identified. Frequently they are so intricately concealed that only the trained clinician is successful in bringing them to light. But before they become so complicated, they usually exist in less potent form and are apparent to one who is aware of their significance. It is at this time that a teacher, armed with understanding, can often forestall the development of more serious maladjustment.

How does the teacher acquire such understanding? How can she investigate a recognized problem in order to find its solution? How much of the child's inner self must she know, how much about the circumstances of his daily life? What information is pertinent, what is of relatively minor consequence? And how can she learn the pertinent facts and so comprehend the child's reactions?

Purpose of the Individual Study Guide

The Individual Study Guide reproduced on pages 323-326 is designed to help the teacher gain a clearer understanding of actual and potential adjustment problems. The Guide comprises what may be termed the *minimum essentials* of understanding a behavior maladjustment. By no means does it intend to restrict investigation to the items it includes, for there will often be cases where more detailed knowledge will be needed; but it does indicate the areas that should not be neglected in studying any child showing evidence of emotional or social maladjustment. These areas—the minimum essentials of understanding—are: (1) a clear formulation of the problem, (2) a picture of the child's physical development, including his present condition of health, (3) his home environment—his parents and brothers and sisters, the attitudes and interrelationships of the entire family, and the physical elements that make up the home and the neighborhood, (4) the child's social and emotional characteristics and reactions, (5) his interests, experiences, and hobbies, (6) a record of his progress and adjustment in school, and (7) the results of whatever standard tests of intelligence and achievement he has taken. The compilation of this information may then be viewed as an overall picture of the child as a total individual.

The interaction and interdependence of the many items of inquiry covered by the Guide must be comprehended before any interpretation can be rightly evolved. Often the unskilled investigator of human behavior snatches at the first apparent cause of maladjustment and directs a plan of management prematurely, only to discover later that the apparent cause had little significance for the real problem, and that the actual cause was bound up in a complexity of details, no one of which seemed particularly vital in itself, but many of which assumed real importance when considered in their effects on one another. To preclude such a contingency and to offer effective guidance, it is wise to withhold final interpretation until *all* possible elements are known, and only then to offer recommendations.

Obtaining essential information

Information is ordinarily sought from the child himself, from his teachers, and from his parents; sometimes additional knowledge may be obtained from other members of the household, from a club leader, or from a playground supervisor. In gathering such information, certain techniques of interviewing help the investigator establish rapport and hence glean useful facts.

No arbitrary rule can be cited, since each interview must be individual—just as each child and each parent is individual. But usually the more informal and conversational the approach of the investigator, and the friendlier the attitude of the person interviewed, the more successful the interview will be. *Harmonious relations must be established before any questioning is attempted.* The skillful investigation is so conducted, once rapport has been established, that, although the person interviewed realizes an interview is in progress, he thinks of the contact primarily as a friendly conversation centering around a mutual interest—the child. Questions must not sound blunt and demanding but sympathetic and interested. The interviewer's manner must never suggest boredom or impatience but always attentive consideration. Neither should there be any suggestion of probing into intimate details of a family's personal relationships. There must be no suggestion of prying; it should be made clear, rather, that the interviewer is seeking to understand existing personal relationships in order to clarify a recognized problem. Tact and patience are essential, but kindliness should not be confused with sentimentality. The interviewer's desire to *help the child* should be stressed initially. Never should the person interviewed receive the impression that he is being criticized or censured because the problem has arisen. Interviewing is an art; a knowledge of *what* to ask is, of course, basic, but that knowledge will not yield the desired results unless the interviewer also knows *how* to ask his questions.

It is poor policy to write down all responses during an interview, for this almost invariably produces unnatural and stilted replies and often a marked hesitation to answer. Never should the investigator page through the Guide asking, as if by rote, about the many items listed and checking them off as the inquiry proceeds. It is *always* wise, however, to *record the facts gathered immediately after* the conclusion of the interview. Delayed recording results in errors and omissions, and often facts recalled after a lapse of time take on an entirely changed tone. If any section of the Guide does not provide enough room to answer questions or add comments, the additional information should be noted on separate sheets and kept with the Guide. Suggestions for filling in the various sections of the Guide are given on pages 327-330.

The organization of the Individual Study Guide gives the investigation of a child's problem a significantly ordered sequence, but it is not essential to follow through each section, point by point, to its conclusion. Often the free conversational comments of the person interviewed will provide information to be inserted later in the various sections. Such a contribution is more natural and the results more satisfactory than if the speaker is constantly interrupted and held to the sequence followed in the record blank. It is desirable, however, that all angles of investigation suggested in the Guide be covered as far as possible. The classroom teacher is not always the one to provide all of this information; the student is never qualified to undertake a complete investigation. The school psychologist, counselor, or adjustment teacher is better prepared to proceed with any extensive inquiry into a child's problem after referral by his teacher.

INDIVIDUAL STUDY GUIDE

Date _____

Name _____ Age _____ Birthdate _____

Address _____ Phone _____

Father's name _____ Occupation _____ Phone _____

School _____ Grade _____

Study requested by _____ Reason for study _____

Résumé of problem:

Résumé of recommendations:

Signed _____

Date _____

PHYSICAL DEVELOPMENT

Early Years

Birth normal _____

       instrumental _____

       premature _____

Walked at _____

Talked: single words at _____

       sentences at _____

       baby talk _____

       any defect _____

Bladder control: days _____ nights _____

Defects of development _____

Injuries _____

Operations _____

Diseases _____

_____

Allergies _____

_____

Present Health

Height _____ Weight _____

Underweight for body build _____

Overweight _____

Vision _____

Hearing _____

Speech _____

Fatigues easily _____

Muscular coordination _____

Characteristic physical reactions: _____

       energetic _____

       slow-moving _____

       lethargic _____

General appearance _____

_____

_____

Vaccination and Inoculation _____

_____

Anecdotal comment: _____

_____

_____

HOME BACKGROUND

	Age	Education	Health	Relations with child
Mother	____	_____	_____	_____
Father	____	_____	_____	_____
Siblings	____	_____	_____	_____
	____	_____	_____	_____

Lives in house _____ Apartment _____ Others in home _____

Own room _____ Shares with _____ Place to play _____

Language spoken at home _____ Mother at home _____

Neighborhood _____ Supervision _____

Anecdotal comment: _____

_____

_____

_____

EMOTIONAL AND SOCIAL REACTIONS

Friendly _____   Shy _____

Cooperative _____   Negativistic _____

Self-assured _____   Dependent _____

Reliable _____   Careless _____

Cheerful_____   Sullen _____

Anxious_____   Rebellious _____

Excitable_____   Placid _____

Temper_____   Fearful _____

Daydreams_____   Nightmares _____

Other_____

_____

_____

Enough time for play_____

Parents join in play _____

Plays with siblings _____

Good athlete _____

Place to play_____

Play equipment _____

Prefers solitary play_____

     group play _____

     active games _____

     solitary games _____

Resourceful in play_____

Imaginative in play _____

Favorite pastime _____

Prefers older playmates _____

     younger playmates_____

     playmates same age _____

Accepted by peers_____

Popular_____

Anecdotal comment: _____

_____

_____

INTERESTS, EXPERIENCES, HOBBIES

Likes to read_____

Prefers being read to _____

Reading materials at home _____

Reading skill _____

Kinds of stories preferred _____

_____

Radio: hours per day_____

     favorite programs _____

     _____

     _____

TV: hours per day_____

     favorite programs _____

     _____

     _____

Has some familiarity with

     farm _____ concerts _____

     city _____ zoo _____

     museums _____ circus _____

     travel _____

Has lessons in music _____ art _____

     dancing _____ other _____

Regular allowance _____

Job experience _____

Ambition for future _____

Parents' ambition _____

_____

Anecdotal comment: _____

_____

_____

_____

▬▬▬▬▬RECORD OF SCHOOL PROGRESS▬▬▬▬▬

Nursery school _____ At age ___   Early adjustment _____

Kindergarten _____ At age ___   _____

Schools attended _____   Reasons for transfer _____

_____   _____

_____   _____

Grades repeated _____   Best work in _____

Reasons for retardation _____   Difficulty with _____

_____   Preferred subject(s) _____

_____

Grades skipped _____   Disliked subject(s) _____

Reasons for acceleration _____   Adjustment in general _____

Anecdotal comment: _____

_____

_____

_____

▬▬▬▬▬STANDARD TEST RESULTS▬▬▬▬▬

Intelligence tests	C A	M A	I Q	Examiner
Binet Rev. _____	___	___	___	_____
WISC _____	___	___	___	_____
Group _____	___	___	___	_____
_____	___	___	___	_____

Achievement tests	C A	E A	GR. Equivalent	Examiner
_____	___	___	_____	_____
_____	___	___	_____	_____
_____	___	___	_____	_____

Other tests:

Anecdotal comment: _____

_____

_____

_____

Suggestions for filling in the Individual Study Guide

1. Descriptive Data

The first page of the Guide may serve, at the conclusion of the study, as a summary of the investigation. The identifying details are simple and self-explanatory:

Name and address
Father's name, occupation, telephone number
School and grade placement
Age and date of birth

The detail of birthdate often assumes greater significance than may be realized; in some homes with a foreign background the individual's age is given as one year immediately after birth, and in many homes the child is taught to give the age of his *next* birthday as his *present* age. From the standpoints of both physical and mental development, as well as social adjustment and emotional maturity, chronological age is important.

The *Reason for study* should be formulated concisely in a word or short phrase such as "truancy," "troublesome in classroom," "has no friends," "bullies younger children," "retarded in academic achievement."

The *Résumé of problem* supplements the *Reason for study*. It should be explanatory, descriptive of the trend of the problem. "Truancy," for example, might be amplified as follows:

Starts for school mornings, but often fails to arrive; truant at least once weekly, sometimes three times a week. Claims he "just walks around"; returns to his home at time he would be expected from school. Deficient in all subjects; disturbing in the classroom; no problem on the playground.

"Troublesome in classroom" might be expanded thus:

A constant annoyance in the classroom because of whispering, fidgeting, poking at children as they pass down the aisle. Achievement satisfactory. Likes to read. Does not enter into playground activities.

The lower half of the first sheet of the Guide is to be completed only *after* salient facts have been obtained, recorded, and assimilated. Interpreting the data is possible only in the light of all available knowledge of the child. The *Résumé of recommendations* can be completed sensibly and helpfully only after the data has been adequately interpreted.

2. Physical Development

This aspect of the child's development must never be neglected, since often an unsuspected physical defect or malfunction is basic to unsatisfactory adjustment. For each item, a word or two may indicate the facts, *unless* some unusual situation obtains, in which case further details should be sought and noted under *Anecdotal comment*. The items of this section are to be interpreted as follows:

Birth: Was birth normal? Instrumental? Premature?
Walked: How old was the child when he first walked alone?
Talked: How old was he when he first used single words? Sentences? Did he use babytalk? How long did babytalk persist?

Bladder control: Was it difficult to establish toilet habits? How old was the child when he kept dry during the day? During the night?

Defects of development: Was there any crippled condition at birth? Were there any conspicuous birthmarks, particularly on the face, neck, or hands? Was the child born with a cleft palate? Harelip? Tongue-tied? Did dental irregularities result in malformation of the mouth?

Injuries: Did the child suffer any serious injury, as from a burn or fall? Were there any obvious effects of such an accident? When did it occur?

Operations: Has the child undergone surgery? Was there a long period of convalescence? How old was he at the time of the operation?

Diseases: What diseases has the child had? At what age? How long was he ill? Were there any resultant defects—scars, sensory deficiency, crippling, cardiac condition?

Weight: How much does the child weigh?

Overweight or underweight: In accordance with height-weight tables, how many pounds above or below expected weight is he? Is there any factor in his skeletal build which might explain this?

Height: How tall is he?

Vision: Have the child's eyes been examined recently? By whom—physician, nurse, optometrist? What is his vision? Does he wear glasses? How long has he worn them? Did he have any trouble in getting accustomed to them? Do they interfere in any way now, such as in football or other sports? Is there any evidence of visual difficulty in the classroom? Can he see the board? Does he have trouble with reading? Do his eyes tear or become inflamed? Does he blink or squint?

Hearing: Has his hearing been tested recently? By whom—physician, school nurse? Does he evidence any auditory difficulty in the classroom? Can he hear from the rear of the room? Does he have to be spoken to often before he carries out requests? Does he seem inattentive?

Speech: Is there any stuttering? Lisping? Prolonged baby talk? Is speech clear and distinct?

Fatigues easily: Does he tire easily? In the classroom? On the playground?

Characteristic physical reactions: Is he normally alert, or dull and slow? Is he hyperactive? Does he appear to be lethargic?

General appearance: Note whether the child is sturdy, well built, has good color, or whether he is thin, puny, pale. Neatness or slovenliness may also be noted here.

Vaccination and inoculation: When was the child vaccinated against small-pox? Has he been inoculated for any other diseases—diphtheria, scarlet fever, whooping cough, infantile paralysis?

Anecdotal comment: Here may be noted anything of interest, for example, an incident during convalescence from illness, attitude toward seeing a physician, or pronounced fear of contracting a disease, in addition to the elaboration of any response to preceding items.

3. Home Background

Sometimes this information about the home provides the clue to the child's difficulty; always it provides a framework for interpreting the problem.

Parents and siblings: The data desired are self-explanatory.

Others in the home: Do relatives live with the family? Are there boarders? Are there servants? What are their respective attitudes toward the child?

Comment on parents: Are their relations amicable? Is there evidence of one dominating the home? Are they divorced? Separated? Are they foster parents? Is there a step-parent? What is the attitude toward the child—overly strict, indulgent? Do the parents agree on what is expected of the child? Are their expectations too great? Do they show marked favoritism? Does the child feel resentful toward them? Is he critical of them?

Comment on neighborhood: Rural, small town, apartment district, residential, business? Are there recreational facilities—park, playground, backyard? Are there undesirable features—taverns, poolrooms?

Comment on economic status: Comfortable economic circumstances? Poverty? Wealth? Anything outstanding concerning the home—few rooms for many people? Does child have his own room? How does status compare with that of schoolmates' homes?

4. Social and Emotional Behavior

The child must be understood as a reacting personality, and the ensuing points help to picture this personality.

Personality characteristics: Both the teacher and the parents should express an opinion regarding the traits listed. Check the traits that apply and use a different color pencil to indicate the judgment of the home and the school so you can easily tell them apart. If the child is fearful, note specific fears. If the child daydreams excessively, note the content of the dreams. For these, the child himself must, of course, be the contributor.

Play preferences: Here, too, both the teacher and the parents should express an opinion; but it is even more important to elicit the child's own reaction. Discrepancies may be noted under *Anecdotal Comment.*

Favorite pastime: What does the child do when he can do as he pleases?

Place to play: Is there a playroom in the home? Is there a backyard? Does the child play on the streets?

Play equipment: Are there toys and equipment satisfactory to the child? Does he have any particular unsatisfied desire for play materials?

Enough time for play: Does the child feel that he has ample time for play? Does he feel that home and school obligations consume too much time?

Play with parents, with siblings: Do the parents enter into play situations? Do the brothers and sisters play together?

5. Interests, Experiences, and Hobbies

Interests: Likes stories of—adventure, romance, mystery? Realistic, fanciful, etc.? How many television programs does he regularly watch each day? Is the radio on immediately before bedtime? Note any other interests in the *Anecdotal Record.*

Experiences and lessons: Note the child's reaction to them, particularly those he enjoys most.

Allowance: Does he receive a certain sum regularly? Does he think it is sufficient? How does he usually use it?

Outside work: What work has he done? Was he satisfactory to his employer? Was he paid for it? Did he undertake it of his own volition? If no longer working, why did he stop?

Ambition for future: What would he like to do when he is grown?

Parents' ambition: What would his parents like him to do? Are they insistent concerning their desires for him?

6. Record of School Progress

The data called for on the last page of the Guide are generally available from the school records.

Early adjustment: The mother should be the source of this information unless the teacher recalls the child clearly. Did he appear eager or reluctant to enter school? Did he adjust readily to the new situation?

Reasons for retardation: Did the family move frequently, necessitating changing schools? Was he ill and absent frequently? Was attendance regular and application satisfactory, yet achievement poor? Was he inattentive and disinterested, hence showed poor achievement?

Reasons for acceleration: Was achievement outstanding in comparison to that of other children? Was he older than the others in the grade? Was he advanced to effect a more equable distribution of students in two classrooms? Did the family bring pressure for advancement?

Reasons for transfer: Did the family move frequently? Did the parents want a different environmental influence for the child? Was there difficulty in school, and placement in another to give him another chance?

Best work in; Difficulty with: Note teacher's judgement.

Preferred subject(s); Disliked subject(s): Note child's reaction.

General adjustment: Does he like school? Does he feel that it is "hard"? "Easy"? Does he feel that his teachers are fair? Play favorites? Have a grudge against him? Does he get along well with his classmates? Is he well liked?

Anecdotal comment: Add here any incident, attitude, or habitual reaction which may supplement the data gathered. Note the teacher's opinion of the child and her attitude toward him.

7. Standard Test Results

These data will be more or less complete as the school's testing program provides for such aids in teaching.

Other tests: Personality tests, diagnostic tests, or special ability tests may have been used. If so, note the results.

Anecdotal Comment: Under what circumstances was the test given? By whom? Was the examiner skilled, or experimenting in testing? Did the child cooperate? Was he antagonistic?

Concluding comment

Throughout the investigation, the aim should be to reach the child's reaction toward the items of inquiry and to understand personality interrelationships and attitudes at home, at school, and on the playground. As the interviewer becomes familiar with the organization of the Individual Study Guide, he can use it to obtain a compact and complete background picture that will help him understand the child's problem. The suggestions incorporated in this section on using the Individual Study Guide should be familiar to the interviewer *before* approaching a parent. At the conclusion of the first several interviews, a review of the suggestions will indicate where a point might have received further emphasis, or where the conversation, wandering too far afield, might have been redirected to more significant paths of inquiry. As the investigator records his information, he should keep these suggestions at hand to insure his inclusion of all pertinent aspects of the study. He can also use the suggestions to help him understand the single words in the blank record form, and so to fill them out in a meaningful and helpful manner. The Guide is not necessarily self-explanatory to the novice; however, after practice in interviewing and in using the Guide, the investigator becomes increasingly aware that he need not be overwhelmed with a mass of details, which for his immediate purpose would present an embarrassment of questionably useful riches. Through the Guide, he can combine the many influences significant in a child's development into an ordered account. Then he can isolate some of the underlying factors responsible for the behavior judged undesirable. Sometimes he will realize, on the basis of his investigation, that the problem is a serious one that should be referred to a psychologist or psychiatrist.

The Individual Study Guide is useful for the teacher or specialist interested in seeking out the cause of undesirable behavior in children and for the student working toward a background of training in understanding children's adjustment problems. Such an inquiry is helpful in guiding children effectively toward successful adjustments in their everyday experiences.

Guide for Parent-Teacher Conferences*

To All Elementary Teachers:

Through reporting to parents we have one of our best means of building good public understanding. As a teacher, you are the most reliable source of information concerning the growth, progress, and achievement of the children in our schools. This reporting process is a vital responsibility. Because of your unique day-to-day relationship with children, you can present a clear, concise, and informative summary of the child's growth. To do it effectively will challenge your resources and talents as a teacher; it will also bring you the rewards that always accompany a significant undertaking. This guide will assist you in this responsibility.

What Reporting Is

It is a way in which the home and school share information about the child.

It furnishes specific information regarding his academic achievement and program.

It helps the child understand his strengths and weaknesses.

It gives direction to teacher-parent-pupil planning for future growth.

What Purposes Does the Parent-Teacher Conference Serve?

For the child

Helps the child to be more specifically aware of his own progress and needs through the *parent-teacher* conference and through the *pupil-teacher* conference which should precede the *parent-teacher* conference.

For the parent

Provides an opportunity to become acquainted with the teacher and the school.
Enables him to gain a better understanding of his own child through shared information.
Serves as a basis for planning with the teacher for the child's continued growth.

*From *Bulletin* of the Arlington Public Schools, Arlington, Virginia.

For the teacher

Supplements the teacher's information of the home and family background of the child.

Enables him to gain a better understanding of the child through shared information.

Allows for intensive discussion of pertinent problems.

Serves as a basis for making plans to meet the child's needs.

Helps the teacher to guide the child in evaluating his own progress in terms of his strengths, weaknesses, and future plans.

How Does a School Staff Prepare for Parent-Teacher Conferences?

Formulates a clear statement of the purposes of the parent-teacher conferences.

Reaches common agreement on good conference techniques.

Decides upon items to be covered under general areas for discussion and specific evidence which can be used to substantiate evaluation.

Decides how to interpret standardized test results to parents.

How Does a Teacher Prepare for a Parent-Teacher Conference?

Determines status and needs of a child by:

Reviewing record in the cumulative record folder and adding new data as obtained.

Collecting dated and evaluated samples of children's work in all areas of instruction. Evaluate children's work by using such devices as check marks, number right, or descriptive terms ("well-written," "neat," "this is not your best work"). Avoid the use of percentage grades, letter and numerical grades, and such symbols that are not consistent with our method of reporting.

Studying results obtained from standardized and informal tests.

Talking informally with the child.

Keeps anecdotal records from observations of:

Work habits
Relationships with others
Display of attitudes
Behavior changes
Special abilities and interest

Becomes acquainted with parents and home background through:

Back-to-School night
P.T.A. and Study Group meetings
Home visits
Telephone conversations
Informal contacts
Studying records
Parent comments on reports

Interpreting children's comments
Parent-Teacher Conferences

Confers with others who have worked with the child

Becomes familiar with the goals normally expected for a child's grade level.

Analyzes progress in terms of the child as an individual:*

His background
His ability
His achievement in relation to his ability
His achievement in relation to standards for his grade level.

Studies achievement test profiles so that he may be able to interpret current test results to the parents. This interpretation should be related to the child's performance and is only one part of the total evaluation.

Prepares questions which might be discussed.

Parent initiated:
1. How does your child feel about school?
2. Has your child any health problems that the teacher should know (sight, hearing, allergies, diet, etc.)?
3. How well does he accept responsibility at home?
4. How does he spend his free time?
5. Does he get along well with other children?
6. Has he any hobbies, special interest, or abilities?

Teacher initiated:
1. Is your child working up to his ability in academic subjects?
2. Is he working on, above, or below grade level in academic subjects?
3. What special interest and abilities does he display in the classroom?
4. What work habits is he developing?
5. How well does he accept responsibility?
6. How does he get along with classmates?
7. What problems or difficulties is he experiencing?
8. What plans for help should be considered?

Sends appointment form and "Parent's Guide for Parent-Teacher Conference" to all parents. In the space provided for the salutation it is suggested that both parents be invited.

Schedules conferences at most convenient time for parent, conforming to building plans already made.

Makes necessary schedule adjustments for parent's convenience.

Contacts parents if necessary to clarify difficult appointments.

Plans a comfortable, attractive, informal setting for the conference.

Arranges chairs away from teacher's desk to promote feeling of partnership.

*See Individual Study Guide.

Plans an attractive place for parent to wait for conference. Arranges a table with pamphlets of interest to parents of the group.

What Pointers Are Helpful in Holding a Parent-Teacher Conference?

Greet parent in a friendly and relaxed manner without hurry or tension.

Establish rapport with parent.

Encourage parents to *talk*.

Teacher needs to be a good listener. Parent often initiates discussion of problem.

Teacher needs to enlist parent cooperation. Develop a feeling that the problems and the solutions are mutual—"What can *we* do about it." The teacher's purpose is to *get* as well as *give* information and help. Learn about all phases of child's development.

Accept parent's reason for child's behavior. Then lead discussion on to a consideration of other possible causes.

Be concrete and specific. Substantiate your evaluations with samples of the child's work.

Avoid comparison with other children.

Help parent to participate in making decisions. Let suggestions grow out of mutual discussion and a growing insight into reasons for behavior. Suggest alternatives for joint consideration. "This *might* be a possibility," or "We might try this and see what happens."

Avoid arguments. Arguing will only arouse resentment and resistance.

Be alert to recognize problems of such serious nature that additional professional help is needed.

Bring up any problems listed on conference sheet which have not been discussed. Discussion should be honest and tactful in presentation.

Avoid assuming role of Family Counselor.

Briefly summarize points covered in discussion.

Mutually make constructive plans for child's progress, ending on note of continued cooperation.

After parent has left, add pertinent information brought out in the conference to the guide sheet and file in child's cumulative folder.

Charting Development

Together with the Summary of Normal Development (pages 356-360), the graphic materials in this section provide a rapid overview of the various areas and stages of growth. In referring to these summaries, the reader should bear in mind several concepts that are basic to any discussion of "normal" development. First, even though all children progress through the same sequence of growth, each individual child grows at his own rate and in his own fashion. Second, there are no clear boundaries between the so-called *stages* of development or between the various *areas* of development. Successive periods of growth merge gradually and almost imperceptibly one into another, and at each stage there is a complex intertwining of physical, mental, emotional, and social development.

The graph at the bottom of the page illustrates yet another concept underlying any generalization about "normal" development. Whatever characteristic we consider—whether height, weight, intelligence, self-reliance, or any other—we find in a large group selected at random that most people possess the trait in an average amount, with about 68 per cent falling within a normal range in the middle of the distribution. Similarly, the development norms established for any age level are those which a *majority* of children—but not all of them—display at that age. Many children will reach this developmental level much earlier than the average, and many will reach it much later.

In short, the following summaries of normal development are dependable and meaningful only if correctly interpreted with the understanding that (1) individual children vary, each being only like himself; (2) "development" refers not to any single area of growth, such as physical growth, but to the overall pattern of growth; and (3) "normal" means not a point on a scale but a *range,* extending over a relatively wide portion of a measure. When interpreted in the light of these qualifications, the charts, graphs, diagrams, and word pictures on the following pages should extend the reader's understanding not only of "normal" development but of the developmental patterns of particular children.

THE "NORMAL" DISTRIBUTION OF SCORES

This is the distribution of scores that would be expected if 1000 randomly selected persons were measured on any biological or psychological trait. Each dot represents one individual's score. Curves actually obtained only approximate this curve, of course, but they come remarkably close to it. (See, for example, FIGURE 1 on page 351.)

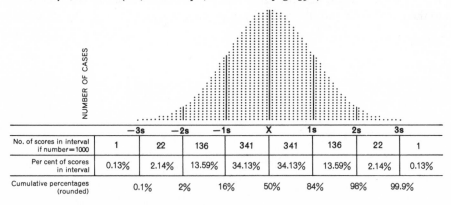

	−3s	−2s	−1s	X	1s	2s	3s
No. of scores in interval if number=1000	1	22	136	341	341	136	22	1
Per cent of scores in interval	0.13%	2.14%	13.59%	34.13%	34.13%	13.59%	2.14%	0.13%
Cumulative percentages (rounded)		0.1%	2%	16%	50%	84%	98%	99.9%

THE DEVELOPMENT OF MOTOR CONTROL

FIGURE I.

FIGURE 2.

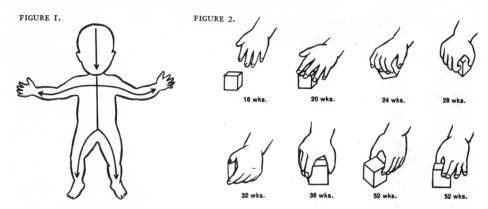

| 16 wks. | 20 wks. | 24 wks. | 28 wks. |
| 32 wks. | 36 wks. | 52 wks. | 52 wks. |

The control of motor functions proceeds from the head downward (the cephalocaudal sequence) and from the center of the body outward (the proximodistal sequence), as shown diagrammatically in FIGURE I. The cephalocaudal sequence is clearly illustrated in the development of posture and locomotion, outlined in FIGURE 3: the infant gains control of his head first, then his shoulders and trunk, finally his legs and feet. The time when a particular child learns to sit or walk will vary with such factors as his weight and body build and his opportunities for practice, but the general sequence of development is the same for all children.

The development of grasping behavior (FIGURE 2) also follows a definite sequence and illustrates the gradual refinement of muscular coordination. At 16 weeks an infant is unable to make voluntary contact with a cube or other small object. At about 20 weeks he can touch or squeeze it but cannot yet really hold it. At about 28 weeks he uses his hand indiscriminately in "palming" the object. The forefinger comes into play at about 36 weeks, and by the time the infant is a year old he is beginning to use thumb and forefinger in opposition, much as an adult would.

FIGURE 3.

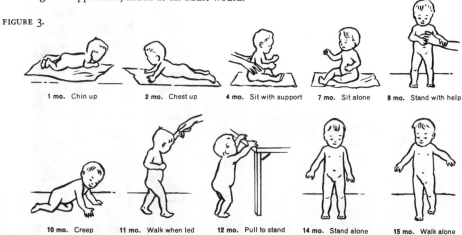

| 1 mo. Chin up | 2 mo. Chest up | 4 mo. Sit with support | 7 mo. Sit alone | 8 mo. Stand with help |
| 10 mo. Creep | 11 mo. Walk when led | 12 mo. Pull to stand | 14 mo. Stand alone | 15 mo. Walk alone |

FIGURE 1: Redrawn from *Developmental Psychology* by Florence L. Goodenough. Appleton Century-Crofts, Inc., 1945 FIGURE 2: Adapted from "An Experimental Study of Prehension in Infants by Means of Systematic Cinema Records," by H. M. Halverson, in *Genetic Psychology Monographs*, 1931, 10: 107-286. By permission of The Journal Press. FIGURE 3: Adapted from Mary M. Shirley, *The First Two Years: A Study of Twenty-Five Babies*, Child Welfare Monograph No. 7, Vol. II. University of Minnesota Press, Minneapolis. Copyright 1933 by the University of Minnesota.

CHANGES IN BODY PROPORTIONS

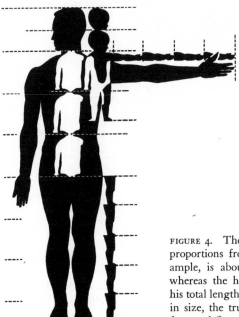

FIGURE 4. The newborn infant has very different body proportions from those of an adult. His head, for example, is about one-fourth of his total body length, whereas the head of an adult is about one-seventh of his total length. In the course of growth the head doubles in size, the trunk triples, and the arms and legs grow four and five times their original lengths.

SKELETAL MATURATION

FIGURE 5. Bone development begins during the sixth week after conception and is not generally completed until the individual is around twenty. These X rays of hand and wrist show skeletal maturation of girls at various stages of development between birth and early adulthood. The development of the wrist (carpal development) is one commonly used measure of skeletal maturation. (See FIGURE 13, page 343.)

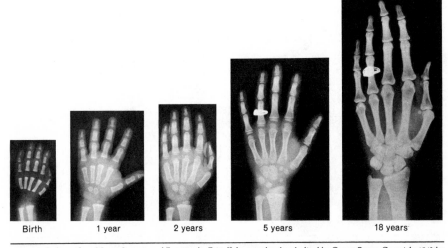

| Birth | 1 year | 2 years | 5 years | 18 years |

FIGURE 4: Redrawn from *Man in Structure and Function*, by Fritz Kahn, translated and edited by George Rosen. Copyright 1943 by Fritz Kahn. Reprinted by permission of Alfred A. Knopf, Inc. FIGURE 5: Reproduced from *Radiographic Atlas of Skeletal Development of the Hand and Wrist*, 2nd edition, by William Walter Greulich and S. Idell Pyle with the permission of the publishers, Stanford University Press. ©1950 and 1959 by the Board of Trustees of the Leland Stanford Junior University.

GROWTH CHART

FIGURE 6. This Growth Chart shows (in the middle column) the average height, at different ages, of girls from birth to nineteen years as shown on the left, and of boys from birth to twenty years as shown on the right. This chart can be used for predicting probable adult stature by taking the height of a child at a given age and figuring from the percentage indicated. A seven-year-old girl, for example, has already attained about 74.3 per cent of her growth in height. If she is an inch taller than average (49 instead of 48), she may grow to be almost 66 inches tall. An eight-year-old boy has attained about 72.4 per cent of his adult height. If he is an inch shorter than the average for his age (50 inches instead of 51), he may grow to be 68 inches tall.

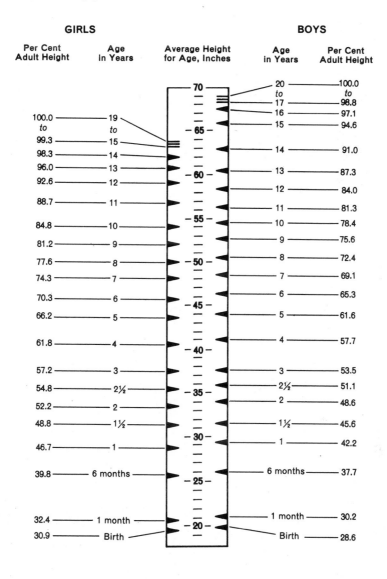

FIGURE 6: From "How Children Grow" by Nancy Bayley, from the book, *The Encyclopedia of Child Care and Guidance* edited by Sidonie Matsner Gruenberg. Copyright ©1954, 1956, 1959, 1963 by Doubleday and Company, Inc. Reprinted by permission of the publisher.

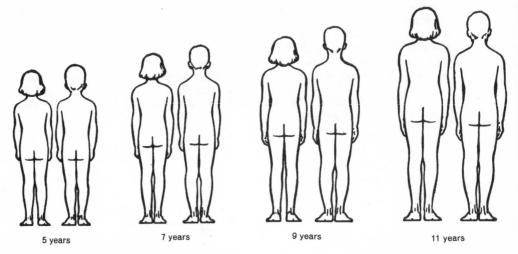

5 years   7 years   9 years   11 years

FIGURE 7. The drawings across the top of this and the next page illustrate the course of growth from five to seventeen, at two-year intervals, for a typical girl and a typical boy. Until nine or ten, the boy and girl are much alike in both size and build, with the boy just a bit taller and heavier. But at eleven, the girl is well into the period of rapid pubertal growth and has overtaken the boy in height. Her figure is beginning to round out, and during the next few years she will become increasingly feminine in physique.

WHEN BOYS AND GIRLS MATURE

FIGURE 8. Each male figure on the chart represents 10 per cent of all boys of a given age measured, and each female figure represents 10 per cent of all girls of a given age measured. Note that the girls, on the average, achieve physical maturity about two years earlier than the boys. This difference in the pattern of maturing for boys and girls is illustrated also in FIGURE 7.

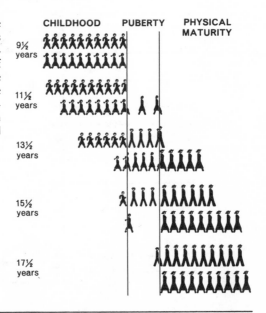

CHILDHOOD   PUBERTY   PHYSICAL MATURITY

9½ years

11½ years

13½ years

15½ years

17½ years

FIGURE 7: From "How Children Grow" by Nancy Bayley, from the book, *The Encyclopedia of Child Care and Guidance* edited by Sidonie Matsner Gruenberg. Copyright ©1954, 1956, 1959, 1963 by Doubleday and Company, Inc. Reprinted by permission of the publisher. FIGURE 8: From *Life and Growth* by Alice V. Keliher. Appleton-Century Company, Inc., 1941. By permission of Pictograph Corporation.

340

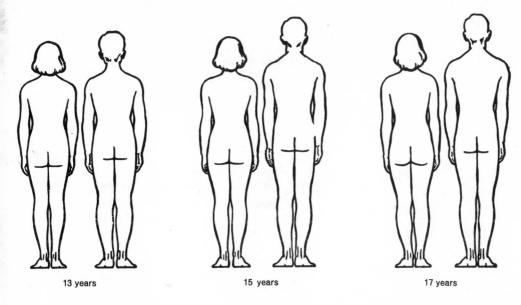

13 years   15 years   17 years

By thirteen the girl's rate of growth has slowed down and the boy, whose pubertal growth spurt starts between ten and twelve, once again is taller. His frame is becoming bigger and heavier, his shoulders are beginning to broaden, and his muscles are increasing in size and strength. Growth in height slows down after the boy is fifteen, but changes in both height and build continue until he is eighteen and a half or nineteen. A girl ordinarily attains her adult height and build by the time she is sixteen.

POSTURE CHANGES

FIGURE 9. These drawings of a girl at various ages from early childhood to preadolescence illustrate the improvement of posture after the preschool years. Probably the most striking change is the disappearance of the protruding abdomen that is so characteristic of early childhood.

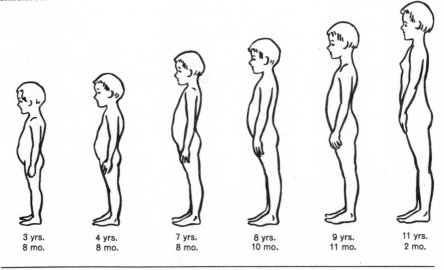

3 yrs.   4 yrs.   7 yrs.   8 yrs.   9 yrs.   11 yrs.
8 mo.   8 mo.   8 mo.   10 mo.   11 mo.   2 mo.

FIGURE 9: From *Growth and Development of the Young Child*, 7th edition, by Marion Breckenridge and Margaret N. Murphy. W. B. Saunders Company, 1963. By permission of the authors and publisher.

CHANGING SLEEP PATTERNS

FIGURE 10. These pie charts show one child's sleeping-awakeness cycle at various ages from three days to four years. The dark segments indicate sleep and the white segments awakeness. Feedings are shown by the markings along the margin of each circle. Other children will show different but similar patterns.

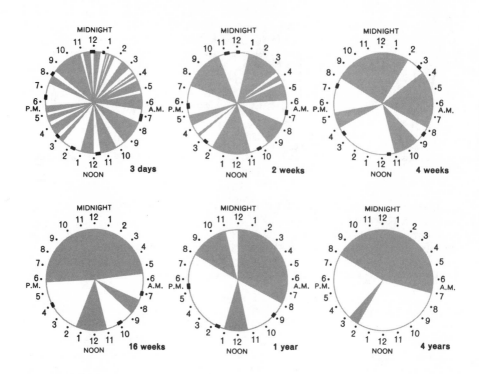

SLEEP NEEDS MUST BE MET

FIGURE 11. Sleep needs vary widely with individuals at all ages. It is especially important to consider this during the early school years when so many new demands face boys and girls. Studies show that an average of eleven hours of sleep per day is needed by these children, but of course some require less and some need much more.

AGE	HOURS	MINUTES
1—6 months	15	3
6—12 months	14	9
12—18 months	13	23
1½—2 years	13	6
2—3 years	12	42
3—4 years	12	7
4—5 years	11	43
5—6 years	11	19
6—7 years	11	4
7—8 years	10	58

FIGURE 10: Redrawn from *The Embryology of Behavior* by Arnold Gesell and Catherine S. Amatruda. Copyright 1945 by Arnold Gesell. By permission of Harper & Row, Publishers. FIGURE 11: Adapted from *Child Care and Training* by Marion L. Faegre and John E. Anderson. University of Minnesota Press, 1947.

SKILLS AND SPEED DEVELOP SLOWLY

FIGURE 12. One index of normal development is the way in which the hands are used. This shows wide differences among little children. Increasingly complex manual activities require greater and greater skill in manipulation. Early play develops such skill. The tendency of the child to carry on a great deal of repetitive activity in his play is productive of better integration of muscular responses and increasing speed of movement.

AVERAGE AGE	ACTIVITY
14 mos.	Unwraps a toy
14 mos.	Takes and holds three cubes
16 mos.	Puts beads into a box
16 mos.	Puts lid on a round box
16 mos.	Puts round block in form board
18 mos.	Puts ten cubes in a cup
20 mos.	Puts square block in form board
22 mos.	Places cover on oblong box
24 mos.	Attempts to fold paper
27 mos.	Imitates drawing a line instead of scribbling
30 mos.	Folds paper successfully

INDIVIDUAL PATTERNS OF GROWTH

FIGURE 13. These graphs show the growth patterns of two children measured at regular intervals over a seven-and-a-half year period. Growth factors plotted are height, weight, dentition (as measured by the eruption of the permanent teeth), skeletal development (as measured by X rays of the wrist bones, or carpus), muscular development (as measured by strength of grip), mental development (as measured by standard tests of mental ability), and reading ability. The base line of each graph shows chronological age and the vertical axis represents growth age. The norms for growth are based on the average measurements of large numbers of children. To show clearly how an individual child compares to the norm, a straight diagonal line is drawn through the points where chronological age and growth age would coincide. Note the high correlation among the various aspects of development and the general stability of each child's pattern of growth.

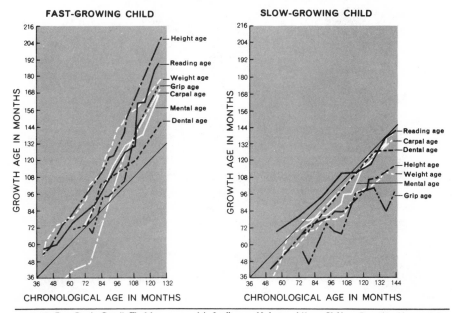

FIGURE 12: From Psyche Cattell, *The Measurement of the Intelligence of Infants and Young Children.* Reproduced by permission. Copyright ©1940, Psyche Cattell. Published by The Psychological Corporation, New York, N.Y. All rights reserved. FIGURE 13: Adapted from "Concepts of Growth—Their Significance to Teachers," by Willard C. Olson and Byron O. Hughes. From *Childhood Education,* October 1944, Vol. 21, No. 2. Reproduced by permission of the Association for Childhood Education International, 3615 Wisconsin Avenue, N.W., Washington, D.C.

DEVELOPMENTAL TASKS

FIGURE I. At each period of growth, the individual is confronted with certain developmental tasks—skills, attitudes, and understandings which he must acquire to meet society's expectations and to satisfy his own needs for growth and accomplishment. The characteristics and continuity of these developmental tasks are represented schematically in the diagram below. Some tasks are compressed into a short period of time (areas striped in black); others persist for many years and span several phases of development (areas striped in white); and some alter and merge into predominant tasks of another phase (areas stippled in white). The discrepant age scales on the left and right margins indicate different developmental rates for individuals. The predominant tasks of a given phase of development (adolescence, for example) can be seen by reading across the age scales. The relative importance of a task at any particular age is indicated by its width. The diagram does not represent all of the developmental tasks for any given age.

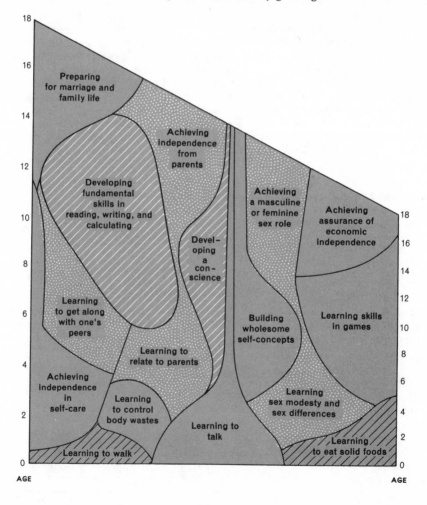

FIGURE 1: Redrawn from *Human Development in Western Culture* by Harold W. Bernard. Allyn and Bacon, Inc., 1962.

DEVELOPMENT OF PERSONAL–SOCIAL BEHAVIOR

FIGURE 2. This chart illustrates types of behavior that are typical at various stages of personal-social development. There are many individual variations on this pattern, however, for the socialization of the child is affected not only by his maturational level but by his individual temperament and the kind of environment in which he is reared.

LEVELS OF MATURITY	
Birth	---
4 weeks	Regards faces.
16 weeks	Plays with hands and dress. Recognizes bottle. Poises mouth for food.
28 weeks	Plays with feet and toys. Expectant in feeding situations.
40 weeks	Plays simple nursery games. Feeds self cracker.
12 months	Cooperates in dressing. Gives toy. Finger feeds.
18 months	Uses spoon with moderate spilling. Toilet regulated.
2 years	Verbalizes toilet needs. Plays with dolls.
3 years	Uses spoon well. Puts on shoes. Takes turns.
4 years	Can wash and dry face. Goes on errands. Plays cooperatively.
5 years	Dresses without assistance. Asks meaning of words.

EMOTIONS GROW AND DEVELOP TOO

FIGURE 3. This diagram, based on a classic study of sixty-two infants, shows the progressive differentiation of overt emotional responses during the first two years of life. For a time after birth, the only discernible emotion is that of general excitement. This nonspecific response continues in evidence throughout infancy (and even into adulthood), but within three months after birth two other general patterns—delight and distress—have become differentiated. Emotional differentiation becomes increasingly evident as the infant matures, and by the time he is two years old he has a quite varied range of responses.

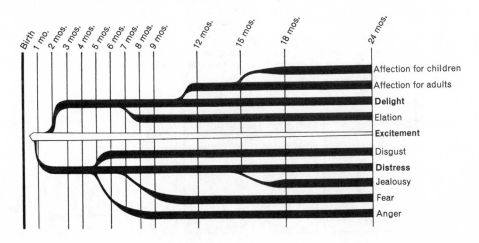

FIGURE 2: Adapted from Fig. 5, p. 15, of Developmental Diagnosis by Arnold Gesell and Catherine S. Amatruda. Copyright 1941, 1947 by Arnold Gesell. Reprinted by permission of Hoeber Medical Division, Harper & Row, Publishers   FIGURE 3: Adapted from "Emotional Development in Early Infancy" by K. M. B. Bridges, in Child Development, 1932, 3: 324-341. © 1932 by the Society for Research in Child Development, Inc.

FRUSTRATION, ANGER, AND AGGRESSION

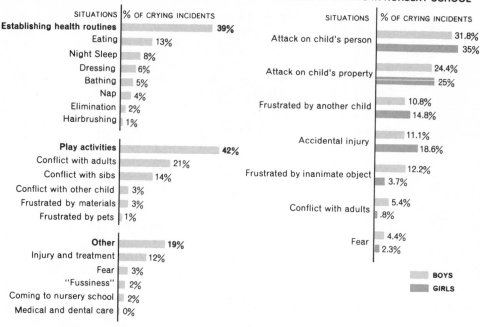

FIGURE 4.   CAUSES OF CRYING AT HOME

SITUATIONS	% OF CRYING INCIDENTS
Establishing health routines	39%
Eating	13%
Night Sleep	8%
Dressing	6%
Bathing	5%
Nap	4%
Elimination	2%
Hairbrushing	1%
Play activities	42%
Conflict with adults	21%
Conflict with sibs	14%
Conflict with other child	3%
Frustrated by materials	3%
Frustrated by pets	1%
Other	19%
Injury and treatment	12%
Fear	3%
"Fussiness"	2%
Coming to nursery school	2%
Medical and dental care	0%

CAUSES OF CRYING IN NURSERY SCHOOL

SITUATIONS	% OF CRYING INCIDENTS
Attack on child's person	31.8% / 35%
Attack on child's property	24.4% / 25%
Frustrated by another child	10.8% / 14.8%
Accidental injury	11.1% / 18.6%
Frustrated by inanimate object	12.2% / 3.7%
Conflict with adults	5.4% / .8%
Fear	4.4% / 2.3%

BOYS
GIRLS

The two graphs in FIGURE 4 illustrate the results of a study investigating the causes of crying among preschool children both in the home and in the nursery school. The immediate causes of crying in the two situations show some interesting differences. In the home, conflicts with adults—over such routine activities as eating, sleeping, and playing—accounted for about 60 per cent of the crying incidents. In the nursery school, on the other hand, conflicts with adults were few and crying was caused in the great majority of instances by conflicts with other children. Note that crying in both situations was usually an expression *not* of fear or hurt but of anger in the face of frustration. Learning to tolerate frustration and to respond to it in constructive and socially approved ways is an important part of growing up. Overt aggression, though a very natural response (FIGURE 5), is almost never a satisfactory way of dealing with frustration. The mature individual is more likely to seek ways of overcoming the obstacles in his path or to find other compensating sources of satisfaction.

FIGURE 5.

FIGURE 4: Redrawn from "Factors Associated with Crying in Young Children in the Nursery School and the Home" by C. Landreth, in *Child Development*, 1941, 12: 81-97. © 1941 by the Society for Research in Child Development, Inc.   FIGURE 5: "Peanuts" cartoon by Charles M. Schulz. Copyright © 1956 by United Feature Syndicate, Inc.

CHANGING PATTERNS OF CHILDREN'S FEARS

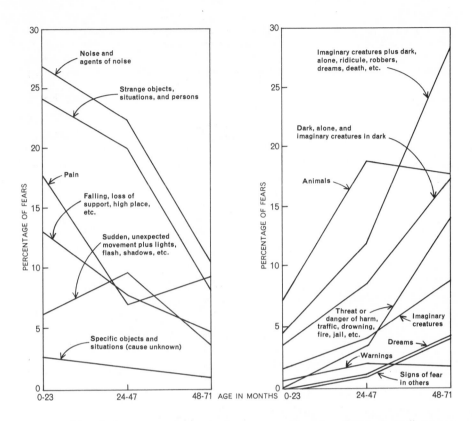

FIGURE 6 (above) shows some changes in the patterns of fear that children typically express between birth and six years. During infancy, fear is aroused primarily by specific situations in the child's immediate environment—sudden noise, strange objects or persons, loss of support, and other new or unexpected stimuli. As shown in the chart at left, these fears tend to diminish with age. There is an increase, however, in imaginary fears and in fears of remote or distant dangers. One reason for this widening range of fears, which is shown in the chart at right, is that the child's imaginative abilities increase, as does his understanding of potential danger. Fear, once incurred, also has a tendency to spread to similar objects and situations. As suggested by FIGURE 7 (below), a sense of humor is sometimes a good antidote to fears that might otherwise prove overwhelming.

FIGURE 6: Adapted from A. T. Jersild and F. B. Holmes, "Children's Fears," Child *Development Monographs*. No. 20. New York: Bureau of Publications, Teachers College, Columbia University, 1935. FIGURE 7: "Miss Peach" cartoon by Mell Lazarus. Courtesy of Mell Lazarus and Publishers Newspaper Syndicate.

SOURCES OF HAPPINESS AND SATISFACTION

FIGURE 8. The table below summarizes the responses children gave in a study where they were asked to describe "one of the happiest days" of their lives. The values represent percentages of children giving one or more responses in each category. Categories mentioned by only small percentages of children are omitted. Although the younger children tended to express happiness in terms of occasions when they received gifts or enjoyed some other special "treat," it should be understood that their joy often had a deeper basis. A gift, for example, might sometimes be more important as a symbol of love or acceptance than as a material possession, though a child would be unlikely to express it in these terms.

DESCRIPTION	GRADES 1-3 AGES 6-9		GRADES 4-6 AGES 9-12		GRADES 7-9 AGES 12-15		GRADES 10-12 AGES 15-18	
	363 BOYS	331 GIRLS	309 BOYS	343 GIRLS	282 BOYS	290 GIRLS	159 BOYS	171 GIRLS
Receiving or having or otherwise enjoying material things, gifts, toys, money, living quarters	8.7	8.1	10.4	7.2	10.1	4.5	5.6	3.1
Holidays, festive occasions, birthdays, Christmas, etc.	39.1	40.5	32.4	38.9	6.3	10.1	0.6	6.5
Sports, games, hiking, hunting, bicycling, etc.	10.2	6.4	9.1	5.5	12.4	5.8	13.0	7.3
Going to miscellaneous places of recreation, going to camps, traveling, going to resorts, to parks	9.6	9.0	10.1	11.4	9.7	13.9	30.2	6.9
Self-improvement, success in school, educational opportunity, evidence of vocational competence, getting a job	2.4	2.3	2.9	1.9	4.8	4.1	13.6	15.9
Happenings connected with school, including last day, end of school, going to a certain school	3.6	3.4	5.4	4.3	14.0	11.1	7.0	5.4
Relationship with people (explicitly described), companionship, being with certain friend, return home of relatives, etc.	7.7	15.9	8.0	15.8	10.5	22.0	8.7	19.9
Residing in, moving to, a certain city or community	1.3	1.0	0.8	2.9	0.9	2.9	1.4	5.0
Benefits befalling others, or mankind in general, including end of war	0.6	0.8	3.2	2.8	2.2	2.6	7.9	9.7

VALUES AND ATTITUDES OF ADOLESCENTS

FIGURE 9. Adolescents tend to look to each other, rather than to the adult community, for social approval and social rewards. Some of the things they consider most important are suggested in the graph at right, which summarizes the responses of teen-age boys and girls to the question, "What does it take to get into the leading crowd in this school?" Nine schools were represented in the study.

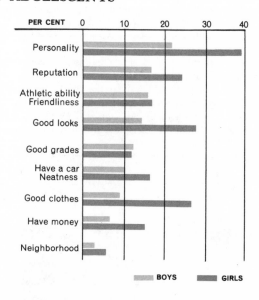

FIGURE 8: From A. T. Jersild and R. J. Tasch, *Children's Interests*. New York: Bureau of Publications, Teachers College, Columbia University, 1949. FIGURE 9: Redrawn from *Social Climates in High Schools, Cooperative Research Monograph No. 4* by J. S. Coleman (Washington, D.C.: U.S. Department of Health, Education, and Welfare).

CAUSES OF ADOLESCENT CONCERN

FIGURE 10. Based on a survey of 15,000 teen-agers, this graph summarizes the problems considered important by adolescents. Information of this sort can be useful to parents and teachers in determining the special kinds of guidance and help teen-agers need.

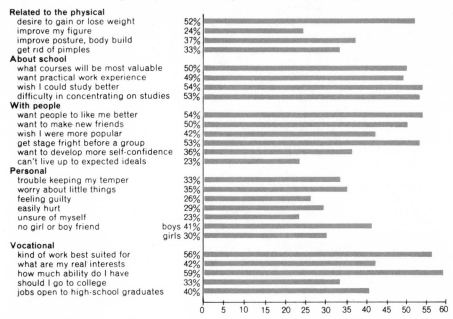

Related to the physical
desire to gain or lose weight	52%
improve my figure	24%
improve posture, body build	37%
get rid of pimples	33%

About school
what courses will be most valuable	50%
want practical work experience	49%
wish I could study better	54%
difficulty in concentrating on studies	53%

With people
want people to like me better	54%
want to make new friends	50%
wish I were more popular	42%
get stage fright before a group	53%
want to develop more self-confidence	36%
can't live up to expected ideals	23%

Personal
trouble keeping my temper	33%
worry about little things	35%
feeling guilty	26%
easily hurt	29%
unsure of myself	23%
no girl or boy friend	boys 41%
	girls 30%

Vocational
kind of work best suited for	56%
what are my real interests	42%
how much ability do I have	59%
should I go to college	33%
jobs open to high-school graduates	40%

0   5   10   15   20   25   30   35   40   45   50   55   60

EMOTIONAL DISTURBANCE AMONG CHILDREN

FIGURE 11. The top graph shows the percentage of emotionally disturbed children, by grade level, in one large elementary school system. The incidence of disturbance increases sharply between kindergarten and first grade, remains fairly stable until eighth grade, then shows another increase. As shown in the second graph, emotionally disturbed children seem to come more frequently than other children do from home conditions generally regarded as unfavorable. The figures also show, however, that many children come from similar home conditions without suffering similar emotional effects. Emotional disturbance seldom if ever can be traced to one simple cause, and the temperament and individual resources of a particular child can be quite as important as his environment in determining the quality of his emotional health.

EMOTIONAL DISTURBANCE BY GRADE LEVEL

GRADE	PER CENT DISTURBED
Kindergarten	5%
1st Grade	11%
2nd Grade	11%
3rd Grade	11%
4th Grade	12%
5th Grade	11%
6th Grade	11%
7th Grade	10%
8th Grade	13%
Special class	21%

EMOTIONAL DISTURBANCE BY HOME CONDITION

HOME CONDITION	PER CENT OF CHILDREN STUDIED
Broken home	36% / 11%
Mother employed	23% / 12%
Serious neglect and deprivation	21% / 3%
Foreign-language background	20% / 10%

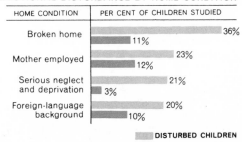

DISTURBED CHILDREN
NORMAL CHILDREN

FIGURE 10: Based on data from *The American Teen-Ager* by H. H. Remmers and D. H. Radler. The Bobbs-Merrill Company, Inc., 1957. FIGURE 11: "Incidence of Emotionally Disturbed Children," redrawn from *Teaching in the Elementary School* by Herbert J. Klausmeier and Katharine Dresden. Harper & Brothers, 1962. Based on data from "A Study of Emotionally Disturbed Children in Santa Barbara County Schools" by N. Clancy and F. Smitter, in *California Journal of Educational Research*, 1953, 4: 209-222.

SERIOUSNESS OF BEHAVIOR PROBLEMS

FIGURE 12. This table shows how common childhood behavior problems were ranked in order of seriousness—from 1 to 46—by groups of parents, teachers, children, and mental hygienists. In general, the ratings of the mental hygienists were more objective than those of parents and teachers, reflecting greater concern with the long-range implications of undesirable behavior and less concern with the immediate problems it might cause.

	Mental Hygienists	Fathers	Mothers	5A Boys	5A Girls	8B Boys	8B Girls	Teachers
Tardiness	39	31	35	41	44	36	43	35
Truancy	23	4	5	6	4	3	7	2
Destroying School Materials	41	8	8	2.5	3	2	10	7
Untruthfulness	23	7	3	19	13	5.5	9	6
Imaginative Lying	30	45	45	44	39	39	42	45
Cheating	23	3	4	12	10	10.5	15	12
Stealing	13.5	1	1	1	1	1	1	1
Profanity	43	30	34	2.5	2	8	2	18
Smoking	45	33	30	7	6	26	12	29
Disorderliness	42	25	24	15	28	23	24	11
Whispering	46	46	46	34	36	45	46	42
Interrupting, Talkativeness	44	44	44	32	26.5	41	33	31
Restlessness	37.5	42	40	35	38	44	44	36
Inattention	31	36	29	24	32	37	29.5	21
Lack of Interest in Work	25	20.5	11	9.5	19	22	20	14
Carelessness in Work	34.5	24	26	14	23	20.5	16	22
Laziness	32.5	27	22	20	29.5	32	22	17
Unreliable, Irresponsible	21	5	7	11	11	13	6	9
Disobedience	37.5	18	18	5	8	14	5	5
Impertinence, Defiance	34.5	10	10	9.5	5	12	13	4
Cruelty, Bullying	6	2	2	4	7	4	8	3
Quarrelsomeness	28	17	17	17	20	24	23	13
Tattling	26	34	33	37	12	28	34.5	46
Stubbornness, Contrariness	20	38	37	38	34	35	31.5	19
Sullenness	12	29	32	18	21	19	26	34
Temper Tantrums	17	20.5	20	23	15	18	18	8
Impudence, Rudeness	29	12	19	8	9	7	4	10
Selfishness	16	11	9	27	16	5.5	11	25
Domineering, Overbearing	11	26	14	21.5	17	15	17	20
Shyness	13.5	37	39	46	46	46	45	44
Sensitiveness	10	41	38	42	42	43	40	43
Unsocial, Withdrawing	1	19	21	33	41	38	34.5	26
Overcritical of Others	9	28	31	26	18	25	14	39
Thoughtlessness	36	35	36	29	33	33	29.5	40
Inquisitiveness	40	39	41	25	29.5	29	27	41
Silliness	27	40	42	36	31	20.5	28	33
Unhappy, Depressed	3	6	6	39	43	30	37	16
Resentfulness	4	22.5	16	28	26.5	34	39	23
Nervousness	18.5	16	12	31	25	31	38	24
Fearfulness	5	14	13	40	45	42	36	32
Dreaminess	18.5	43	43	45	40	40	41	38
Slovenly in Appearance	32.5	22.5	27	30	14	17	3	30
Suspiciousness	2	32	28	43	35	27	31.5	37
Physical Coward	15	13	25	16	37	9	25	27
Easily Discouraged	7	9	15	13	24	16	21	28
Suggestible	8	15	23	21.5	22	10.5	19	15

FIGURE 12: Adapted from *Children's Behavior* by Sophie Ritholz. Bookman Associates, Inc., 1959. By permission of Twayne Publishers, Inc., N.Y.

THE DISTRIBUTION OF INTELLIGENCE

FIGURE 1 shows the I.Q. distribution of 2970 children (ages 2½ to 18 years) on the Revised Stanford-Binet Intelligence Scale. Note how closely the actual plotting of I.Q.'s (ragged line) follows the smooth normal curve. (See page 336 for a discussion of normal distribution.) FIGURE 2 shows the diagnostic equivalents of statistically expressed intelligence levels on the Wechsler Intelligence Scale for Children.

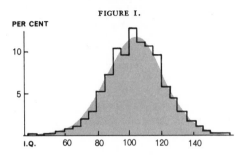

FIGURE 1.

FIGURE 2.

I.Q.	CLASSIFICATION	PER CENT INCLUDED
130 and above	Very superior	2.2
120-129	Superior	6.7
110-119	Bright normal	16.1
90-109	Average	50.0
80-89	Dull normal	16.1
70-79	Borderline	6.7
69 and below	Mental defective	2.2

INDIVIDUAL CURVES OF INTELLIGENCE

FIGURE 3. The two graphs below show individual curves of intelligence for five boys (left) and for five girls (right), selected to represent wide variations in adult intelligence. The curves of these ten individuals suggest differences both in rates of maturing and in inherent capacity. Minor fluctuations in the general pattern for a given individual may be caused by motivational factors, emotional distractions, or differences in the content of the tests given at different ages. Note how closely together the scores cluster during the first two or three years and how the differences between individuals become progressively more pronounced as the children grow older. This suggests the difficulty of predicting adult intelligence on the basis of scores achieved during infancy.

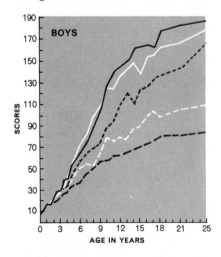 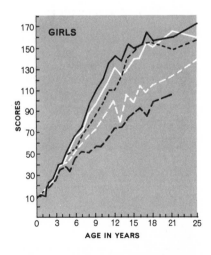

FIGURE 1: From *The Revision of the Stanford-Binet Scale: An Analysis of the Standardization Data* by Q. McNemar. Houghton-Mifflin Company, 1942. FIGURE 2: From *Manual of the Wechsler Intelligence Scale for Children* by David Wechsler. Reproduced by permission. Copyright ©1949, The Psychological Corporation, New York, N.Y. All rights reserved. FIGURE 3: Adapted from "Individual Patterns of Development" by Nancy Bayley, in *Child Development*, 1956, 27: 45-74. © 1956 by the Society for Research in Child Development, Inc.

THE SPAN OF ATTENTION

FIGURE 4. Characteristically, attention in little children is fleeting. Personality characteristics have been found to be an important governing factor: extrovertive traits are associated with a short attention span, while introvertive traits are associated with a long attention span. Sex differences are generally very definite. Interest is a factor, too, as suggested by the differences in attention span for simple and complex situations.

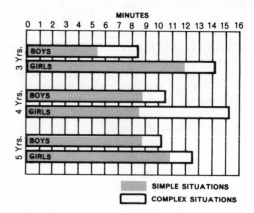

DEVELOPMENT OF LANGUAGE BEHAVIOR

FIGURE 5. This chart illustrates some kinds of language behavior that are typical at various stages of development. Language maturity is estimated in terms of articulation, vocabulary, adaptive use, and comprehension.

LEVELS OF MATURITY	LANGUAGE BEHAVIOR
Birth	--
4 weeks	Small throaty sounds. Heeds bell.
16 weeks	Coos. Laughs. Vocalizes socially.
28 weeks	Crows. Vocalizes eagerness. Listens to own vocalizations.
40 weeks	Says one word. Heeds his name.
12 months	Says two or more words.
18 months	Jargons. Names pictures.
2 years	Uses phrases. Understands simple directions.
3 years	Talks in sentences. Answers simple questions.
4 years	Uses conjunctions. Understands prepositions.
5 years	Speaks without infantile articulation. Asks "Why?"

VOCABULARY GROWTH

FIGURE 6. This table shows the average rise in oral vocabulary of children from the age of eight months to six years. Vocabulary increases slowly for six months or so after the first few words are learned, which is usually near the end of the first year. It takes its biggest jump between two and a half and three. Differences in personality and environment both account for wide differences in early speech.

AGE	NUMBER OF WORDS	GAIN
8 mos.	0	—
10 mos.	1	1
12 mos.	3	2
15 mos.	19	16
18 mos.	22	3
21 mos.	118	96
2 yrs.	272	154
2½ yrs.	446	174
3 yrs.	896	450
3½ yrs.	1222	326
4 yrs.	1540	318
4½ yrs.	1870	330
5 yrs.	2072	202
5½ yrs.	2289	219
6 yrs.	2562	273

FIGURE 4: Adapted from "A Method for Measuring Sustained Attention of Preschool Children" by Helen Shacter, in *Journal of Genetic Psychology*, June 1933: 362. By permission of The Journal Press. FIGURE 5: Adapted from Fig. 4, p. 13, of *Developmental Diagnosis* by Arnold Gesell and Catherine S. Amatruda. Copyright 1941, 1947 by Arnold Gesell. Reprinted by permission of Hoeber Medical Division, Harper & Row, Publishers. FIGURE 6: Adapted from "An Investigation of the Development of the Sentence and the Extent of Vocabulary in Young Children" by M. E. Smith, in *University of Iowa Studies in Child Welfare*, 1926, 3, No. 5, p. 54.

CHILDREN'S USE OF THE MASS MEDIA

The information and ideas to which children are exposed by the mass media comprise an important part of their learning environment. Of special concern to today's parents and teachers is the impact of television, the one medium that children use almost universally (FIGURE 7). Television viewing dominates the leisure time of most children from the age of five or six, rising from an average of about 2 hours a day at the start of elementary school to over 3 hours a day in the seventh and eighth grades (FIGURE 8). The decline among teen-agers in viewing time and in the valuation of television (FIGURE 9) reflects the adolescent's growing preference for leisure-time activities that involve his friends.

Although bright children tend to spend less time watching television than do children with average or low I.Q.'s, there is no real evidence that television viewing has a deleterious effect on school performance or even that it interferes seriously with homework. Television does, nonetheless, have a significant impact on children—not only through the information and ideas it imparts but also through the effect it has of reducing participation in other leisure-time activities. The influence of the medium is not all bad, but studies show that it has failed, by and large, to achieve its potential for stimulating children's intellectual growth and for exerting a positive influence on their development.

FIGURE 7. **PERCENTAGE OF CHILDREN WHO HAD BEGUN BY GIVEN AGE TO USE GIVEN MEDIUM**

AGE	TV	RADIO	MAGAZINES	COMIC BOOKS	MOVIES	BOOKS		NEWSPAPERS	
						Read to them	They read	Read to them	They read
2	14%	11%	3%	1%	1%	38%	0%	0%	0%
3	37%	20%	11%	6%	8%	58%	0%	0%	0%
4	65%	27%	20%	17%	21%	72%	2%	4%	0%
5	82%	40%	33%	35%	39%	74%	9%	9%	0%
6	91%	47%	41%	50%	60%	75%	40%	12%	9%
7	94%	53%	53%	61%	70%	75%	73%	12%	44%
8	95%	62%	59%	68%	76%	75%	86%	12%	59%
9	96%	65%	62%	70%	77%	75%	89%	12%	71%

(382 CHILDREN)

FIGURE 8. **ESTIMATED HOURS OF TELEVISION VIEWING**

GRADE	WEEKDAY		SUNDAY	
	Boys	Girls	Boys	Girls
2	2.2	2.1	2.5	2.8
4	2.2	2.2	2.1	2.6
6	2.5	2.6	2.3	2.6
8	3.2	3.2	3.6	3.2
10	2.8	2.5	3.5	3.4
12	2.5	2.1	2.8	3.1

(1740 CHILDREN)

FIGURE 9. **MEDIUM THAT WOULD BE MISSED MOST**

MEDIUM	BOYS			GIRLS		
	8TH	10TH	12TH	8TH	10TH	12TH
Books	6%	5%	5%	7%	6%	13%
Magazines	4%	2%	2%	0%	1%	2%
Newspapers	5%	11%	20%	4%	3%	11%
Comic Books	3%	1%	0%	2%	1%	0%
Television	71%	58%	33%	61%	45%	38%
Radio	4%	17%	32%	22%	39%	33%
Movies	3%	5%	4%	3%	3%	4%

(650 CHILDREN. NO RESPONSE FROM ABOUT 3%.)

FIGURES 7, 8, and 9: From "Television in the Life of the Child: Implications for the School" by Wilbur Schramm, in *New Teaching Aids for the American Classroom* by C. R. Carpenter et al. The Institute for Communication Research, Stanford, California, 1960.

353

INTELLIGENCE AND CREATIVITY

FIGURE 10. Although a high I.Q. is necessary for creativity in fields such as science and mathematics, creativity is not simply a matter of intelligence. People who are highly intelligent may rank very low in creativity, and, conversely, people who are highly creative do not always have exceptionally high I.Q.'s. What distinguishes the creative individual more than his intelligence level is his originality and independence of thought. Some of the differences between intelligence and creativity are suggested by the drawings on this page. The first was made by an adolescent who was highly intelligent but not highly creative; the second, by one who was highly creative but not highly intelligent. The directions to both youngsters were indentical: "Draw a picture appropriate to the title, 'Playing Tag in the School Yard.' You may draw any picture you like—whatever you may imagine for the theme." The highly creative adolescent has used these instructions merely as a point of departure for expressing himself. His drawing is not only freer than that of the highly intelligent youngster, but also more playful and humorous.

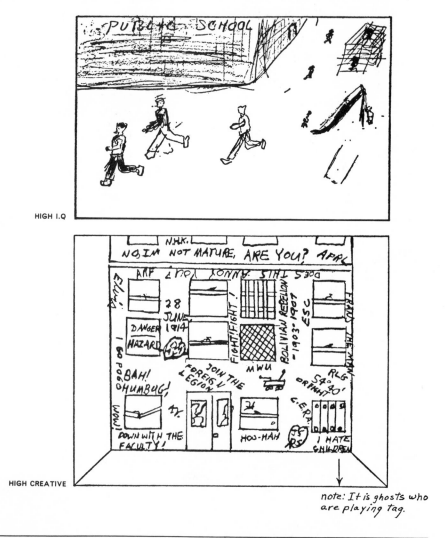

HIGH I.Q

HIGH CREATIVE

note: It is ghosts who are playing tag.

FIGURE 10: From *Creativity and Intelligence: Explorations with Gifted Students* by Jacob W. Getsels and Philip W. Jackson. John Wiley & Sons, Inc., 1962.

354

PERCEPTION OF A BRAIN-INJURED CHILD

FIGURE 11. How the brain-injured child's perceptual handicap alters his view of the world can be determined to some extent by psychological tests. It may be illustrated, for example, by the response of a brain-injured child to the following sequence.

For example, what does this drawing represent? Two rectangles. It seems to.

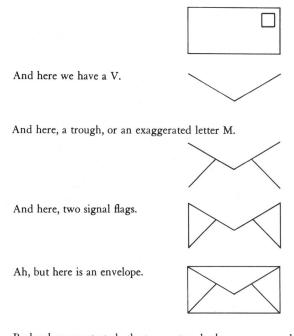

And here we have a V.

And here, a trough, or an exaggerated letter M.

And here, two signal flags.

Ah, but here is an envelope.

Back where we started—the two rectangles become an envelope with a stamp on it.

The normal person sees the progression:

The brain-injured may see this:

Would he be led to perceive the rectangles as an envelope? Perhaps not. Does this mean he is less intelligent? No, it indicates he is not perceiving what the normal person perceives.

FIGURE 11: From *The Other Child—the Brain-Injured Child* by Richard S. Lewis with Laura E. Lehtinen and Alfred A. Strauss. Grune & Stratton, Inc., New York, 1960. Reprinted by permission of the publisher and author.

A Summary of Normal Development

But allowance must always be made for individual differences

THE INFANT

Physical Development

Continued neuromuscular development. Progression from head downward—gains control of eye movements, swallowing, smiling, and using hands before he gains control of leg movements.

Most rapid growth rate of any period—often triples birth weight by age one.

Develops from crying as only form of language expression to smiling, cooing, laughing, babbling, using one or two words.

Gradually develops some motor control—from random movements to ability to pick up small objects with fingers.

Begins to cut teeth by six or seven months.

Sleep pattern changes from almost constant sleep to twelve hours a night and one or two naps.

Learns to eat solid food, drink from a cup.

Characteristic Behavior

Develops from no social perception to recognizing parents, brothers, sisters, environment, and routine.

Responds to people he knows. Usually withdraws from strangers.

Gradually becomes social—likes watching people and being played with, talked to, or held.

May be startled or cry at sudden, loud sounds or voices. May pull back or cry at strange objects. Disturbed by sudden movements.

Special Needs

Physical care—is dependent on adults for satisfaction of all physical needs. Should have prompt response to his needs.

Certainty of parents' love. Consistency and patience in handling. Cuddling, holding, rocking.

Consistent care by one or two people.

Verbal response to his babbling to help his language development.

Activity, opportunity to move about and to develop the large muscles.

THE TODDLER

Physical Development

Growth rate slower than during infancy.

Decrease in appetite from infancy.

Walks between twelve and eighteen months. Runs awkwardly and may fall.

Tries to feed himself, but manipulating spoon and cup still difficult. Finger feeds. Will be messy.

Constantly in motion. Into everything. Explores his environment—pushing, pulling, climbing, dragging, lifting everything within reach.

Learns by touching, feeling, and putting in mouth.

Short attention span.

Vocabulary increase in second half of year. May use words, but can't always express his wants.

Characteristic Behavior

Responds to his mother and likes to be near her. Enjoys his father and siblings, but usually wants his mother to do things for him.

Unable to play cooperatively with others.

Likes simple stories about himself, jingles, rhymes, and picture books.

Beginning to be negativistic and may develop some fears. Developing likes and dislikes.

Becomes angry when frustrated.

Special Needs

Love, affection, and a secure, happy relationship with parents.

Acceptance of his constant activity. Patience and encouragement as he tries to learn to do things for himself.

Training with a light touch rather than by commanding and scolding.

A safe environment in which to explore, with dangerous objects put out of reach. Also a fenced-in, outdoor play area. Playpen outgrown near beginning of period.

Recognition that the toddler is not old enough to be responsible for himself, even though he may seem to understand directions.

356

THE RUNABOUT

Physical Development

Motor skills unevenly developed—marked development in large muscle coordination, but small muscles and eye-hand coordination still not well developed.

Full set of temporary teeth by three years.

Gradually acquires ability to feed and dress himself with greater skill.

Rapid language development—from a few words to an average of 2000.

Change in sleep pattern—twelve hours needed at night with daytime naps gradually given up. But still needs rest period because children of this age fatigue easily.

Toilet habits established. Child usually takes care of his own needs by end of period.

Characteristic Behavior

Learning to understand his environment and comply with many of its demands.

Often negativistic at beginning of period, but gradually becomes able to accept necessary limits and restraints. Wants adult approval.

Likes to be close to his mother, but his father is becoming increasingly important to him.

Likes to help around the house.

Imitative in language, manners, and habits.

Constantly active, but capable of longer stretches of quiet activity toward end of period.

Shows fatigue by being irritable or restless.

Gradually learning what is acceptable behavior and what is not.

Great curiosity. Asks countless questions.

Special Needs

Security of love and affection from parents.

Guidance and a pattern of behavior to follow.

Time, patience, understanding, and genuine interest from adults.

Simple, clear routines. Limited choices.

Opportunity to learn to give and take, to play cooperatively with other children.

Wider scope of activity. Limited freedom to move about and to move away from immediate home environment by end of period.

ABOUT FIVE

Physical Development

Period of slow growth. Body lengthens out and hands and feet grow larger. Girls usually about a year ahead of boys in physical development.

Good general motor control, though small muscles not so fully developed as large ones.

Sensory-motor equipment usually not ready for reading. Eye-hand coordination improving, but still poor. Apt to be far-sighted.

Activity level high.

Attention span still short, but increasing.

Little infantile articulation in speech.

Handedness established.

Characteristic Behavior

Stable—good balance between self-sufficiency and sociability.

Home-centered.

Beginning to be capable of self-criticism. Eager and able to carry some responsibility.

Noisy and vigorous, but activity has definite direction.

Purposeful and constructive—knows what he's going to draw before he draws it.

Uses language well, enjoys dramatic play.

Can wash, dress, eat, and go to the toilet by himself, but may need occasional help.

Individuality and lasting traits beginning to be apparent.

Interested in group activity.

Special Needs

Assurance that he is loved and valued.

Wise guidance.

Opportunity for plenty of activity, equipment for exercising large muscles.

Opportunity to do things for himself, freedom to use and develop his own powers.

Background training in group effort, in sharing, and in good work habits that he will need next year in first grade.

Opportunity to learn about his world by seeing and doing things.

Kindergarten experience if possible.

ABOUT SIX

Physical Development

Growth proceeding more slowly, a lengthening out.

Large muscles better developed than small ones.

Eleven to twelve hours of sleep needed.

Eyes not yet mature, tendency toward far-sightedness.

Permanent teeth beginning to appear.

Heart in period of rapid growth.

High activity level—can stay still only for short periods.

Characteristic Behavior

Eager to learn, exuberant, restless, overactive, easily fatigued.

Self-assertive, aggressive, wants to be first, less cooperative than at five, keenly competitive, boastful.

Whole body involved in whatever he does.

Learns best through active participation.

Inconsistent in level of maturity evidenced—regresses when tired, often less mature at home than with outsiders.

Inept at activities using small muscles.

Relatively short periods of interest.

Has difficulty making decisions.

Group activities popular, boys' and girls' interests beginning to differ.

Much spontaneous dramatization.

Special Needs

Encouragement, ample praise, warmth, and great patience from adults.

Ample opportunity for activity of many kinds, especially for use of large muscles.

Wise supervision with minimum interference.

Friends—by end of period, a best friend.

Concrete learning situations and active, direct participation.

Some responsibilities, but without pressure and without being required to make complicated decisions or achieve rigidly set standards.

Help in developing acceptable manners and habits.

ABOUT SEVEN

Physical Development

Growth slow and steady.

Annual expected growth in height—two or three inches. In weight—three to six pounds.

Losing teeth. Most seven-year-olds have their six-year molars.

Better eye-hand coordination.

Better use of small muscles.

Eyes not yet ready for much close work.

Characteristic Behavior

Sensitive to feelings and attitudes of both other children and adults. Especially dependent on approval of adults.

Interests of boys and girls diverging. Less play together.

Full of energy but easily tired, restless and fidgety, often dreamy and absorbed.

Little abstract thinking. Learns best in concrete terms and when he can be active while learning.

Cautious and self-critical, anxious to do things well, likes to use hands.

Talkative, prone to exaggerate, may fight verbally instead of physically, competitive.

Enjoys songs, rhythms, fairy tales, myths, nature stories, comics, television, movies.

Able to assume some responsibility.

Concerned about right and wrong, but often prone to take small things.

Rudimentary understanding of time and monetary values.

Special Needs

The right combination of independence and encouraging support.

Chances for active participation in learning situations with concrete objects.

Adult help in adjusting to the rougher ways of the playground without becoming too crude or rough.

Warm, encouraging, friendly relationships with adults.

Acceptance at own level of development.

ABOUT EIGHT

Physical Development

Growth still slow and steady—arms lengthening, hands growing.

Eyes ready for both near and far vision. Nearsightedness may develop this year.

Permanent teeth continuing to appear.

Large muscles still developing. Small muscles better developed, too. Manipulative skills are increasing.

Attention span getting longer.

Poor posture may develop.

Characteristic Behavior

Often careless, noisy, argumentative, but also alert, friendly, interested in people.

More dependent on his mother again, less so on his teacher. Sensitive to criticism.

New awareness of individual differences.

Eager, more enthusiastic than cautious. Higher accident rate.

Gangs beginning. Best friends of same sex.

Allegiance to other children instead of to an adult in case of conflict.

Greater capacity for self-evaluation.

Much spontaneous dramatization, ready for simple classroom dramatics.

Understanding of time and of use of money.

Responsive to group activities, both spontaneous and adult-supervised.

Fond of team games, comics, television, movies, adventure stories, collections.

Special Needs

Praise and encouragement from adults.

Reminders of his responsibilities.

Wise guidance and channeling of his interests and enthusiasms, rather than domination or unreasonable standards.

A best friend.

Experience of belonging to peer group—opportunity to identify with others of same age and sex.

Adult-supervised groups and planned after-school activities.

Exercise of both large and small muscles.

ABOUT NINE OR TEN

Physical Development

Slow, steady growth continues—girls forge further ahead. Some children reach the plateau preceding the preadolescent growth spurt.

Lungs as well as digestive and circulatory systems almost mature. Heart especially subject to strain.

Teeth may need straightening. First and second bicuspids appearing.

Eye-hand coordination good. Ready for crafts and shop work.

Eyes almost adult size. Ready for close work with less strain.

Characteristic Behavior

Decisive, responsible, dependable, reasonable, strong sense of right and wrong.

Individual differences distinct, abilities now apparent.

Capable of prolonged interest. Often makes plans and goes ahead on his own.

Gangs strong and of one sex only, of short duration and changing membership.

Perfectionistic—wants to do well, but loses interest if discouraged or pressured.

Interested less in fairy tales and fantasy, more in his community and country and in other countries and peoples.

Loyal to his country and proud of it.

Spends a great deal of time in talk and discussion. Often outspoken and critical of adults, although still dependent on adult approval.

Frequently argues over fairness in games.

Wide discrepancies in reading ability.

Special Needs

Active rough and tumble play.

Friends and membership in a group.

Training in skills, but without pressure.

Books of many kinds, depending on individual reading level and interest.

Reasonable explanations without talking down.

Definite responsibility.

Frank answers to his questions about coming physiological changes.

THE PREADOLESCENT

Physical Development

A "resting period," followed by a period of rapid growth in height and then growth in weight. This usually starts sometime between 9 and 13. Boys may mature as much as two years later than girls.

Girls usually taller and heavier than boys.

Reproductive organs maturing. Secondary sex characteristics developing.

Rapid muscular growth.

Uneven growth of different parts of the body.

Enormous but often capricious appetite.

Characteristic Behavior

Wide range of individual differences in maturity level.

Gangs continue, though loyalty to the gang stronger in boys than in girls.

Interest in team games, pets, television, radio, movies, comics. Marked interest differences between boys and girls.

Teasing and seeming antagonism between boys' and girls' groups.

Awkwardness, restlessness, and laziness common as result of rapid and uneven growth.

Opinion of own group beginning to be valued more highly than that of adults.

Often becomes overcritical, changeable, rebellious, uncooperative.

Self-conscious about physical changes.

Interested in earning money.

Special Needs

Understanding of the physical and emotional changes about to come.

Skillfully planned school and recreation programs to meet needs of those who are approaching puberty as well as those who are not.

Opportunities for greater independence and for carrying more responsibility without pressure.

Warm affection and sense of humor in adults. No nagging, condemnation, or talking down.

Sense of belonging, acceptance by peer group.

THE ADOLESCENT

Physical Development

Rapid weight gain at beginning of adolescence. Enormous appetite.

Sexual maturity, with accompanying physical and emotional changes. Girls are usually about two years ahead of boys.

Sometimes a period of glandular imbalance.

Skeletal growth completed, adult height reached, muscular coordination improved.

Heart growing rapidly at beginning of period.

Characteristic Behavior

Going to extremes, emotional instability with "know-it-all" attitude.

Return of habits of younger child—nail biting, tricks, impudence, day-dreaming.

High interest in philosophical, ethical, and religious problems. Search for ideals.

Preoccupation with acceptance by the social group. Fear of ridicule and of being unpopular. Oversensitiveness and self-pity.

Strong identification with an admired adult.

Assertion of independence from family as a step toward adulthood.

Responds well to group responsibility and group participation. Groups may form cliques.

High interest in physical attractiveness.

Girls usually more interested in boys than boys in girls, resulting from earlier maturing of the girls.

Special Needs

Acceptance by and conformity with others of own age.

Adequate understanding of sexual relationships and attitudes.

Kind, unobtrusive, adult guidance which does not threaten the adolescent's feeling of freedom.

Assurance of security. Adolescents seek both dependence and independence.

Opportunities to make decisions and to earn and save money.

Provision for constructive recreation. Some cause, idea, or issue to work for.

360

Name Index

General Index

of child, 290-292, 294, 297-298, 300-301; punishment within, 296-298; relationship with, at ten, 188; shrinking size of, 9

Family living, preparation for: 260-273

Far-sightedness: 110, 130

Fatigue: at five, 111; of preadolescents, 201, 214; at seven, 143

Favoritism, effects of: 208-212

Fear: causes of, 347; of failure, at ten, 186-187; in insecure child, 208-210, 279-280; in toddlers, 63-64, 68

Feeding: of infants, 38-39, 40, 44, 46-47, 50-53; of toddlers, 61-63, 69-70

Fighting: in rebellious children, 276-279; for rights, 145

Five year olds: 108-123, 357; activities, 110-111; anxieties, 115, 117; attention span, 111; conformity, 117; conscience and responsibility, 117; coordination, 109-110; effect of television programs, 113, 115; enjoyment of music and dramatic play, 114; food preferences, 115; independence, 115-117; language development, 114-115; needs, 111, 115-117; physical development, 108-110; preparation for reading, 112-113; sociability, 114; temper tantrums, 97

Foster-home placement: 152-153, 277, 291-292

Four year olds: 84-97, 102-107; activities and interests, 85-86; attitude toward parents, 95-96; behavior, 84-86, 90-93, 95-96; curiosity, 90-92; effects of television, 90; flexibility, 86; friendships, 93; independence, 87-88, 97; language development, 88-89; muscle development and coordination, 85; needs, 93-94, 97; nursery school, 94-95, 102-107; play, 93-94; rest, 86; sharing, 93, 96; social development, 89; stories, 89

Friendships: during adolescence, 238-239; at eight, 156-158; at nine, 174-176; during preadolescence, 204-205; at six, 134; at ten, 188; at three and four, 93

Frustration: 19-20, 66, 130; effects of, 207-212, 274-276, 279-282, 300-301, 346

Future, preparation for: 6-8, 242

Gangs: adolescent, 225-226, 240; delinquent, 278-279; at eight, 157-158; at nine, 169, 174-175; preadolescent, 204; redirecting activities of, 175

Grasping, development of: 337

Group, importance during adolescence: 238-241. See also Gangs

Group activities: at five, 114; at nine, 169-170; of preadolescents, 206, 207; at six, 134; at ten, 186-188, 189-190

Group discussion, value of: 191-197

Growth: 13-15, 16, 338, 339, 340, 343. See also Development

Guidance: 3-11, 292-301; for disturbed children, 276-284; for family living, 260, 264-273; group, 191-197; vocational, 249-254

Guide for Parent-Teacher Conferences: 328-331

Guilt: in model child, 140-142; in rebellious child, 231-235

Handedness: 110

Handicapped child: mentally, 285-289; physically, 284-285

Hands, dexterity of: 337, 343; at eight, 155-156; at nine, 168; at seven, 144; at six, 132-133

Happiness, source of: 348

Height, at different ages: 339, 340-341

Heredity: 12-13; in mental retardation, 285; role of genes and chromosomes, 28-29

Hero worship: during preadolescence, 202; at ten, 190

Hobbies, at eight: 156

Home: 290-301; affection within, 292-294; consistency in attitudes and expectations within, 295-296; participation within, 298-299; providing for needs of child, 290-292, 294, 297-298, 300-301; strongest factor in adjustment, 12, 13, 17-19, 20, 207, 274-275, 290-301

Homework: 308-309

Honesty: at nine, 173, 177; at seven, 149; at six, 135

Hostility: to adults, 278-279; to new baby, 98, 101-102, 151; to society, 276-278

Humor: appeal to preadolescents, 202; sense of, at six, 135

Hypothyroidism: 162-167

Identification: with adults, 136, 147, 154, 185; with own sex, 263-264

Improvement, desire for, at nine: 170-171

Inconsistency of parental demands: 97, 279, 295-296

Independence: of adolescent, 221-222, 236-239; at eight, 154, 160-161; at five, 115-117; at nine, 173, 177; of preadolescent, 203; of runabout, 87-88; at seven, 147, 149; at six, 129, 133-134; at ten, 187; of toddler, 57

Individual differences: in ability, 113-114, 127-128, 147, 159, 172, 230-231; in environment, 4-6; in intelligence, 351; and "normality," 13-14, 22, 336; patterning of, 343, 351; in physical development, 39, 47-53, 66, 77, 168, 198-199, 224; in social development, 20, 228

Individual Study Guide: 320-331

Infants: 39-53, 356; activity needs, 43-45, 47, 49; communication, 39-41; cooperation, 48; coordination, 40-42, 44-45, 47; feeding, 38-39, 40, 44, 46-47, 50-53; guiding, 46; individual differences, 47-53; insecurity in, 43-44; interests, 42, 47; language development, 48; needs, 39-40, 48, 52-53; physical development, 39-48; siblings, 18, 96, 98, 101-102, 177-180; sleep needs, 40; teething, 42-43; thumb-sucking, 39-40, 51; walking, 46, 48

Inferiority feelings, during later adolescence: 239-240

Intelligence: and creativity, 354; differences in: 351. See also Mental development

Interests: at eight, 156-158, 160-161; at five, 111-114; at nine, 169-172; of preadolescents, 206-207; related to reproduction and sex differences, 264-268; of runabouts, 85-86, 89, 93; at six, 133-135; at ten, 185, 189-190; of toddlers, 58-61

Judgment: at nine, 173; during later adolescence, 239, 269-270

367

Kindergarten: 108; value of, 117

Language development: 352; at five, 114-115; in lower-class homes, 305; of runabout, 88-89; at seven, 144-145; of toddler, 66-67
Laziness, of preadolescents: 201
Learning, active participation in: during adolescence, 243; at five, 112; for runabouts, 89-94; at six, 132, 136; for toddlers, 54-56, 58-59, 69, 71-72
Left-out child: 146, 171, 175-176
Lonely child: 20; helped to better adjustment, 150-153, 162-167, 276-278, 280-281
Longitudinal studies: 21
Love, need for: 12-13, 17-18, 48, 53, 180, 231-235, 275, 290, 292, 294
Loyalty: during adolescence, 227; at eight, 157; at nine, 172, 173, 175

Maladjustment: 274-284; adult-hating child, 278-279; guide for studying, 320-331; insecure child, 177-180; preadolescents, 212-215; over-anxious child, 279-280; overweight child, 162-167; rebellious child, 231-235, 276-278; unloved child, 150-153; withdrawn child, 207-212, 280-281
Marital happiness of parents, effect on child: 177-180, 274, 278-279
Marriage, preparation for: 260-273
Mass media: 11, 353. See also Television
Maturation. See Physical development and Physical maturity
Maturity: in early adolescence, 224, 228; in later adolescence, 236, 244-245; at nine, 176-177
Menstruation, preparation for: 215
Mental development: 15-18, 351-355
Mentally handicapped child: 285-289; classes for, 286-287; culturally retarded, 287; dependent retarded, 285; educable retarded, 287; needs, 287-289; trainable retarded, 286-287. See also Brain damage
Mobility of modern family, 9
Model child: 138-142
Money, understanding of: 160
Moods: during early adolescence, 223; during later adolescence, 236-238; during preadolescence, 201-202
Mother, dependence on: at eight, 154; at five, 117; of runabout, 95; of toddler, 68
Motor control, development of: 337, 343. See also Muscles
Movies: 145-146, 159, 353
Muscles, development of: 337, 343; at eight, 155-156; at five, 109; in runabout, 85; at seven, 143; at six, 130
Music, enjoyment of: at five, 114; during infancy, 48; during preadolescence, 207; at seven, 145; in toddlers, 60

Nagging, ineffectiveness of: 203, 297
Name-calling: at eight, 156-157, 164; among runabouts, 83, 93; at seven, 145; at ten, 188
Near-sightedness: 155

Needs: 4, 197, 290-292, 294, 297-298, 300-301; approaches to understanding, 21-22; basic to emotional development, 17-18; of brain-damaged child, 122-123; of left-out child, 175-176; of mentally handicapped child, 287-289; for mother's affection, 47; for routine, 136-137, 140-142; for self-confidence, 19-20; summary of, for different ages, 356-360
Newborns: 35-39; brain damage to, 35; immunity to disease, 33; individual differences, 39; mother's influence, 38; needs, 37-38; physical development, 35-37, 337
Nine year olds: 168-184, 359; acceptance of criticism and punishment, 173-174, 177; activity needs, 169-170; attention span, 169; awareness of differences, 176; competition, 171; conformity, 174-176; decision-making, 173, 174, 177; desire to improve, 170; development of standards, 173, 177; eye-hand coordination, 168; gangs, 169; independence and responsibility, 173, 177; individual differences, 168; interest in skills, 170-171; need for group acceptance, 174-175; original ideas, 169; patriotism, 172; physical development, 168; reading differences, 172; sex differences in play, 169
Normal development: defined, 336; summarized, 356-360
Normal distribution: 336; of intelligence, 351
Nursery school: 94-95, 102-107; causes of crying in, 346; role of teacher, 94

One year olds. See Toddlers
Original ideas, at nine: 169
Over-active child: 282-283
Over-anxious child: 279-280
Overweight, effect on adjustment: 162-167

Parallel play: among runabouts, 92; at six, 134
Parent-counselor cooperation: for parental adjustment, 245-249; for rebellious adolescent, 231-235; for vocational guidance, 249-254
Parent-school cooperation: 304-305, 310-313; for family-life education, 270-271, 272-273
Parent-teacher conferences: 303; guide, 328-331
Parent-teacher cooperation: 302-313; for brain-damaged child, 283; for children with problems, 280, 281, 283; for early maturing preadolescent, 200, 212-215; for handicapped child, 284, 287; for left-out child, 176; necessity for, 3
Parental problems, effect on child: 177-180, 207-212, 245-249, 249-254, 274, 278-279, 305-306
Parenthood, education for: 260-273
Parents: attitude toward handicapped child, 287-289; conflict with adolescent child, 237-238, 254; need for consistency, 295-296; providing affection, 292-294; role during adolescence, 241, 244-245
Participation: in family, 298-299; in gangs, 157-158, 169, 204, 225-226, 240; in learning, 132, 243
Past and future, concept of: 136, 148, 160
Patriotism, at nine: 172